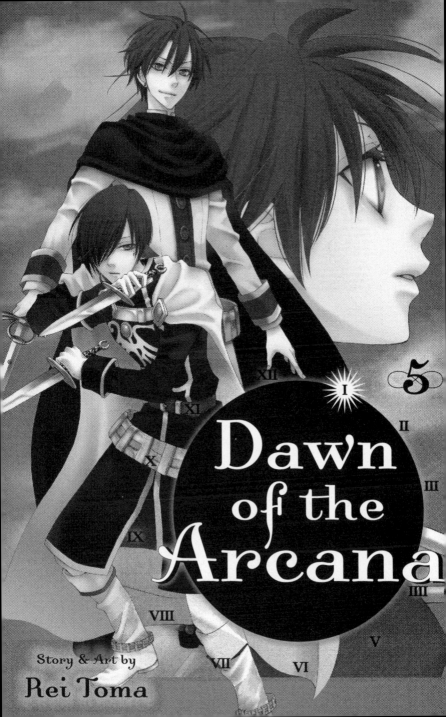

Dawn of the Arcana

5

Story & Art by
Rei Toma

characters

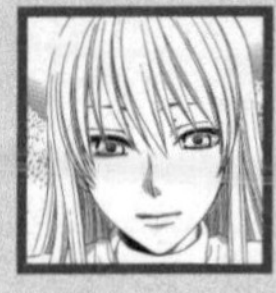

Sara
King Guran's concubine. Deceased.

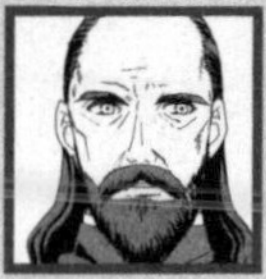

Guran
King of Belquat.

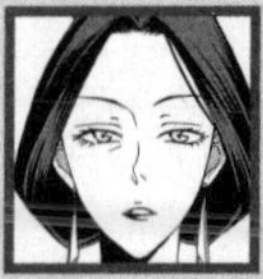

Rosenta
Queen of Belquat.

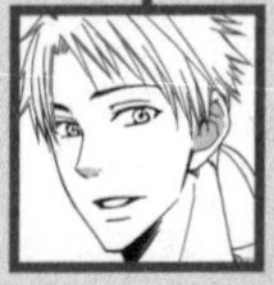

Cain
First-born prince of Belquat. Caesar's brother.

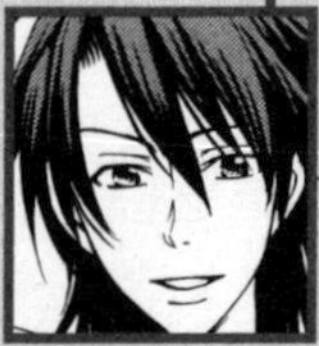

Caesar
The second-born prince of Belquat. Nakaba's husband through a marriage of political convenience. Headstrong and selfish.

Married

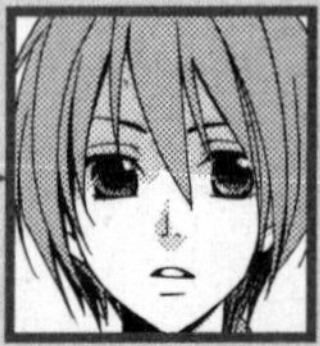

Nakaba
The princess royal of Senan. Strong of will and noble of spirit, she possesses a strange power.

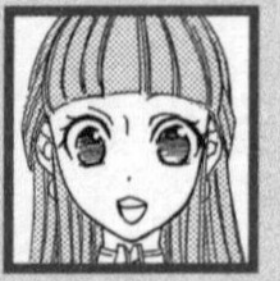

Lemiria
Bellinus's younger sister. Fond of her big brother.

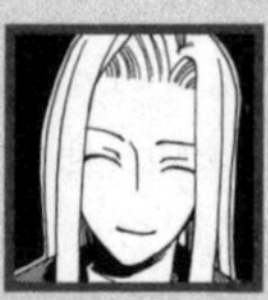

Bellinus
Caesar's attendant. Always cool and collected.

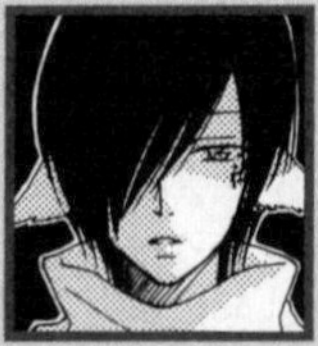

Loki
Nakaba's attendant. His senses of perception are unmatched.

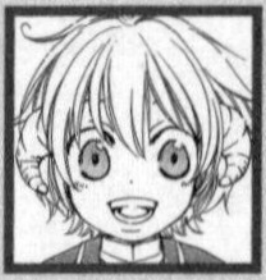

Rito
Nakaba's attendant. Recently arrived from Senan.

story

Seran

Belquat

• Wed to Prince Caesar as a symbol of the peace between their two countries, Nakaba is actually little more than a hostage. Unbeknownst to King Guran, she is a survivor of the race he tried to destroy for fear of their power.

• The political marriage between Nakaba and Caesar gets off to a rocky start, but as they grow to know each other, the gulf between them begins to close. Together they discover a secret armory beneath the castle and learn that King Guran plans to test the new weapons on an Ajin village.

• They set out to stop the attack under the pretext of going on a honeymoon, but soon find that Bellinus's sister, Lemiria, has stowed away on the journey. Nakaba insists she turn back—the Arcana of Time showed her Lemiria's death at the Ajin village—but Lemiria steadfastly refuses.

• At last they reach the royal villa, only to be taken prisoner by Bellinus on King Guran's orders. While the others are confined, Lemiria goes missing. Nakaba convinces Bellinus to let her out to search for her.

• Though wounded in the process, Nakaba uses the Arcana to save Lemiria. Moved by her selflessness, Bellinus agrees to join Nakaba in their attempt to stop the senseless battle!

Dawn of the Arcana

Volume 5

XII

XI

X

CONTENTS

IX

VIII

VII   VI

Chapter 16

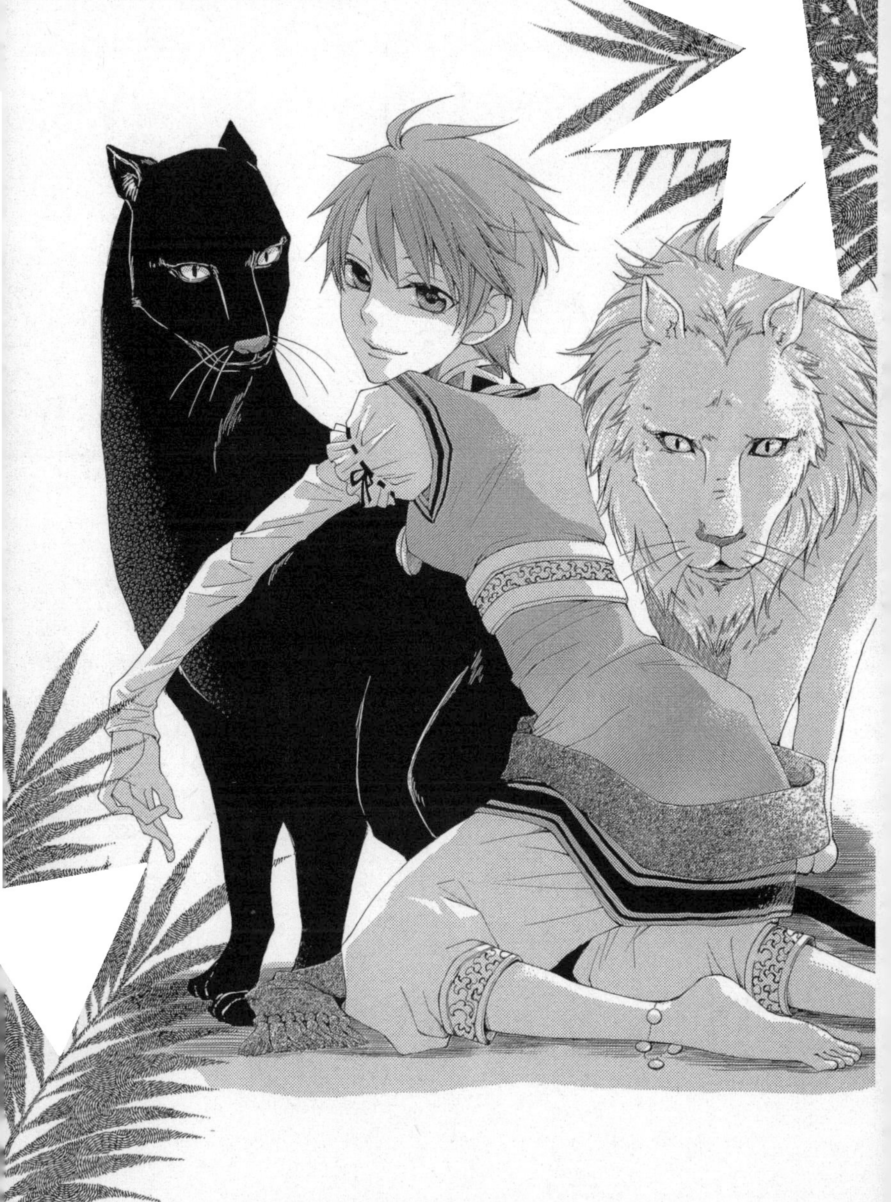

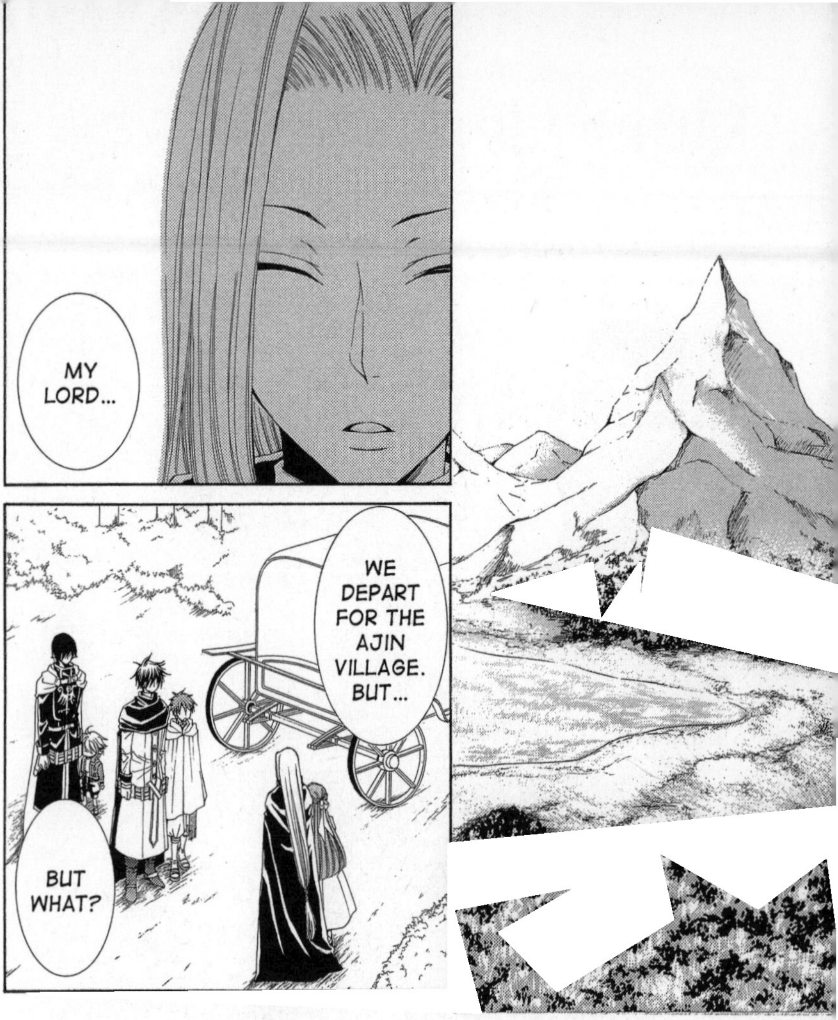
MY LORD...
WE DEPART FOR THE AJIN VILLAGE. BUT...
BUT WHAT?

Dawn of the Arcana

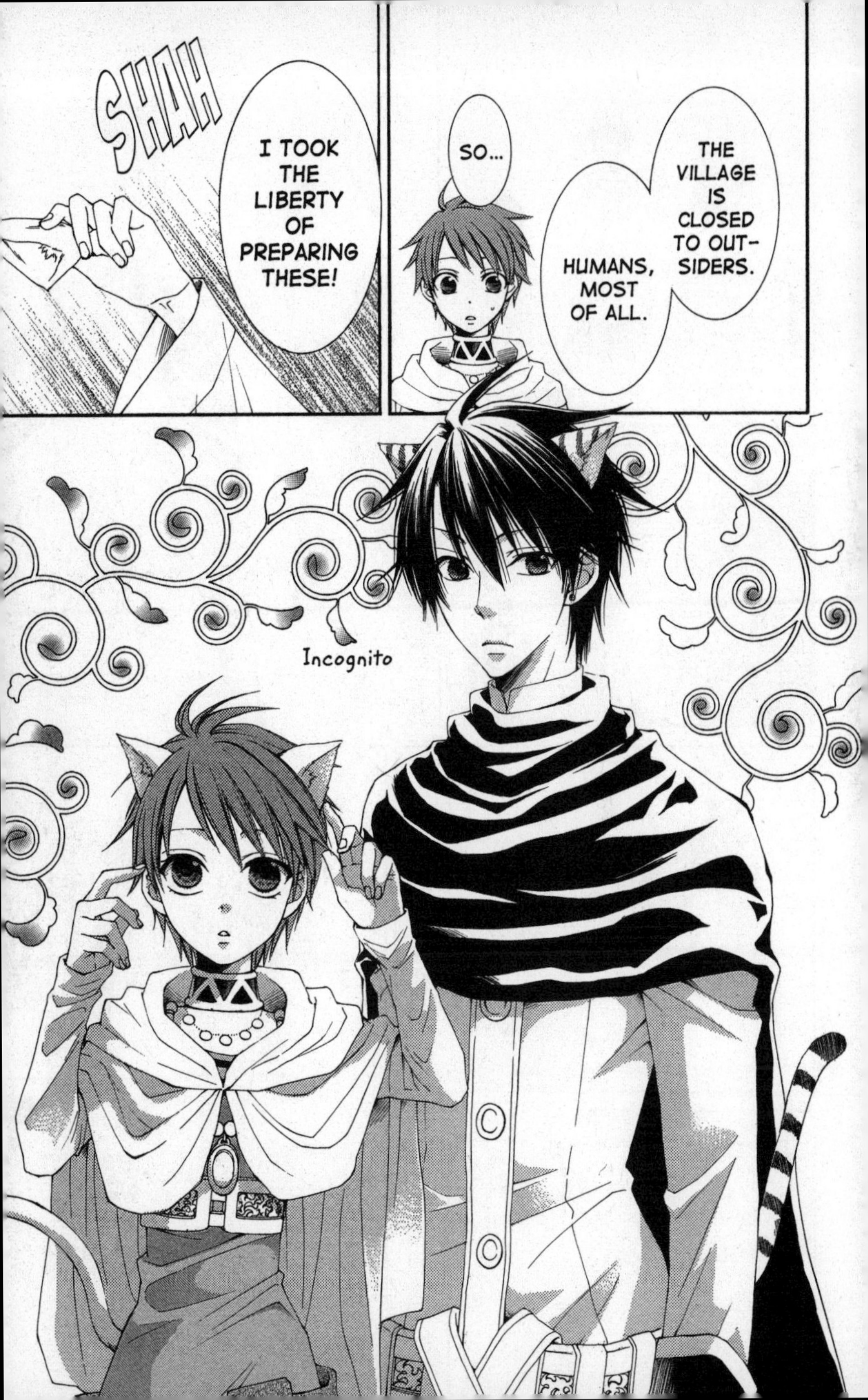
THE VILLAGE IS CLOSED TO OUTSIDERS.
HUMANS, MOST OF ALL.
SO...
I TOOK THE LIBERTY OF PREPARING THESE!
SHAH
Incognito

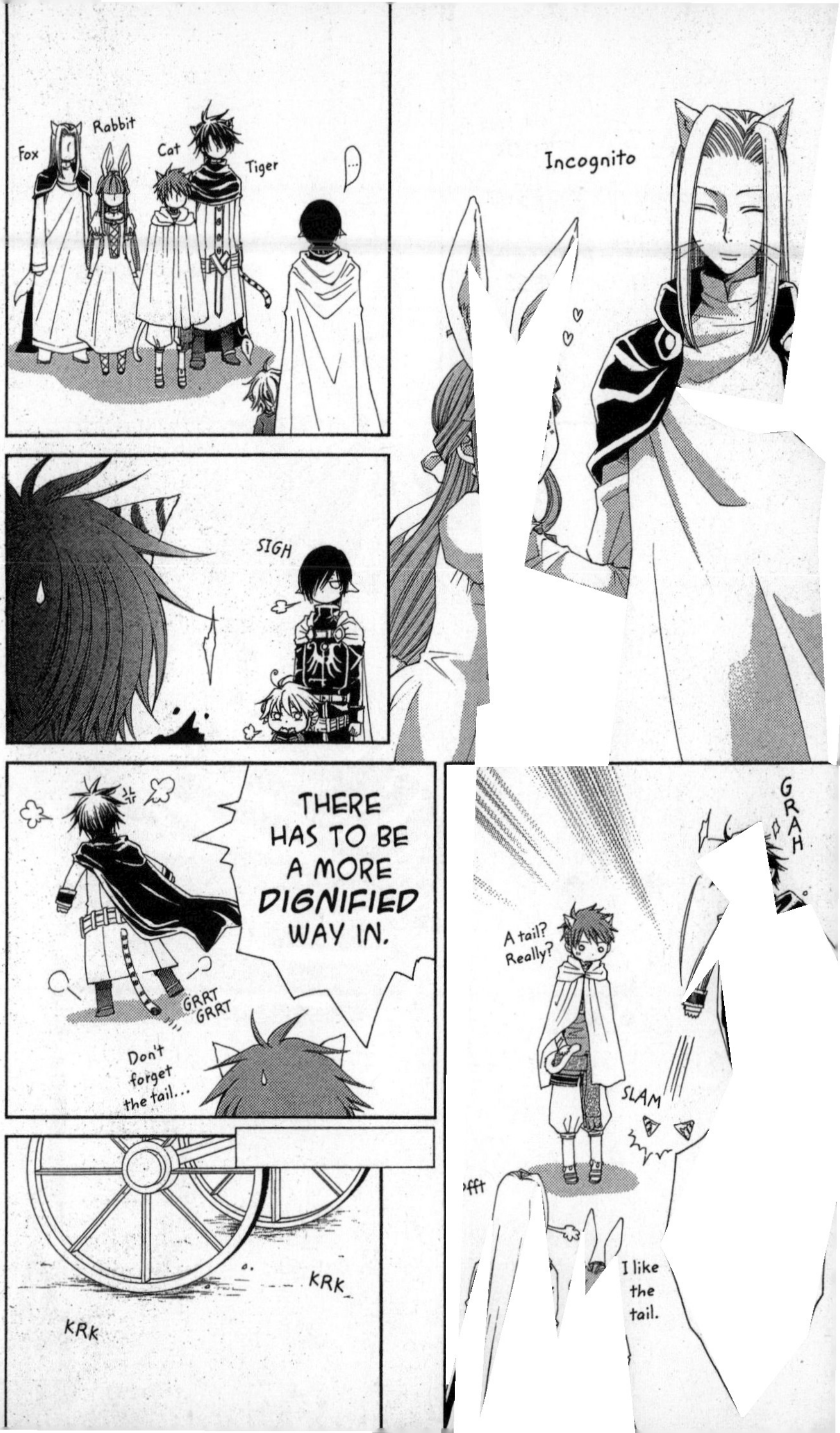
Incognito
Fox
Rabbit
Cat
Tiger
...
SIGH
GRAH
A tail? Really?
SLAM
pfft
I like the tail.
THERE HAS TO BE A MORE DIGNIFIED WAY IN.
GRRT GRRT
Don't forget the tail...
KRK
KRK

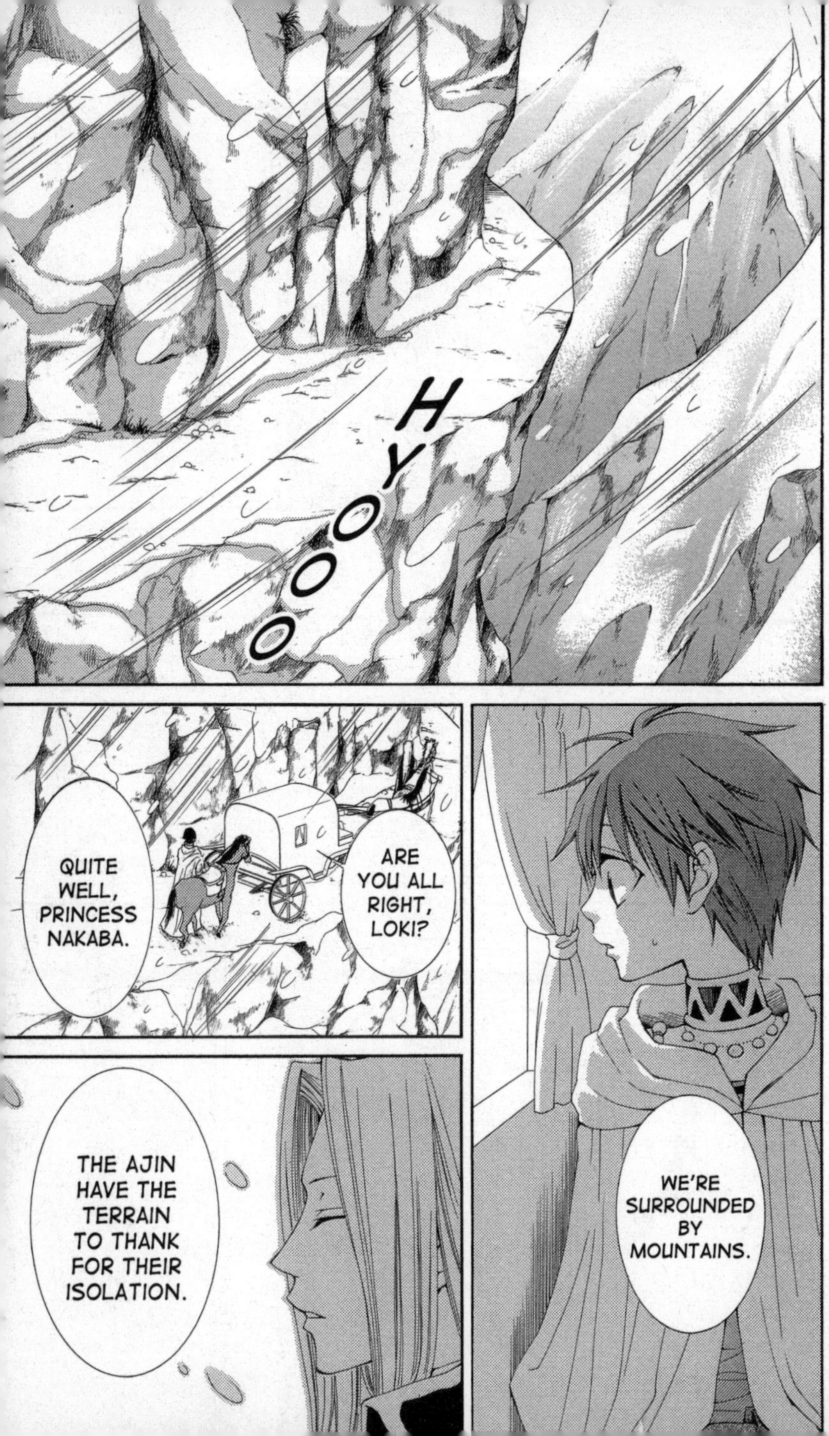
HYOOOO
WE'RE SURROUNDED BY MOUNTAINS.
ARE YOU ALL RIGHT, LOKI?
QUITE WELL, PRINCESS NAKABA.
THE AJIN HAVE THE TERRAIN TO THANK FOR THEIR ISOLATION.

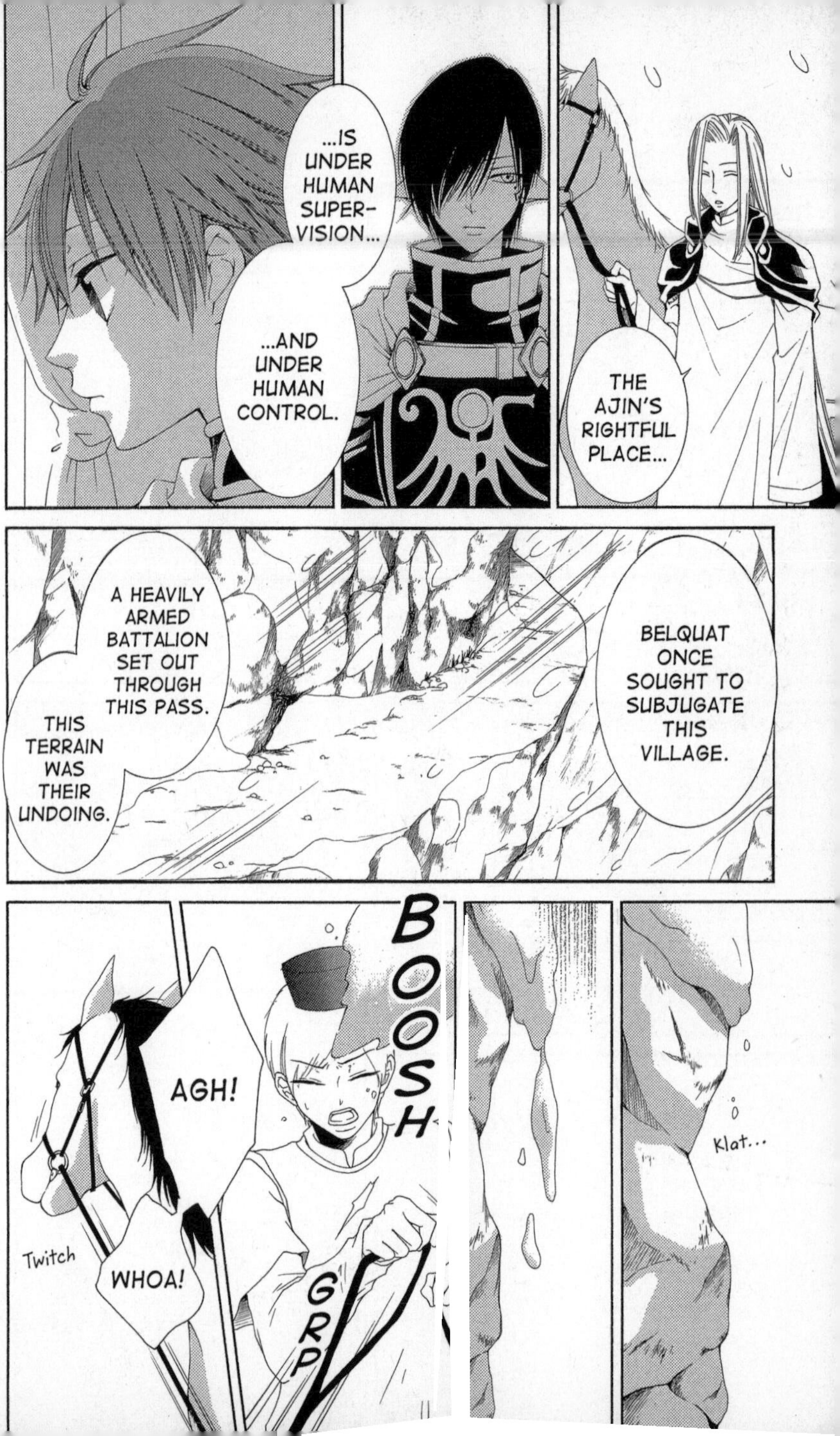
THE AJIN'S RIGHTFUL PLACE...
...IS UNDER HUMAN SUPER-VISION...
...AND UNDER HUMAN CONTROL.
BELQUAT ONCE SOUGHT TO SUBJUGATE THIS VILLAGE.
A HEAVILY ARMED BATTALION SET OUT THROUGH THIS PASS.
THIS TERRAIN WAS THEIR UNDOING.
Klat...
BOOOSH
AGH!
GRP
WHOA!
Twitch

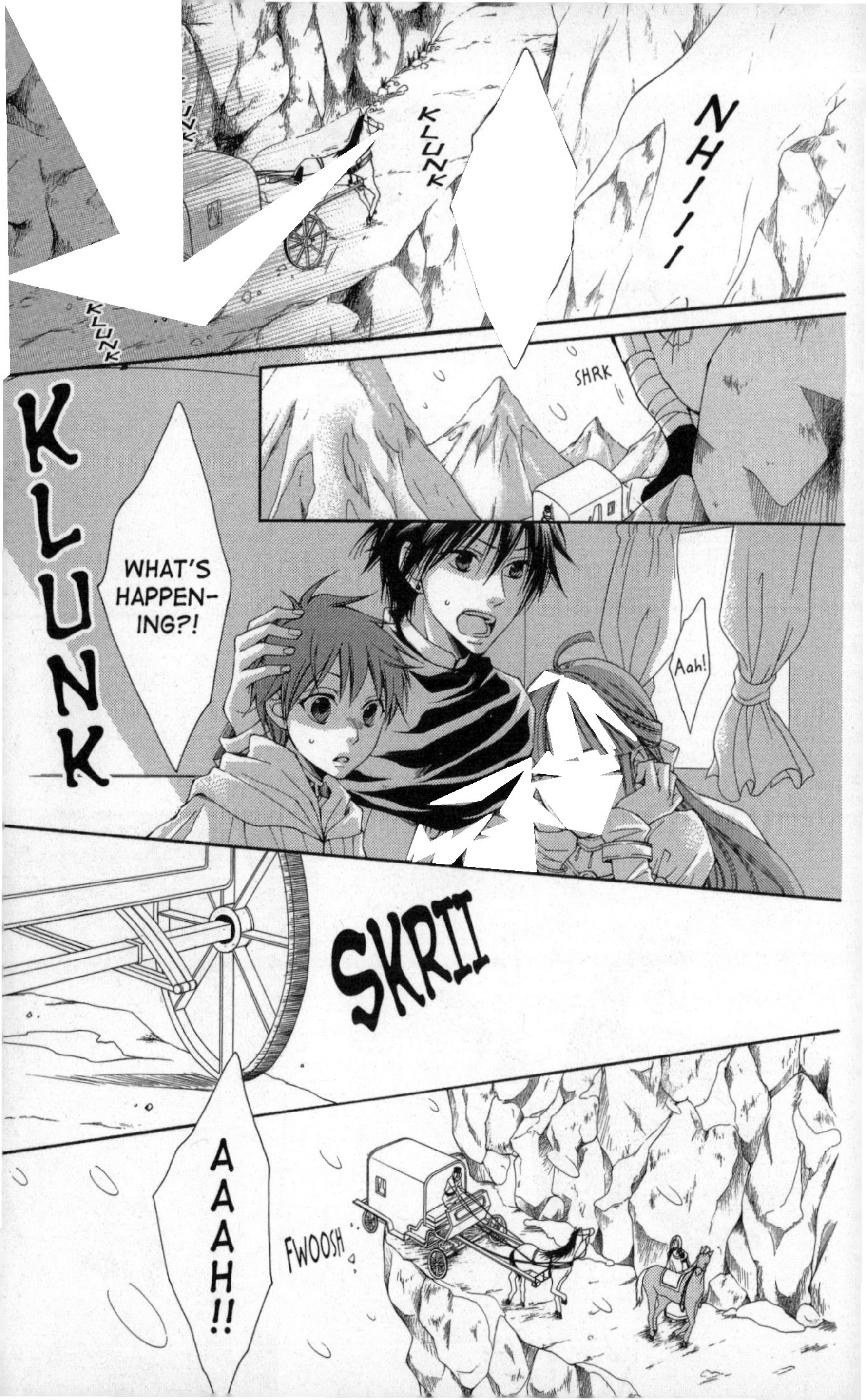
NHIIII
KLUNK
KLUNK
SHRK
Aah!
WHAT'S HAPPEN-ING?!
KLUNK
SKRII
FWOOSH
AAAAH!!

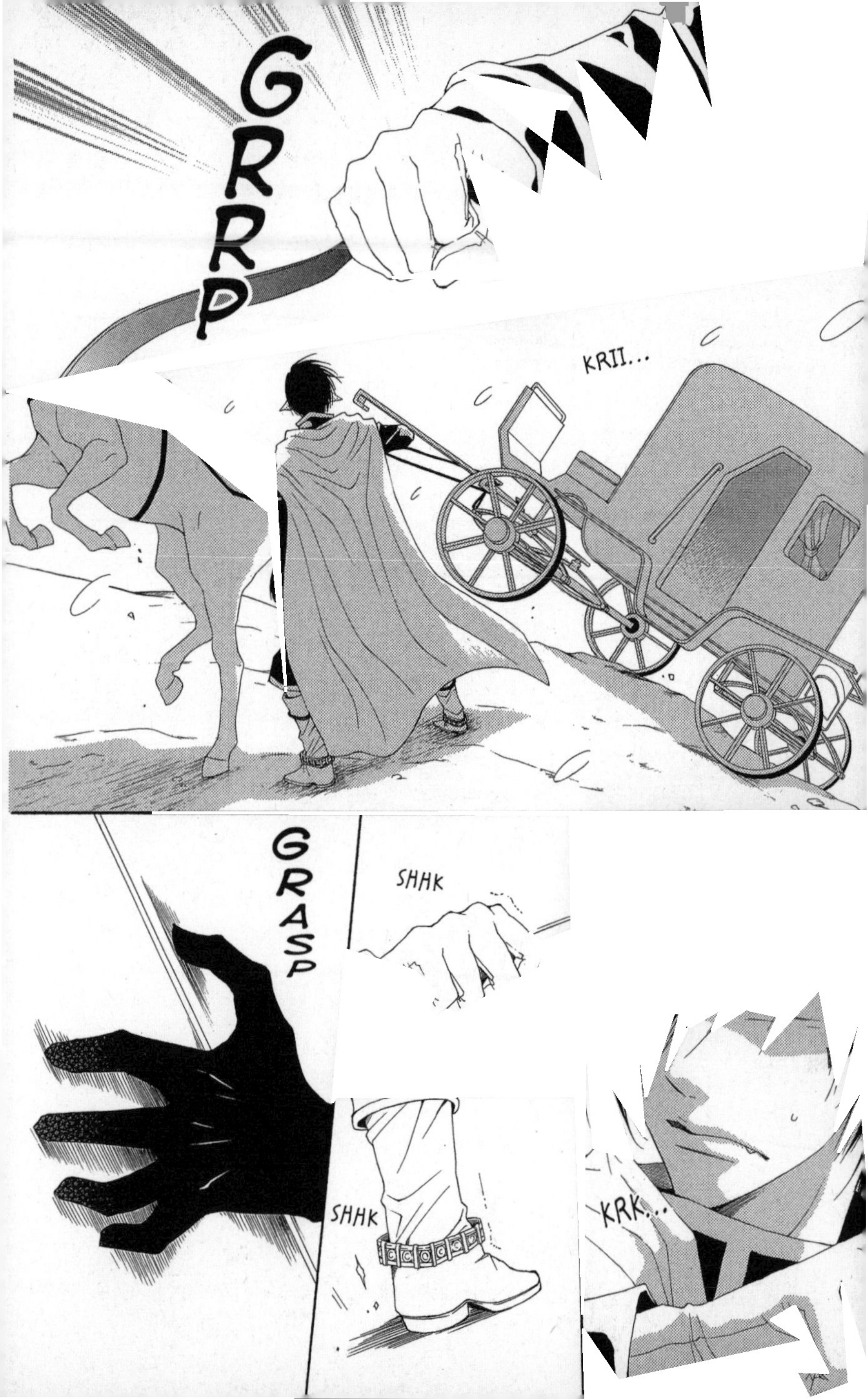
GRRP
KRII...
KRK...
SHHK
SHHK
GRASP

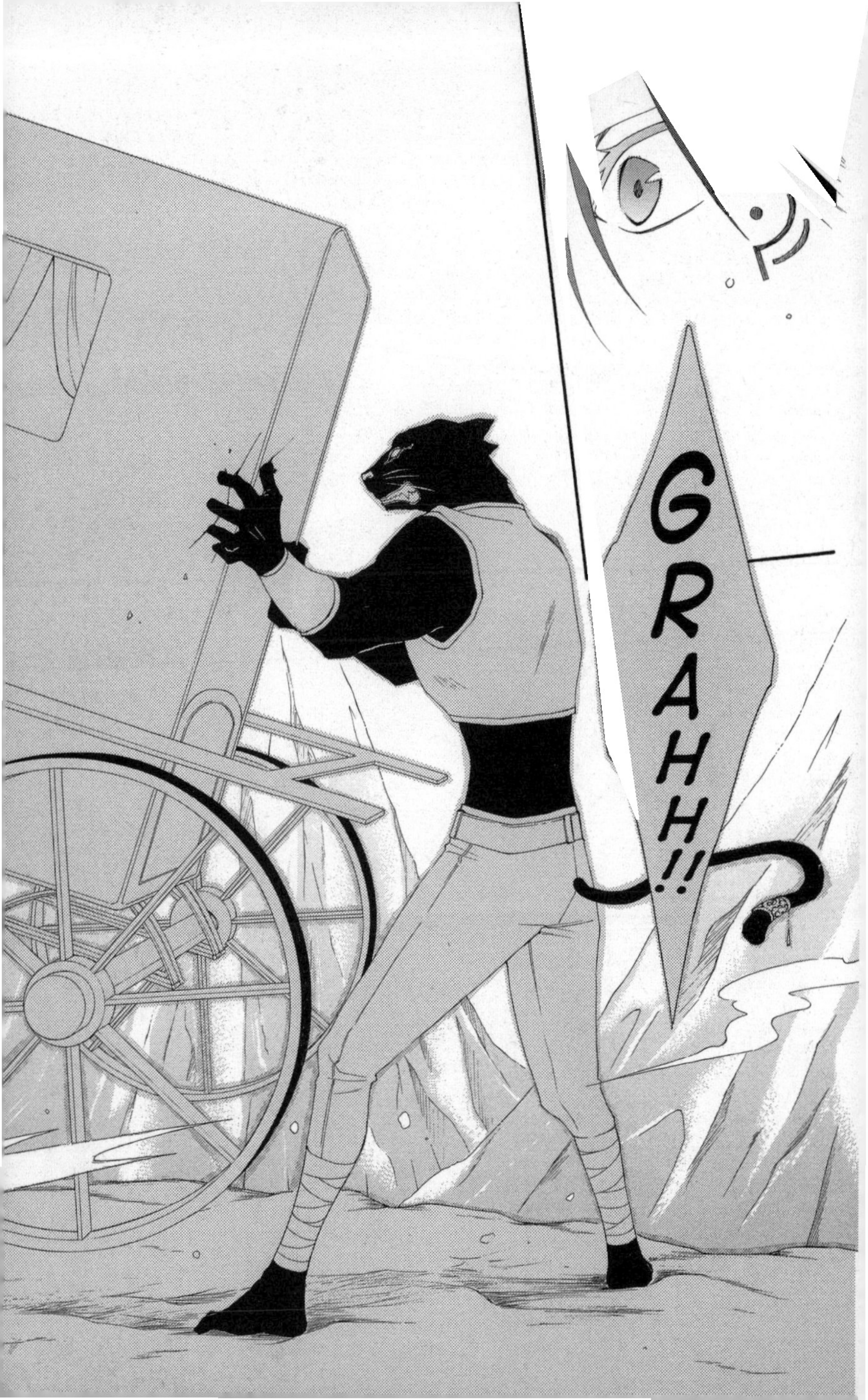
GRAHH!!

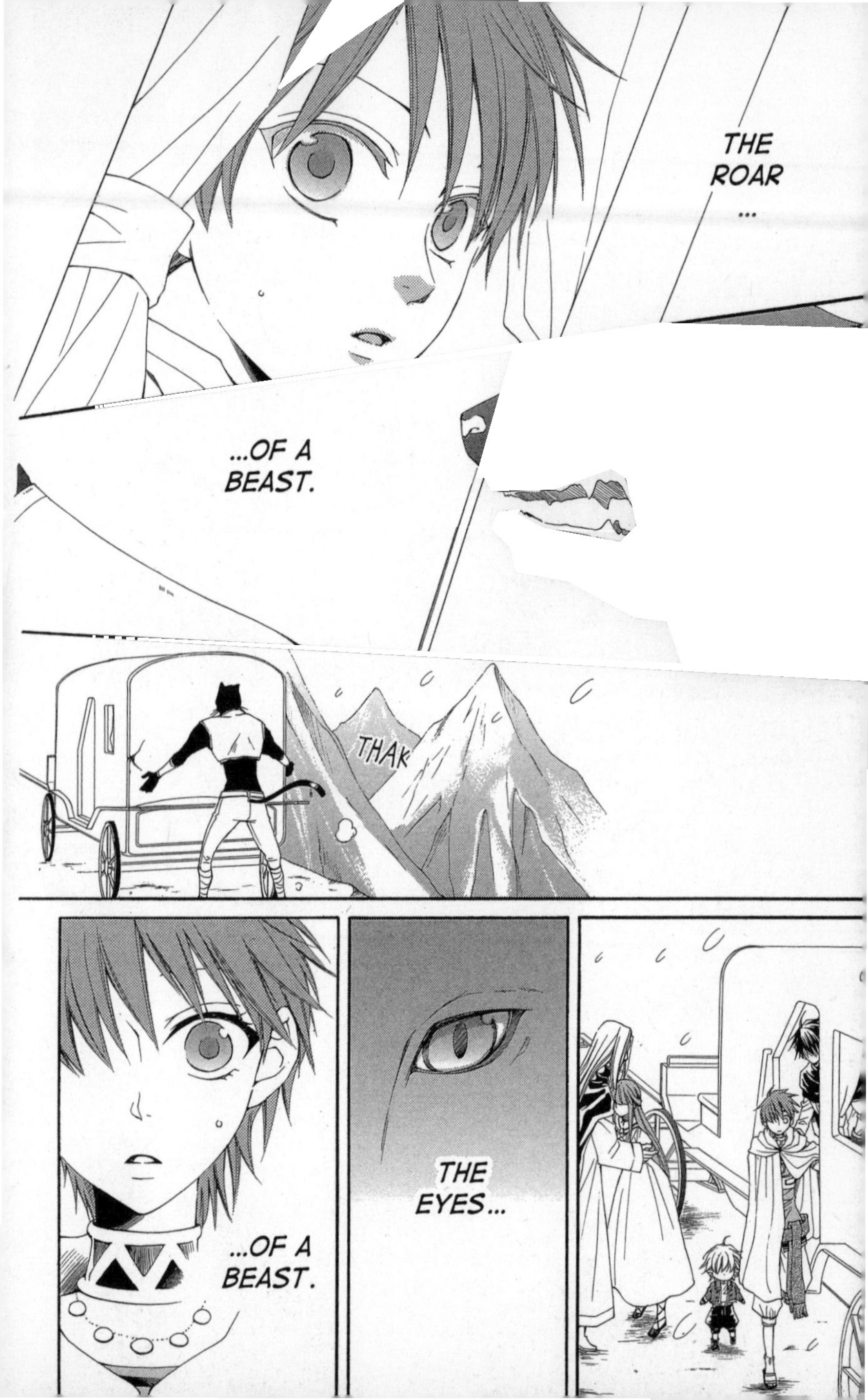
THE ROAR ...
...OF A BEAST.
THAK
THE EYES...
...OF A BEAST.

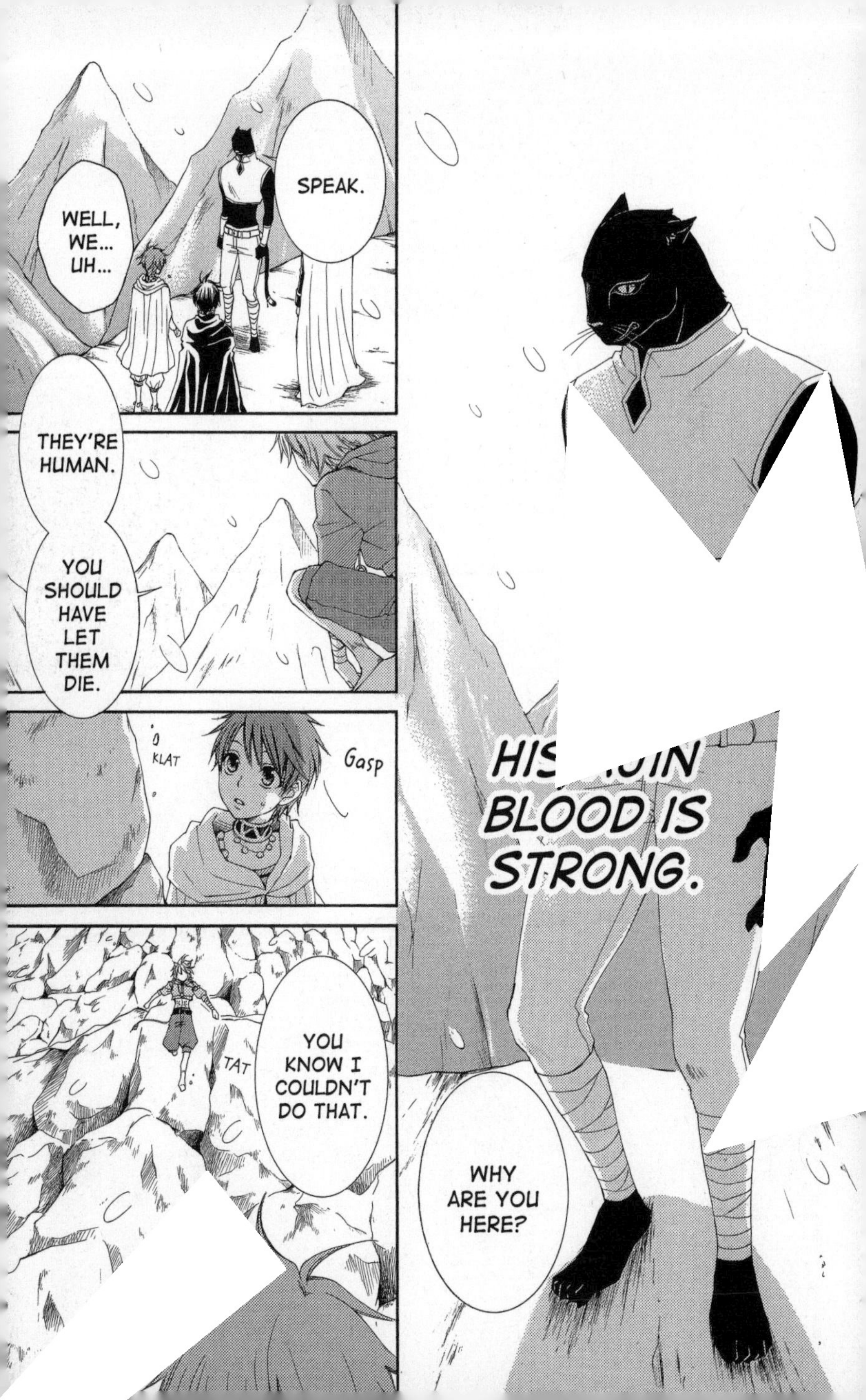
HIS IN
BLOOD IS
STRONG.
WHY ARE YOU HERE?
SPEAK.
WELL, WE... UH...
THEY'RE HUMAN.
YOU SHOULD HAVE LET THEM DIE.
Gasp
KLAT
TAT
YOU KNOW I COULDN'T DO THAT.

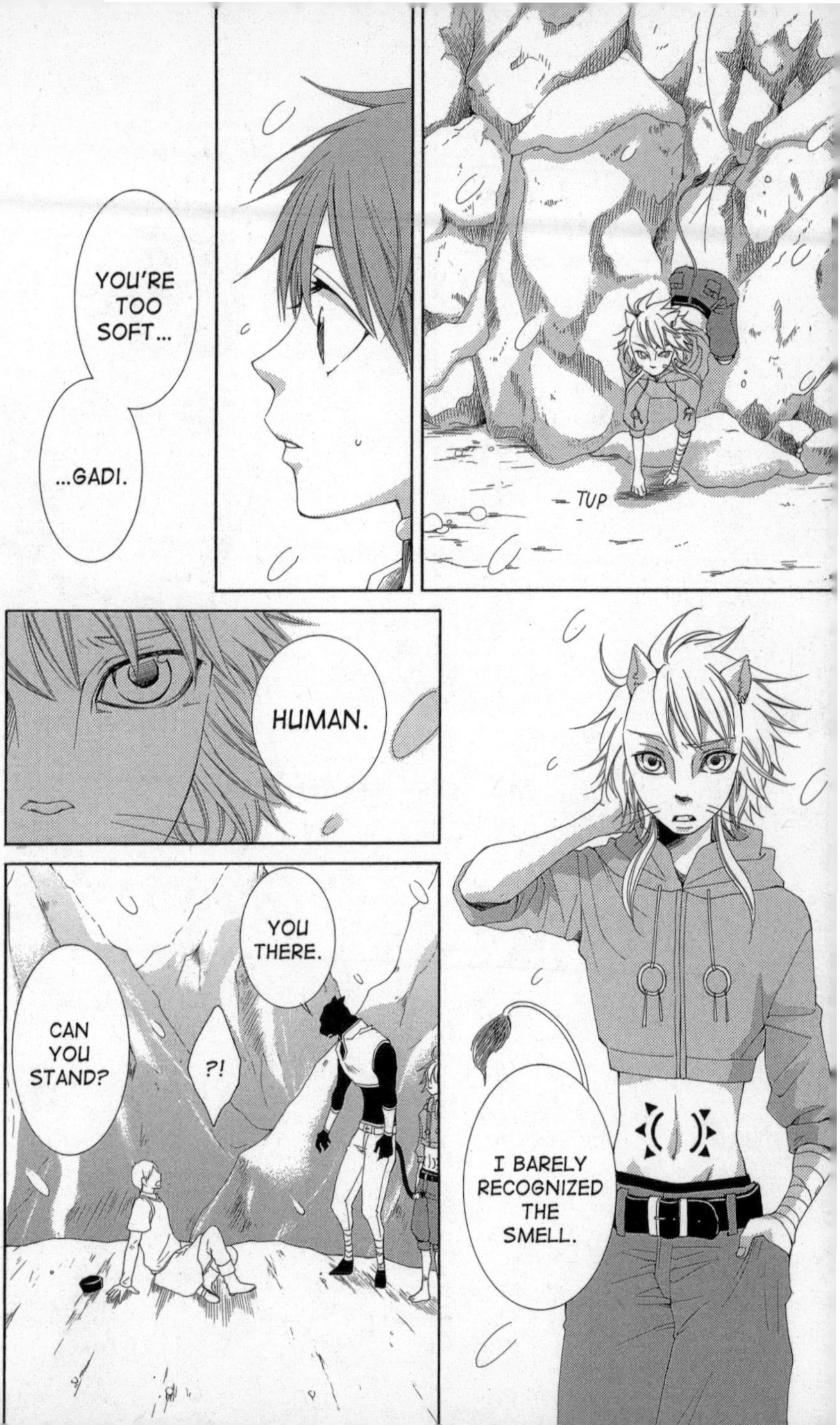
TUP
YOU'RE TOO SOFT...
...GADI.
I BARELY RECOGNIZED THE SMELL.
HUMAN.
YOU THERE.
CAN YOU STAND?
?!

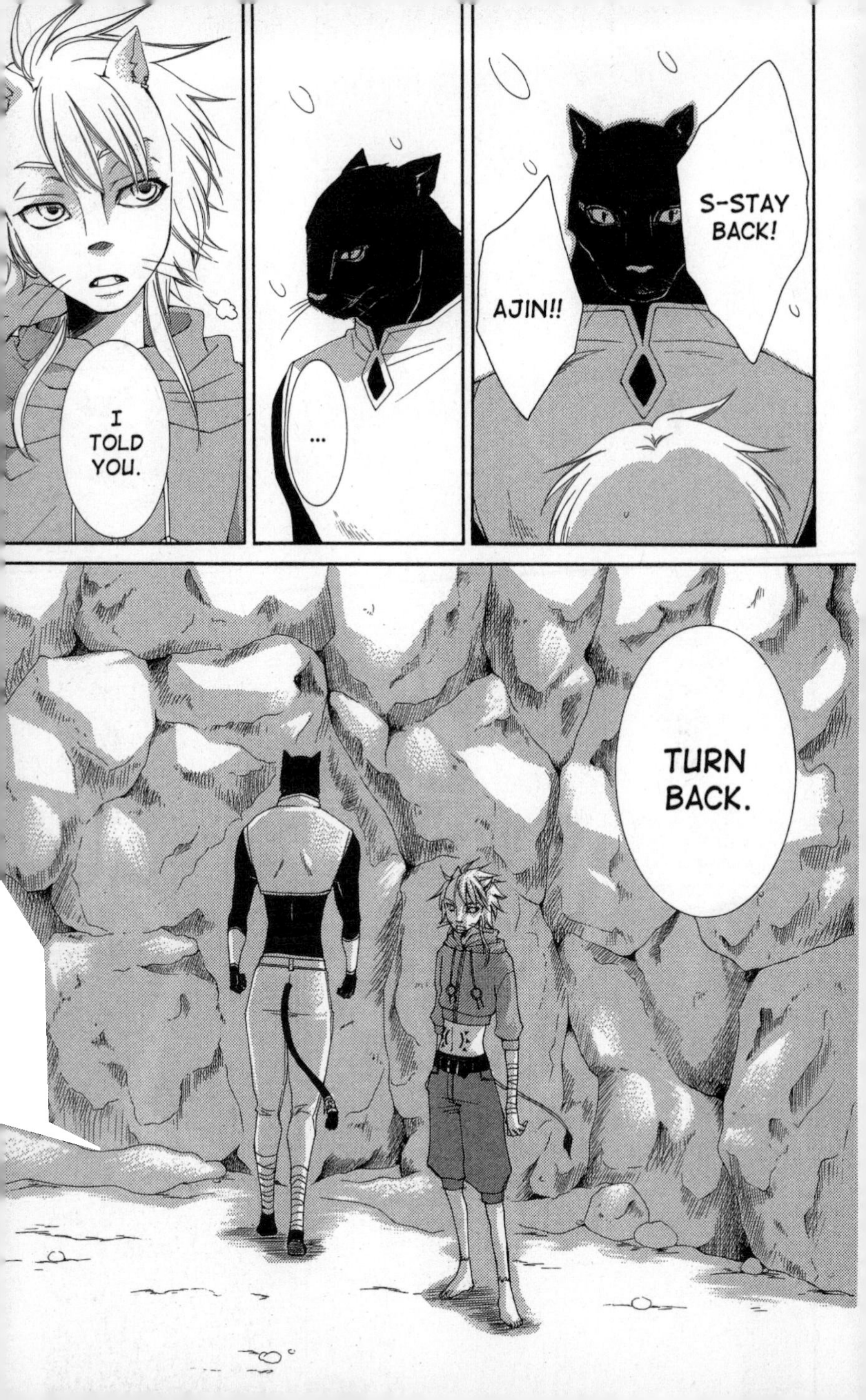
S-STAY BACK!
AJIN!!
...
I TOLD YOU.
TURN BACK.

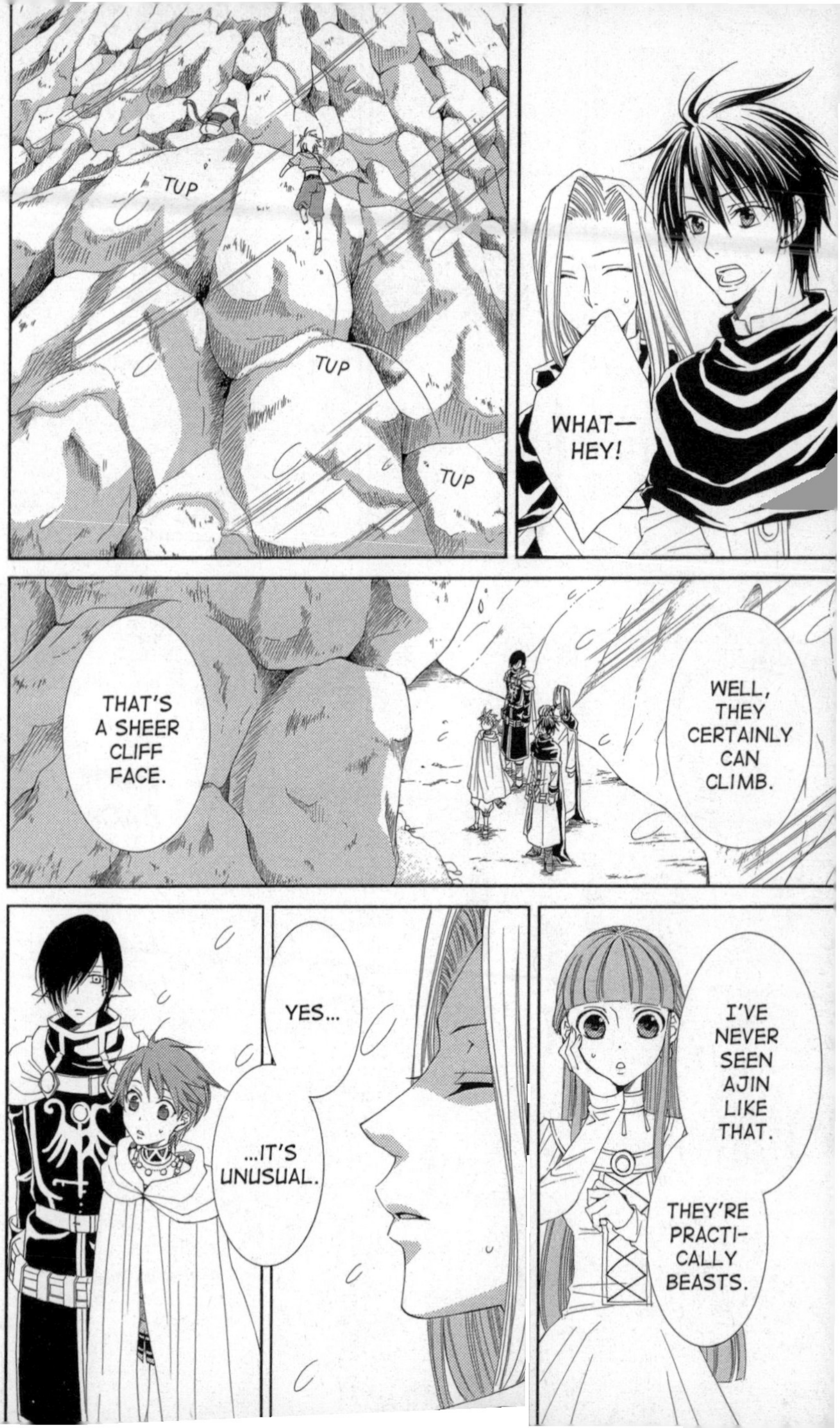
WHAT—
HEY!
TUP
TUP
TUP
WELL, THEY CERTAINLY CAN CLIMB.
THAT'S A SHEER CLIFF FACE.
I'VE NEVER SEEN AJIN LIKE THAT.
THEY'RE PRACTI- CALLY BEASTS.
YES...
...IT'S UNUSUAL.

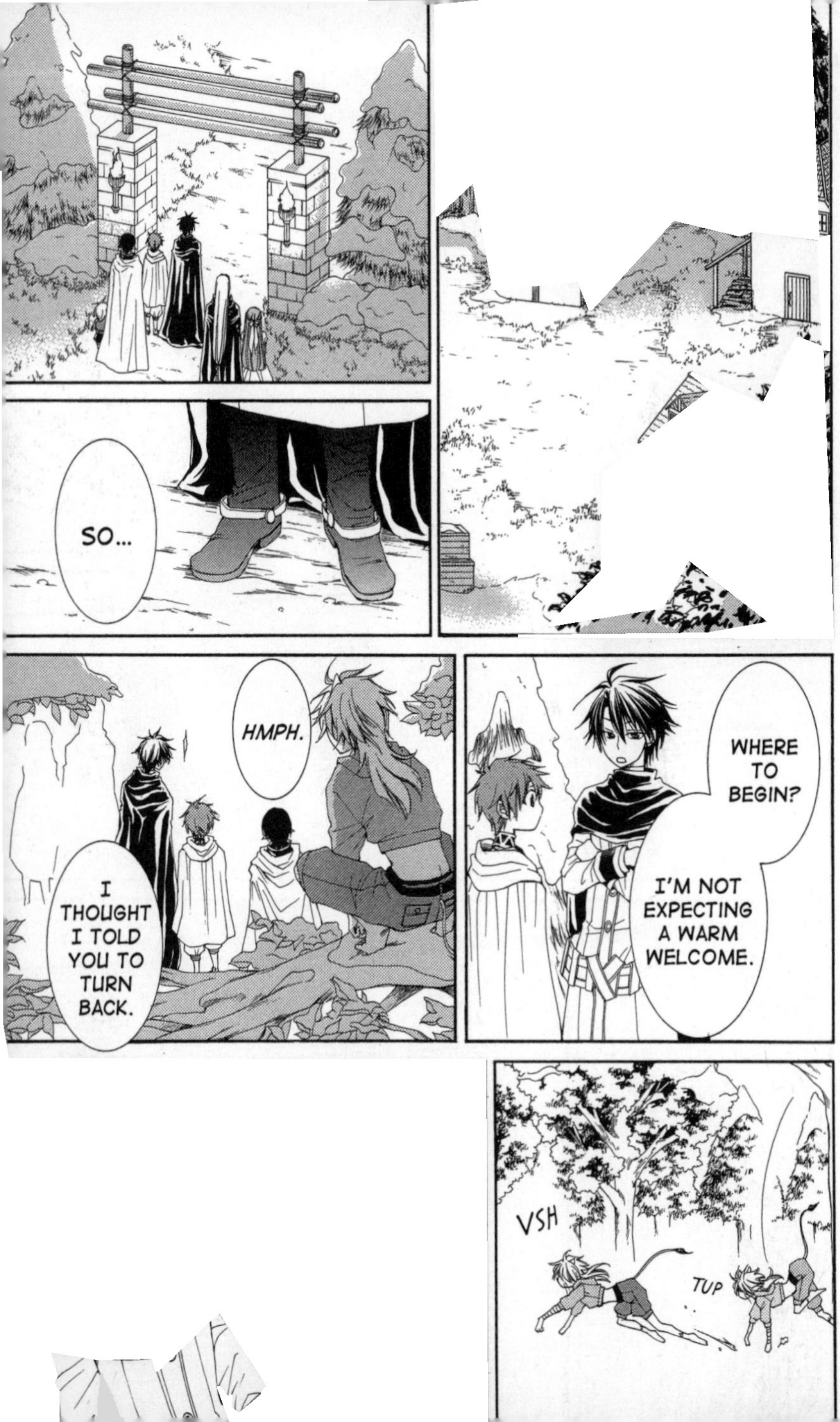
SO...
WHERE TO BEGIN?
I'M NOT EXPECTING A WARM WELCOME.
HMPH.
I THOUGHT I TOLD YOU TO TURN BACK.
VSH
TUP

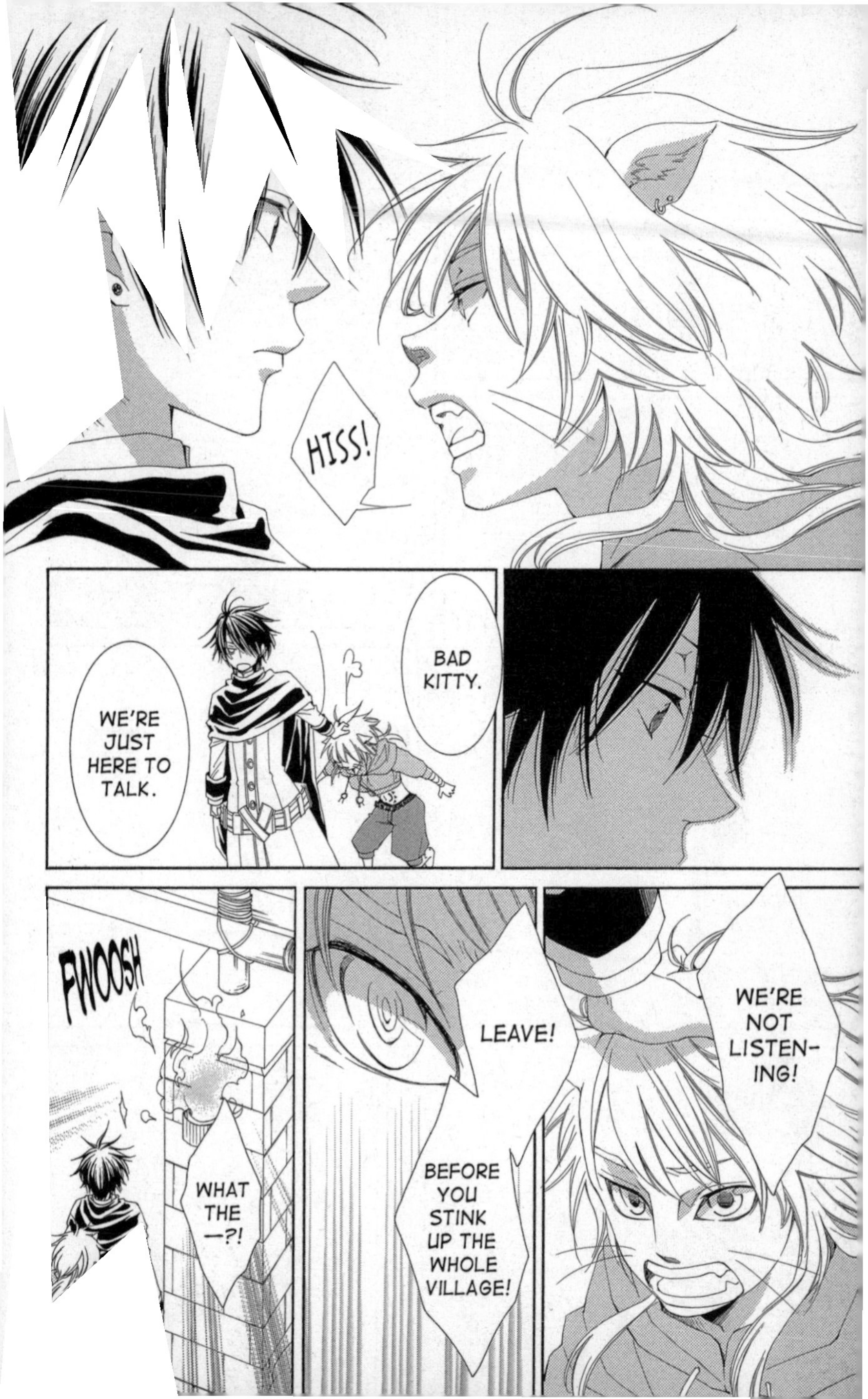
HISS!
BAD KITTY.
WE'RE JUST HERE TO TALK.
WE'RE NOT LISTEN-ING!
LEAVE!
BEFORE YOU STINK UP THE WHOLE VILLAGE!
FWOOSH
WHAT THE—?!

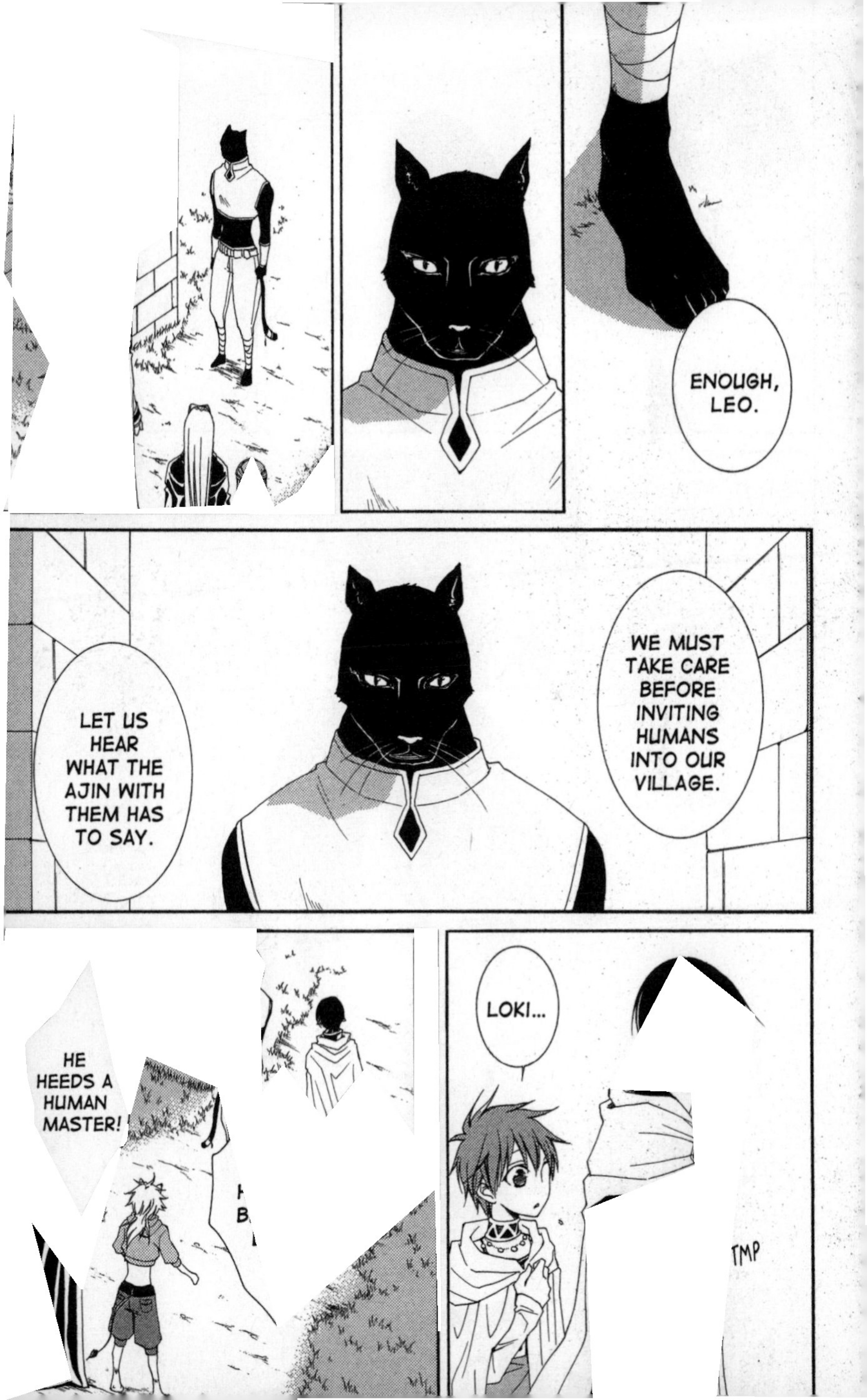
ENOUGH, LEO.
WE MUST TAKE CARE BEFORE INVITING HUMANS INTO OUR VILLAGE.
LET US HEAR WHAT THE AJIN WITH THEM HAS TO SAY.
LOKI...
TMP
HE HEEDS A HUMAN MASTER!

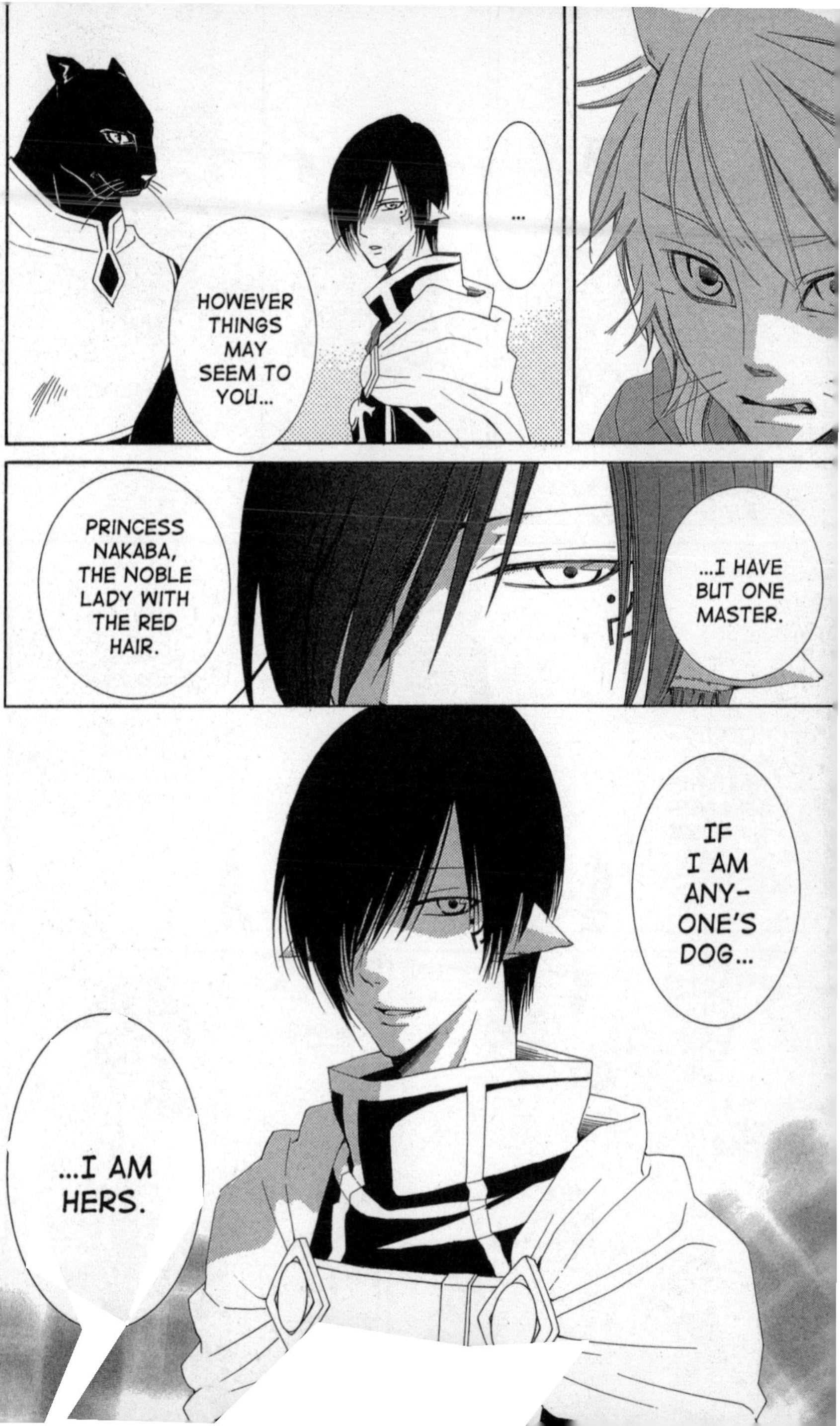
...
HOWEVER THINGS MAY SEEM TO YOU...
...I HAVE BUT ONE MASTER.
PRINCESS NAKABA, THE NOBLE LADY WITH THE RED HAIR.
IF I AM ANY-ONE'S DOG...
...I AM HERS.

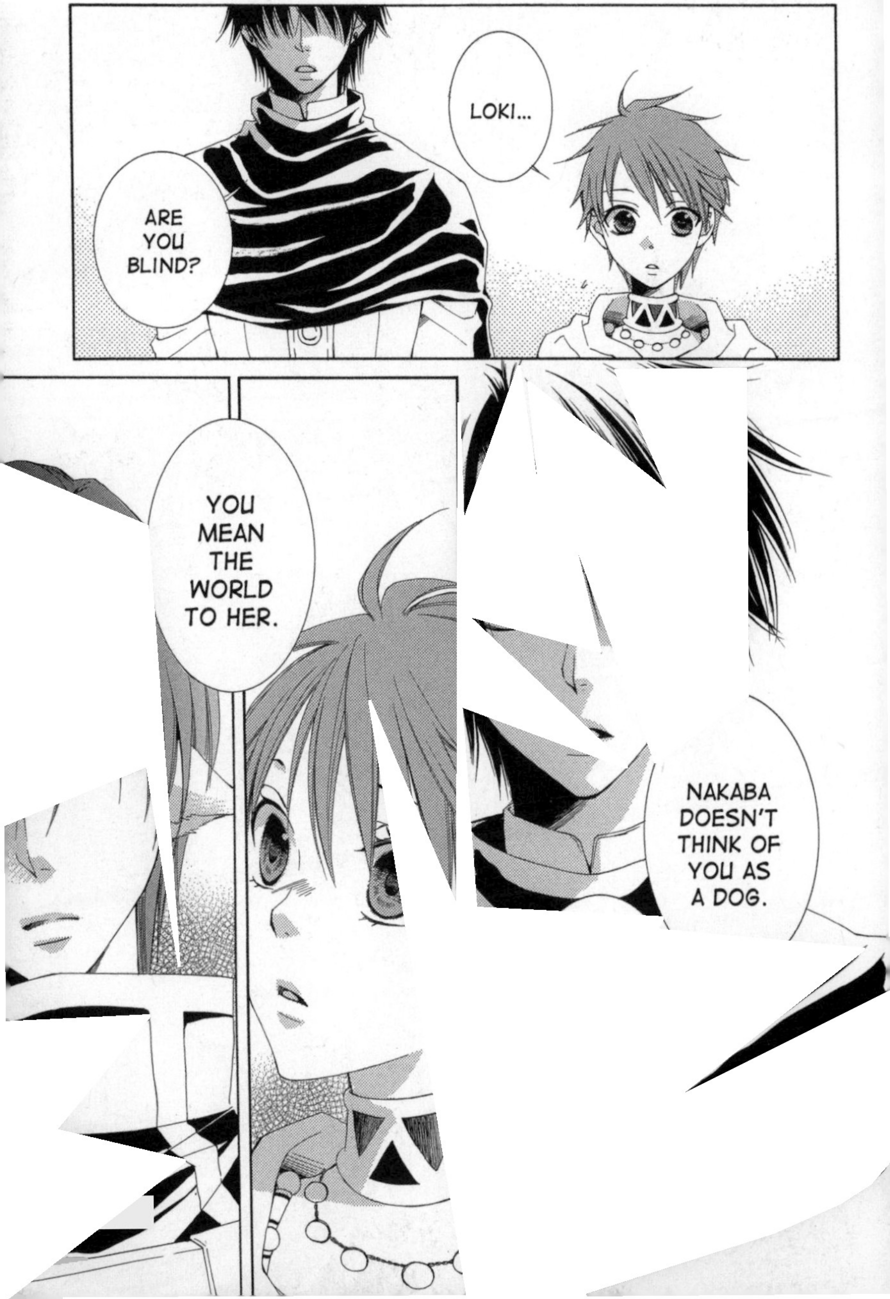
LOKI...
ARE YOU BLIND?
NAKABA DOESN'T THINK OF YOU AS A DOG.
YOU MEAN THE WORLD TO HER.

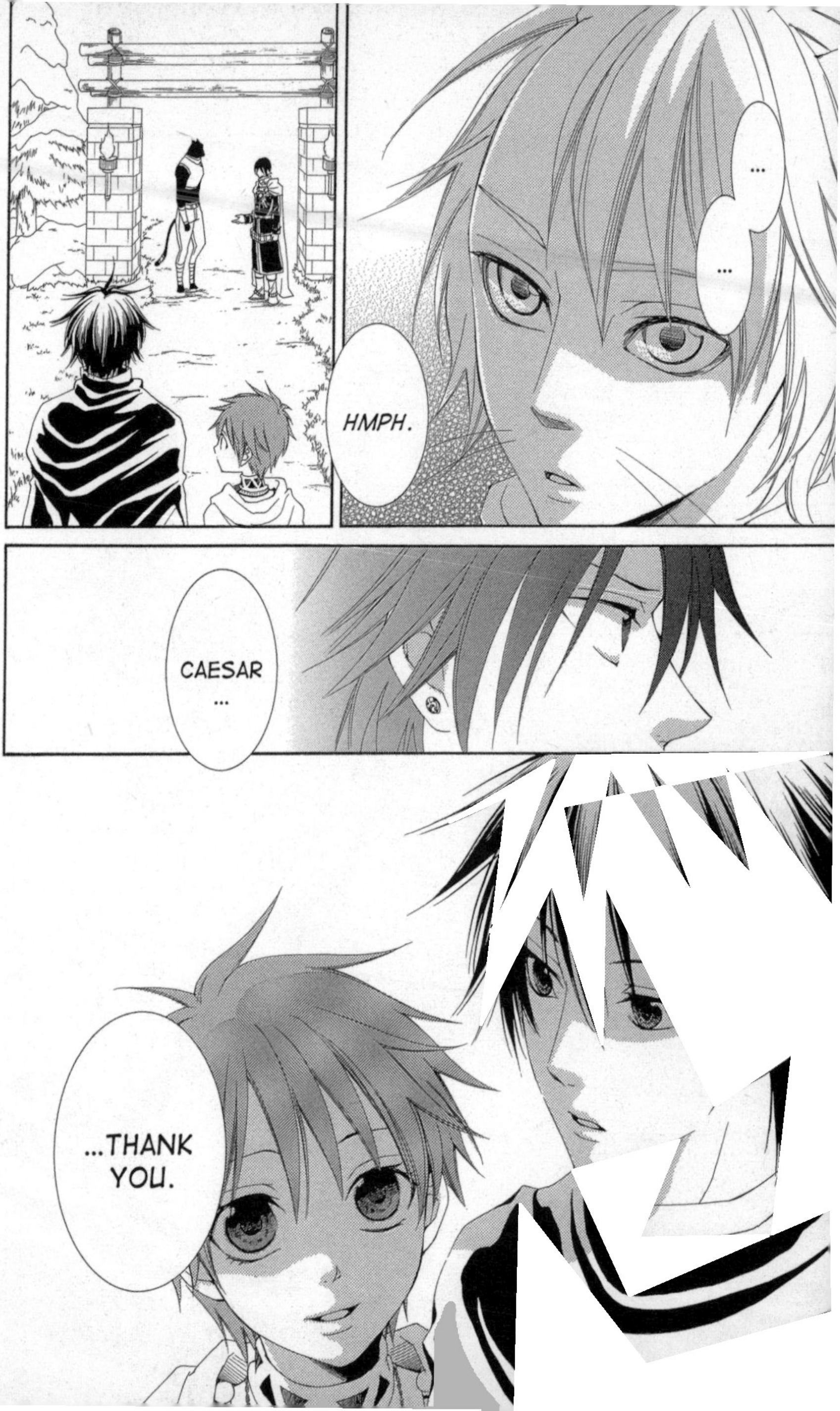
...
...
HMPH.
CAESAR ...
...THANK YOU.

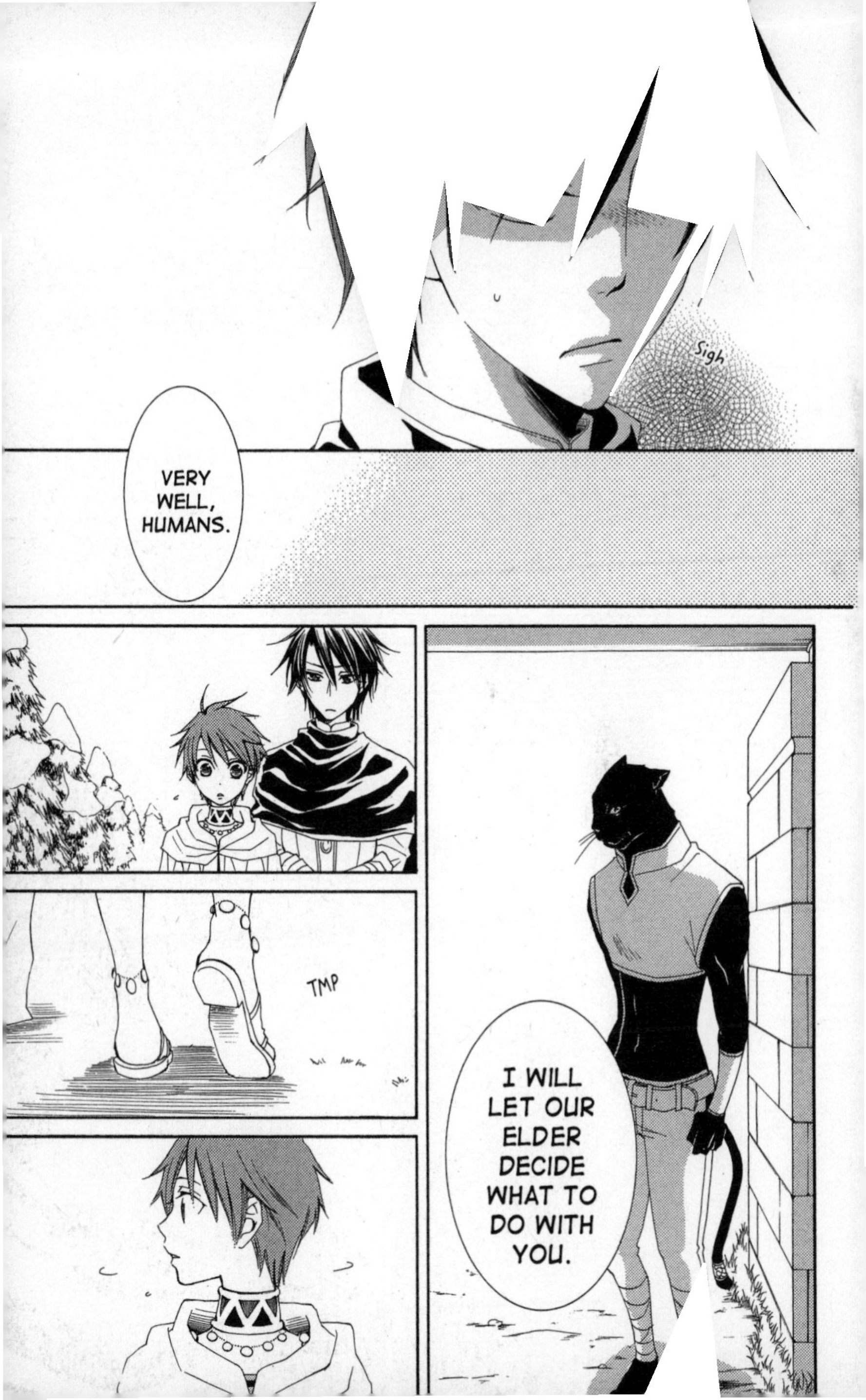
Sigh
VERY WELL, HUMANS.
I WILL LET OUR ELDER DECIDE WHAT TO DO WITH YOU.
TMP

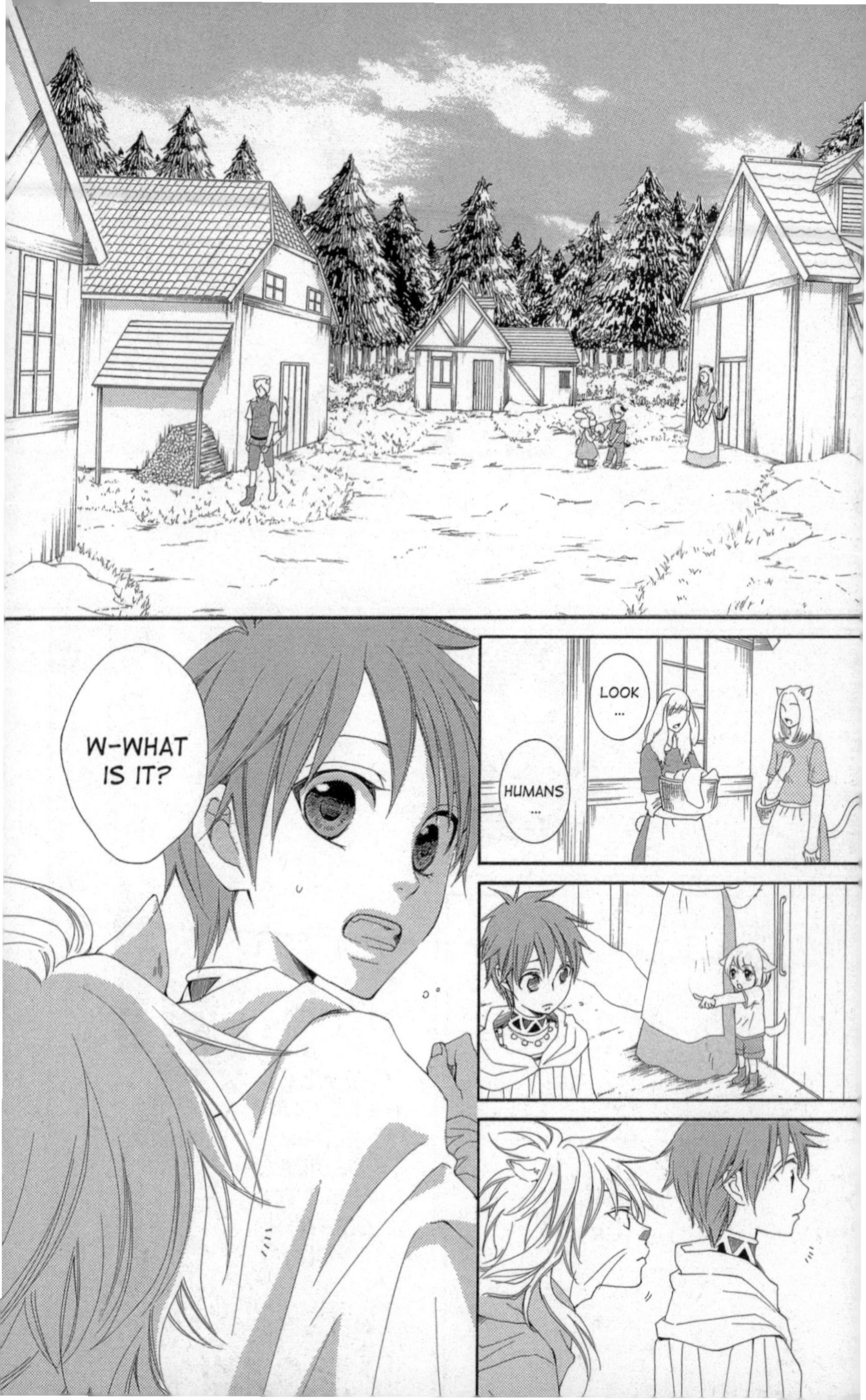
LOOK ...
HUMANS ...
W-WHAT IS IT?

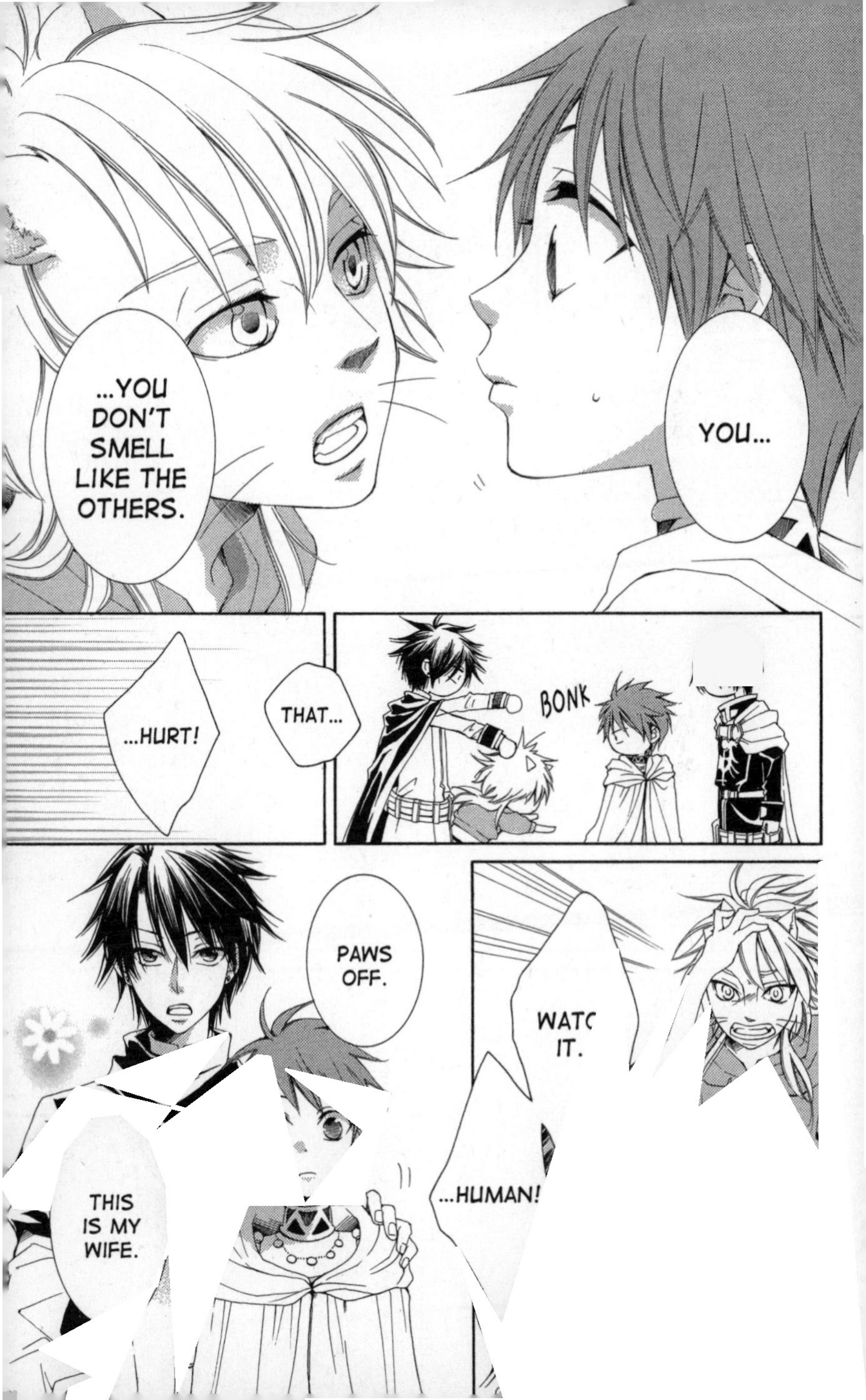
YOU...
...YOU DON'T SMELL LIKE THE OTHERS.
BONK
THAT...
...HURT!
WATC IT.
...HUMAN!
PAWS OFF.
THIS IS MY WIFE.

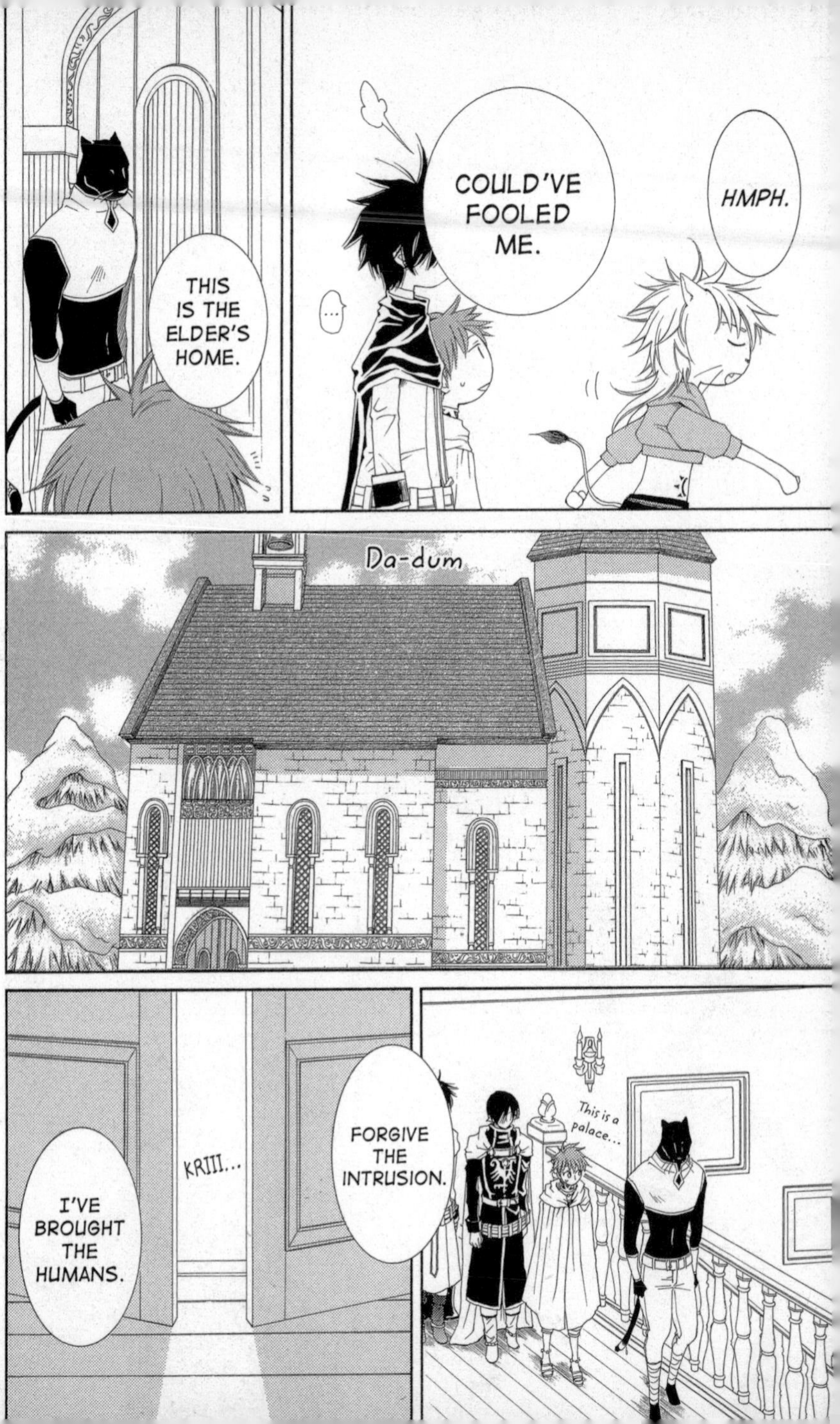
HMPH.
COULD'VE FOOLED ME.
...
THIS IS THE ELDER'S HOME.
Da-dum
FORGIVE THE INTRUSION.
This is a palace...
KRIII...
I'VE BROUGHT THE HUMANS.

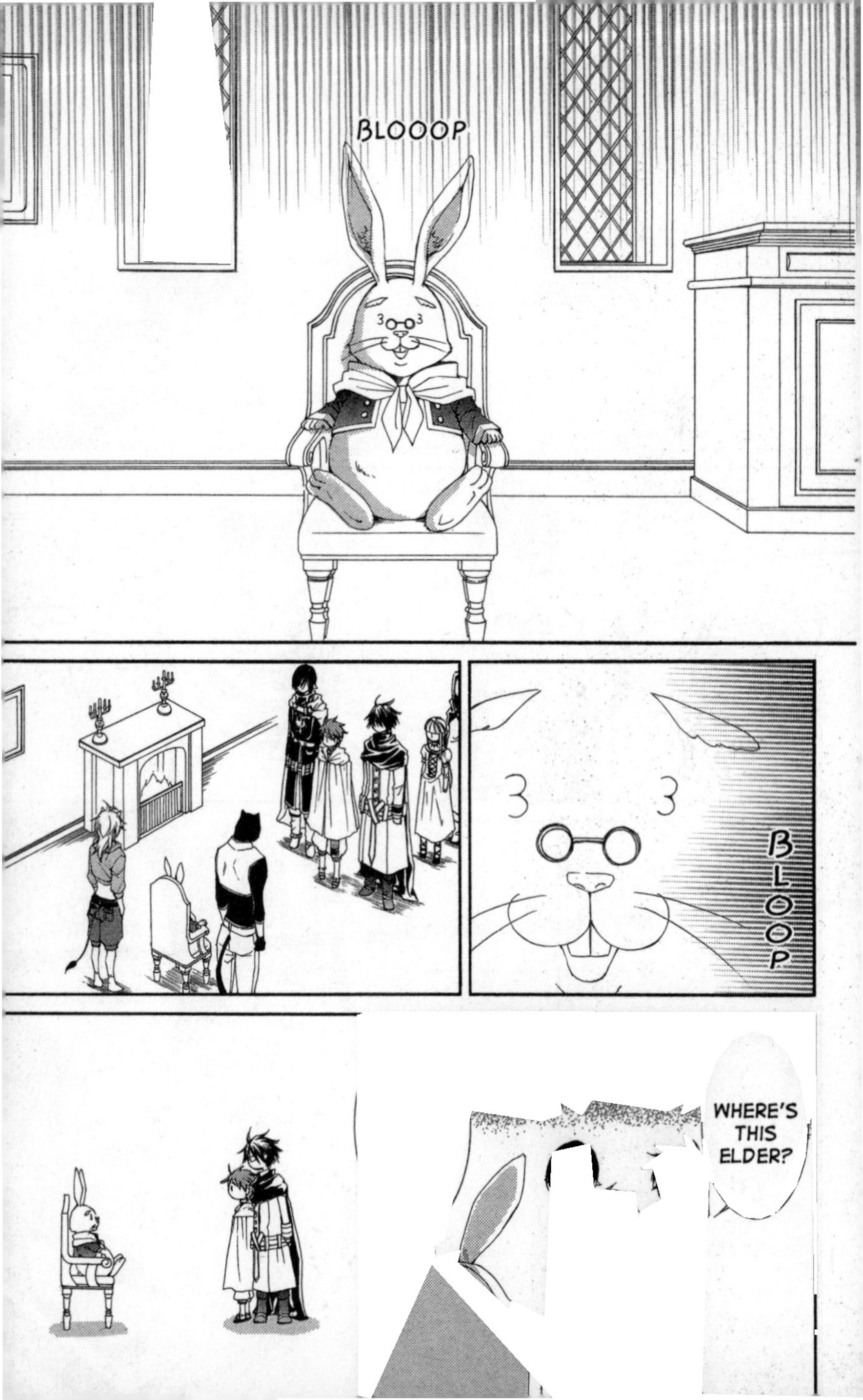
BLOOOP
BLOOOP
WHERE'S THIS ELDER?

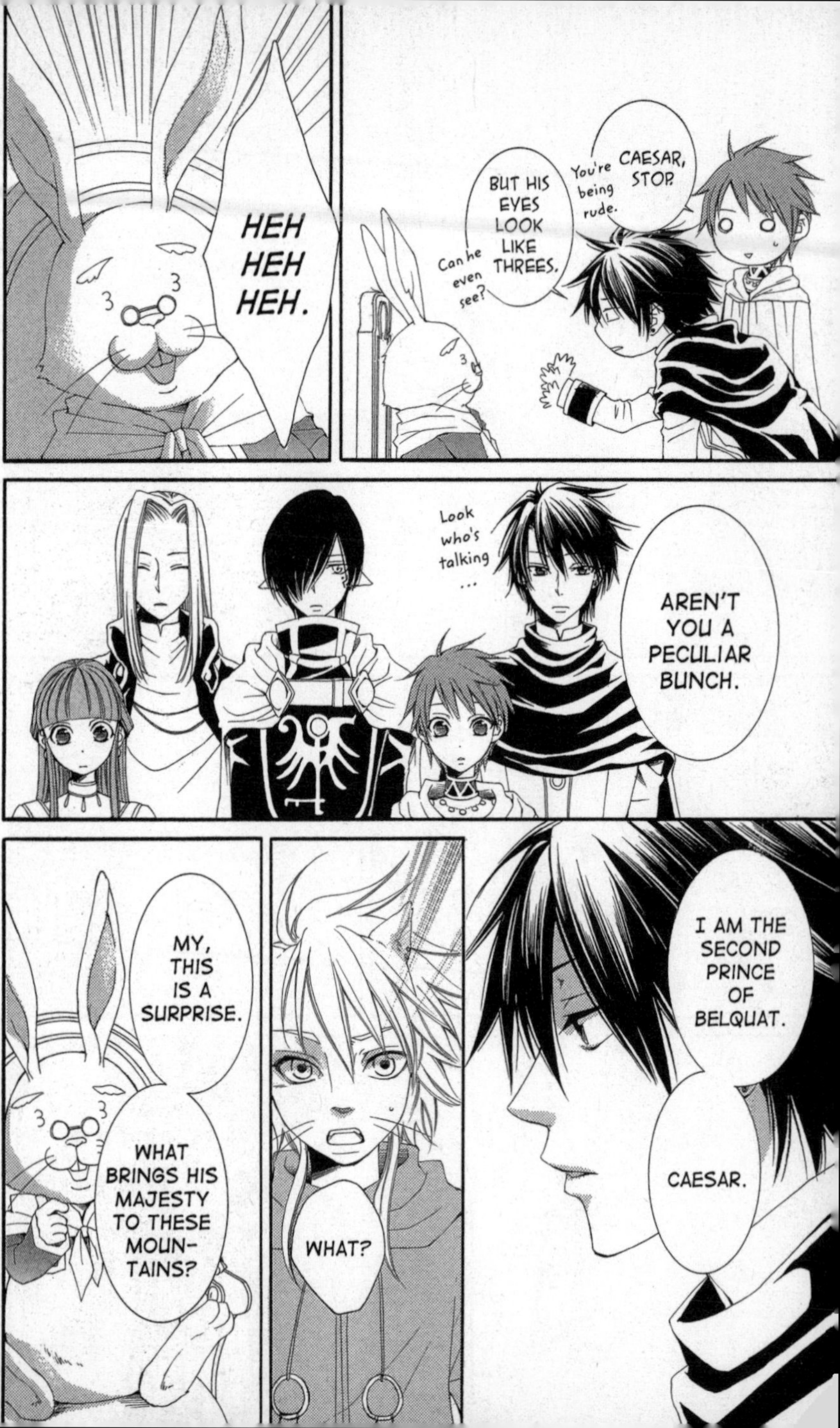
CAESAR, STOP.
You're being rude.
BUT HIS EYES LOOK LIKE THREES.
Can he even see?
HEH HEH HEH.
AREN'T YOU A PECULIAR BUNCH.
Look who's talking ...
I AM THE SECOND PRINCE OF BELQUAT.
CAESAR.
WHAT?
MY, THIS IS A SURPRISE.
WHAT BRINGS HIS MAJESTY TO THESE MOUN-TAINS?

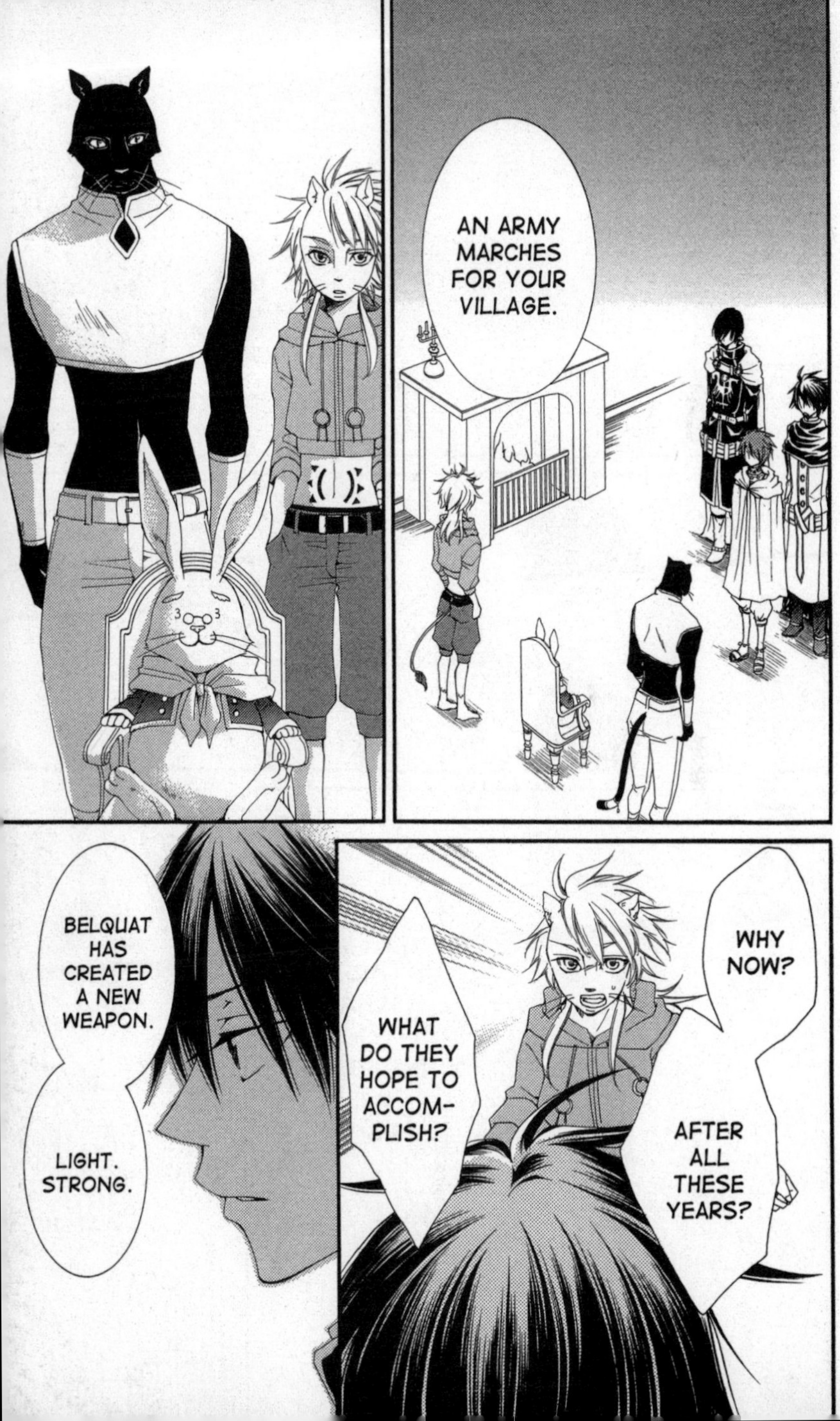
AN ARMY MARCHES FOR YOUR VILLAGE.
WHY NOW?
AFTER ALL THESE YEARS?
WHAT DO THEY HOPE TO ACCOMPLISH?
BELQUAT HAS CREATED A NEW WEAPON.
LIGHT. STRONG.

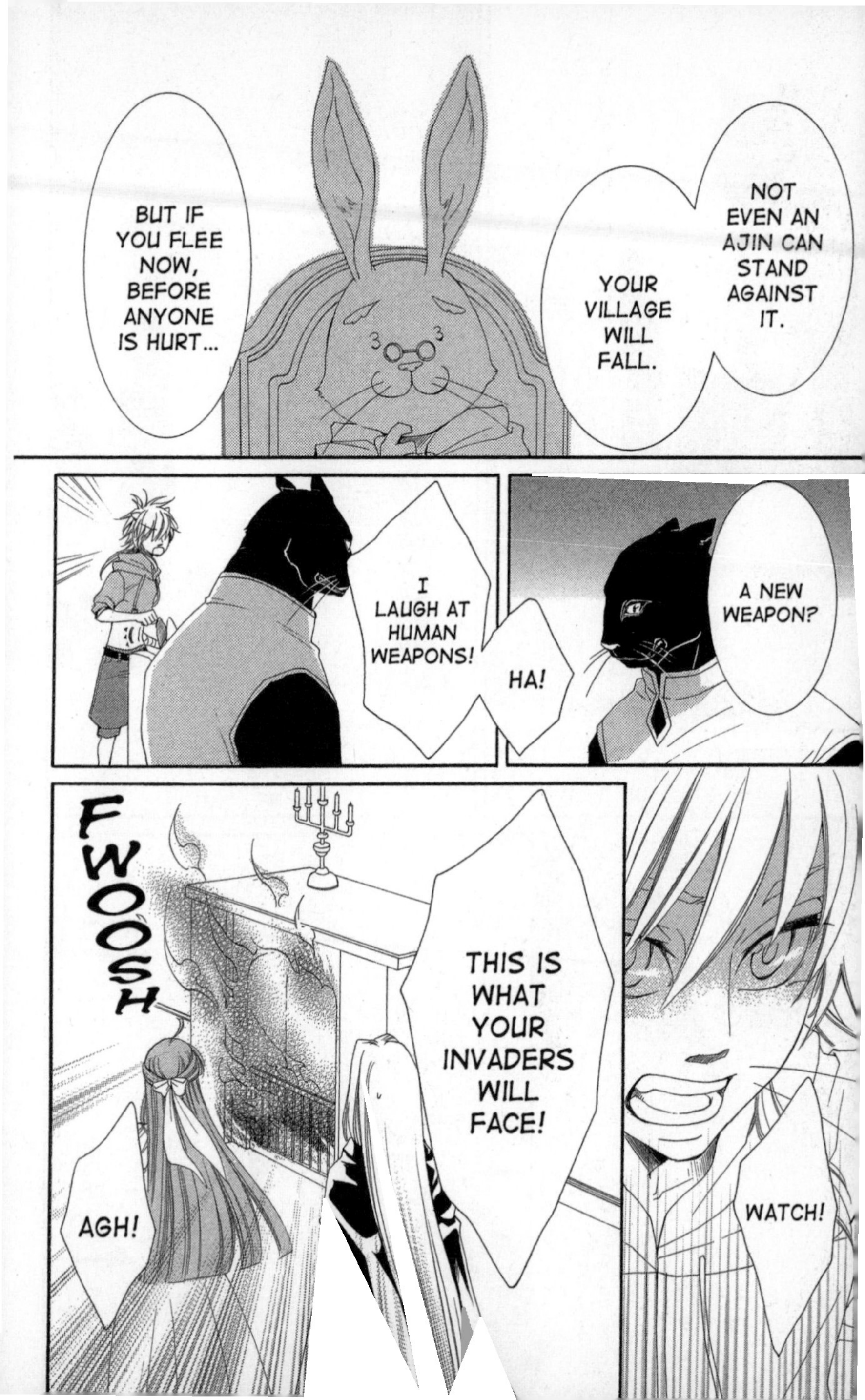
NOT EVEN AN AJIN CAN STAND AGAINST IT.
YOUR VILLAGE WILL FALL.
BUT IF YOU FLEE NOW, BEFORE ANYONE IS HURT...
A NEW WEAPON?
HA!
I LAUGH AT HUMAN WEAPONS!
WATCH!
THIS IS WHAT YOUR INVADERS WILL FACE!
FWOOSH
AGH!

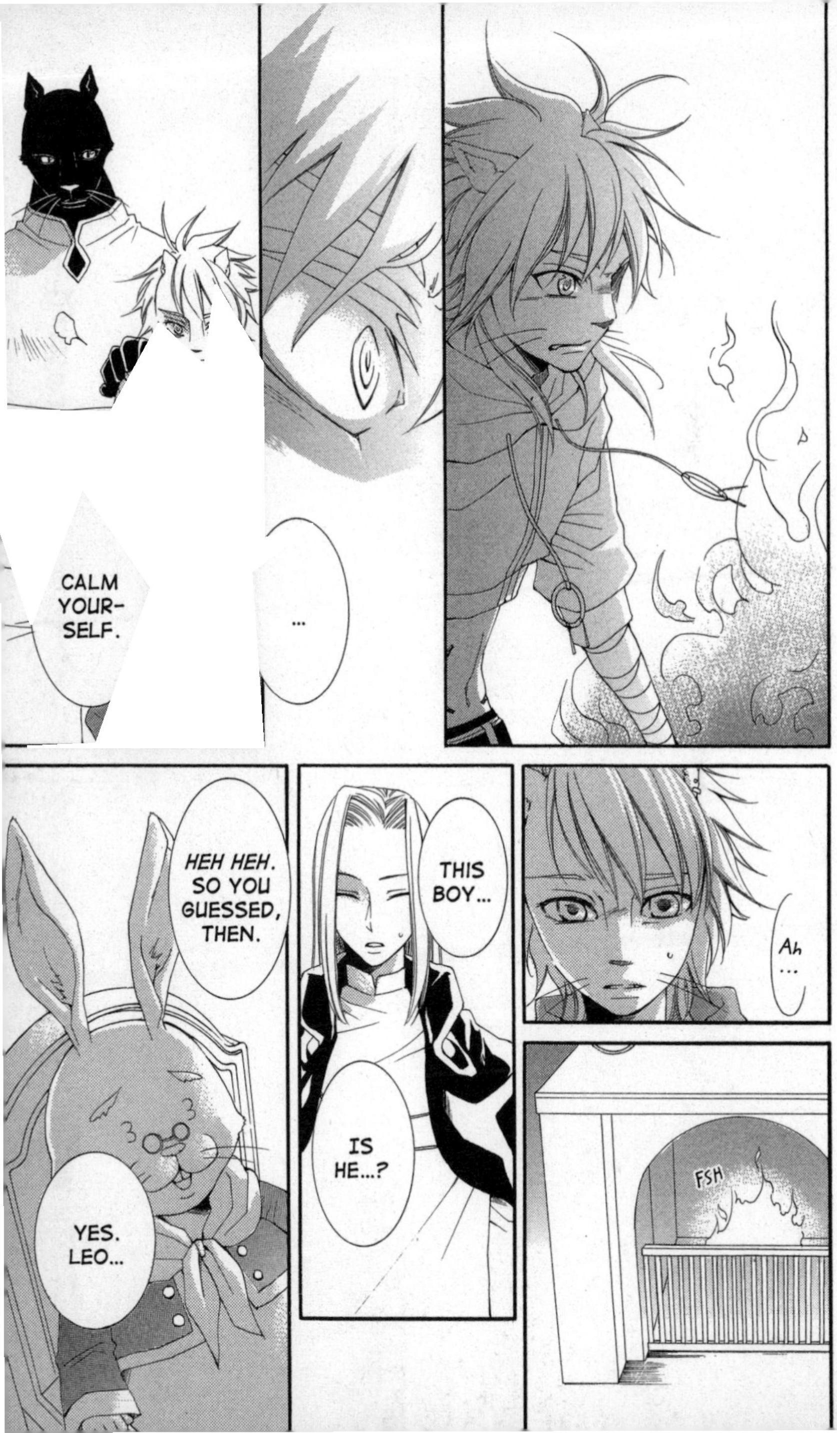
...
CALM YOUR-SELF.
Ah...
FSH
THIS BOY...
IS HE...?
HEH HEH. SO YOU GUESSED, THEN.
YES. LEO...

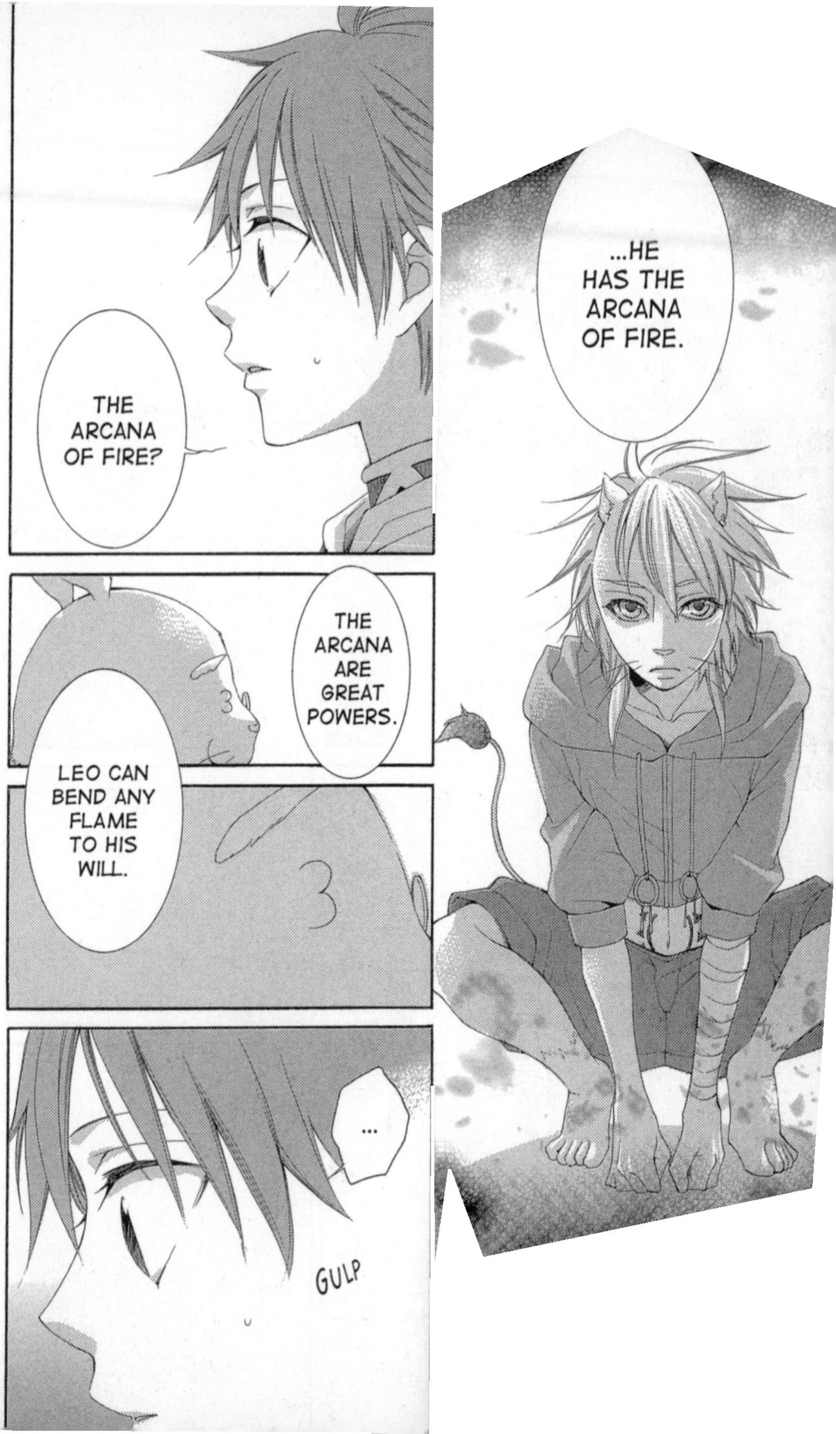
...HE HAS THE ARCANA OF FIRE.
THE ARCANA OF FIRE?
THE ARCANA ARE GREAT POWERS.
LEO CAN BEND ANY FLAME TO HIS WILL.
...
GULP

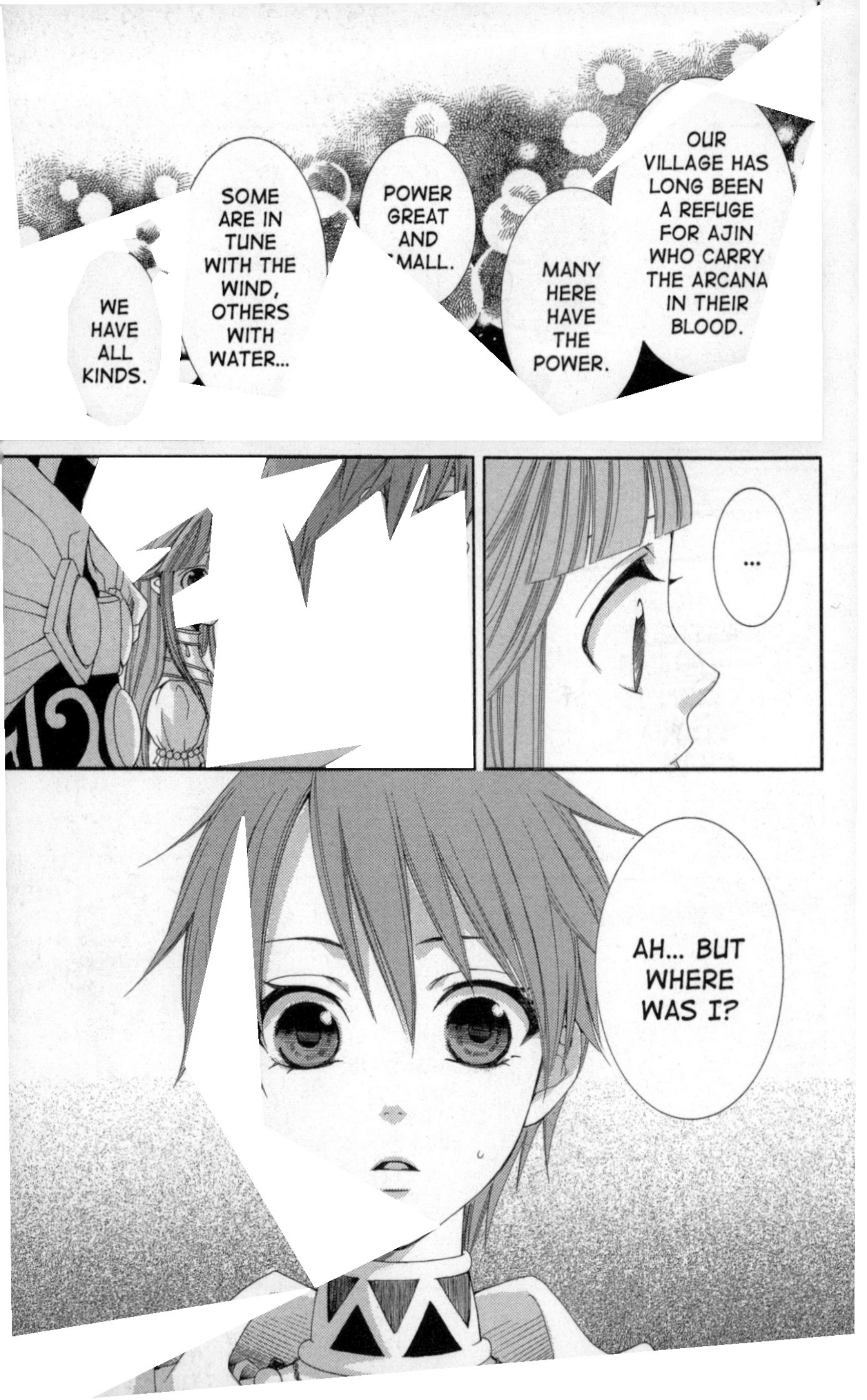
OUR VILLAGE HAS LONG BEEN A REFUGE FOR AJIN WHO CARRY THE ARCANA IN THEIR BLOOD.
MANY HERE HAVE THE POWER.
POWER GREAT AND SMALL.
SOME ARE IN TUNE WITH THE WIND, OTHERS WITH WATER...
WE HAVE ALL KINDS.
...
AH... BUT WHERE WAS I?

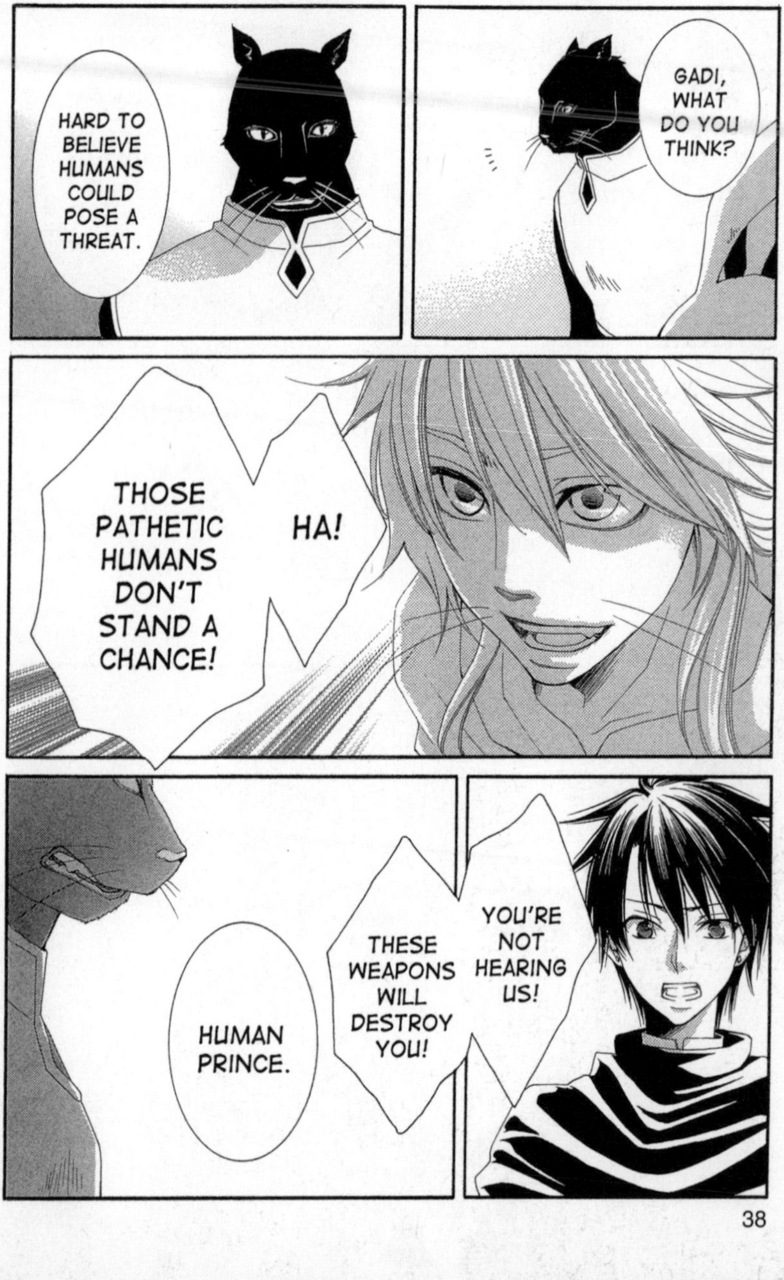
GADI, WHAT DO YOU THINK?
HARD TO BELIEVE HUMANS COULD POSE A THREAT.
HA!
THOSE PATHETIC HUMANS DON'T STAND A CHANCE!
YOU'RE NOT HEARING US!
THESE WEAPONS WILL DESTROY YOU!
HUMAN PRINCE.

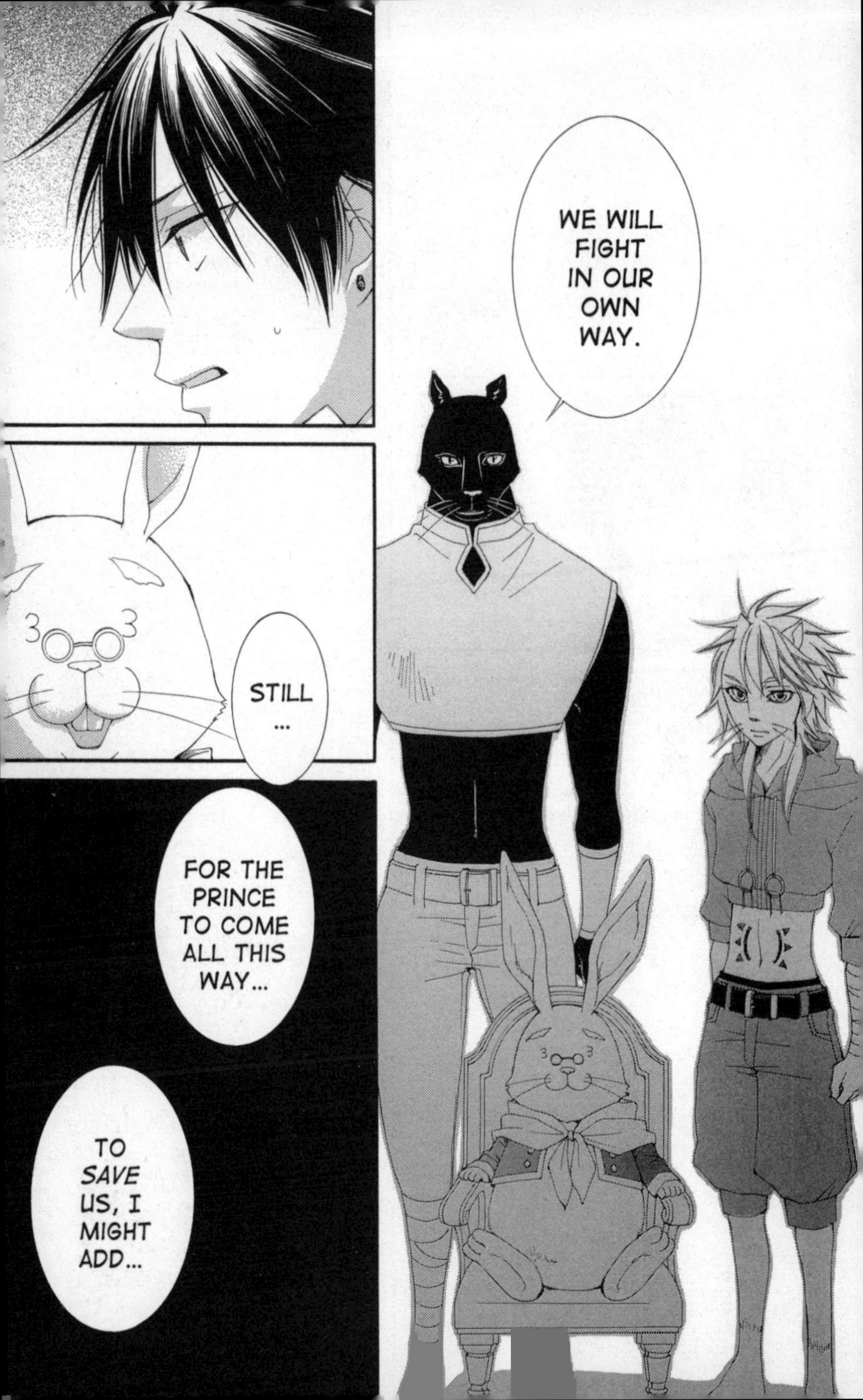
WE WILL FIGHT IN OUR OWN WAY.
STILL ...
FOR THE PRINCE TO COME ALL THIS WAY...
TO *SAVE* US, I MIGHT ADD...

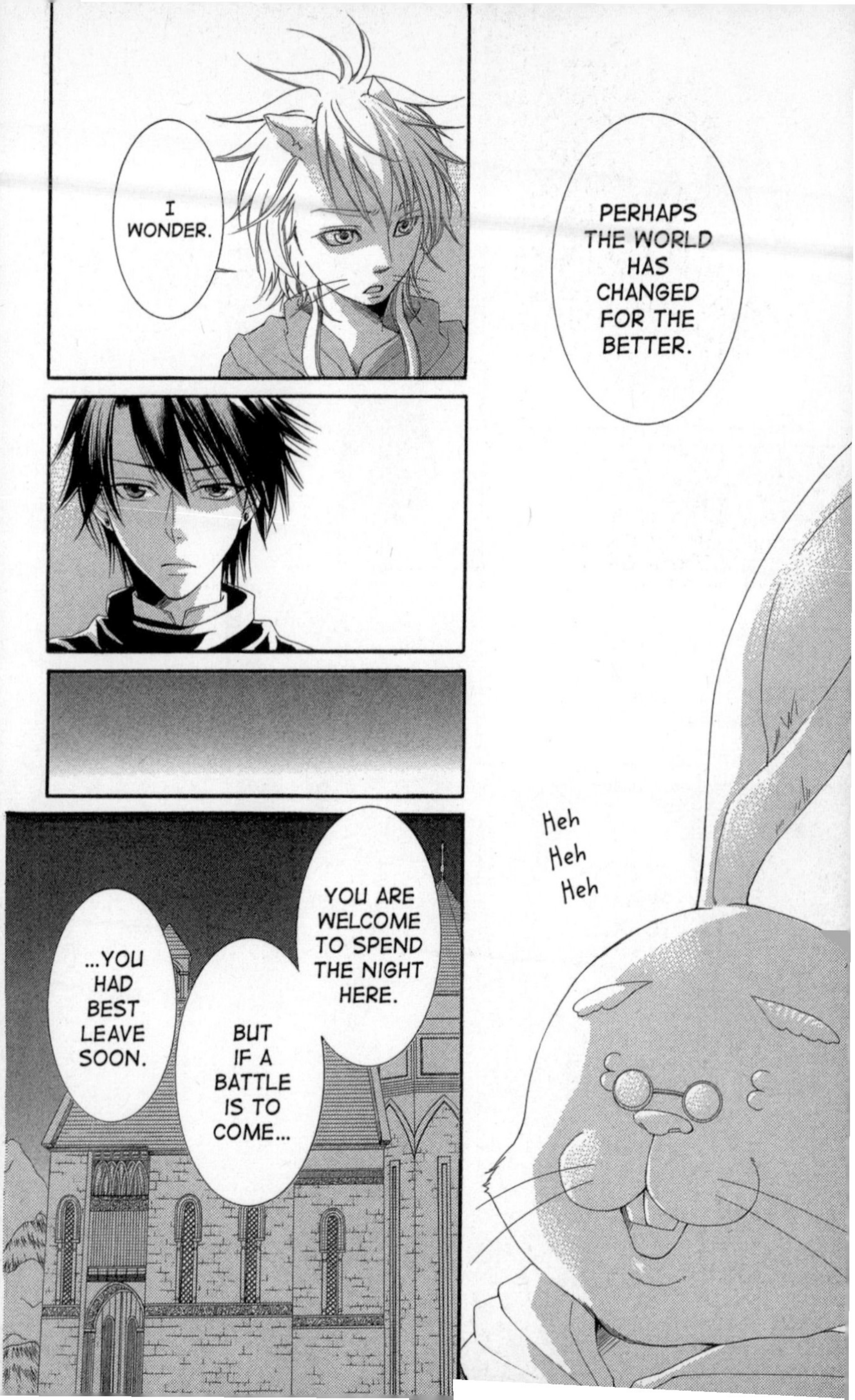
PERHAPS THE WORLD HAS CHANGED FOR THE BETTER.
Heh Heh Heh
I WONDER.
YOU ARE WELCOME TO SPEND THE NIGHT HERE.
BUT IF A BATTLE IS TO COME...
...YOU HAD BEST LEAVE SOON.

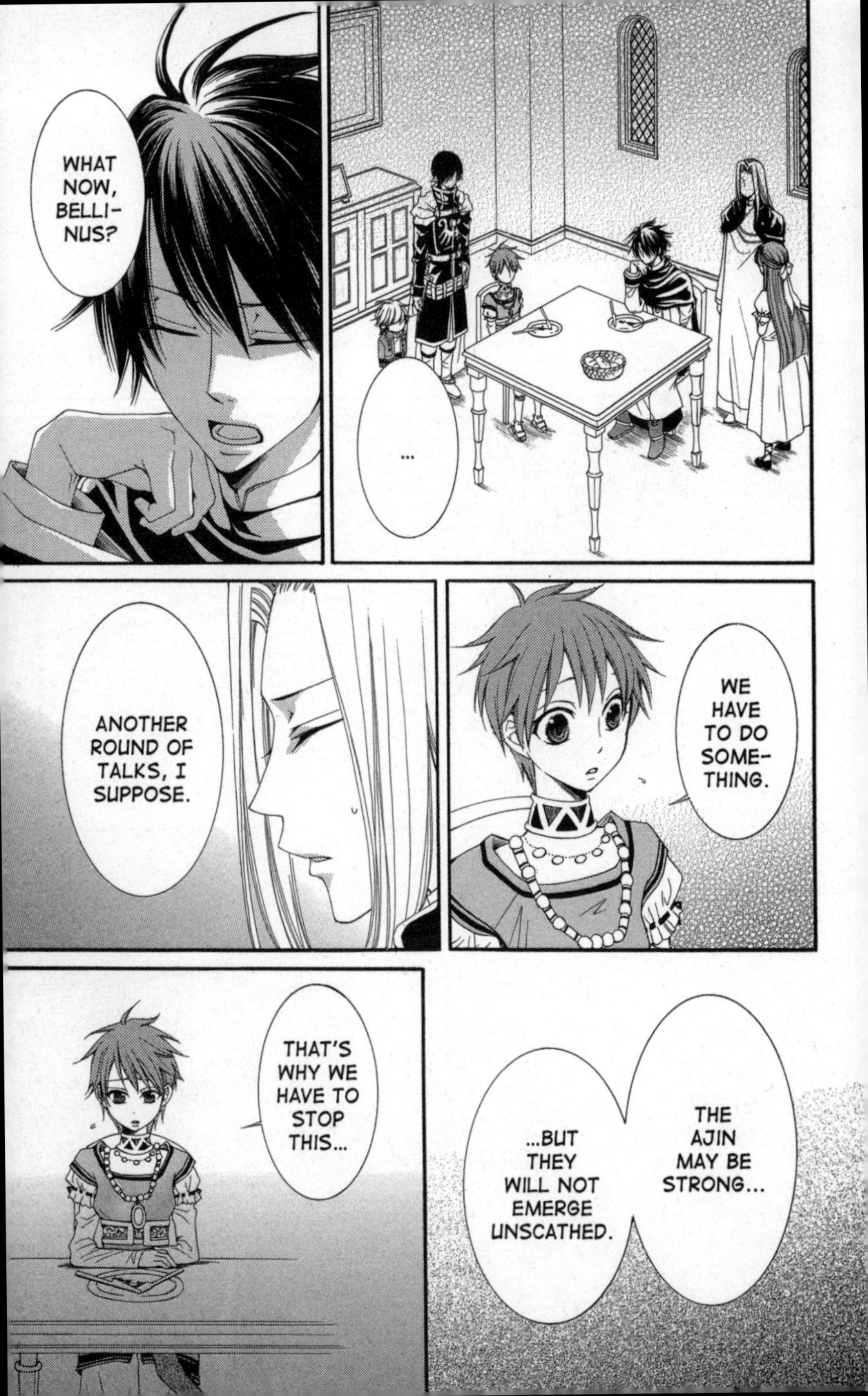
...
WHAT NOW, BELLINUS?
WE HAVE TO DO SOMETHING.
ANOTHER ROUND OF TALKS, I SUPPOSE.
THE AJIN MAY BE STRONG...
...BUT THEY WILL NOT EMERGE UNSCATHED.
THAT'S WHY WE HAVE TO STOP THIS...

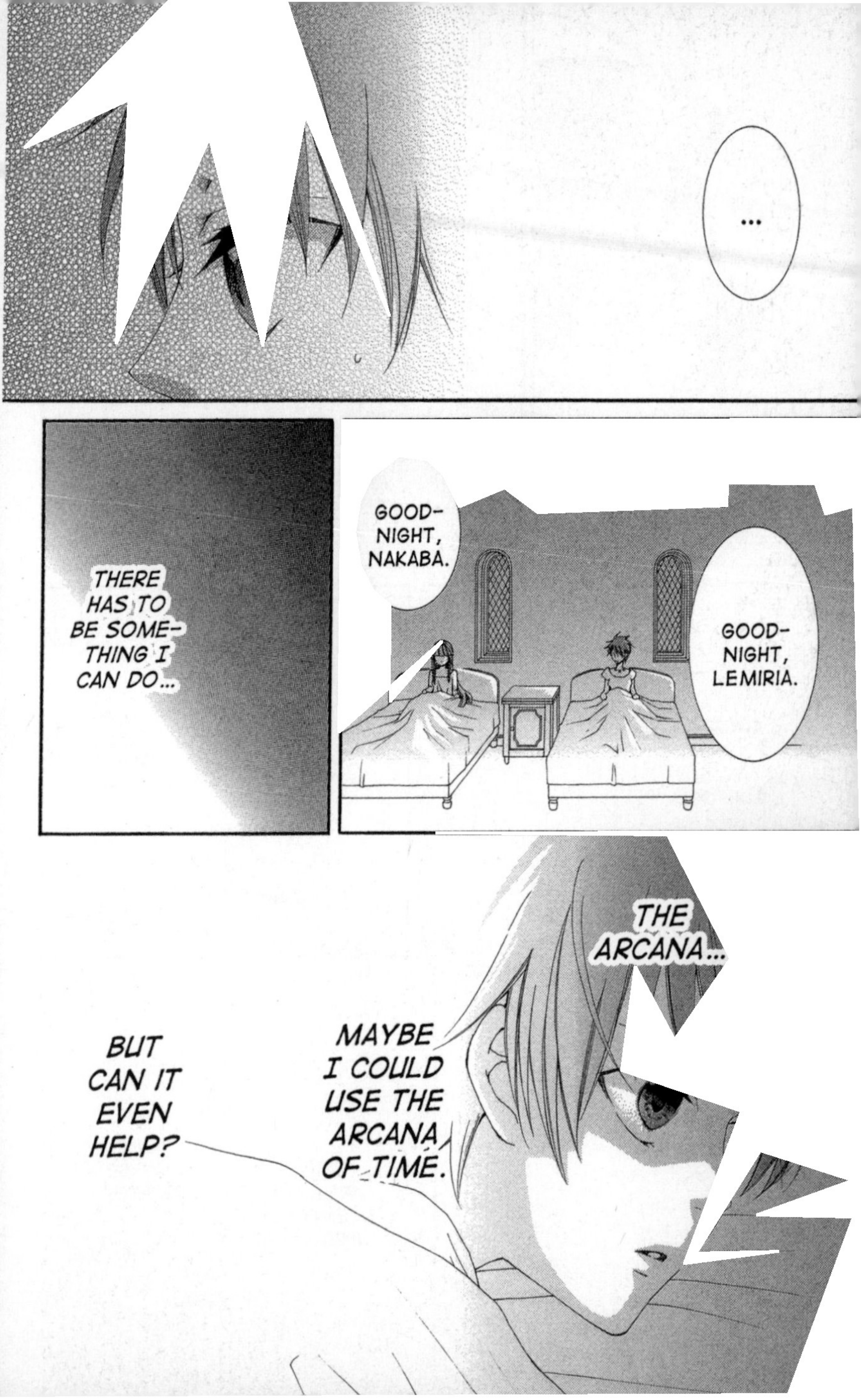
...
GOOD-NIGHT, LEMIRIA.
GOOD-NIGHT, NAKABA.
THERE HAS TO BE SOMETHING I CAN DO...
THE ARCANA...
MAYBE I COULD USE THE ARCANA OF TIME.
BUT CAN IT EVEN HELP?

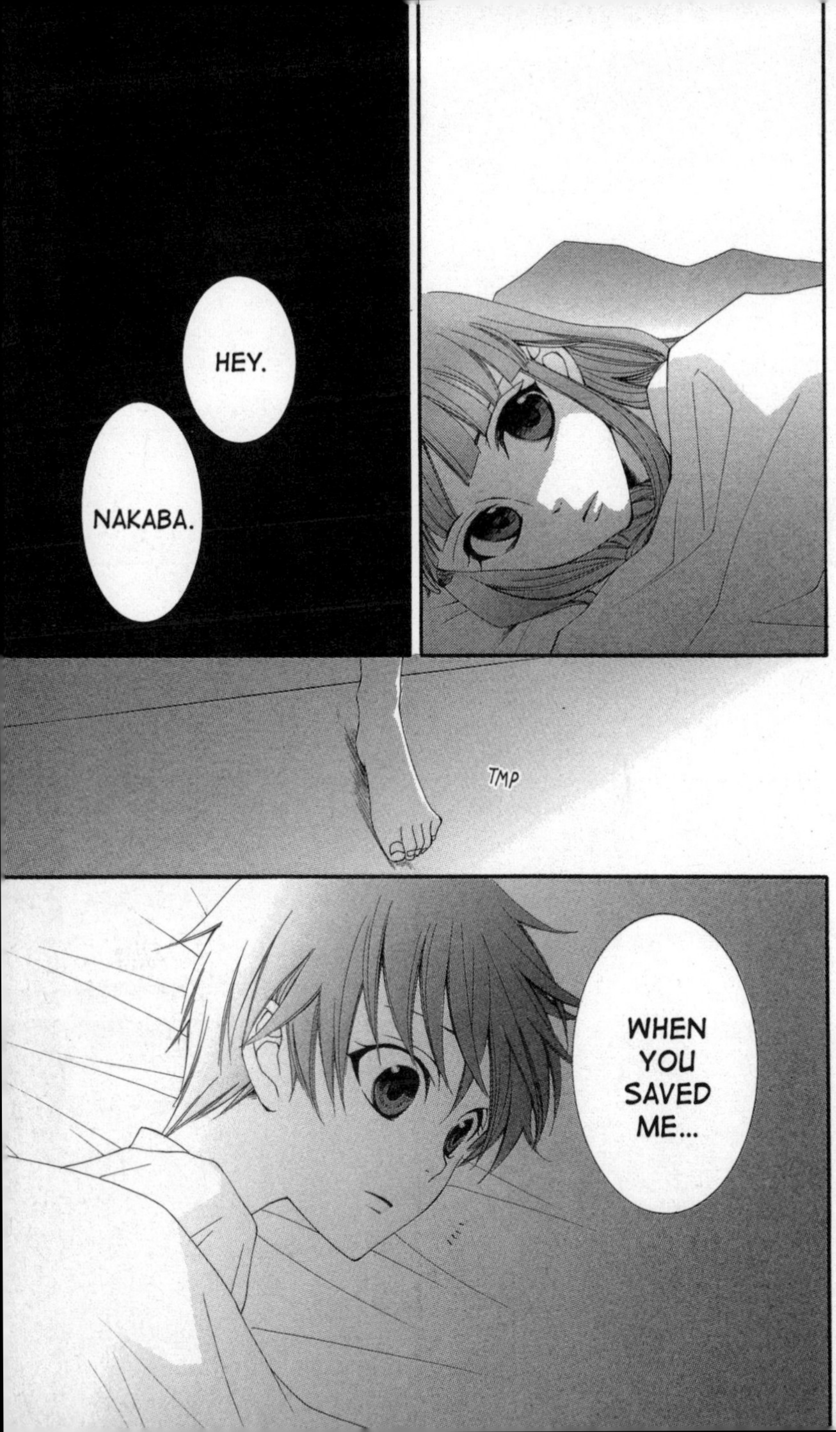
HEY.
NAKABA.
TMP
WHEN YOU SAVED ME...

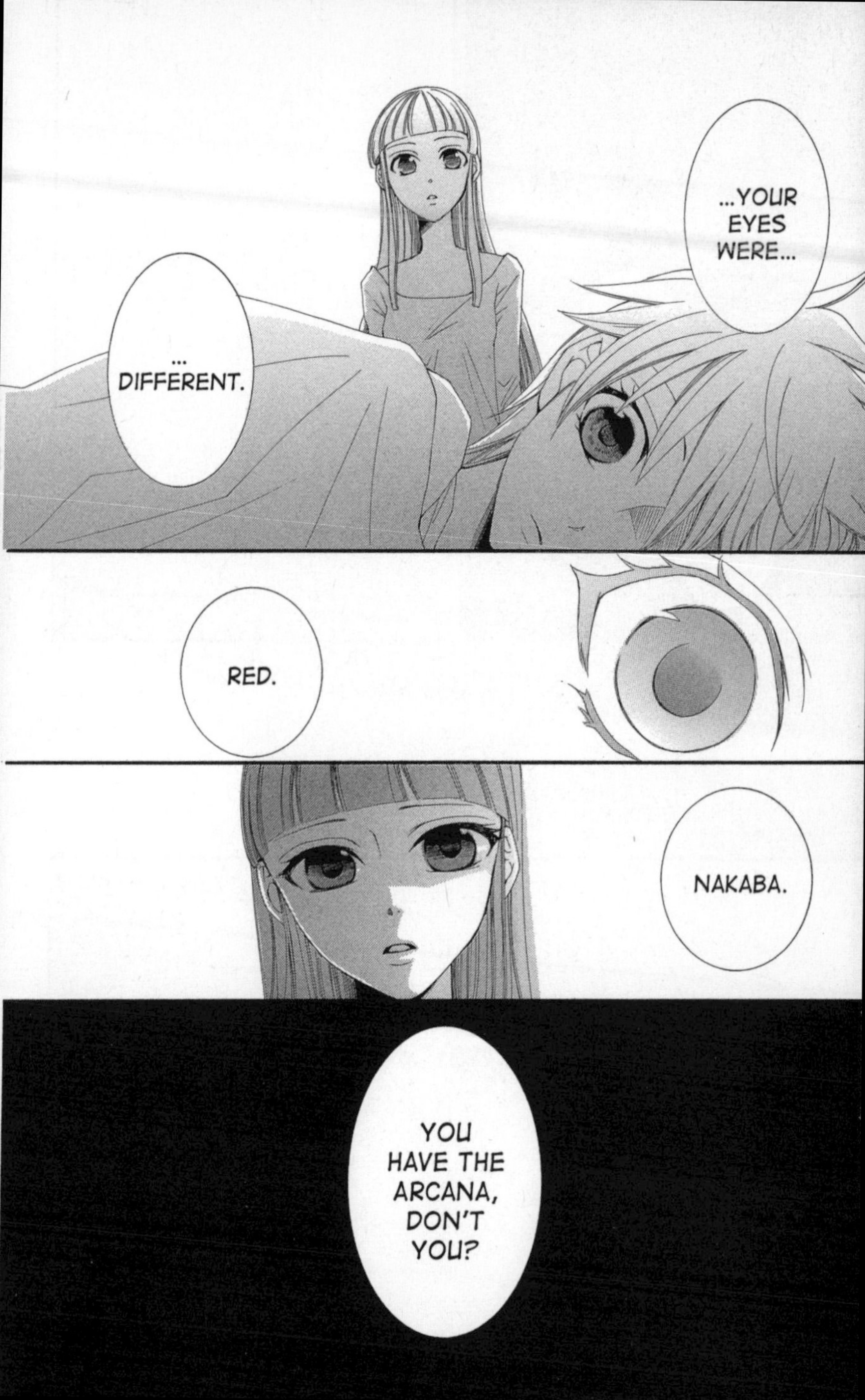
...YOUR EYES WERE...
... DIFFERENT.
RED.
NAKABA.
YOU HAVE THE ARCANA, DON'T YOU?

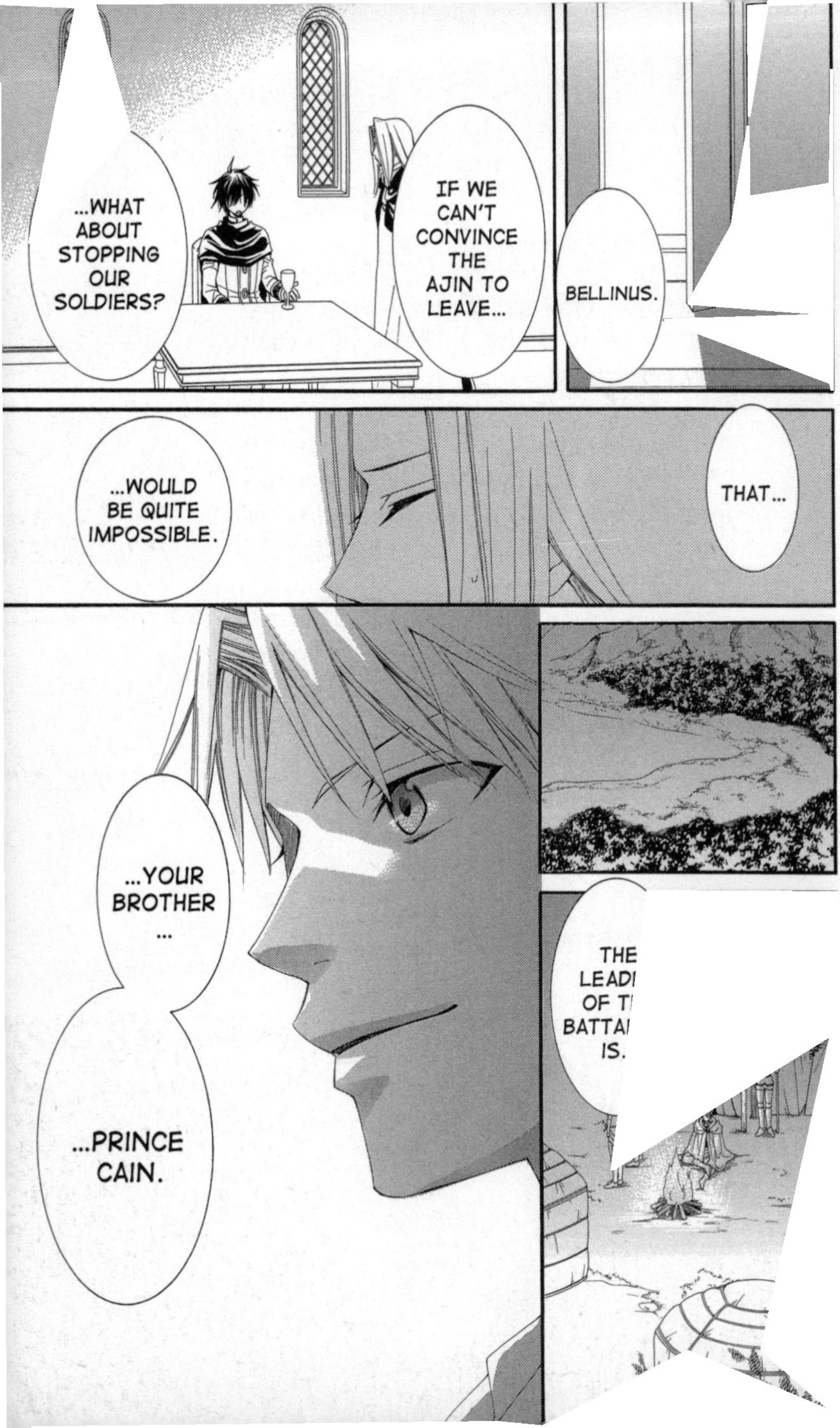
BELLINUS.
IF WE CAN'T CONVINCE THE AJIN TO LEAVE...
...WHAT ABOUT STOPPING OUR SOLDIERS?
THAT...
...WOULD BE QUITE IMPOSSIBLE.
THE LEAD OF T BATTA IS.
...YOUR BROTHER ...
...PRINCE CAIN.

Hello! Rei Toma here. *Dawn of the Arcana* is at five volumes now. I'd be happy if you've been enjoying it.

Ah! Now it's time for round two of the "Assistant-Drawings-of-Arcana-Characters-from-Memory Corner"! We played *Amidakuji* to see who would draw which characters.

First up is Joan's rendition of Rito. Joan opted to employ a sheep to compensate for her lack of confidence. It actually turned out pretty cute, and not far off the mark. I give it 97% for accuracy, 3% for humor. *Hmph*.

Chapter 17

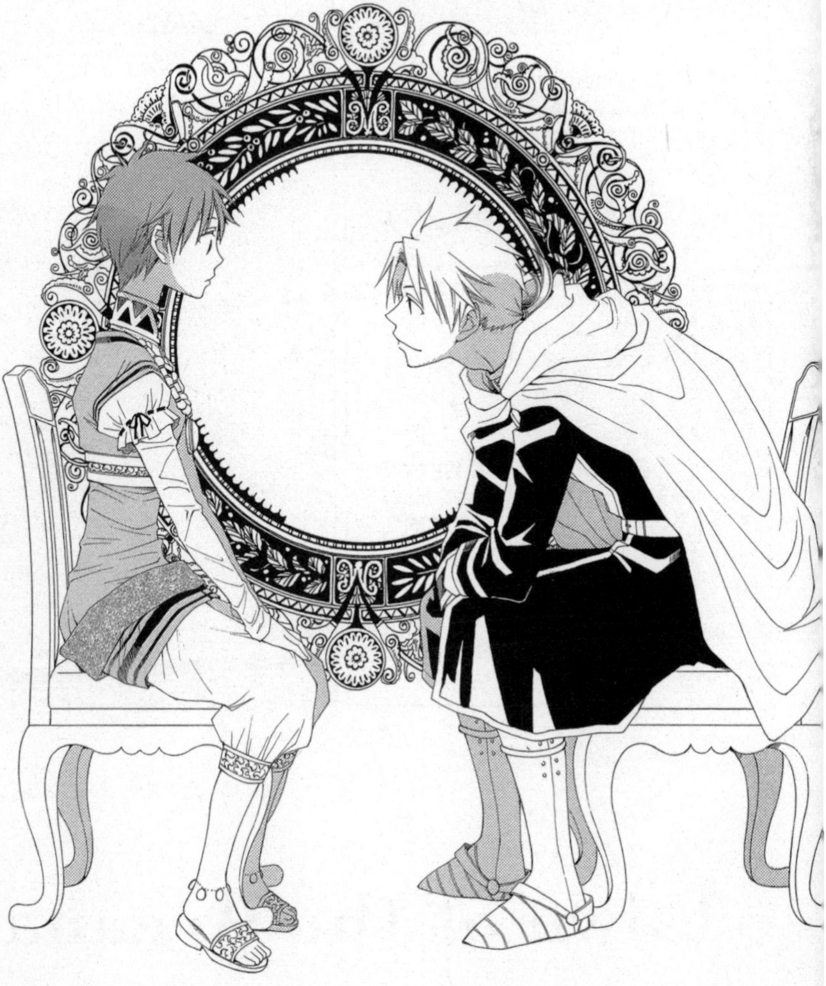

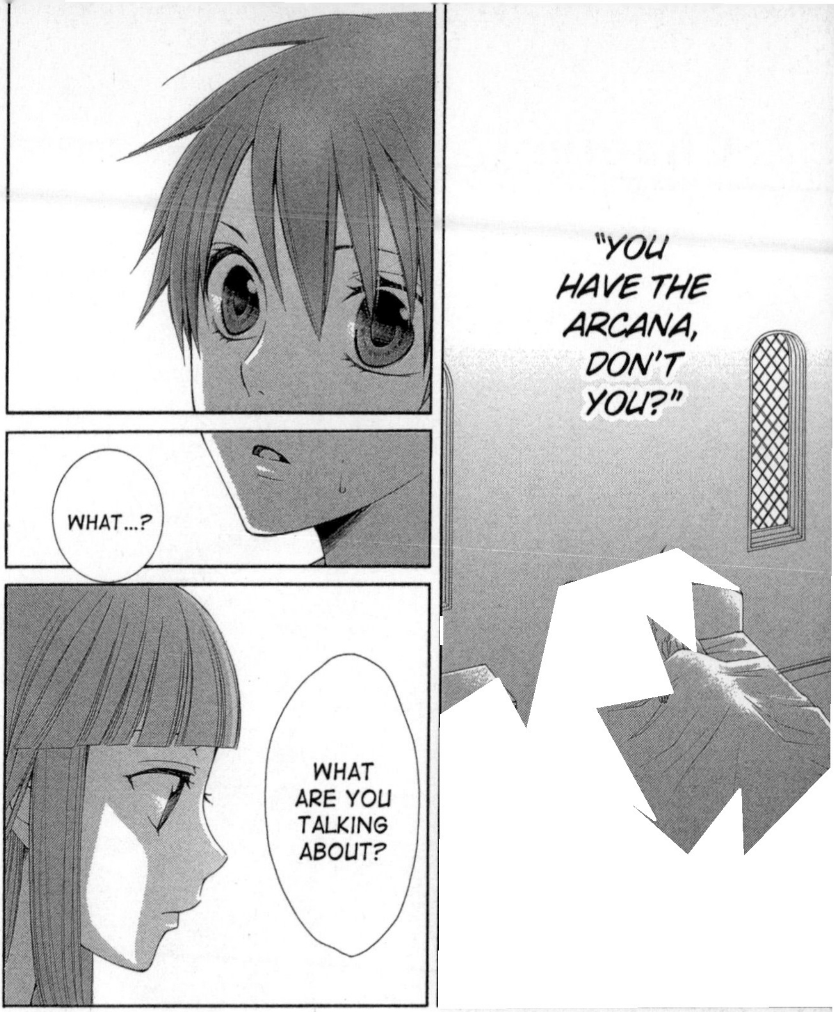
"YOU HAVE THE ARCANA, DON'T YOU?"
WHAT...?
WHAT ARE YOU TALKING ABOUT?

Dawn of the Arcana

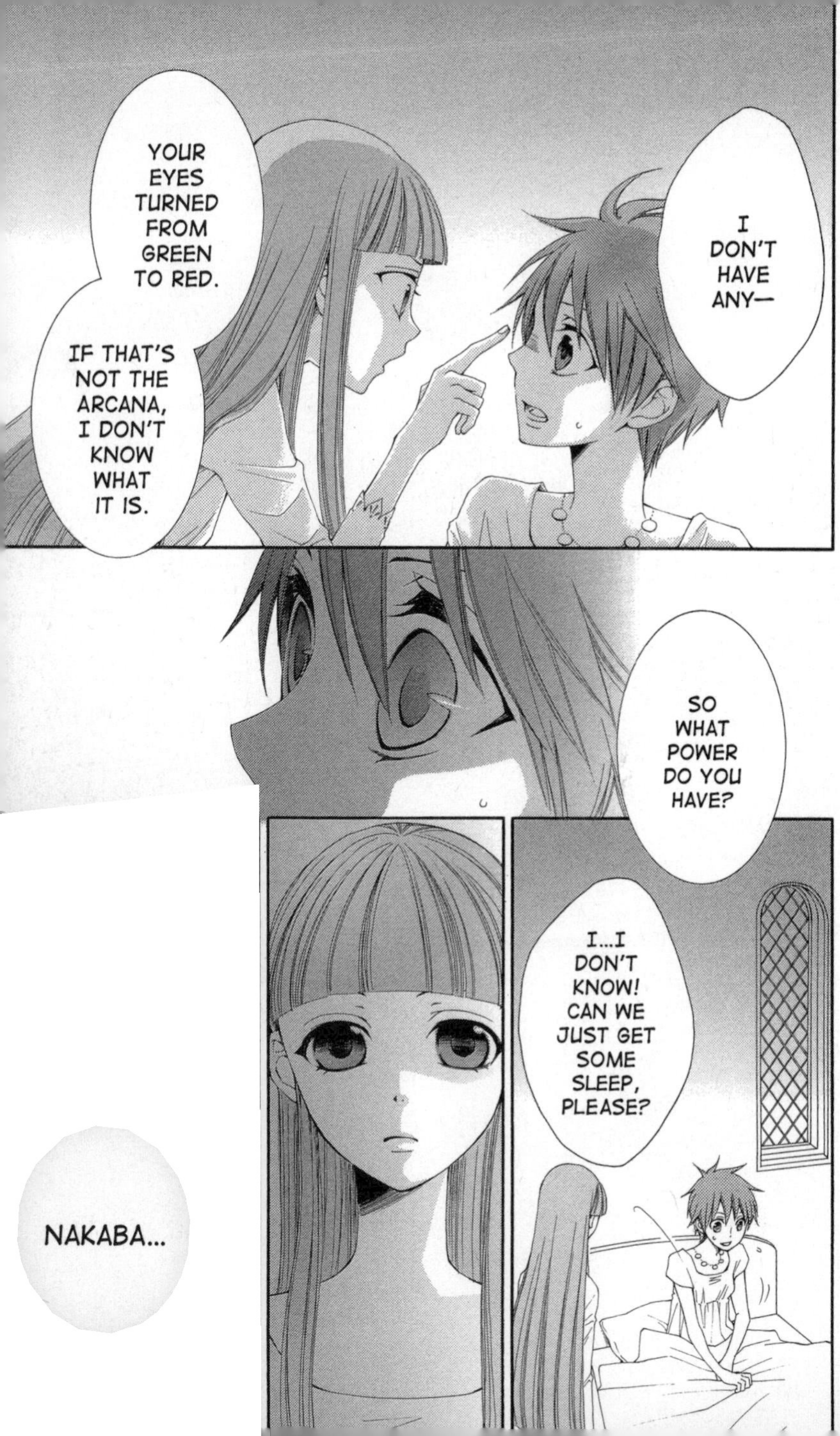
I DON'T HAVE ANY—
YOUR EYES TURNED FROM GREEN TO RED.
IF THAT'S NOT THE ARCANA, I DON'T KNOW WHAT IT IS.
SO WHAT POWER DO YOU HAVE?
I...I DON'T KNOW! CAN WE JUST GET SOME SLEEP, PLEASE?
NAKABA...

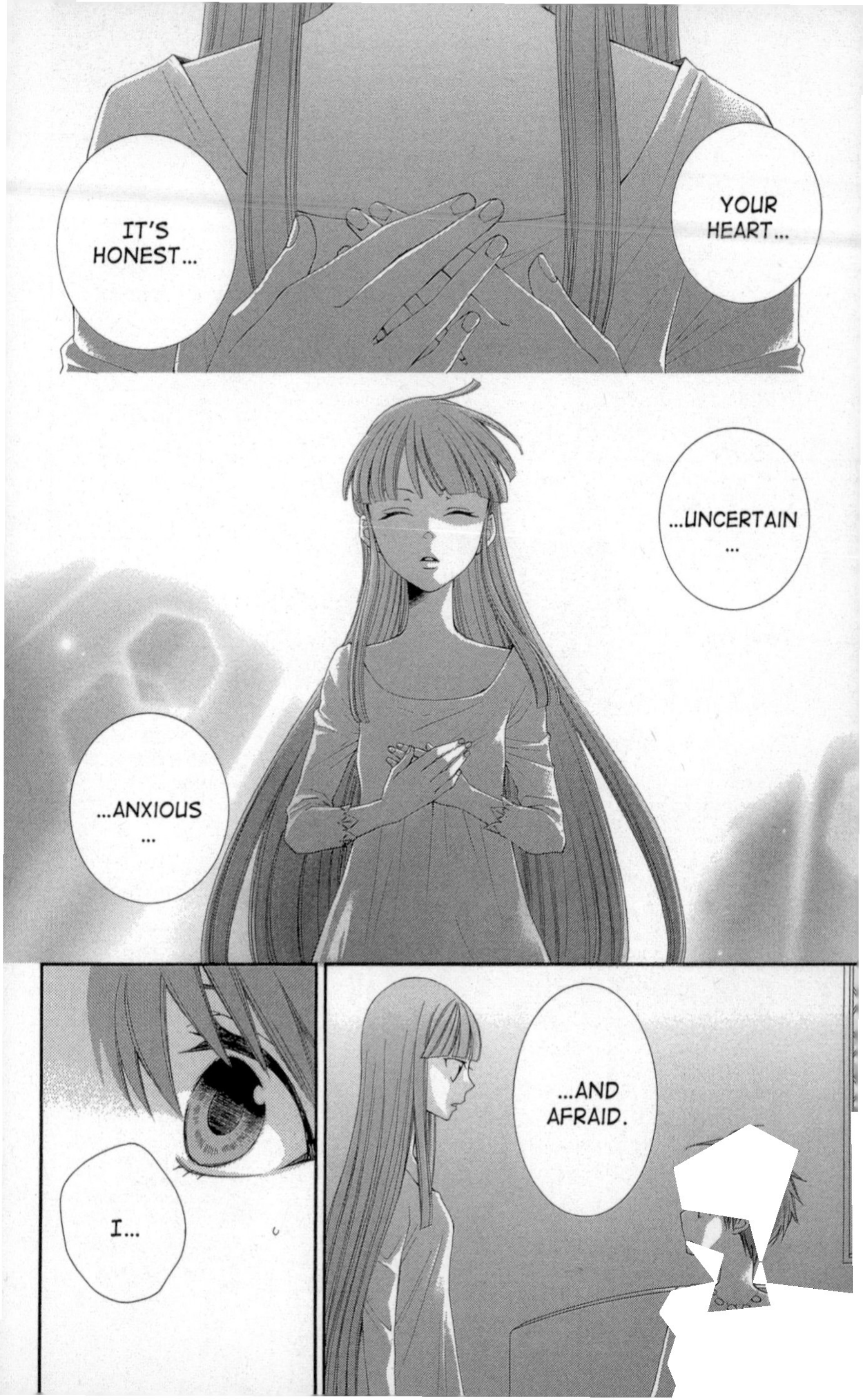
YOUR HEART...
IT'S HONEST...
...UNCERTAIN ...
...ANXIOUS ...
...AND AFRAID.
I...

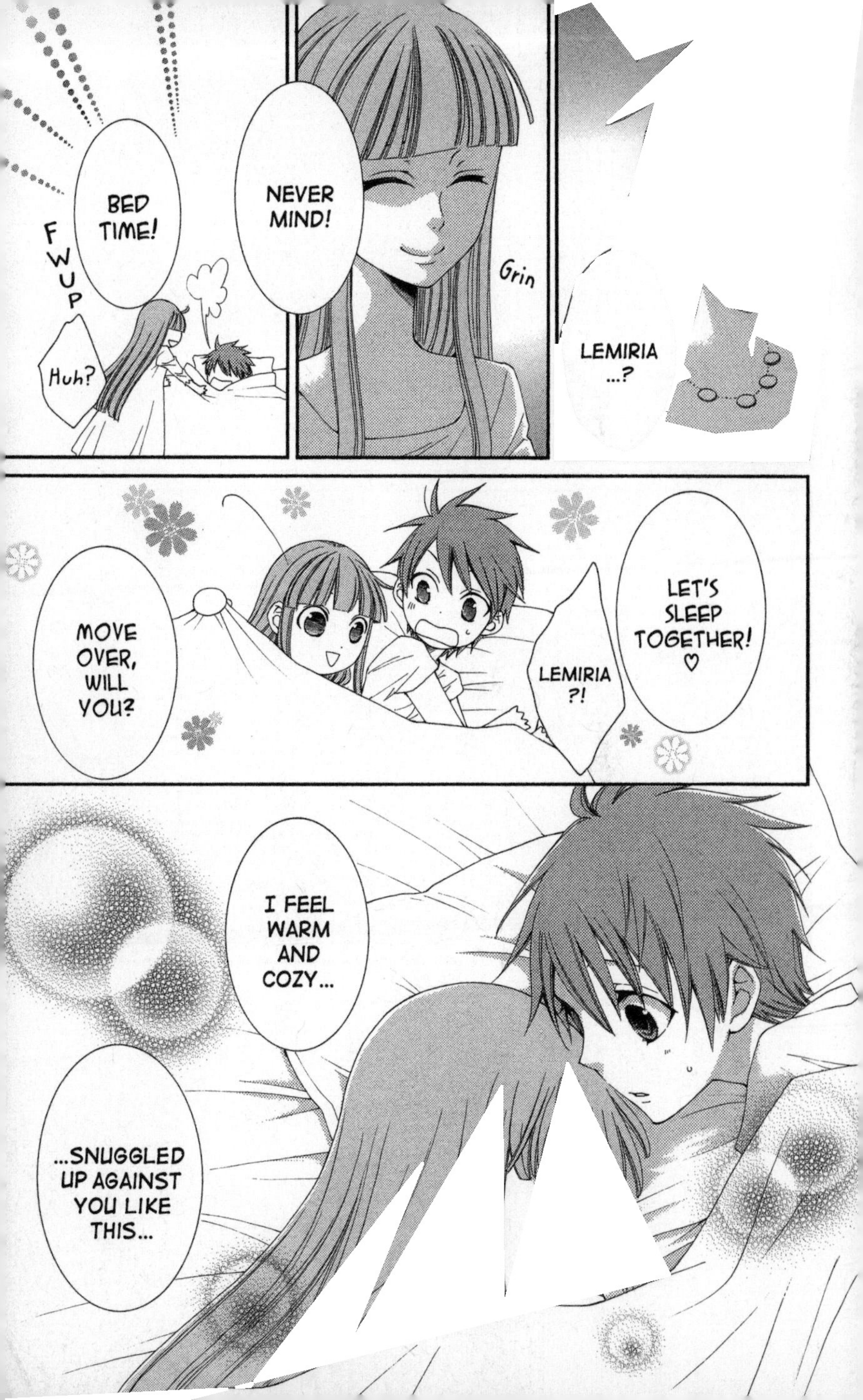
LEMIRIA ...?
NEVER MIND!
Grin
BED TIME!
FWUP
Huh?
LET'S SLEEP TOGETHER! ♡
LEMIRIA ?!
MOVE OVER, WILL YOU?
I FEEL WARM AND COZY...
...SNUGGLED UP AGAINST YOU LIKE THIS...

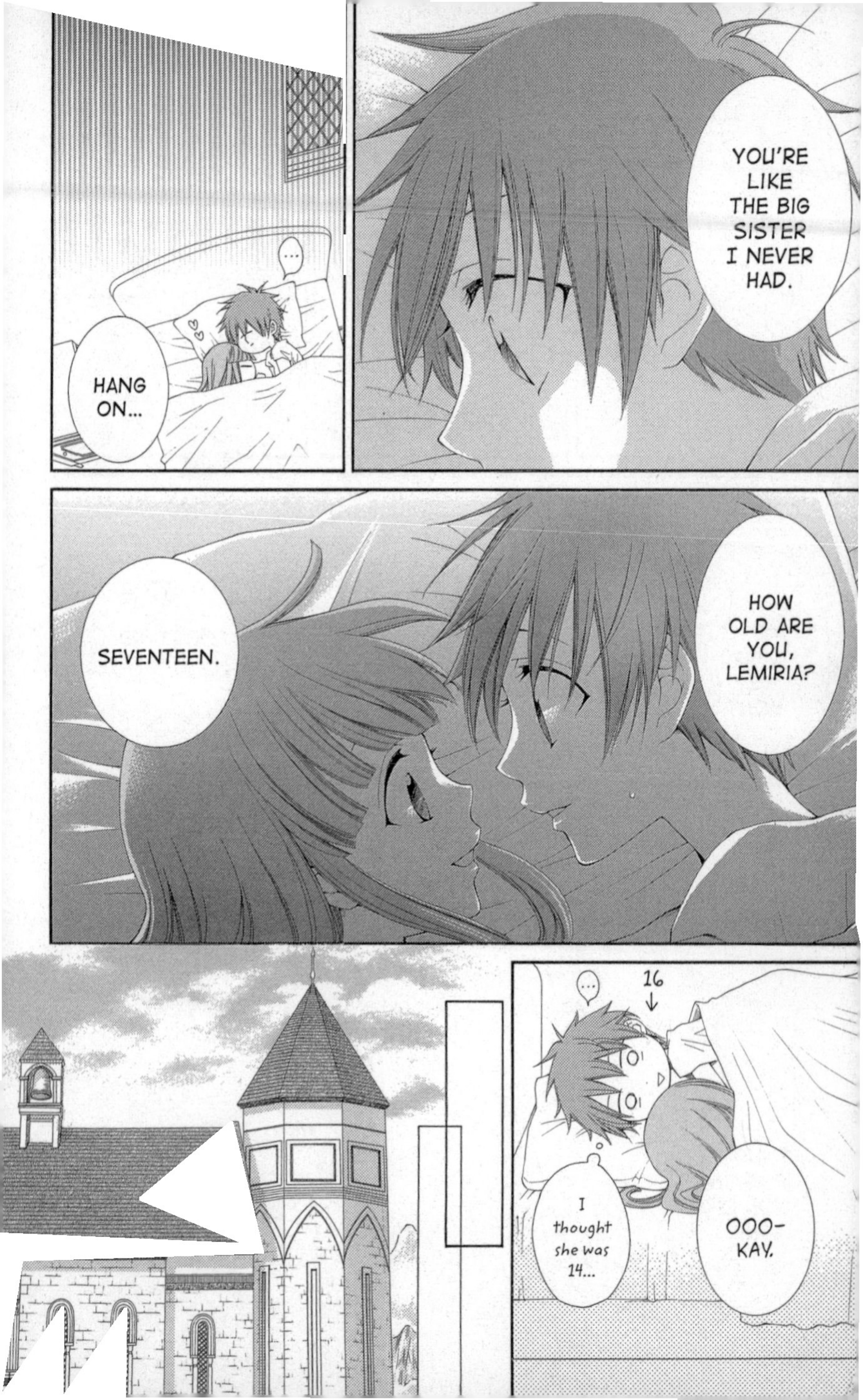
YOU'RE LIKE THE BIG SISTER I NEVER HAD.
...
HANG ON...
HOW OLD ARE YOU, LEMIRIA?
SEVENTEEN.
16
...
OOO-KAY.
I thought she was 14...

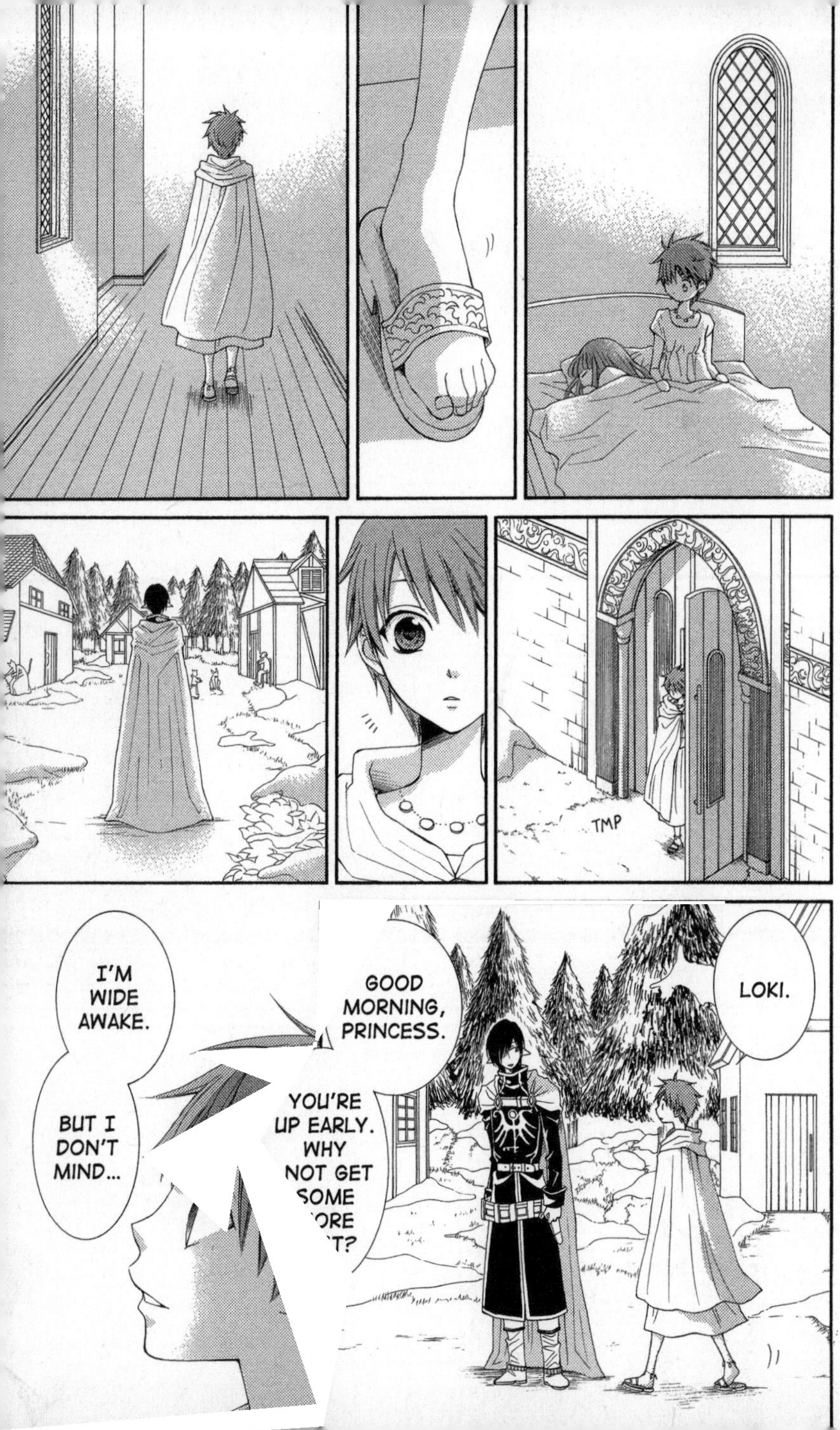
TMP
LOKI.
GOOD MORNING, PRINCESS.
YOU'RE UP EARLY. WHY NOT GET SOME
I'M WIDE AWAKE.
BUT I DON'T MIND...

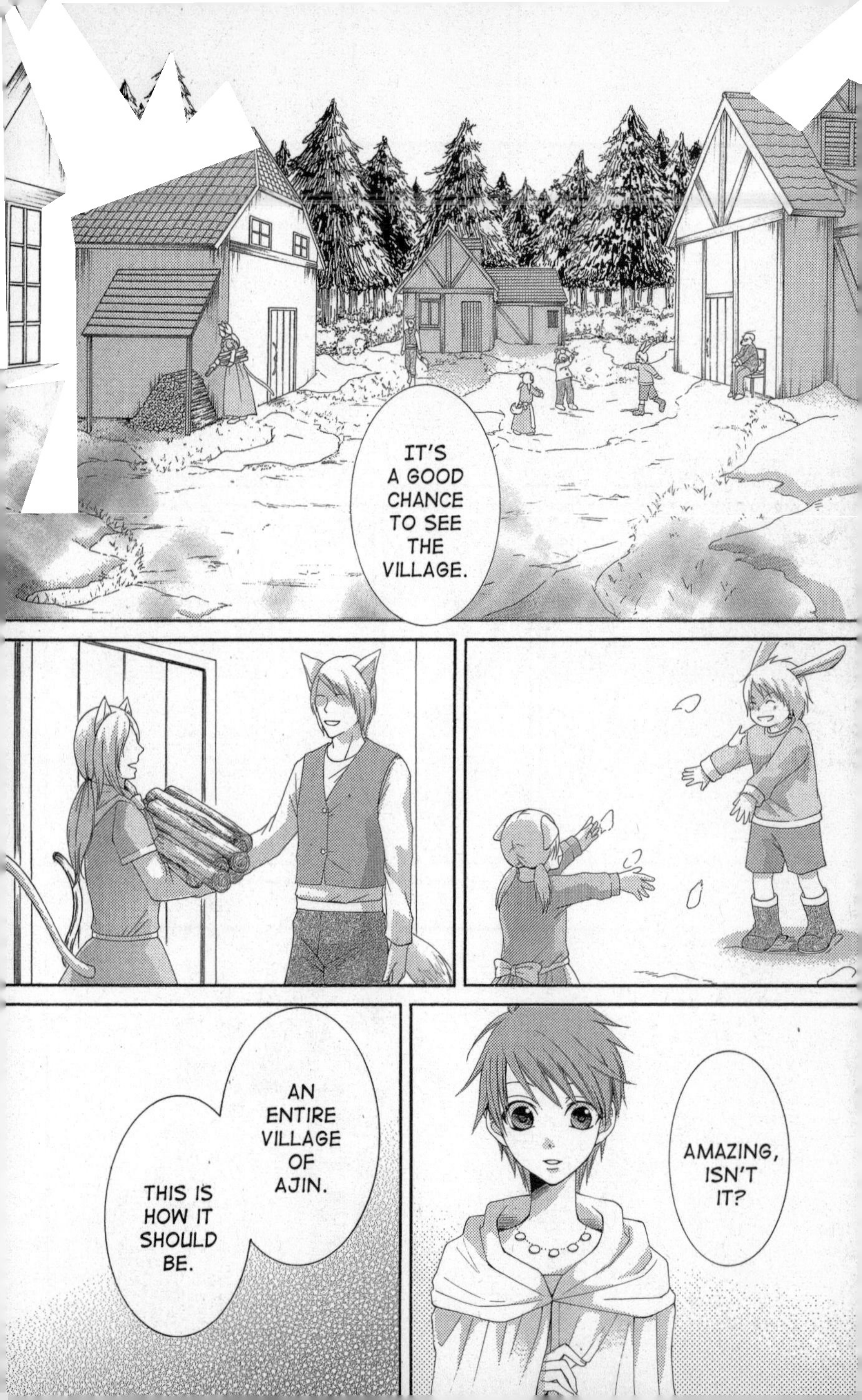
IT'S A GOOD CHANCE TO SEE THE VILLAGE.
AMAZING, ISN'T IT?
AN ENTIRE VILLAGE OF AJIN.
THIS IS HOW IT SHOULD BE.

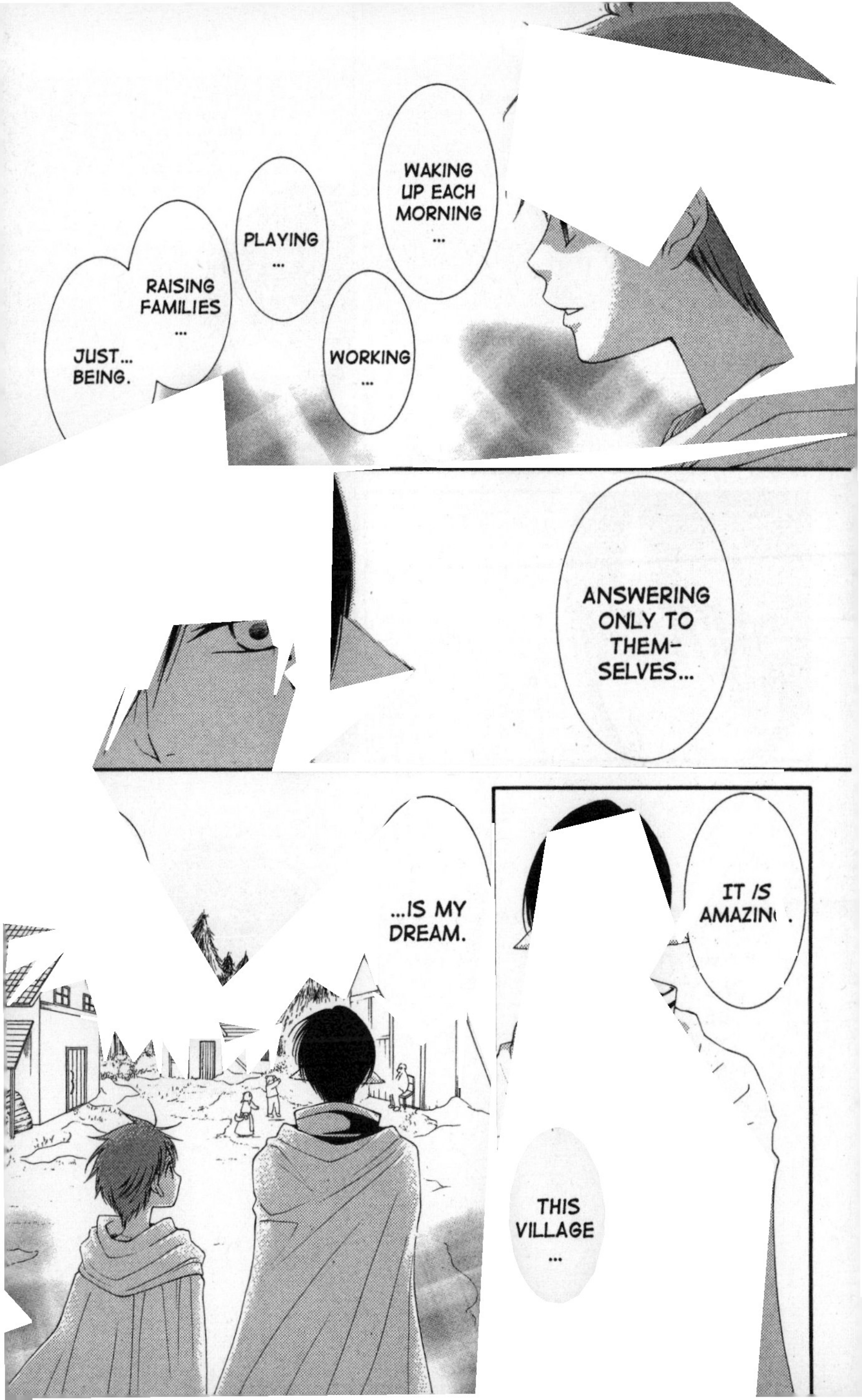
WAKING UP EACH MORNING ...
WORKING ...
PLAYING ...
RAISING FAMILIES ...
JUST... BEING.
ANSWERING ONLY TO THEM-SELVES...
IT IS AMAZIN .
THIS VILLAGE ...
...IS MY DREAM.

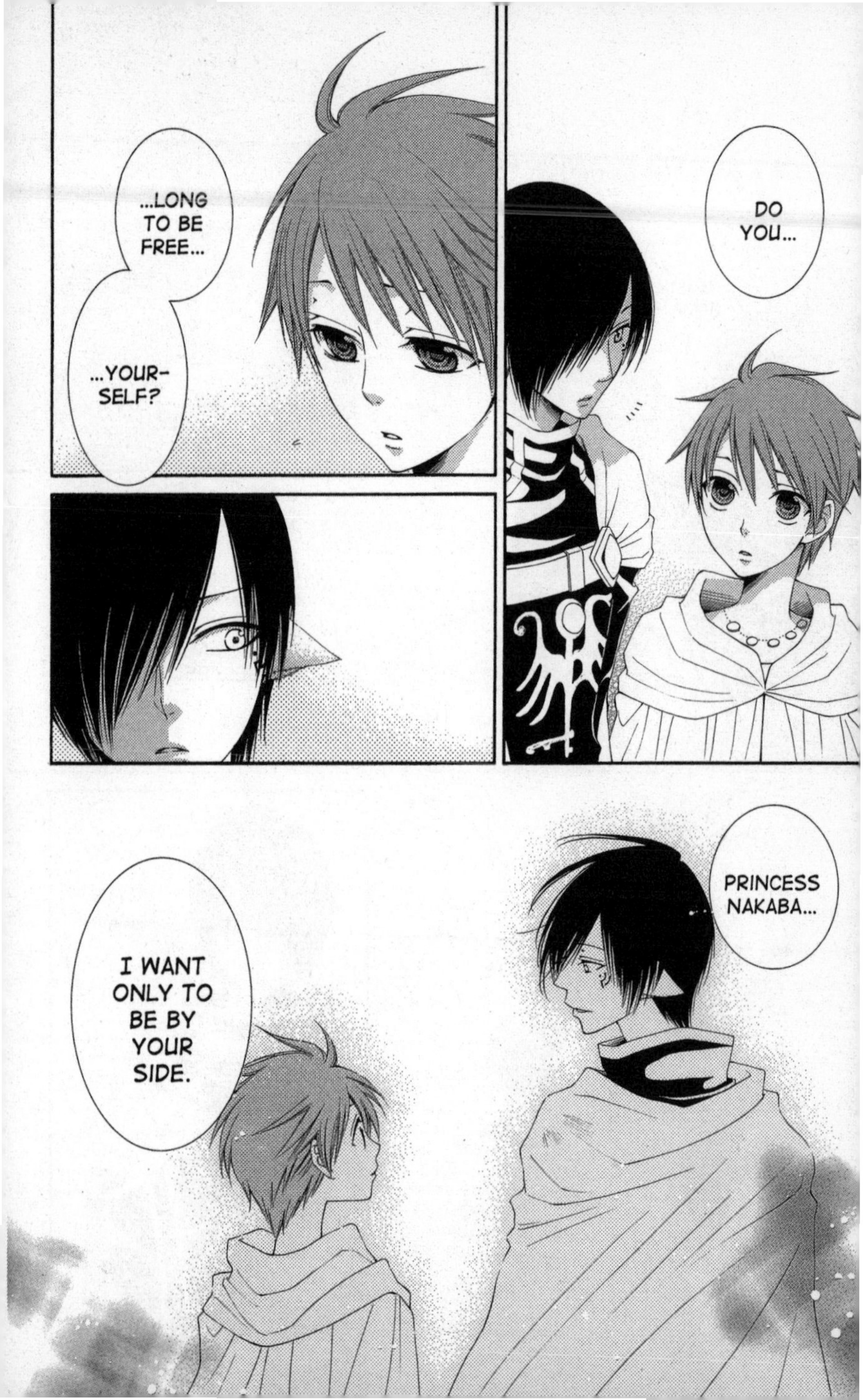
DO YOU...
...LONG TO BE FREE...
...YOUR-SELF?
PRINCESS NAKABA...
I WANT ONLY TO BE BY YOUR SIDE.

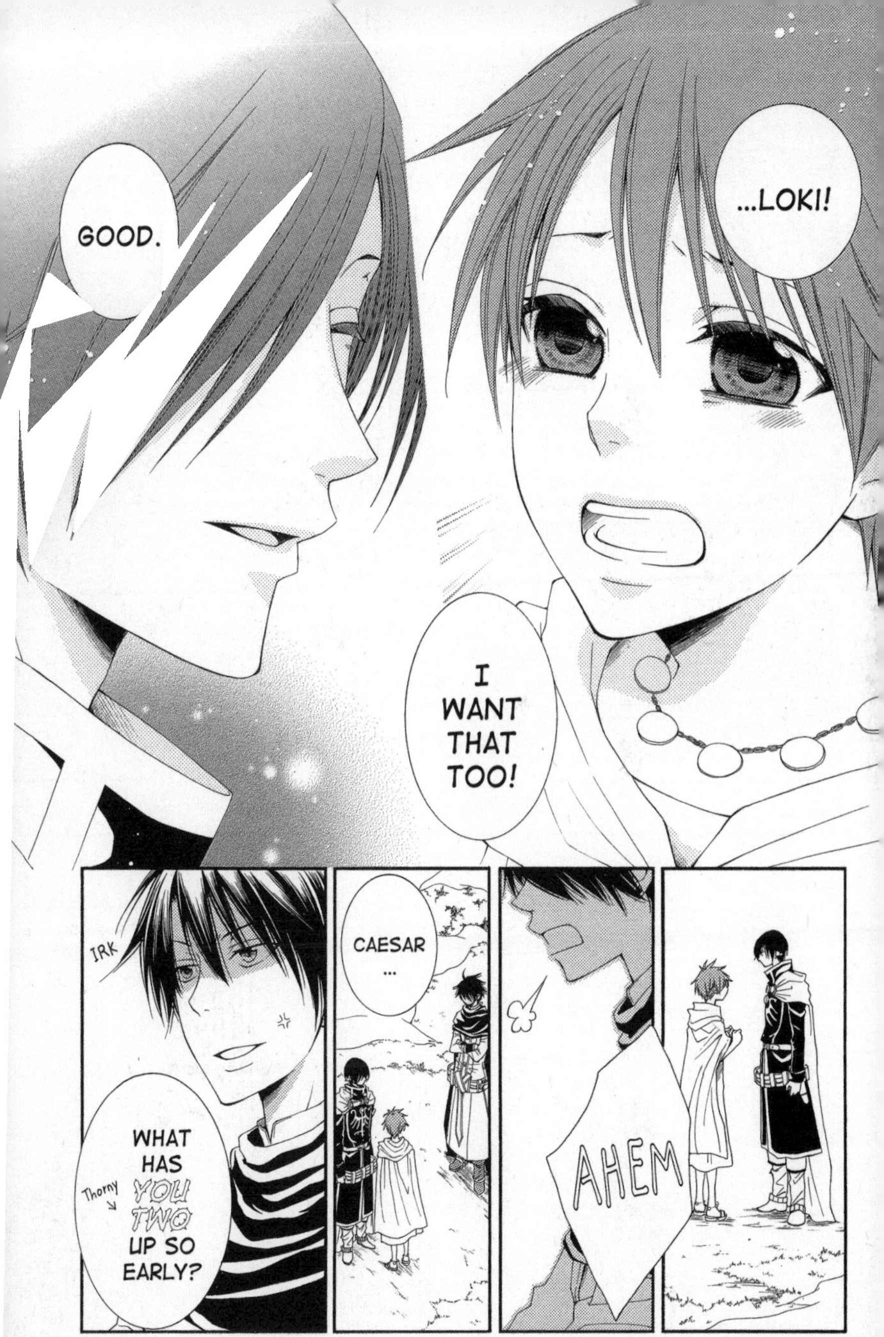
...LOKI!
GOOD.
I WANT THAT TOO!
AHEM
CAESAR ...
IRK
WHAT HAS YOU TWO UP SO EARLY?
Thorny

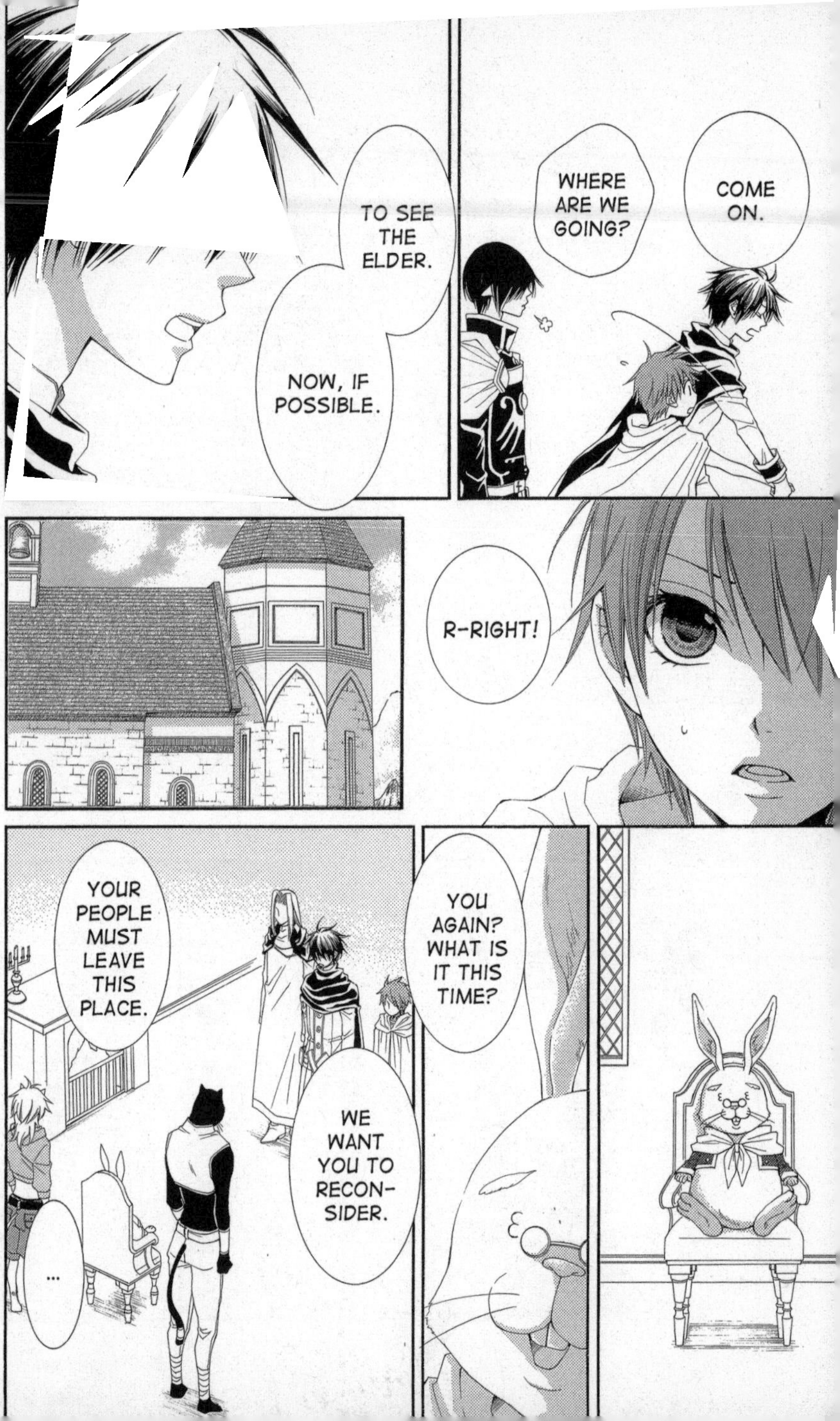
COME ON.
WHERE ARE WE GOING?
TO SEE THE ELDER.
NOW, IF POSSIBLE.
R-RIGHT!
YOU AGAIN? WHAT IS IT THIS TIME?
WE WANT YOU TO RECON-SIDER.
YOUR PEOPLE MUST LEAVE THIS PLACE.
...

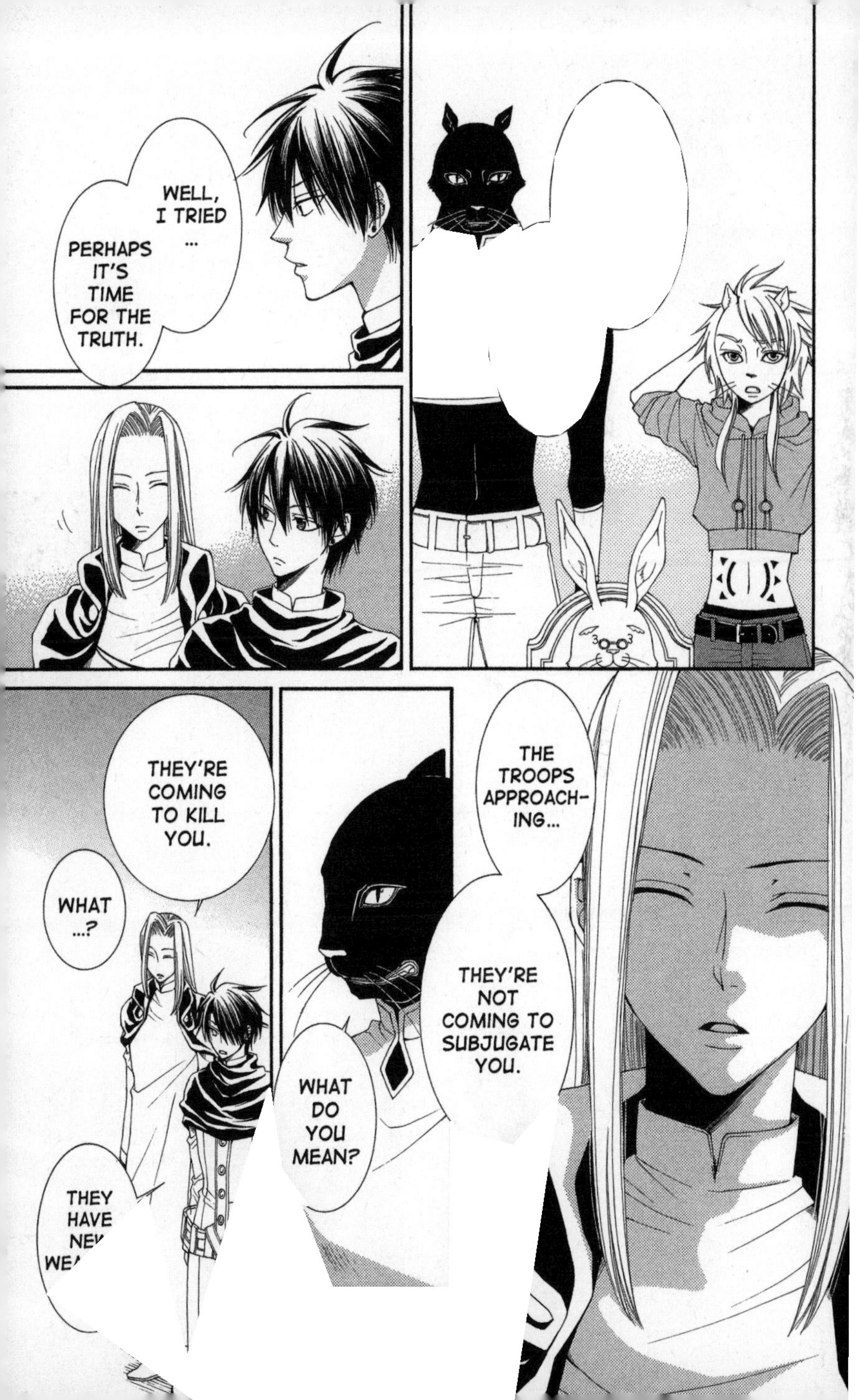
WELL, I TRIED ...
PERHAPS IT'S TIME FOR THE TRUTH.
THE TROOPS APPROACHING...
THEY'RE NOT COMING TO SUBJUGATE YOU.
WHAT DO YOU MEAN?
THEY'RE COMING TO KILL YOU.
WHAT ...?
THEY HAVE

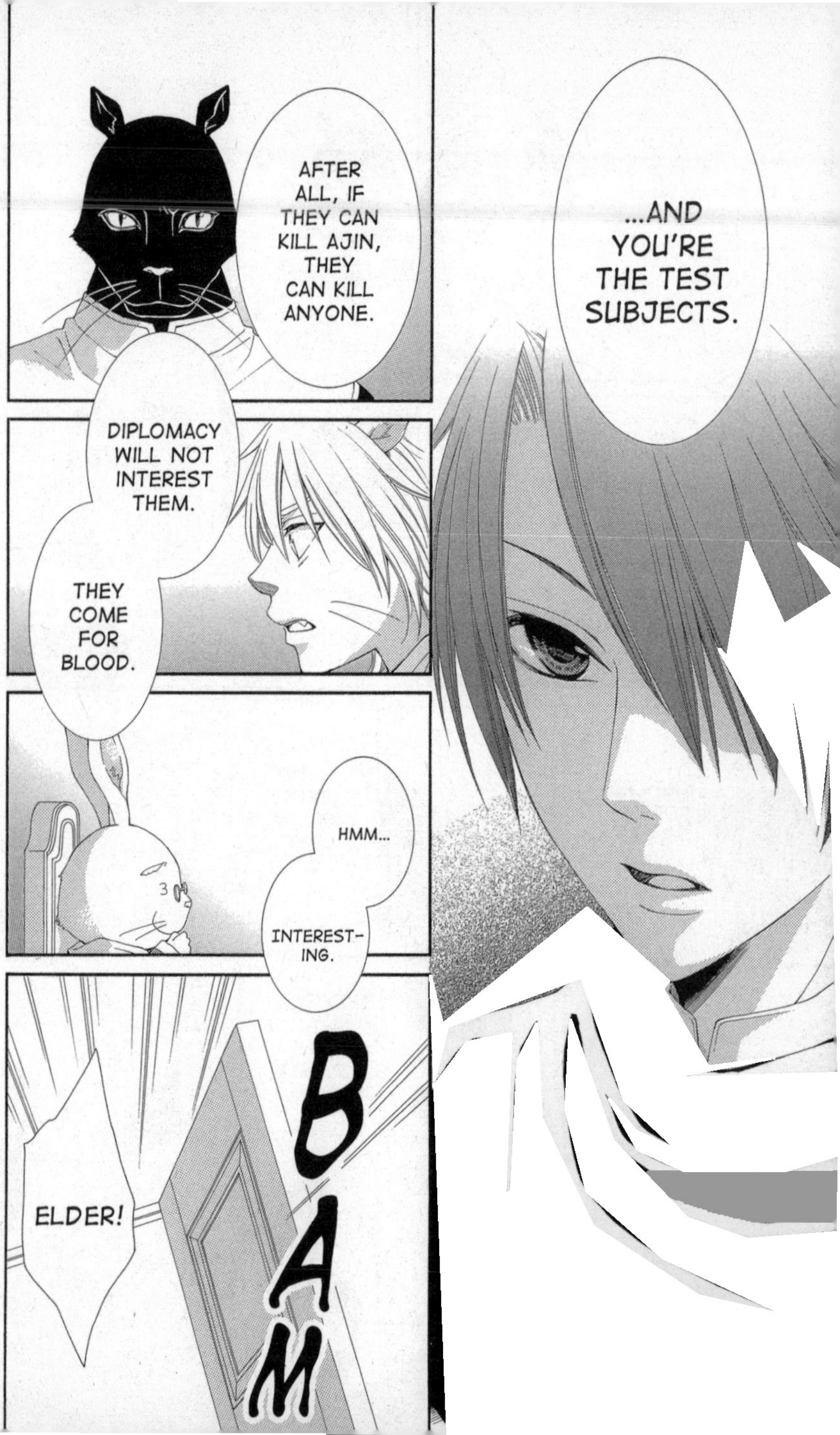
...AND YOU'RE THE TEST SUBJECTS.
AFTER ALL, IF THEY CAN KILL AJIN, THEY CAN KILL ANYONE.
DIPLOMACY WILL NOT INTEREST THEM.
THEY COME FOR BLOOD.
HMM...
INTEREST-ING.
BAM
ELDER!

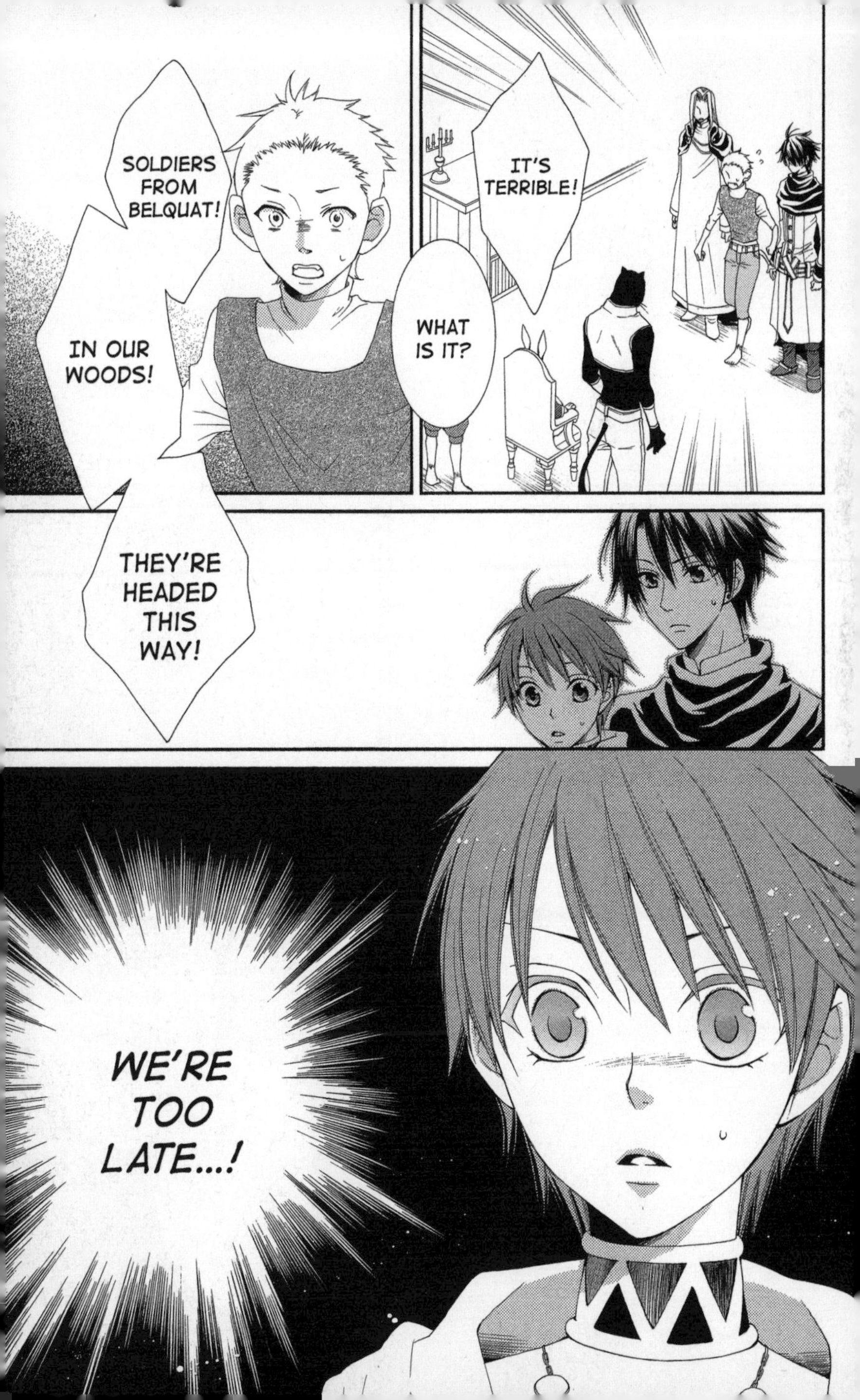
IT'S TERRIBLE!
WHAT IS IT?
SOLDIERS FROM BELQUAT!
IN OUR WOODS!
THEY'RE HEADED THIS WAY!
WE'RE TOO LATE...!

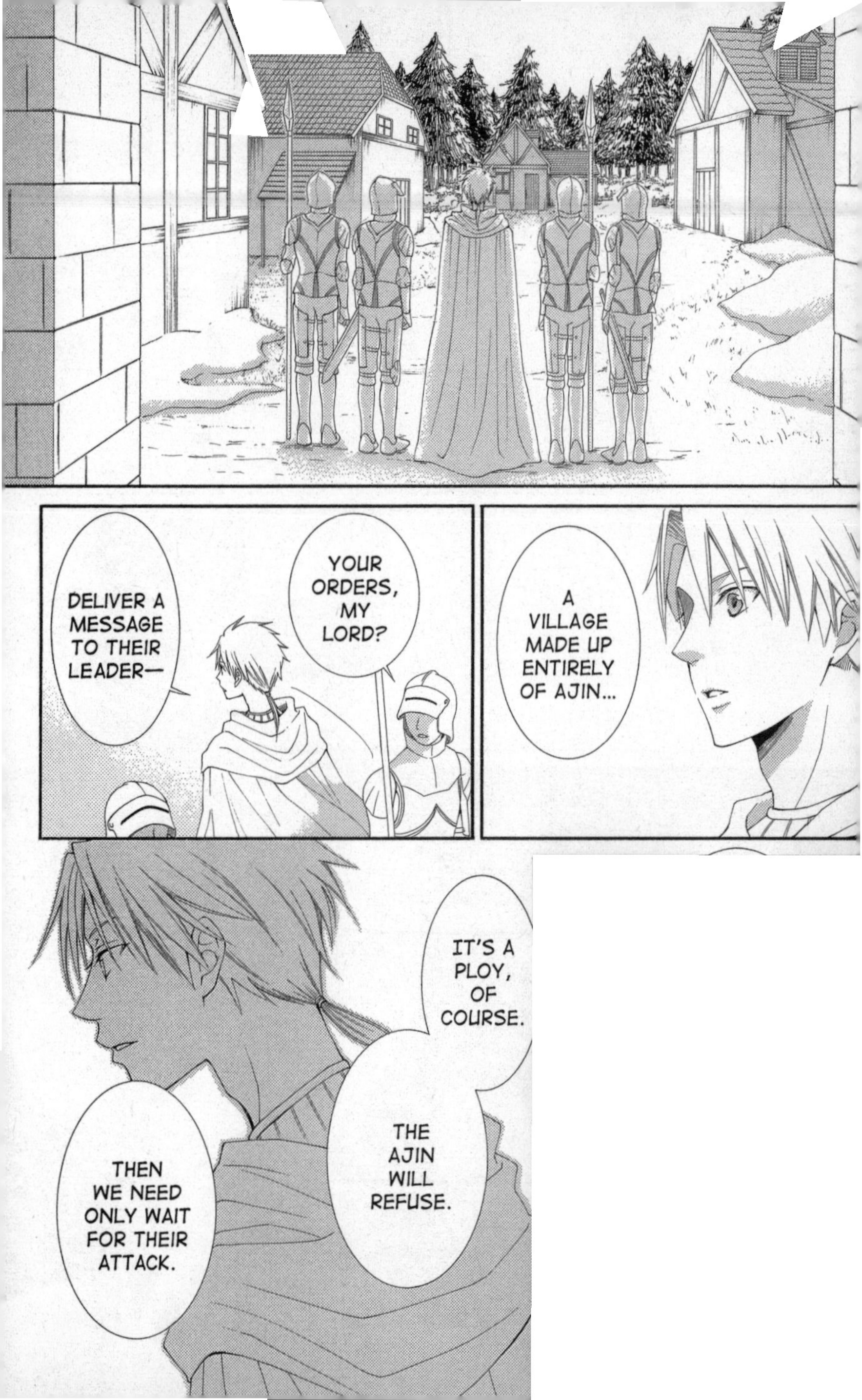
A VILLAGE MADE UP ENTIRELY OF AJIN...
YOUR ORDERS, MY LORD?
DELIVER A MESSAGE TO THEIR LEADER—
IT'S A PLOY, OF COURSE.
THE AJIN WILL REFUSE.
THEN WE NEED ONLY WAIT FOR THEIR ATTACK.

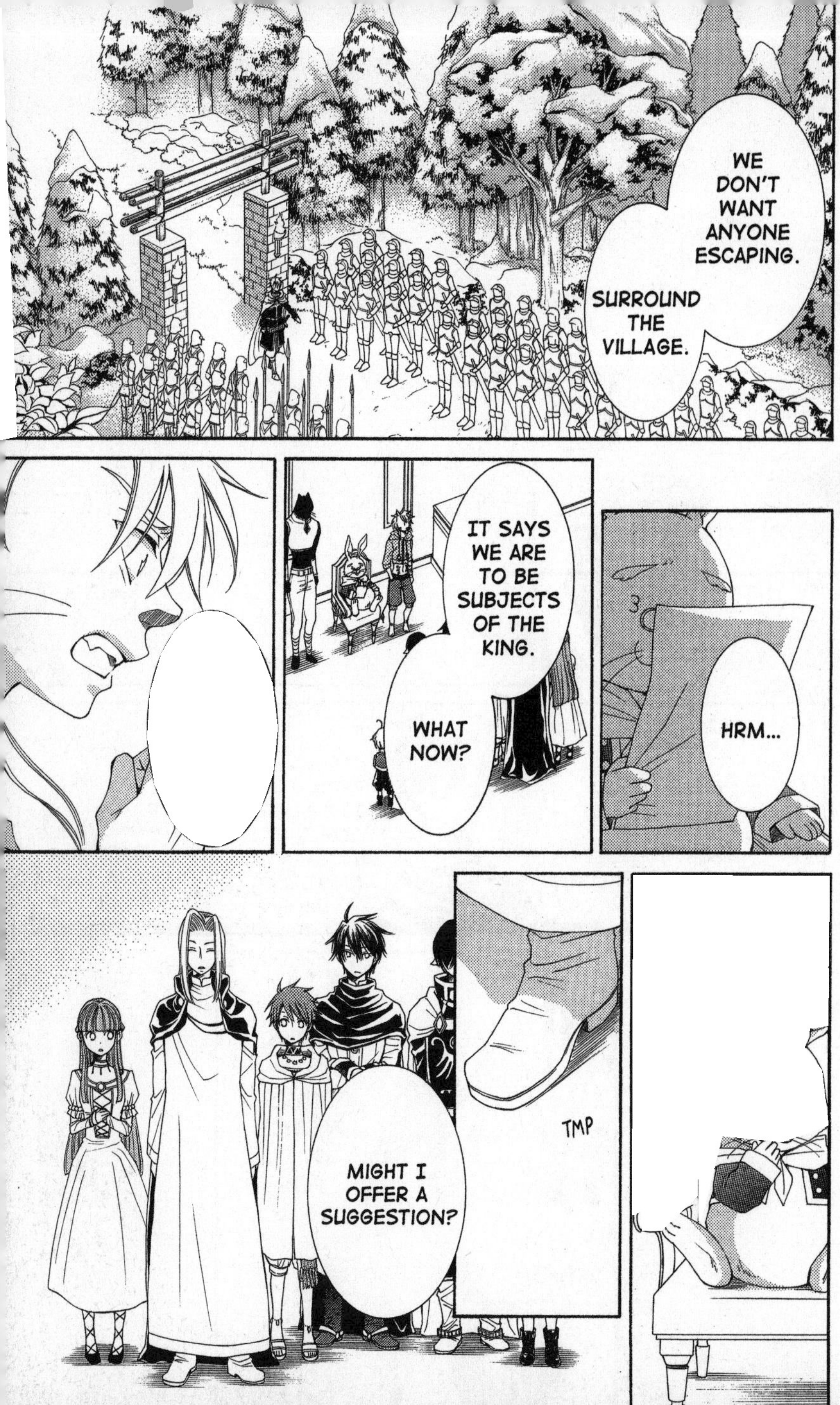
WE DON'T WANT ANYONE ESCAPING.
SURROUND THE VILLAGE.
HRM...
IT SAYS WE ARE TO BE SUBJECTS OF THE KING.
WHAT NOW?
TMP
MIGHT I OFFER A SUGGESTION?

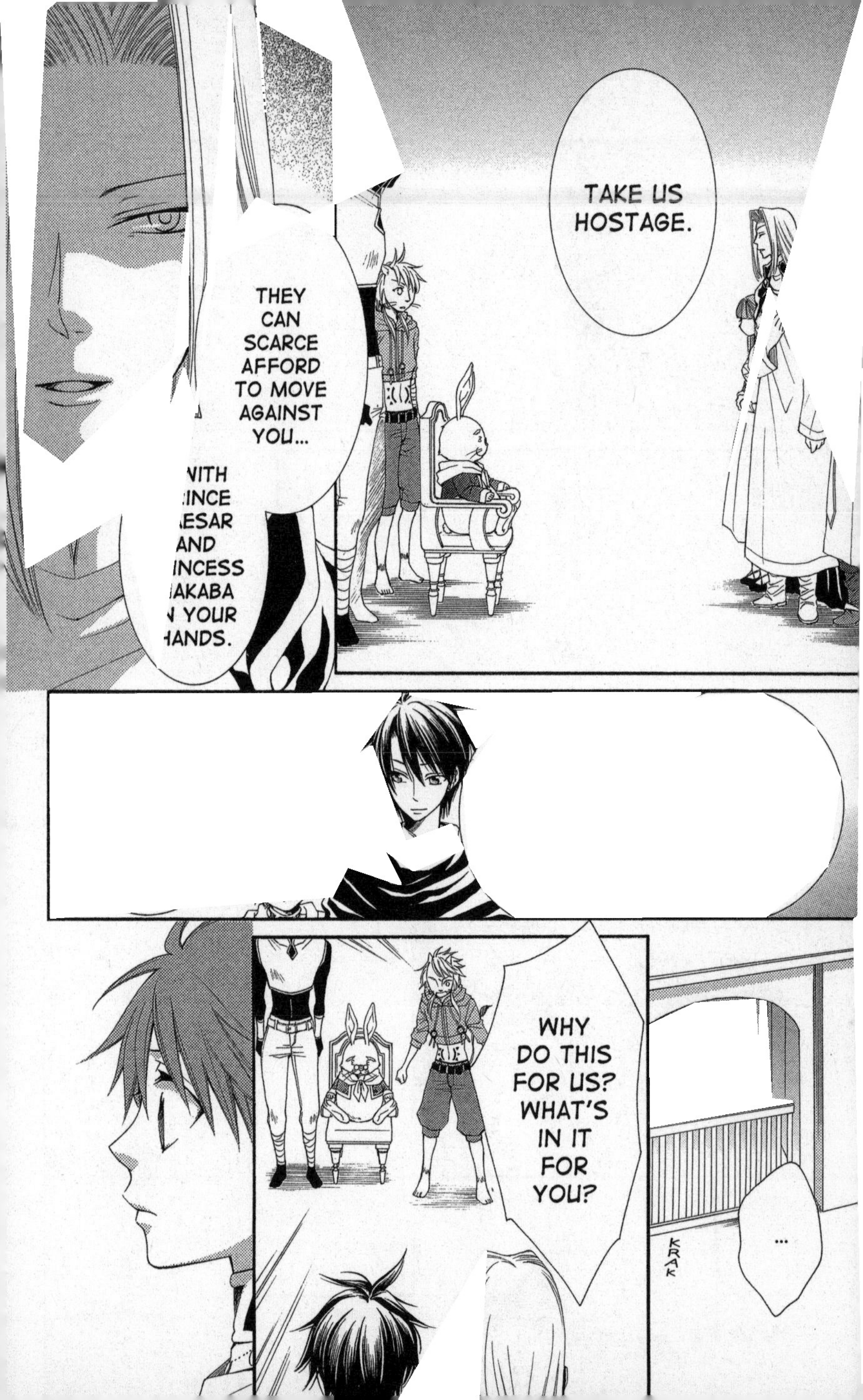
TAKE US HOSTAGE.
THEY CAN SCARCE AFFORD TO MOVE AGAINST YOU...
WITH
INCE
ESAR
AND
INCESS
AKABA
N YOUR
HANDS.
WHY DO THIS FOR US? WHAT'S IN IT FOR YOU?
...
KRAK

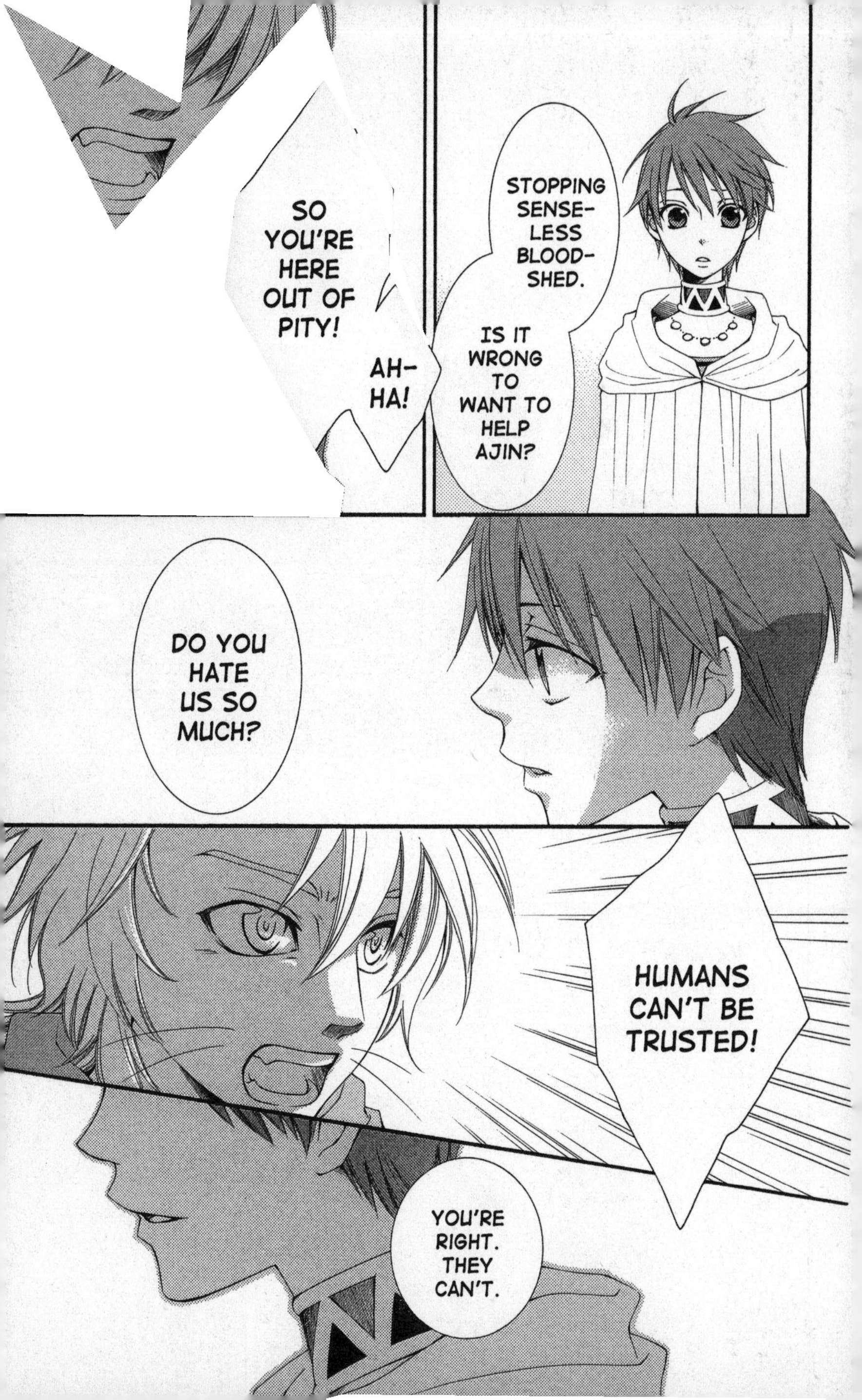
STOPPING SENSE-LESS BLOOD-SHED.
IS IT WRONG TO WANT TO HELP AJIN?
AH-HA!
SO YOU'RE HERE OUT OF PITY!
DO YOU HATE US SO MUCH?
HUMANS CAN'T BE TRUSTED!
YOU'RE RIGHT. THEY CAN'T.

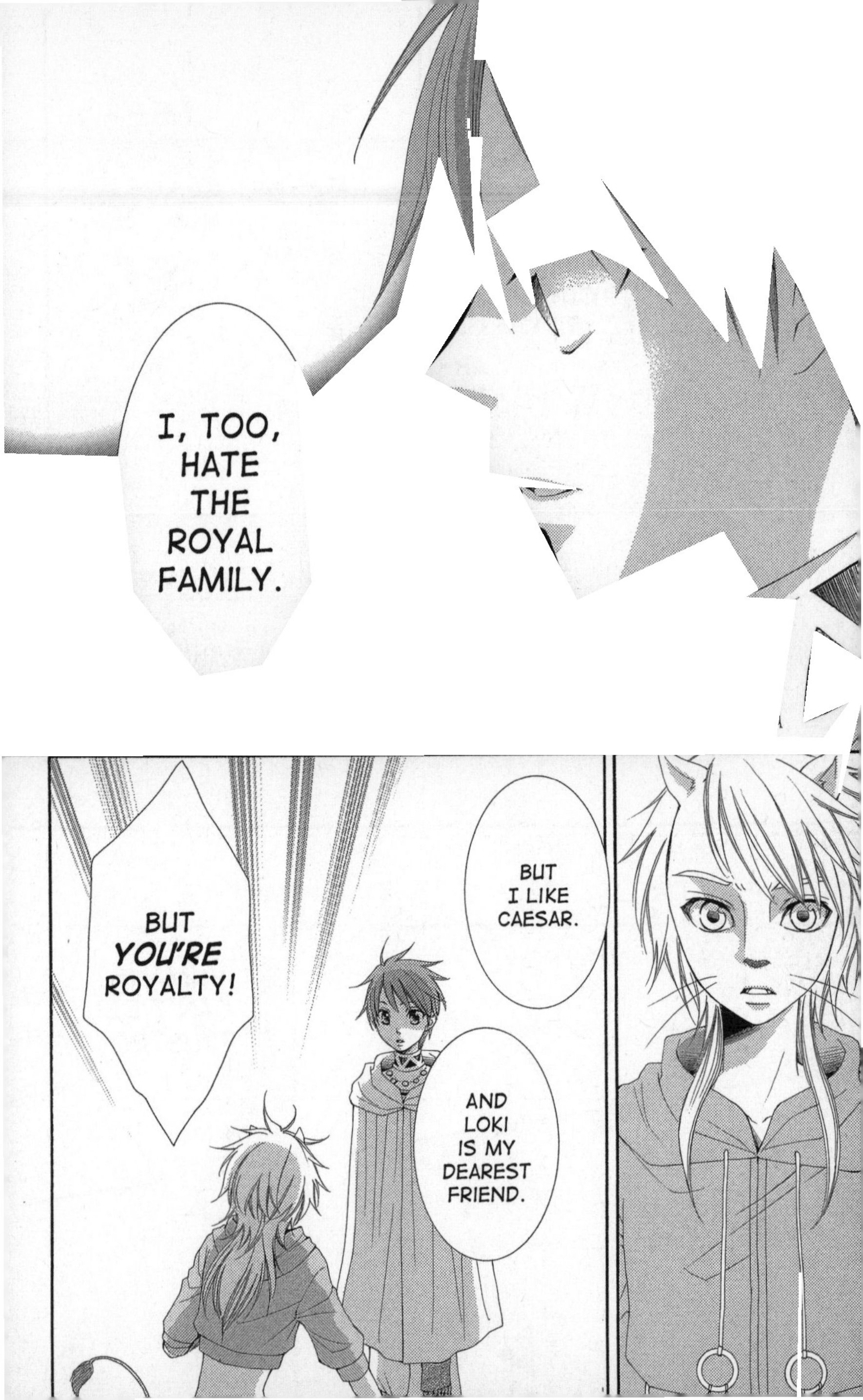
I, TOO, HATE THE ROYAL FAMILY.
BUT I LIKE CAESAR.
AND LOKI IS MY DEAREST FRIEND.
BUT *YOU'RE* ROYALTY!

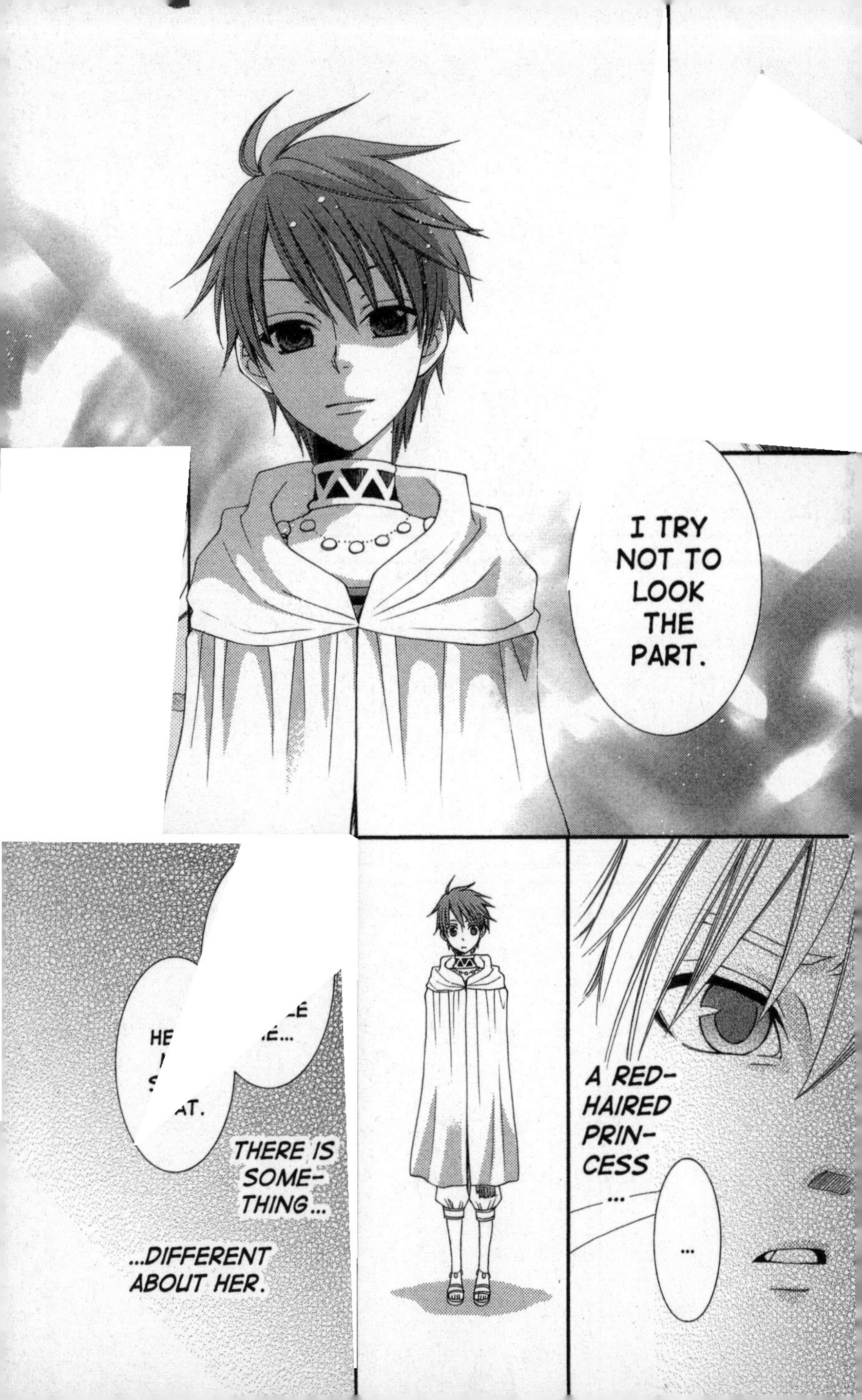
I TRY NOT TO LOOK THE PART.
A RED-HAIRED PRINCESS...
...
THERE IS SOMETHING...
...DIFFERENT ABOUT HER.

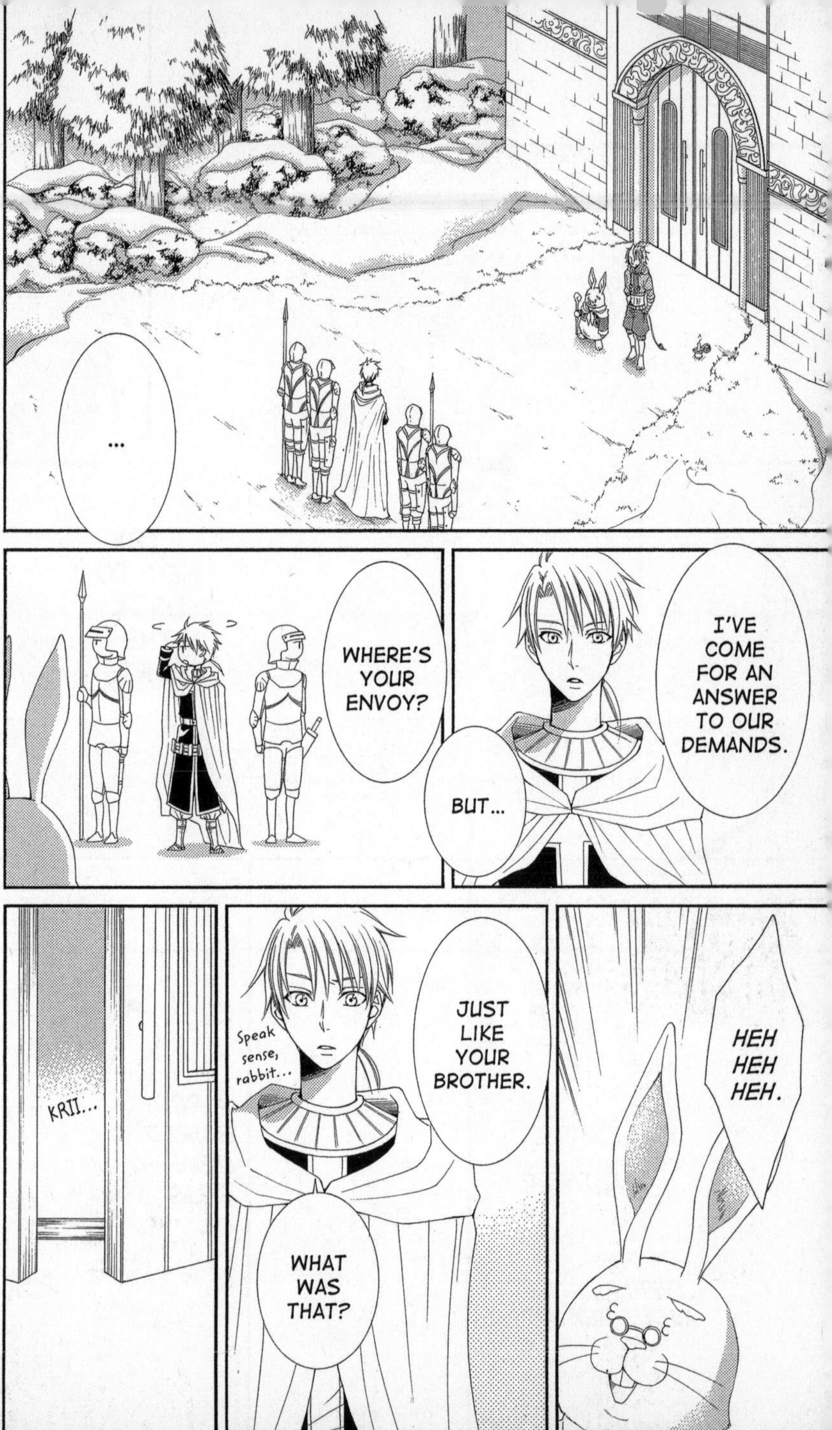
...
I'VE COME FOR AN ANSWER TO OUR DEMANDS.
BUT...
WHERE'S YOUR ENVOY?
HEH HEH HEH.
JUST LIKE YOUR BROTHER.
Speak sense, rabbit...
WHAT WAS THAT?
KRII...

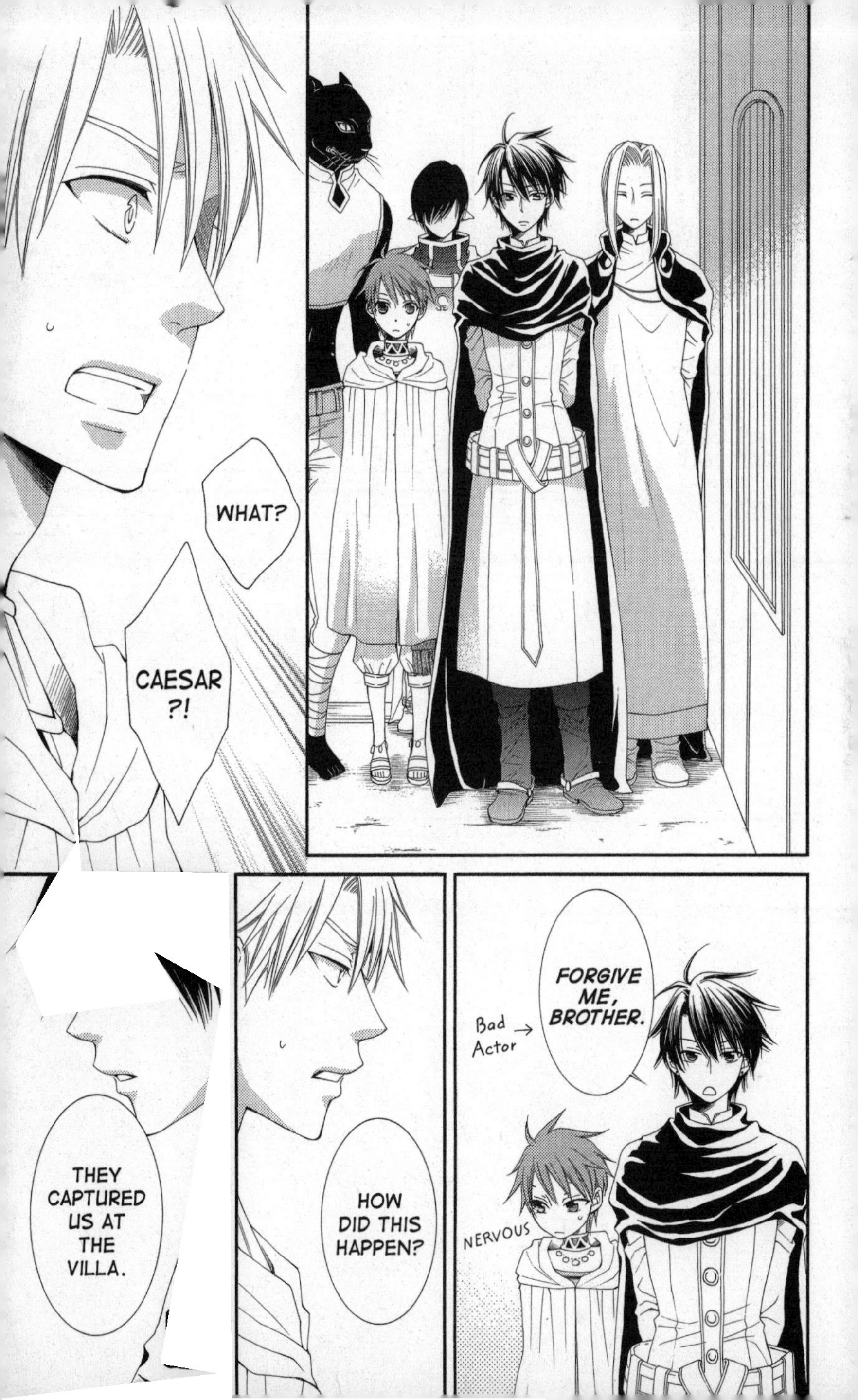
WHAT?
CAESAR ?!
FORGIVE ME, BROTHER.
Bad Actor →
NERVOUS
HOW DID THIS HAPPEN?
THEY CAPTURED US AT THE VILLA.

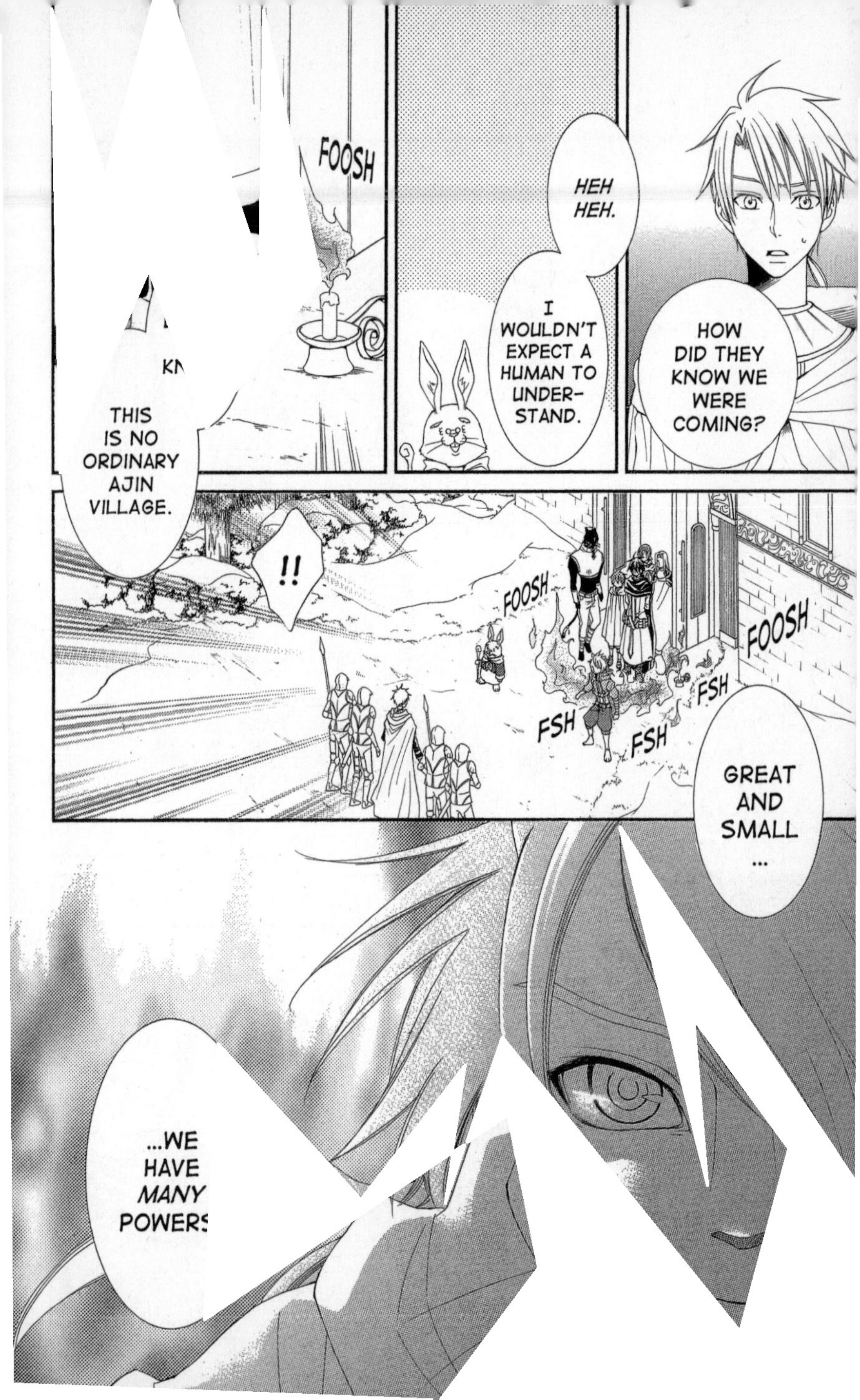
HOW DID THEY KNOW WE WERE COMING?
HEH HEH.
I WOULDN'T EXPECT A HUMAN TO UNDER-STAND.
FOOSH
THIS IS NO ORDINARY AJIN VILLAGE.
FOOSH
FSH
FSH
FOOSH
FSH
!!
GREAT AND SMALL...
...WE HAVE MANY POWERS

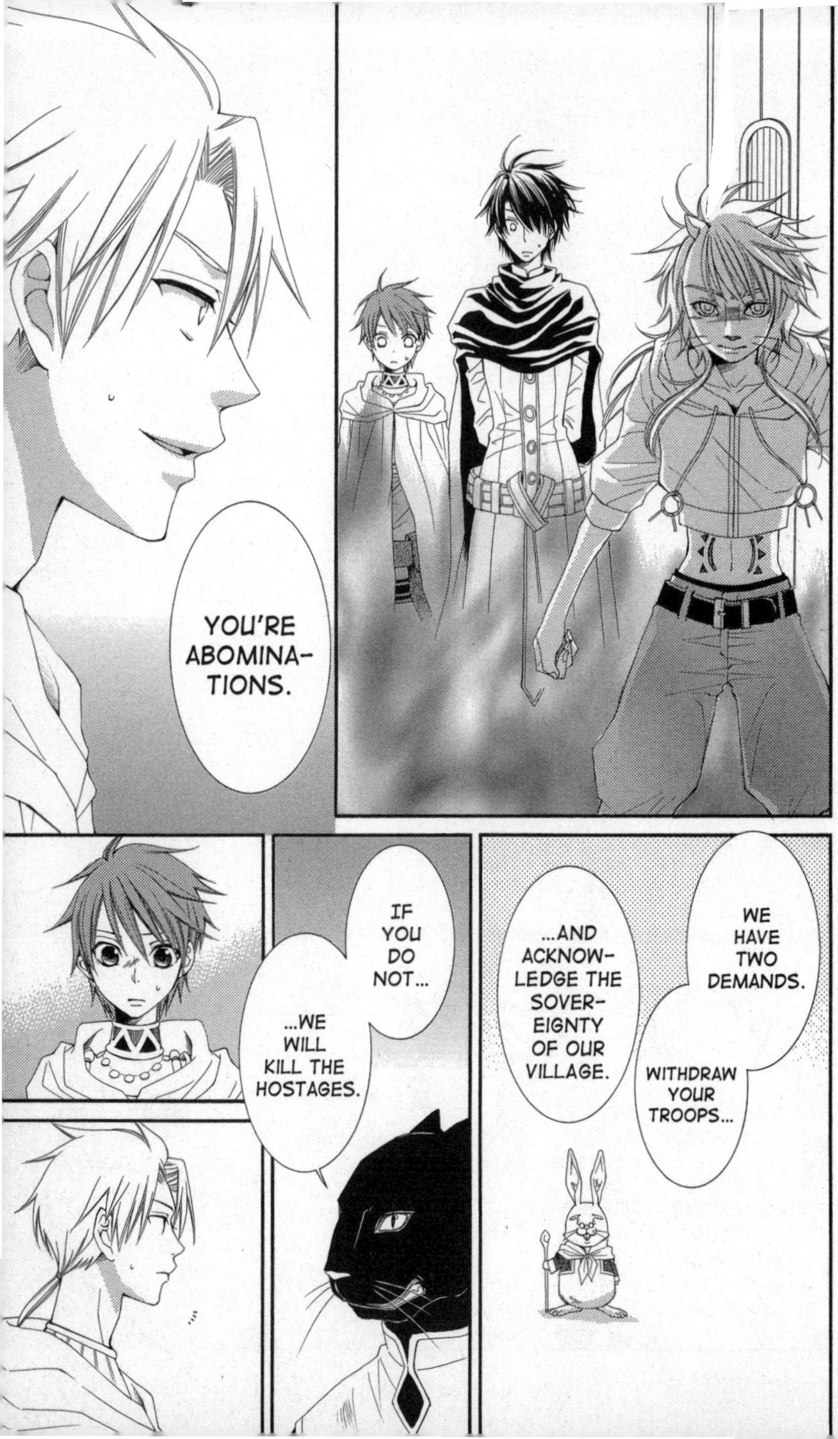
YOU'RE ABOMINA-TIONS.
WE HAVE TWO DEMANDS.
WITHDRAW YOUR TROOPS...
...AND ACKNOW-LEDGE THE SOVER-EIGNTY OF OUR VILLAGE.
IF YOU DO NOT...
...WE WILL KILL THE HOSTAGES.
...

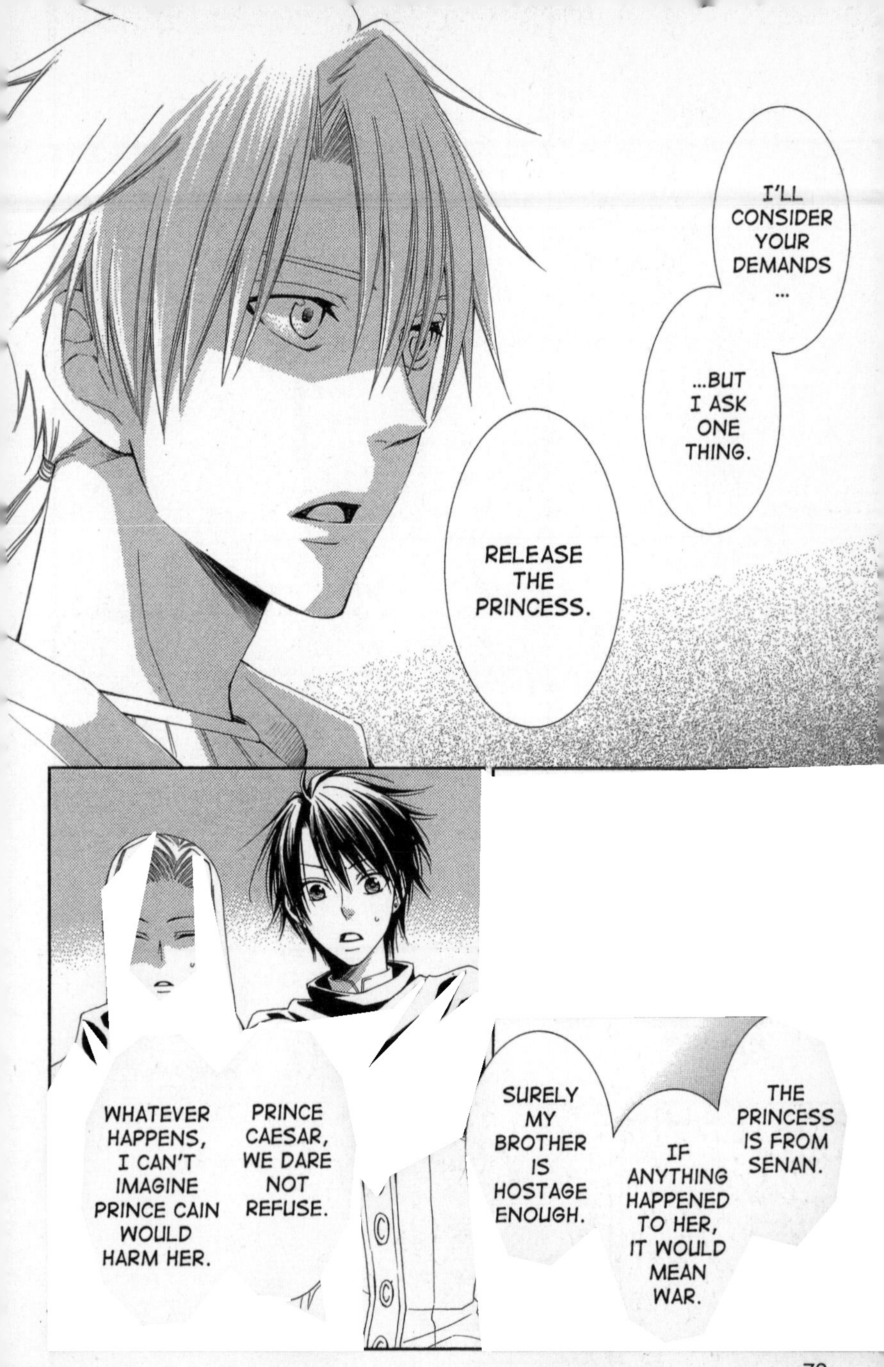
I'LL CONSIDER YOUR DEMANDS ...
...BUT I ASK ONE THING.
RELEASE THE PRINCESS.
THE PRINCESS IS FROM SENAN.
IF ANYTHING HAPPENED TO HER, IT WOULD MEAN WAR.
SURELY MY BROTHER IS HOSTAGE ENOUGH.
PRINCE CAESAR, WE DARE NOT REFUSE.
WHATEVER HAPPENS, I CAN'T IMAGINE PRINCE CAIN WOULD HARM HER.

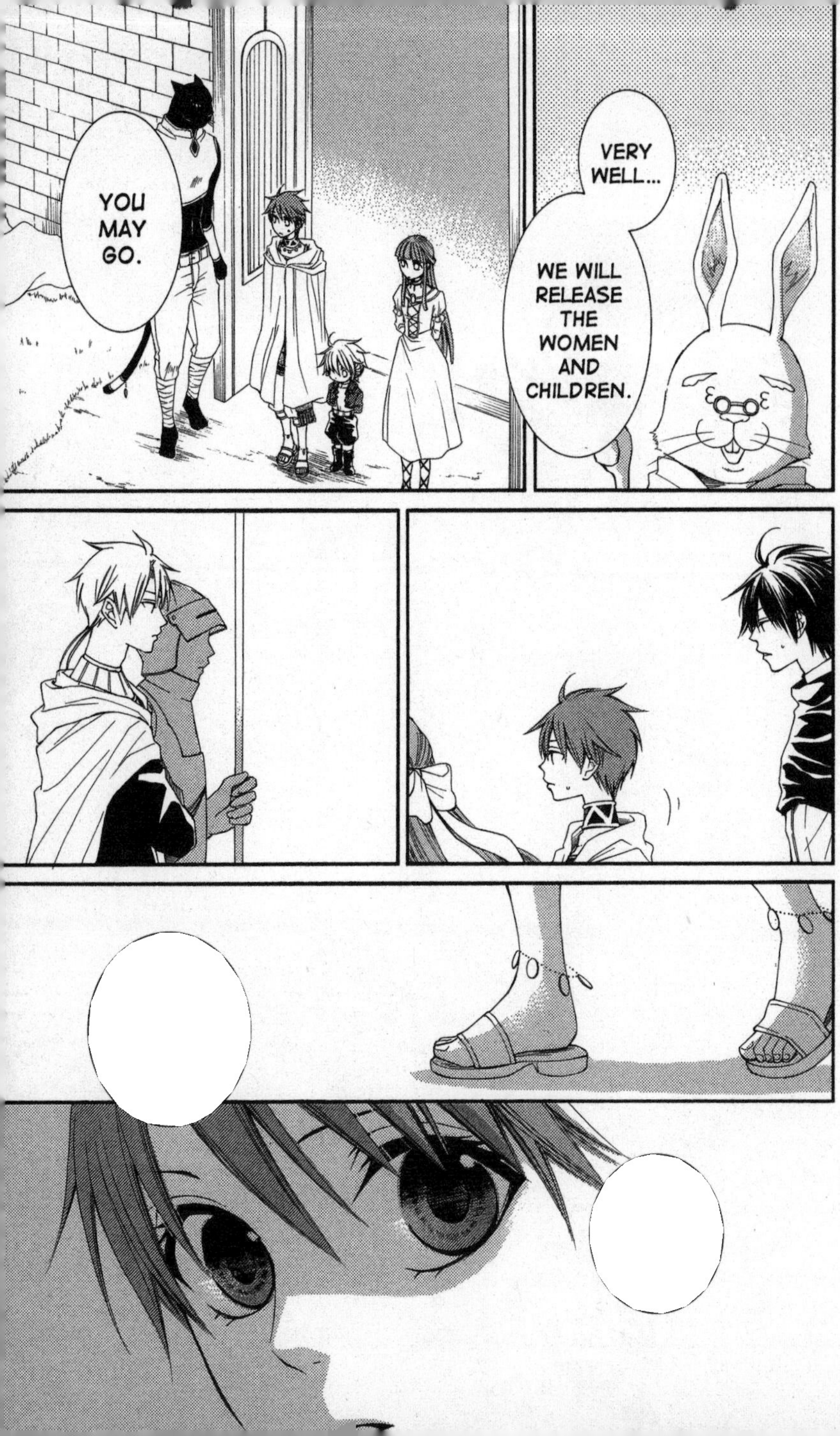
VERY WELL...
WE WILL RELEASE THE WOMEN AND CHILDREN.
YOU MAY GO.

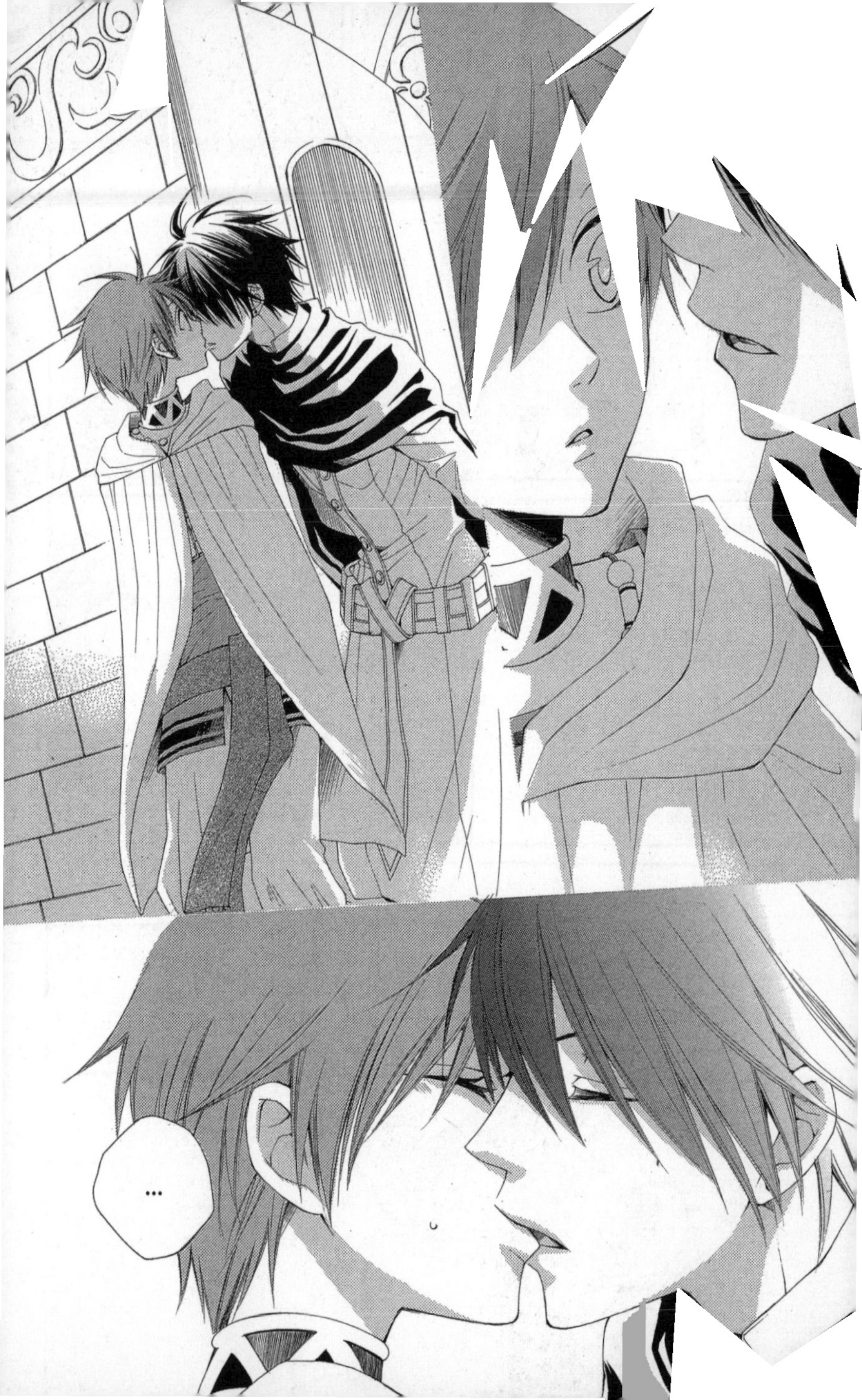
...

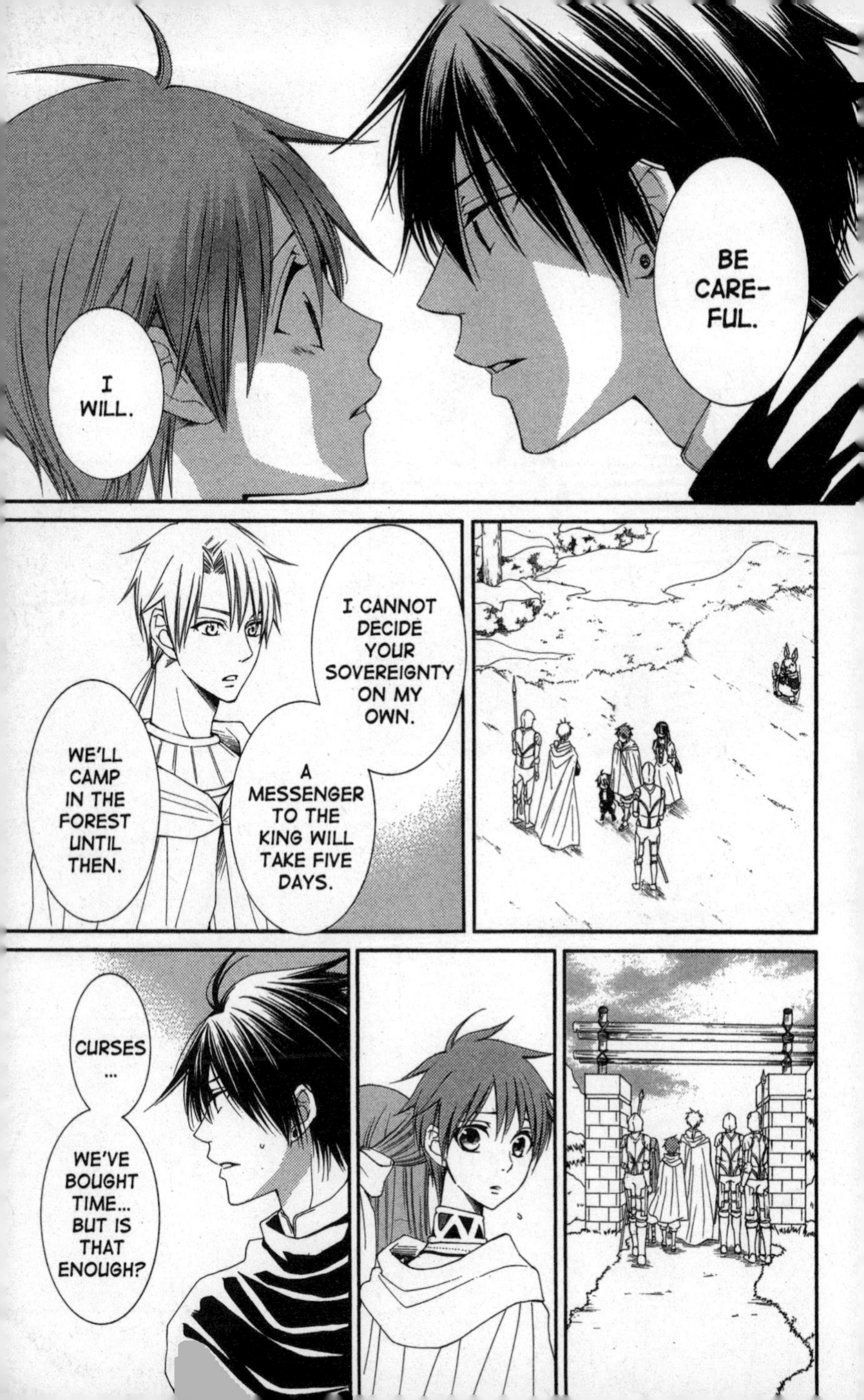
BE CARE-FUL.
I WILL.
I CANNOT DECIDE YOUR SOVEREIGNTY ON MY OWN.
A MESSENGER TO THE KING WILL TAKE FIVE DAYS.
WE'LL CAMP IN THE FOREST UNTIL THEN.
CURSES...
WE'VE BOUGHT TIME... BUT IS THAT ENOUGH?

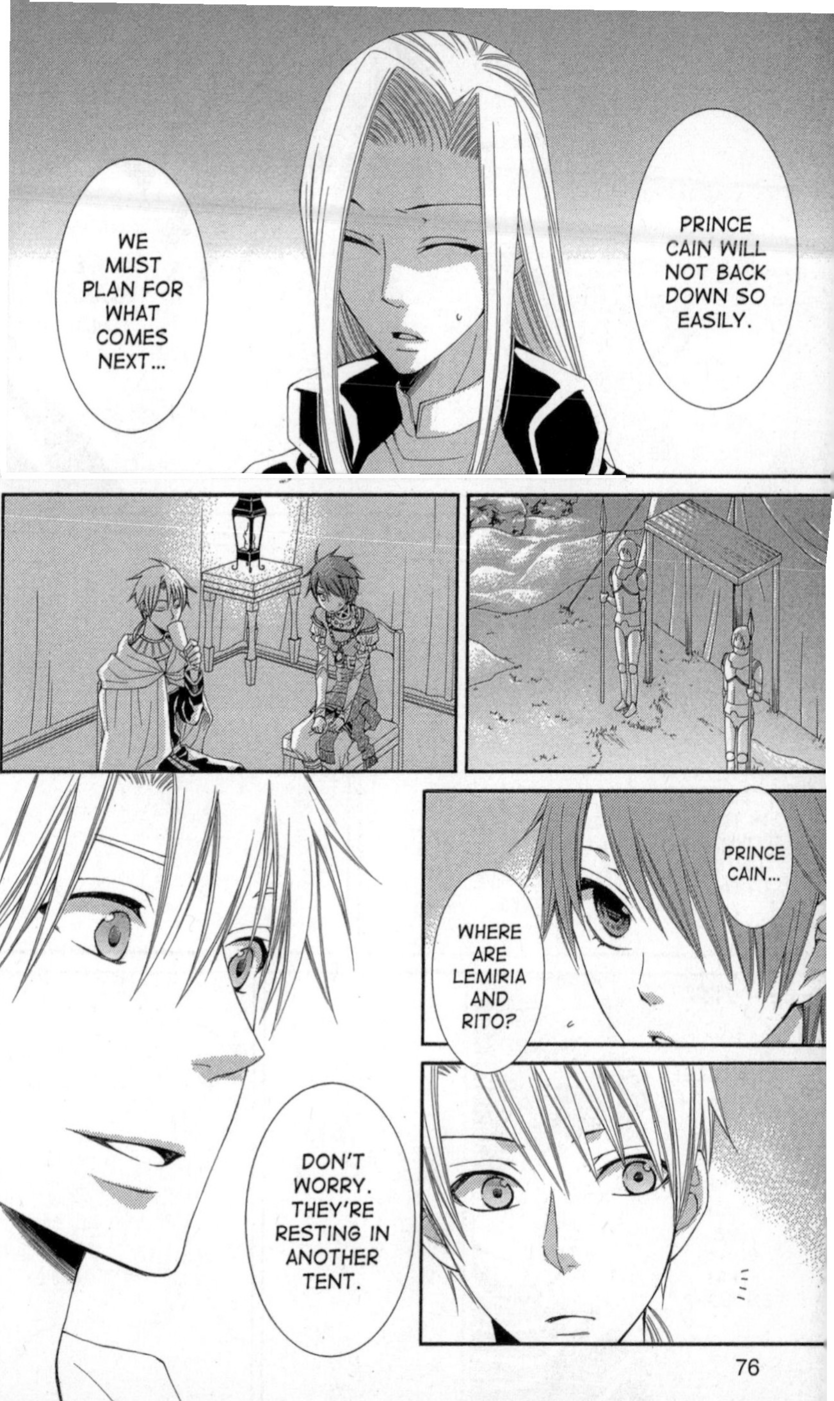
PRINCE CAIN WILL NOT BACK DOWN SO EASILY.
WE MUST PLAN FOR WHAT COMES NEXT...
PRINCE CAIN...
WHERE ARE LEMIRIA AND RITO?
DON'T WORRY. THEY'RE RESTING IN ANOTHER TENT.

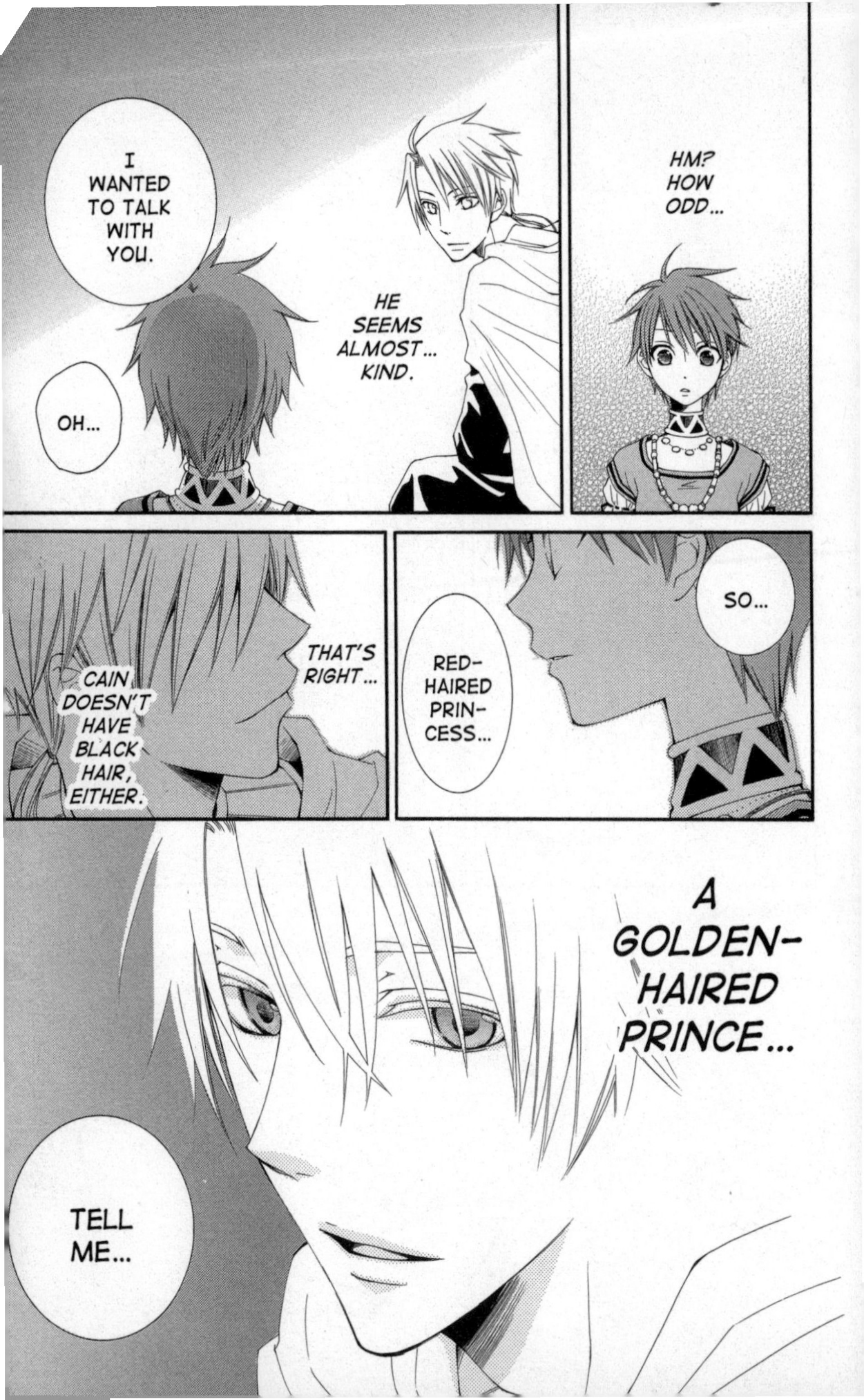
HM? HOW ODD...
I WANTED TO TALK WITH YOU.
HE SEEMS ALMOST... KIND.
OH...
SO...
RED-HAIRED PRIN-CESS...
THAT'S RIGHT...
CAIN DOESN'T HAVE BLACK HAIR, EITHER.
A GOLDEN-HAIRED PRINCE...
TELL ME...

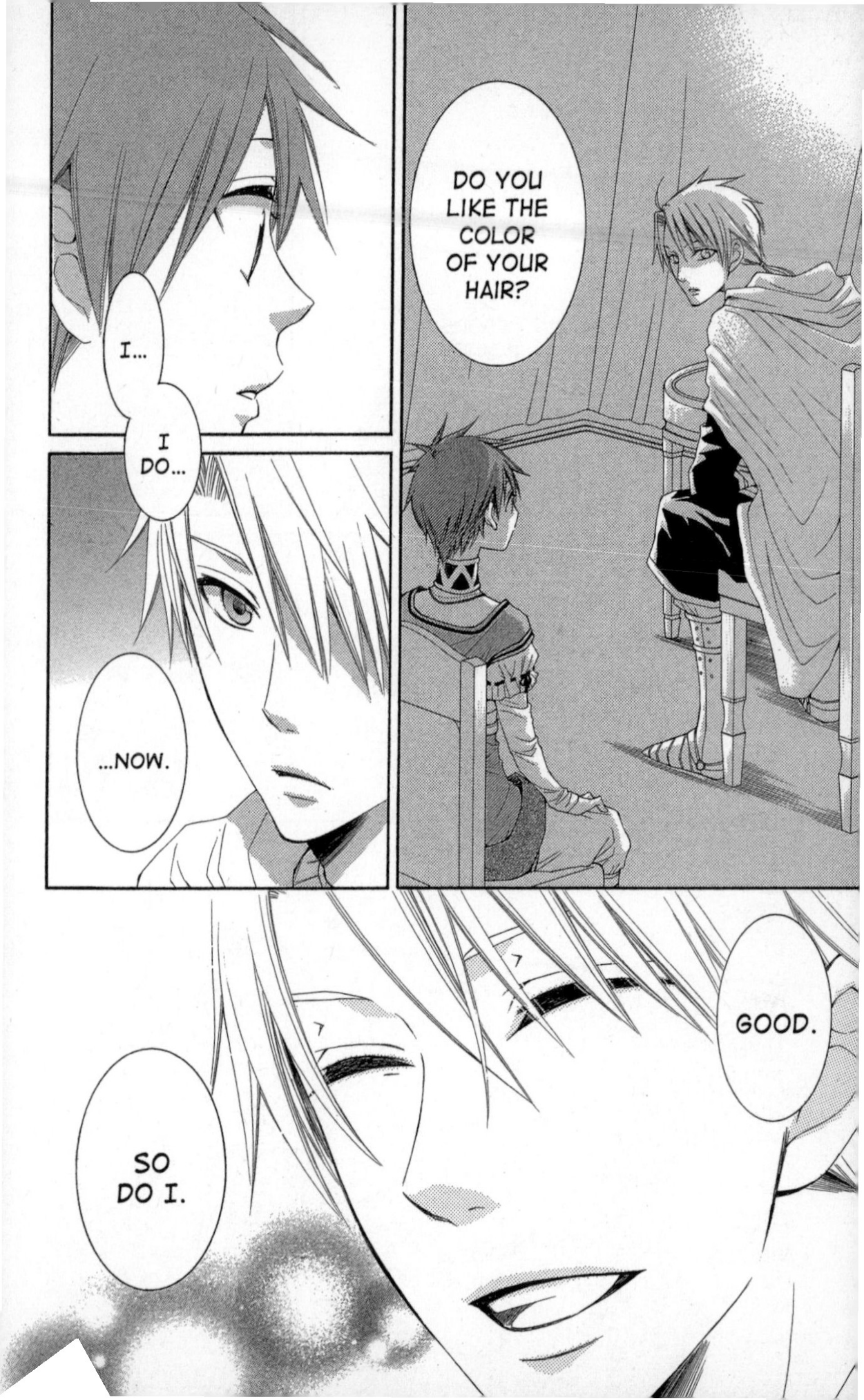
DO YOU LIKE THE COLOR OF YOUR HAIR?
I...
I DO...
...NOW.
GOOD.
SO DO I.

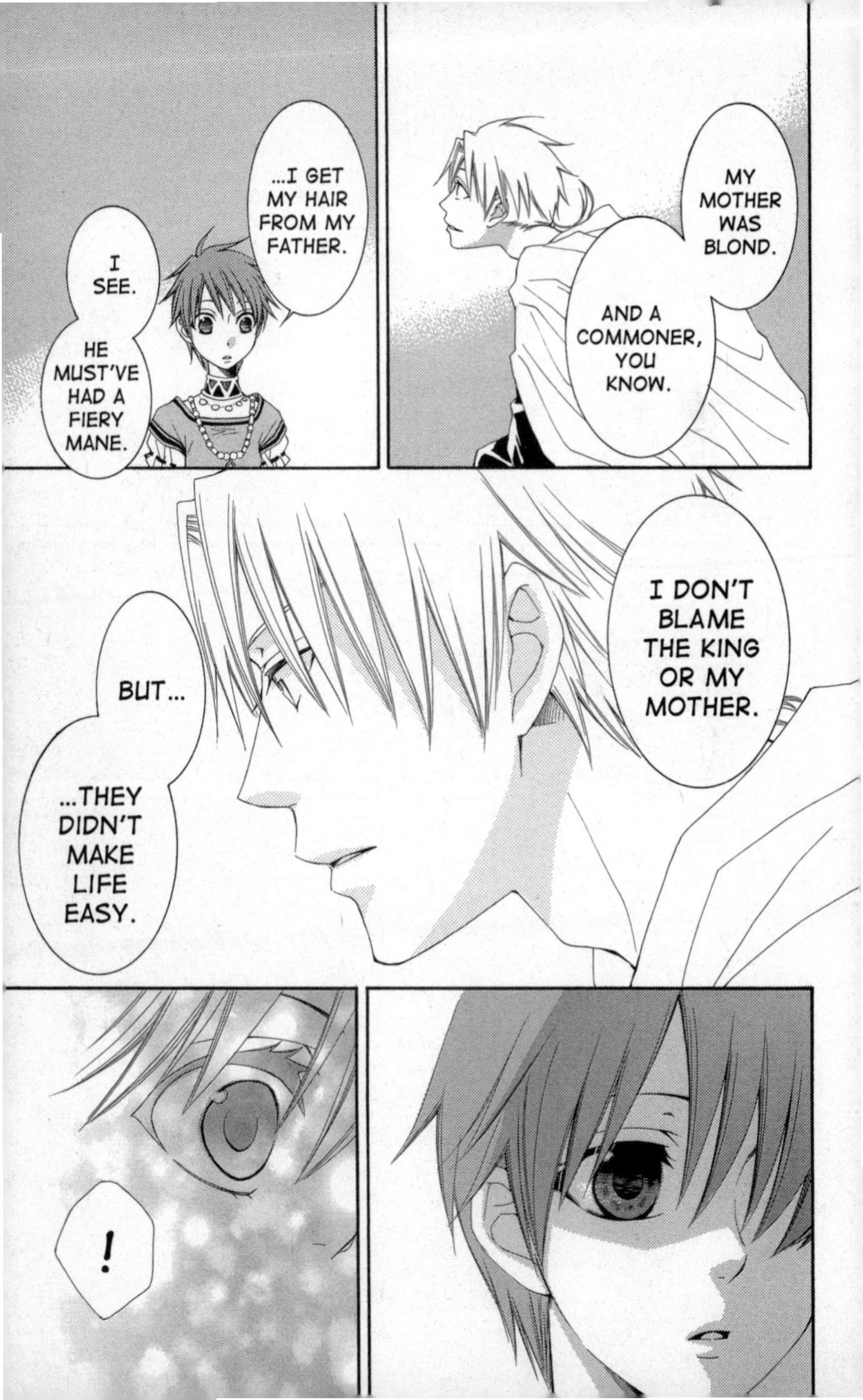
MY MOTHER WAS BLOND.
AND A COMMONER, YOU KNOW.
...I GET MY HAIR FROM MY FATHER.
I SEE.
HE MUST'VE HAD A FIERY MANE.
I DON'T BLAME THE KING OR MY MOTHER.
BUT...
...THEY DIDN'T MAKE LIFE EASY.
!

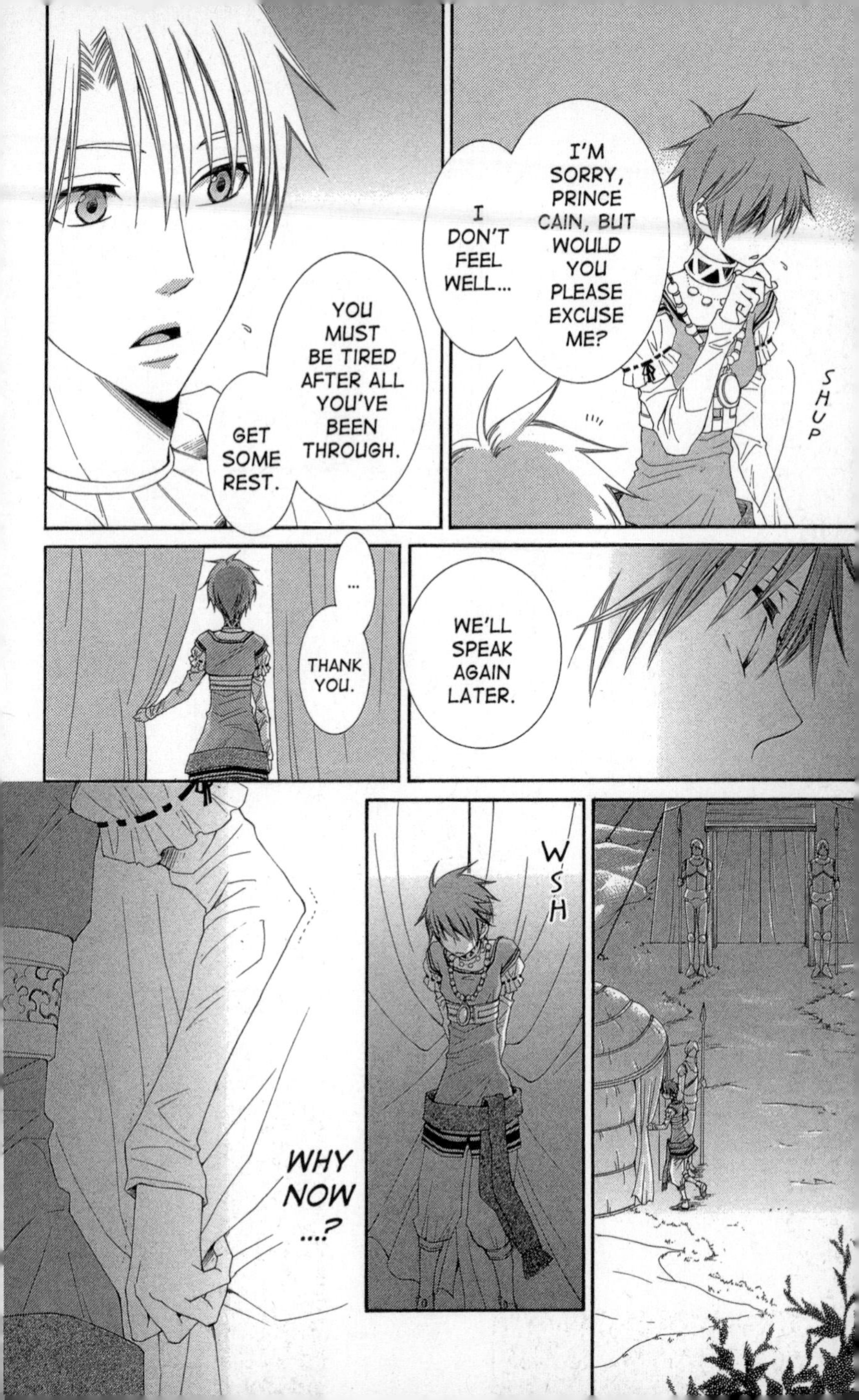
I'M SORRY, PRINCE CAIN, BUT WOULD YOU PLEASE EXCUSE ME?
I DON'T FEEL WELL...
SHUP
YOU MUST BE TIRED AFTER ALL YOU'VE BEEN THROUGH.
GET SOME REST.
WE'LL SPEAK AGAIN LATER.
...
THANK YOU.
WSH
WHY NOW ...?

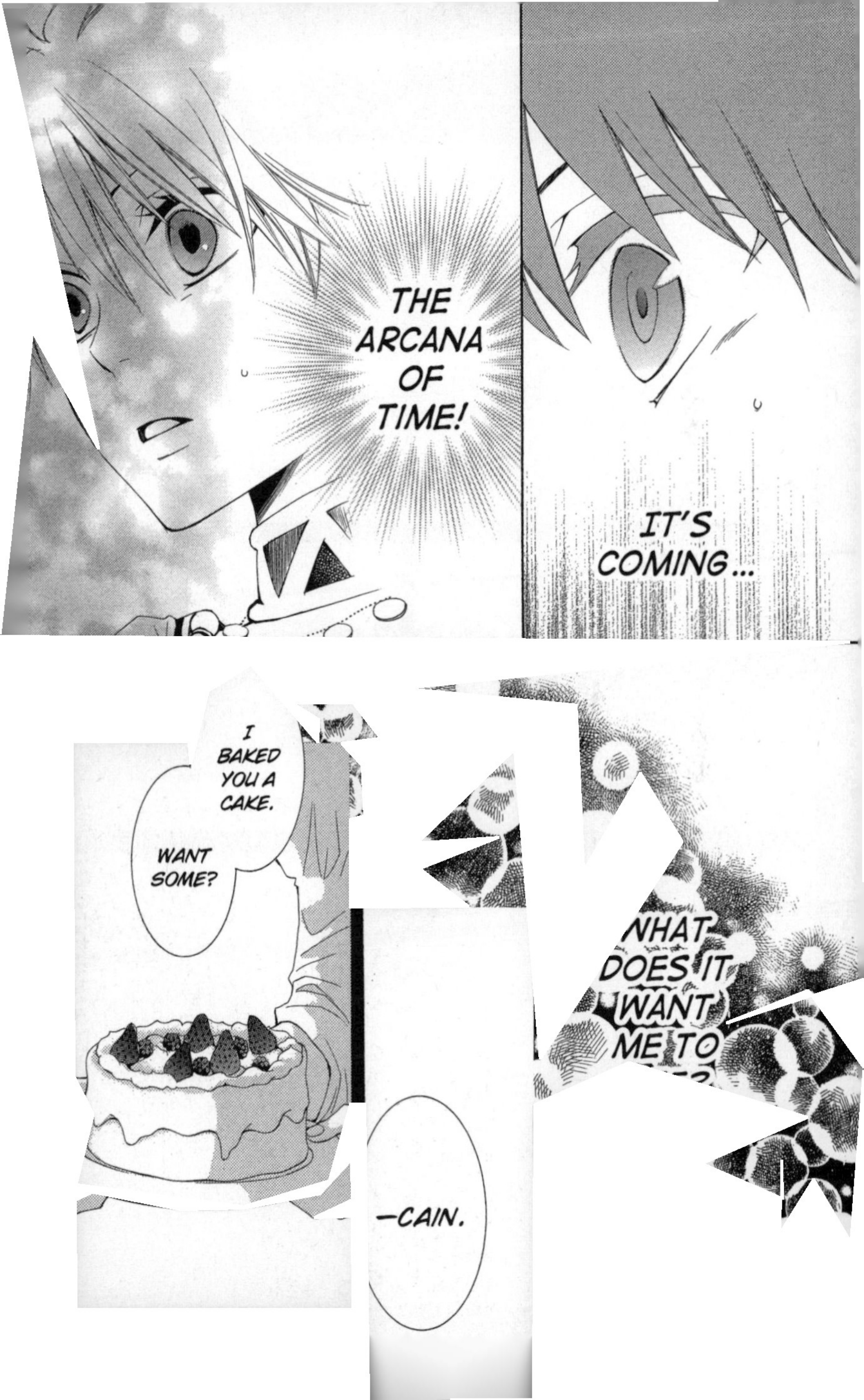
IT'S COMING...
THE ARCANA OF TIME!
WHAT DOES IT WANT ME TO
—CAIN.
I BAKED YOU A CAKE.
WANT SOME?

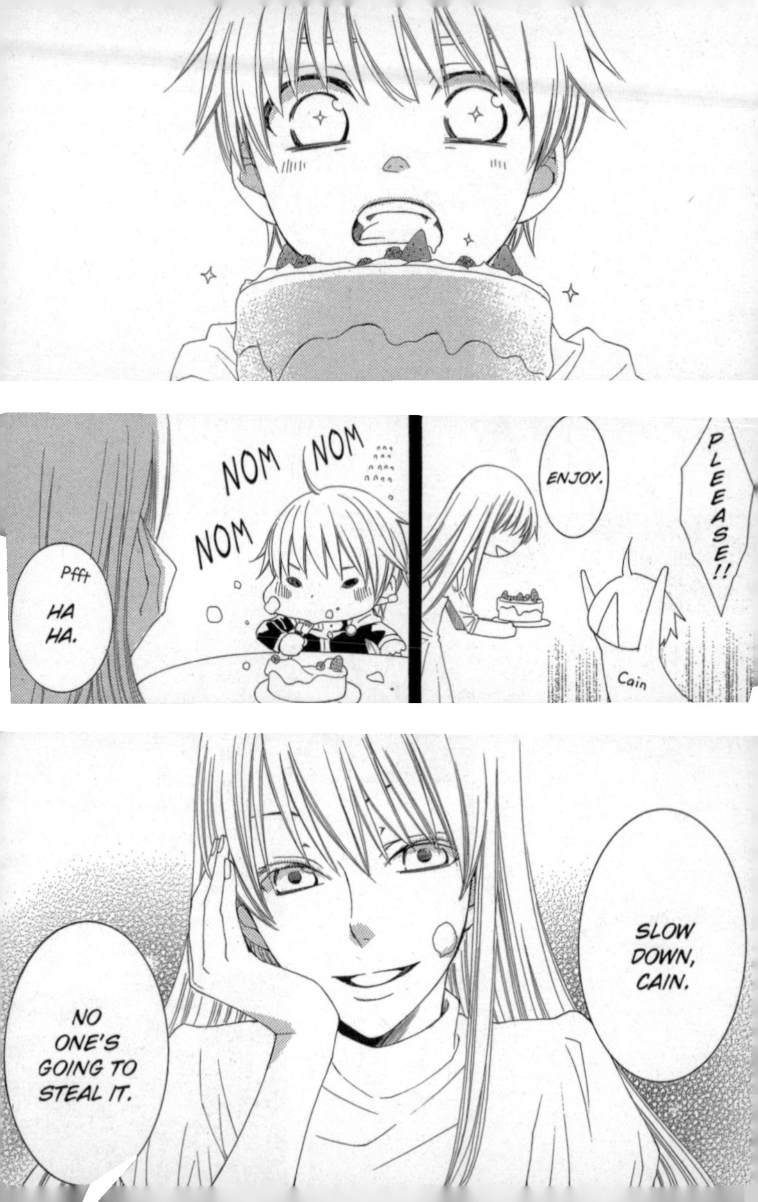
PLEEASE!!
ENJOY.
Cain
NOM NOM
NOM
Pfft
HA HA.
SLOW DOWN, CAIN.
NO ONE'S GOING TO STEAL IT.

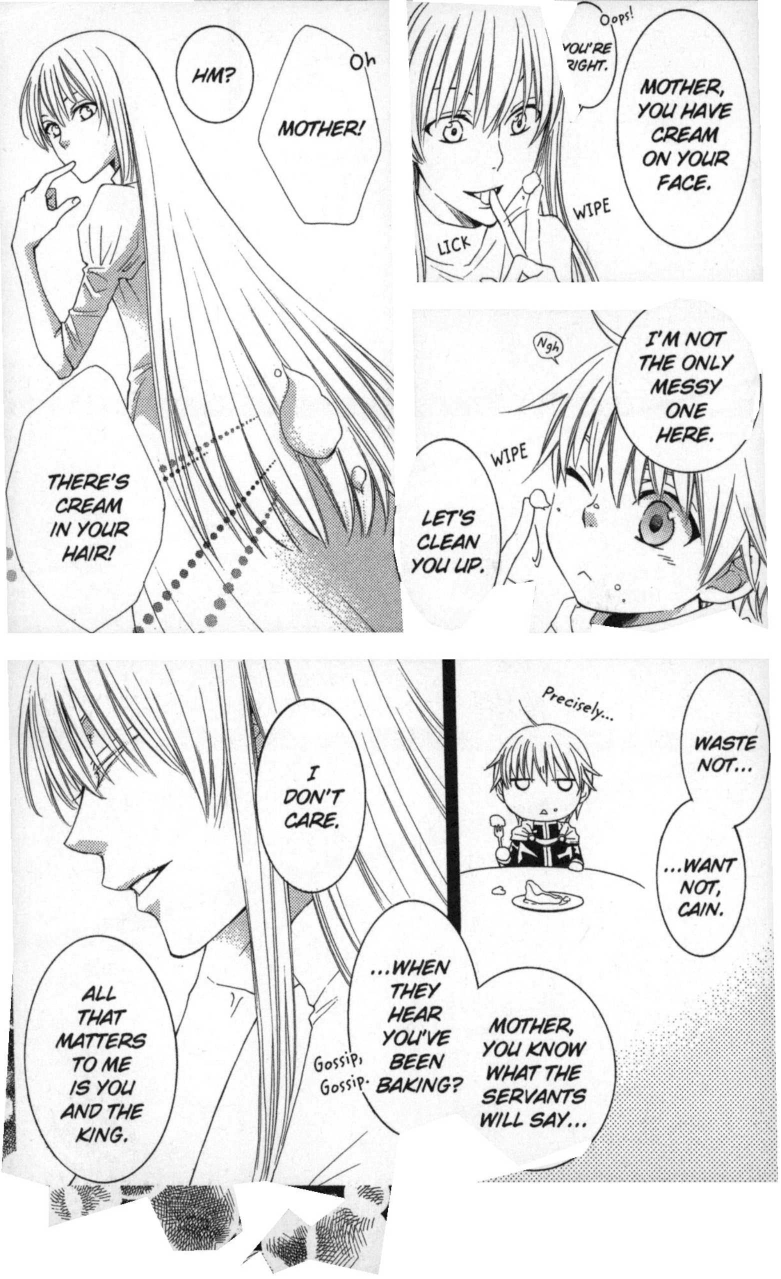
MOTHER, YOU HAVE CREAM ON YOUR FACE.
Oops!
YOU'RE RIGHT.
WIPE
LICK
I'M NOT THE ONLY MESSY ONE HERE.
Ngh
WIPE
LET'S CLEAN YOU UP.
Oh
MOTHER!
HM?
THERE'S CREAM IN YOUR HAIR!
WASTE NOT...
...WANT NOT, CAIN.
Precisely...
MOTHER, YOU KNOW WHAT THE SERVANTS WILL SAY...
...WHEN THEY HEAR YOU'VE BEEN BAKING?
Gossip, Gossip.
I DON'T CARE.
ALL THAT MATTERS TO ME IS YOU AND THE KING.

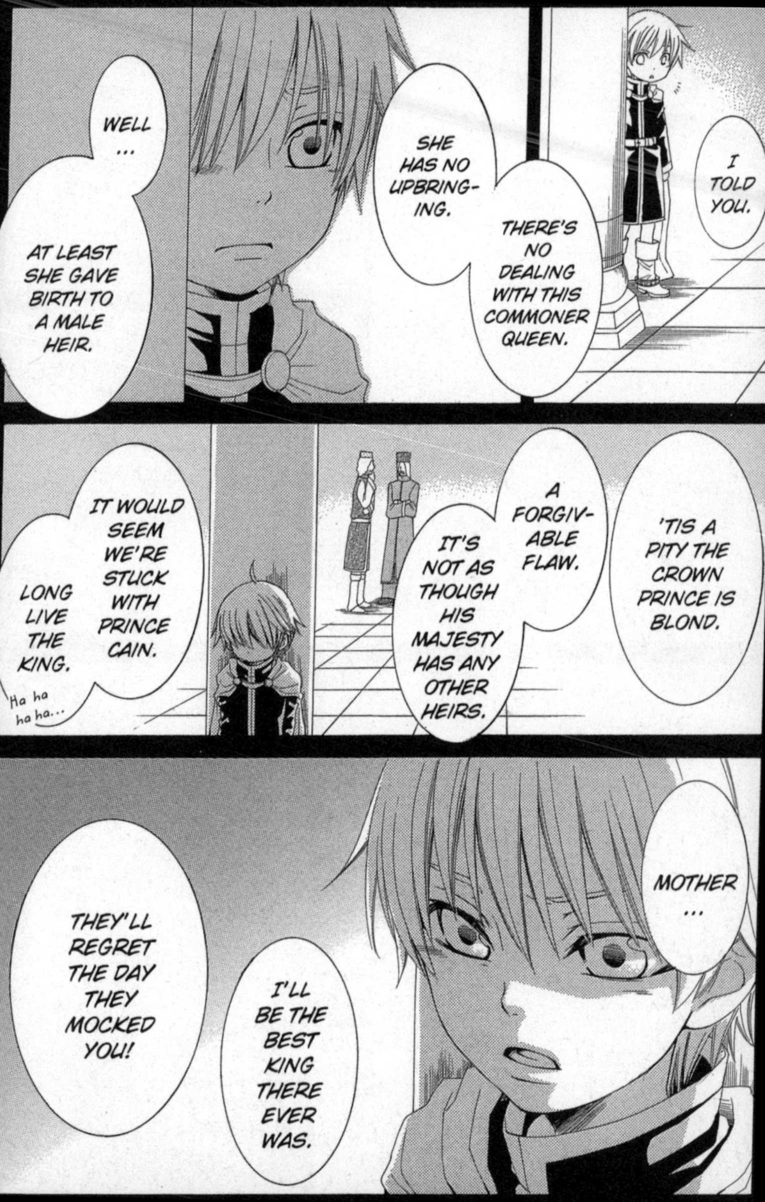
I TOLD YOU.
SHE HAS NO UPBRING-ING.
THERE'S NO DEALING WITH THIS COMMONER QUEEN.
WELL ...
AT LEAST SHE GAVE BIRTH TO A MALE HEIR.
'TIS A PITY THE CROWN PRINCE IS BLOND.
A FORGIV-ABLE FLAW.
IT'S NOT AS THOUGH HIS MAJESTY HAS ANY OTHER HEIRS.
IT WOULD SEEM WE'RE STUCK WITH PRINCE CAIN.
LONG LIVE THE KING.
Ha ha ha ha...
MOTHER ...
I'LL BE THE BEST KING THERE EVER WAS.
THEY'LL REGRET THE DAY THEY MOCKED YOU!

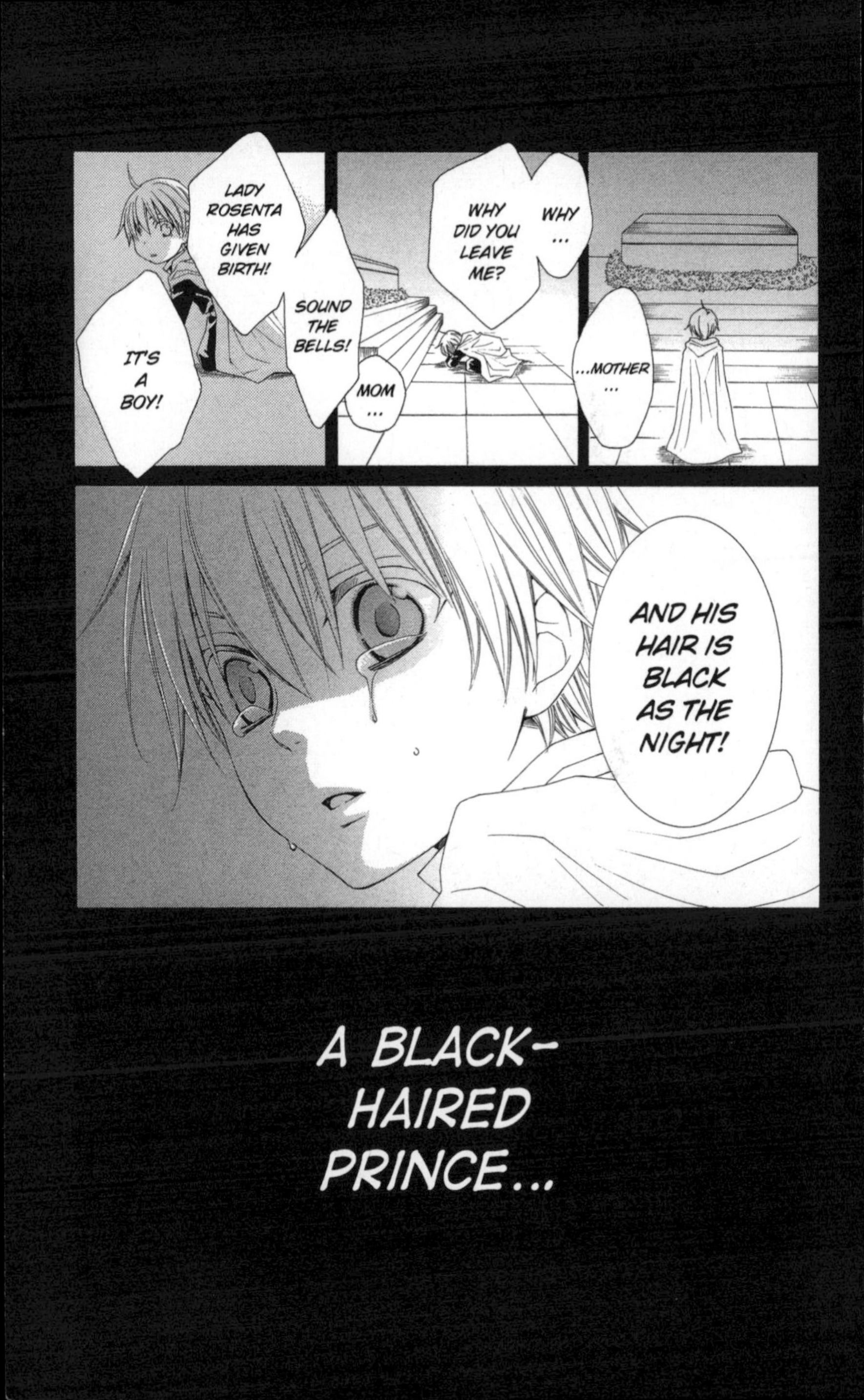
...MOTHER ...
WHY ...
WHY DID YOU LEAVE ME?
MOM ...
LADY ROSENTA HAS GIVEN BIRTH!
SOUND THE BELLS!
IT'S A BOY!
AND HIS HAIR IS BLACK AS THE NIGHT!
A BLACK-HAIRED PRINCE...

Chapter 18

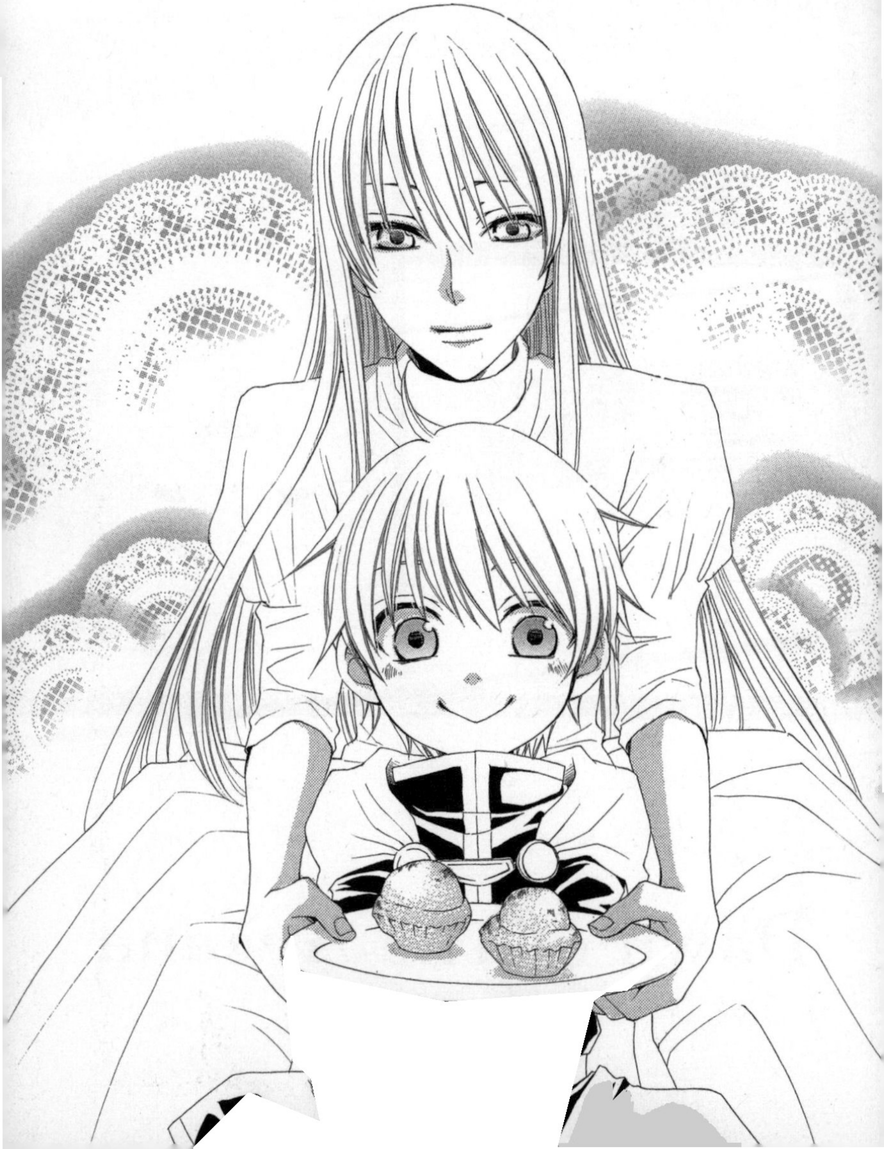

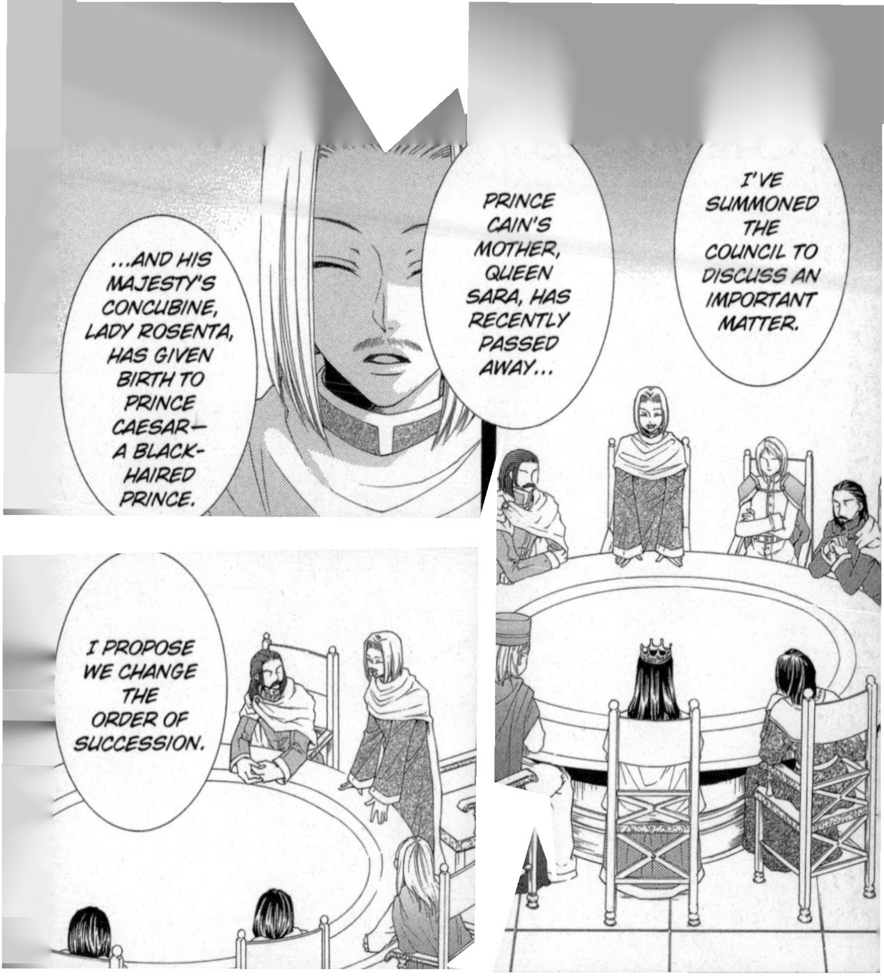
I'VE SUMMONED THE COUNCIL TO DISCUSS AN IMPORTANT MATTER.
PRINCE CAIN'S MOTHER, QUEEN SARA, HAS RECENTLY PASSED AWAY...
...AND HIS MAJESTY'S CONCUBINE, LADY ROSENTA, HAS GIVEN BIRTH TO PRINCE CAESAR—A BLACK-HAIRED PRINCE.
I PROPOSE WE CHANGE THE ORDER OF SUCCESSION.

Dawn of the Arcana

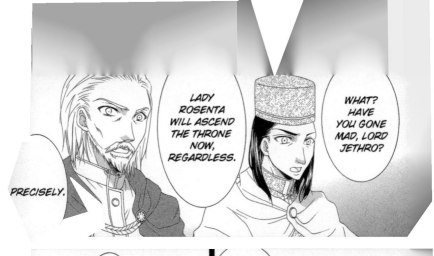

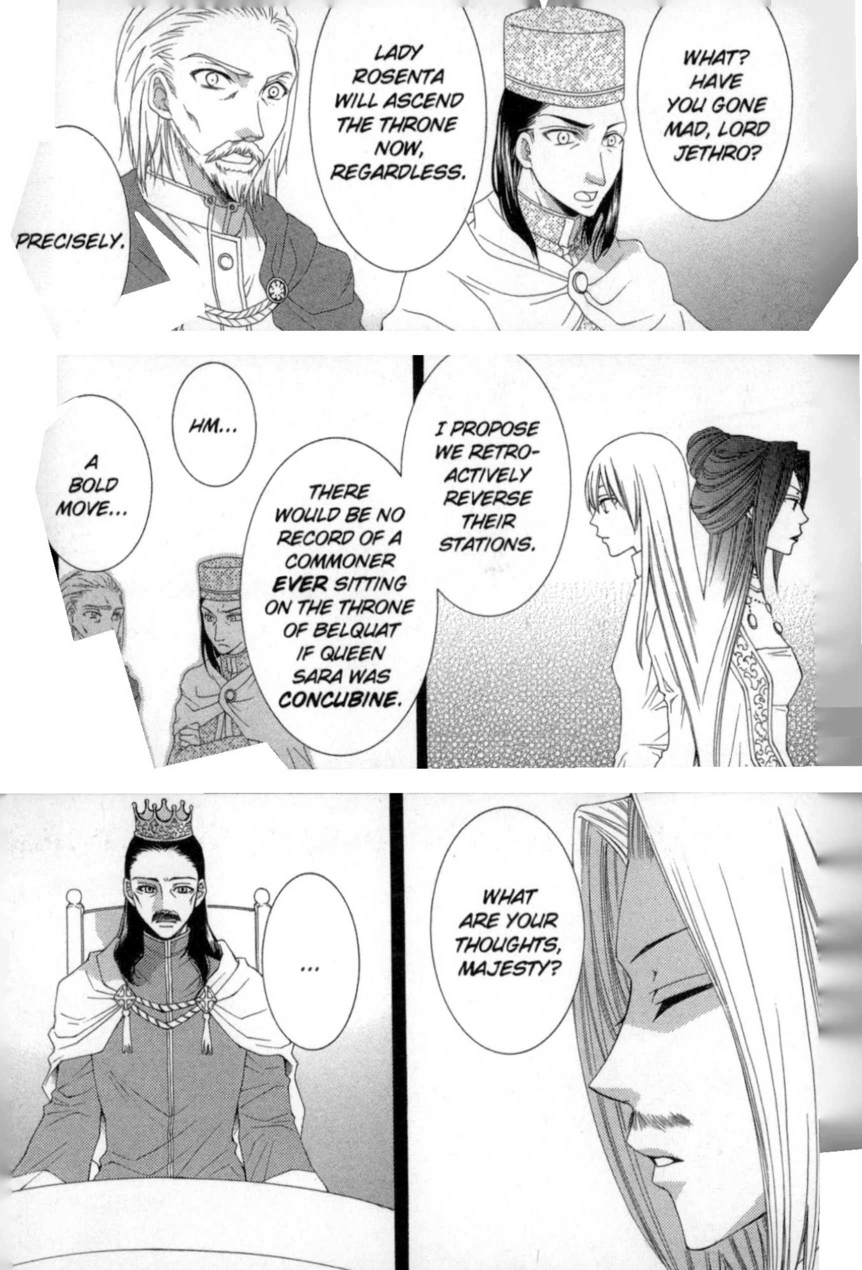
WHAT? HAVE YOU GONE MAD, LORD JETHRO?
LADY ROSENTA WILL ASCEND THE THRONE NOW, REGARDLESS.
PRECISELY.
I PROPOSE WE RETRO-ACTIVELY REVERSE THEIR STATIONS.
THERE WOULD BE NO RECORD OF A COMMONER **EVER** SITTING ON THE THRONE OF BELQUAT IF QUEEN SARA WAS **CONCUBINE.**
HM...
A BOLD MOVE...
WHAT ARE YOUR THOUGHTS, MAJESTY?
...

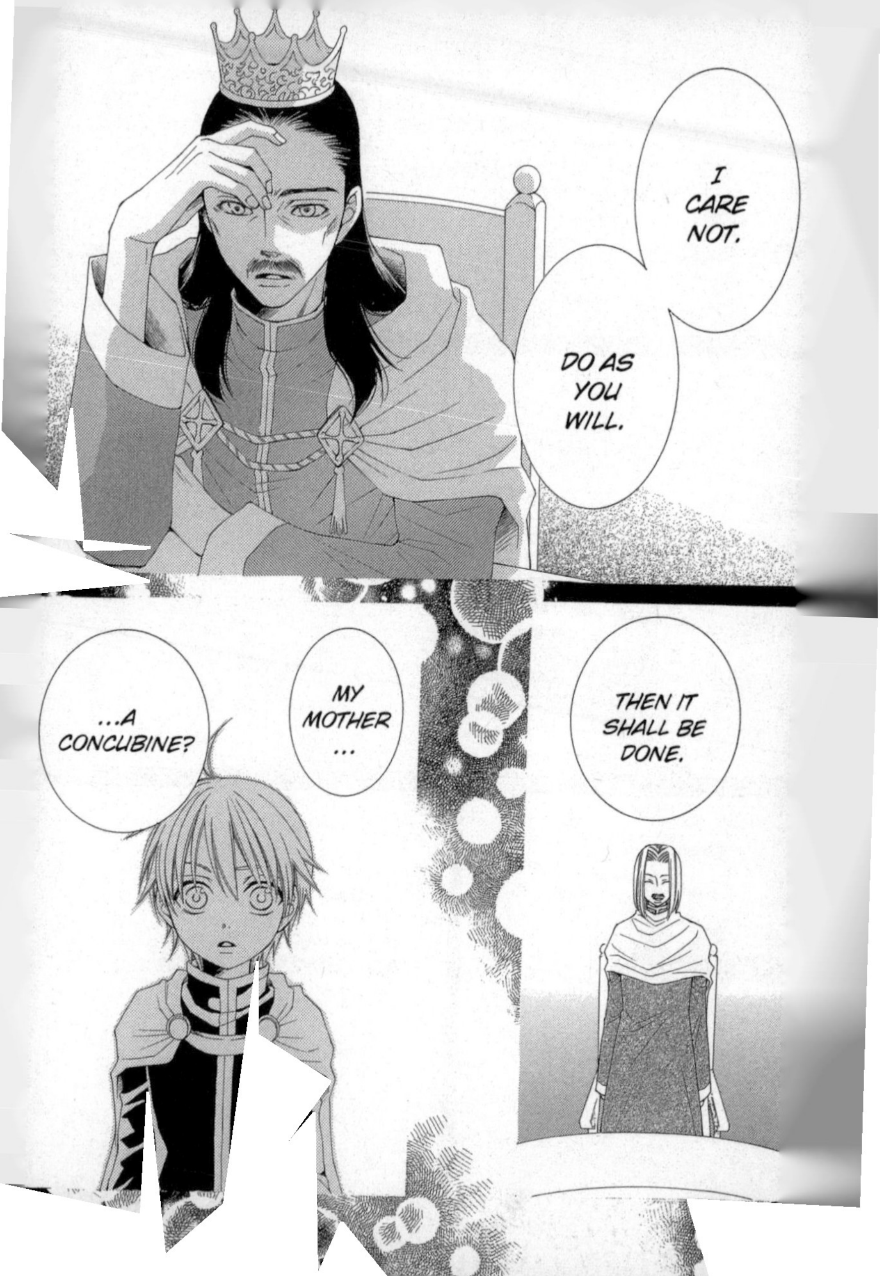
I CARE NOT.
DO AS YOU WILL.
THEN IT SHALL BE DONE.
MY MOTHER ...
...A CONCUBINE?

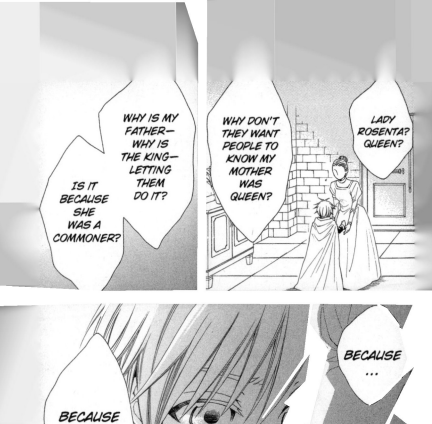

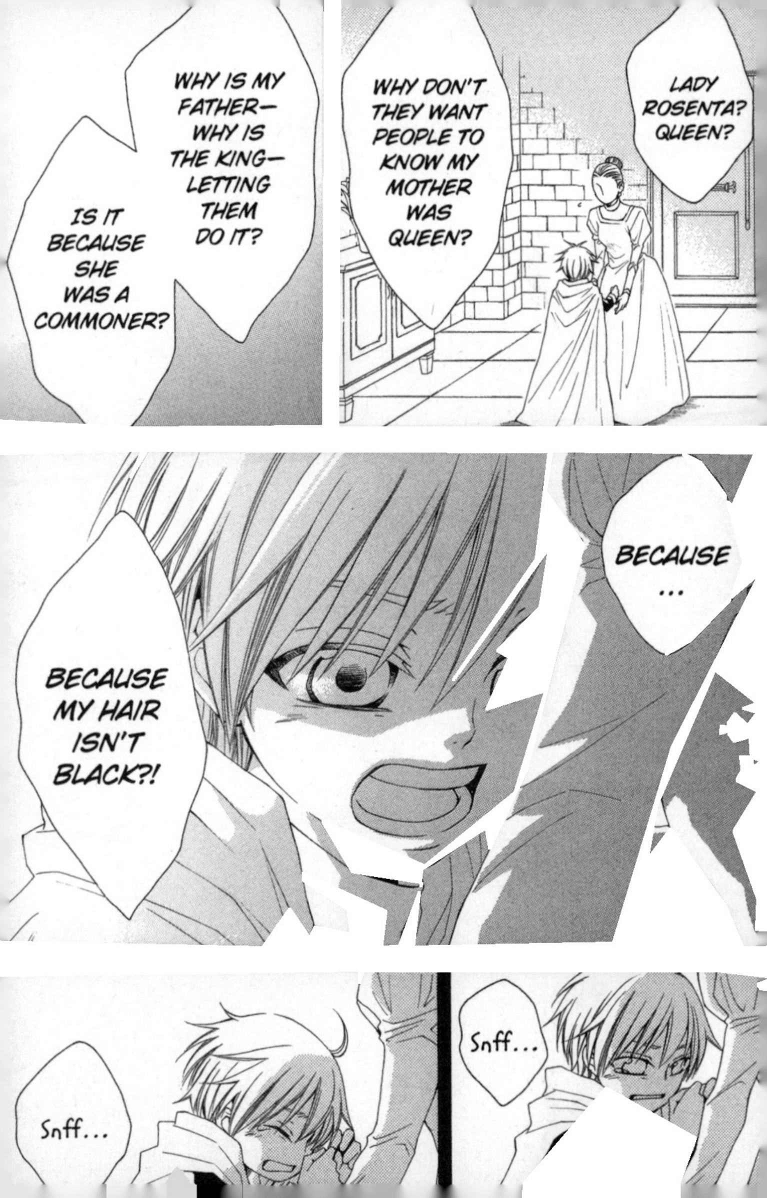
LADY ROSENTA? QUEEN?
WHY DON'T THEY WANT PEOPLE TO KNOW MY MOTHER WAS QUEEN?
WHY IS MY FATHER— WHY IS THE KING— LETTING THEM DO IT?
IS IT BECAUSE SHE WAS A COMMONER?
BECAUSE ...
BECAUSE MY HAIR ISN'T BLACK?!
Snff...
Snff...

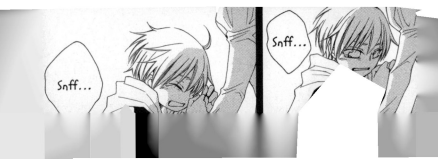

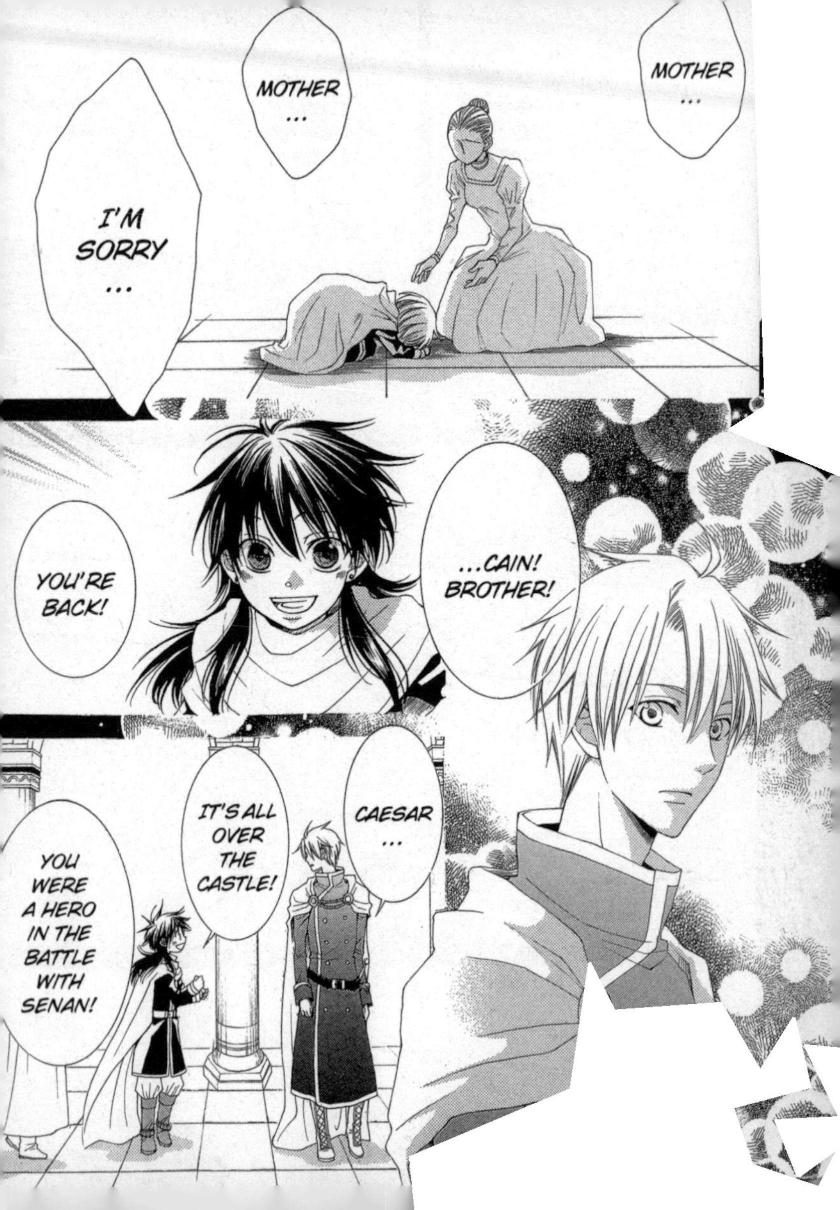

MOTHER ...
MOTHER ...
I'M SORRY ...
...CAIN! BROTHER!
YOU'RE BACK!
CAESAR ...
IT'S ALL OVER THE CASTLE!
YOU WERE A HERO IN THE BATTLE WITH SENAN!

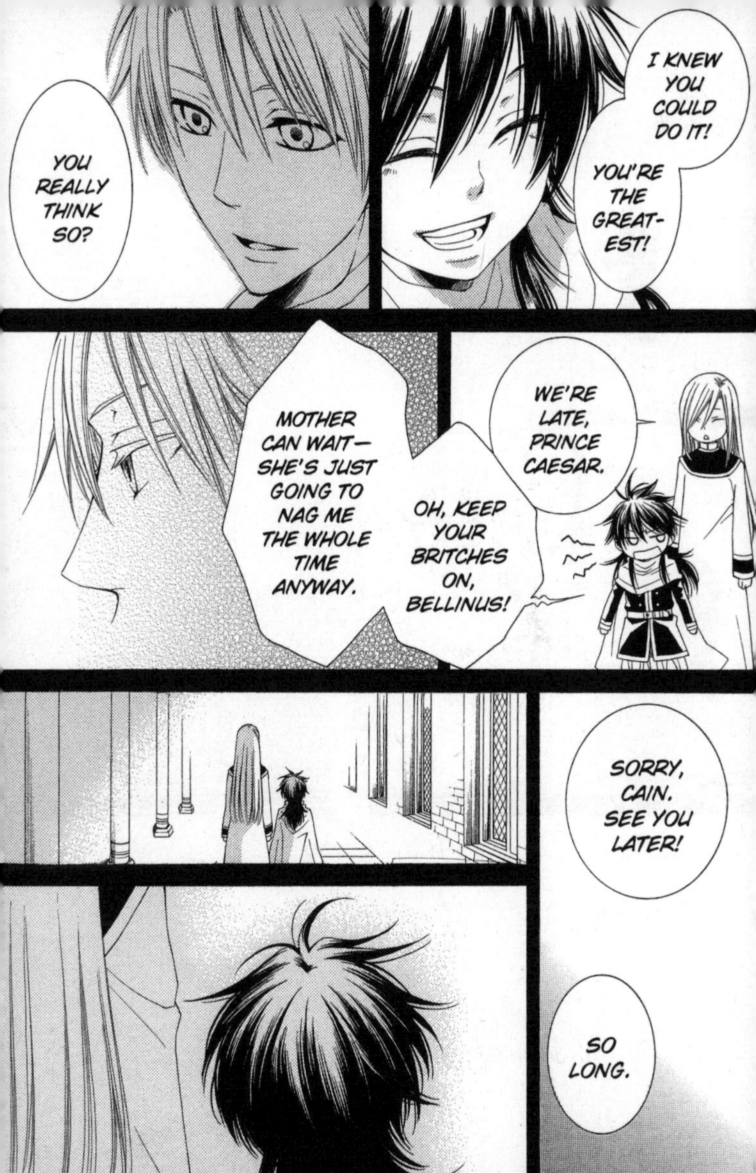
I KNEW YOU COULD DO IT!
YOU'RE THE GREAT-EST!
YOU REALLY THINK SO?
WE'RE LATE, PRINCE CAESAR.
OH, KEEP YOUR BRITCHES ON, BELLINUS!
MOTHER CAN WAIT—SHE'S JUST GOING TO NAG ME THE WHOLE TIME ANYWAY.
SORRY, CAIN. SEE YOU LATER!
SO LONG.

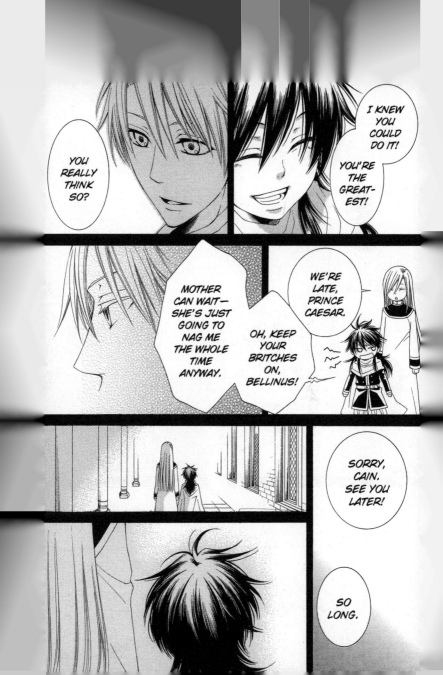

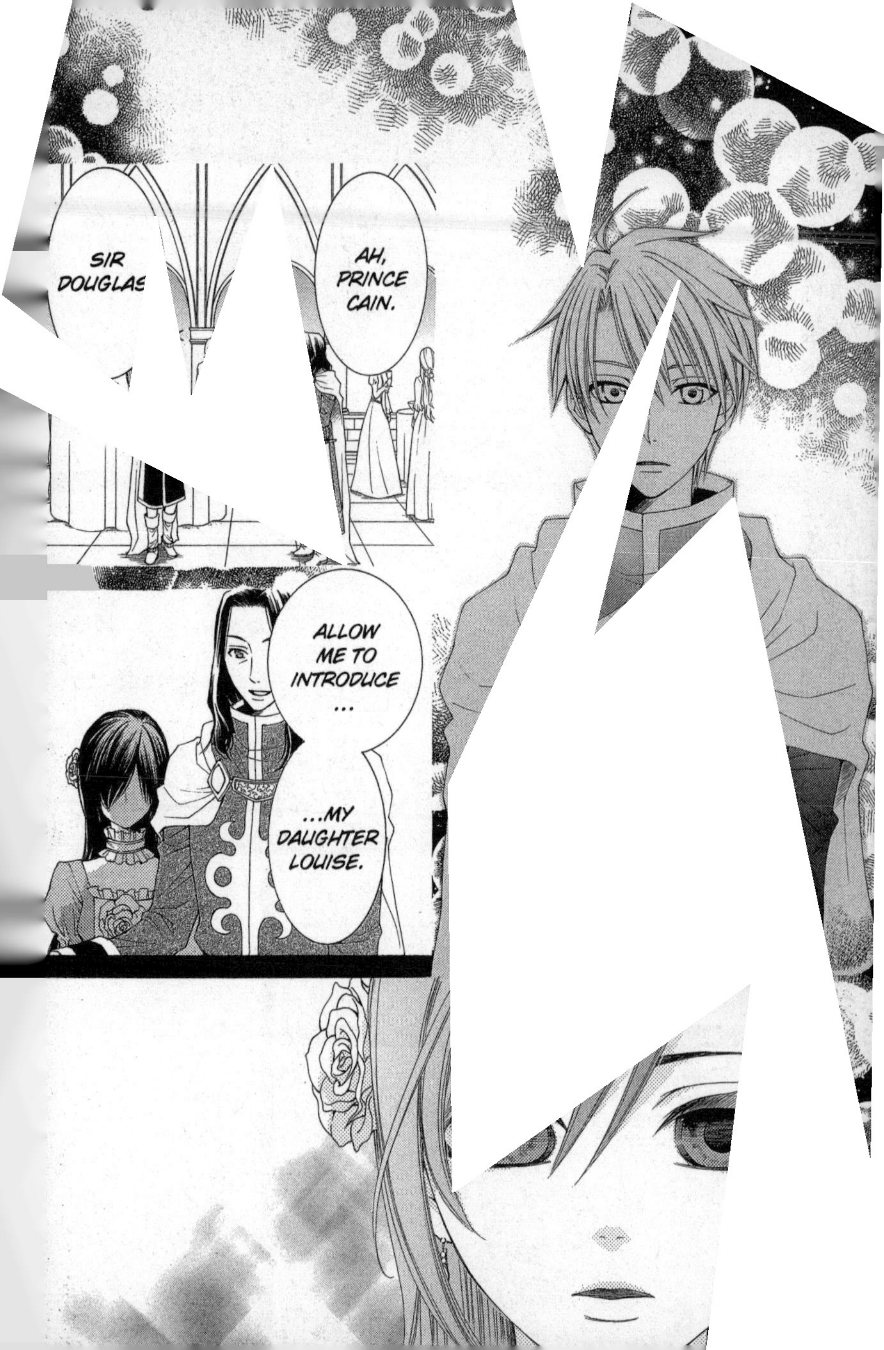
AH, PRINCE CAIN.
SIR DOUGLAS
ALLOW ME TO INTRODUCE ...
...MY DAUGHTER LOUISE.

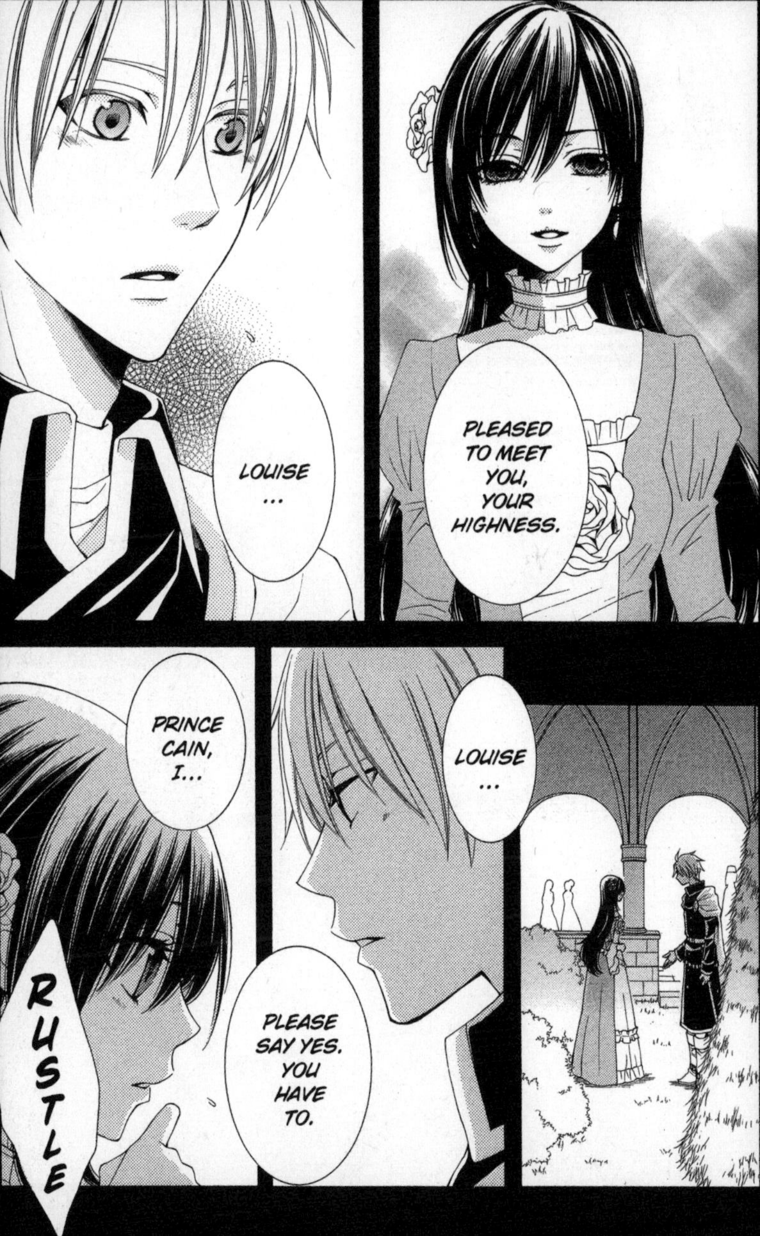
PLEASED TO MEET YOU, YOUR HIGHNESS.
LOUISE ...
LOUISE ...
PLEASE SAY YES. YOU HAVE TO.
PRINCE CAIN, I...
RUSTLE

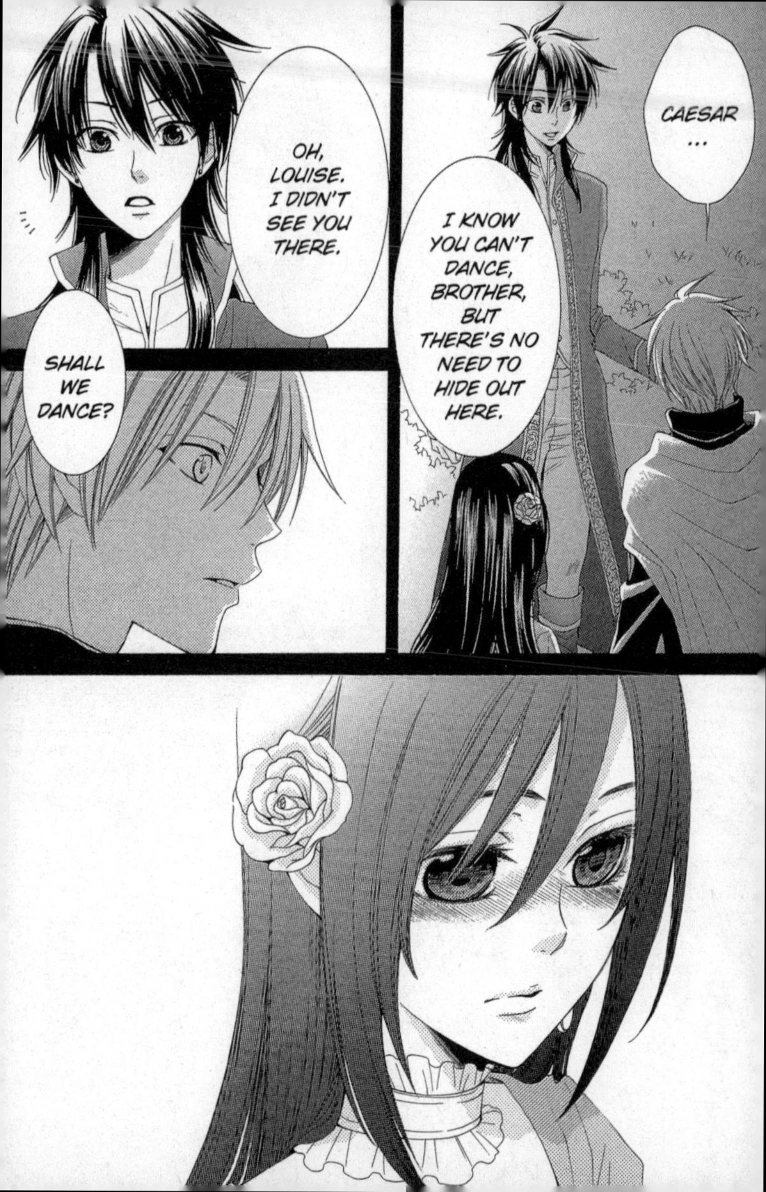
CAESAR ...
I KNOW YOU CAN'T DANCE, BROTHER, BUT THERE'S NO NEED TO HIDE OUT HERE.
OH, LOUISE. I DIDN'T SEE YOU THERE.
SHALL WE DANCE?

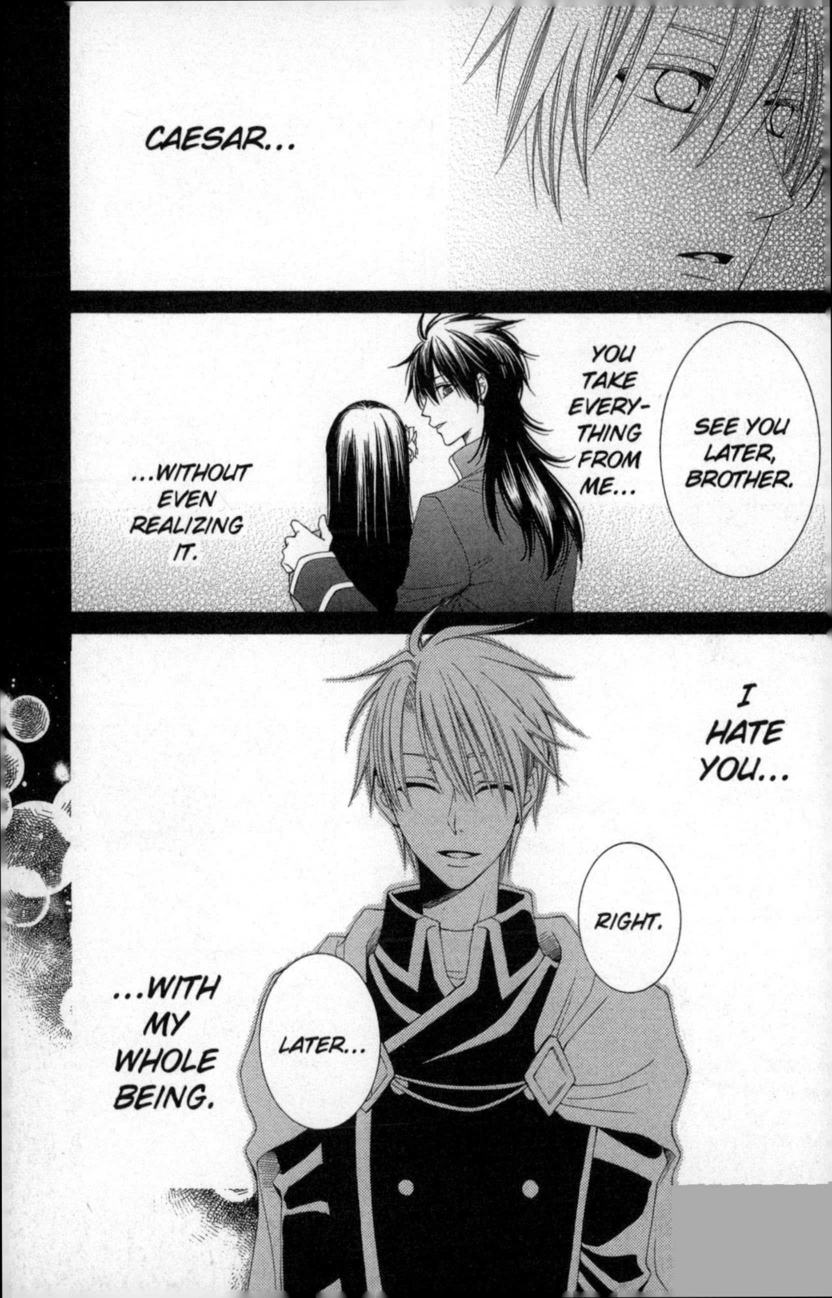
CAESAR...
SEE YOU LATER, BROTHER.
YOU TAKE EVERYTHING FROM ME...
...WITHOUT EVEN REALIZING IT.
I HATE YOU...
RIGHT.
LATER...
...WITH MY WHOLE BEING.

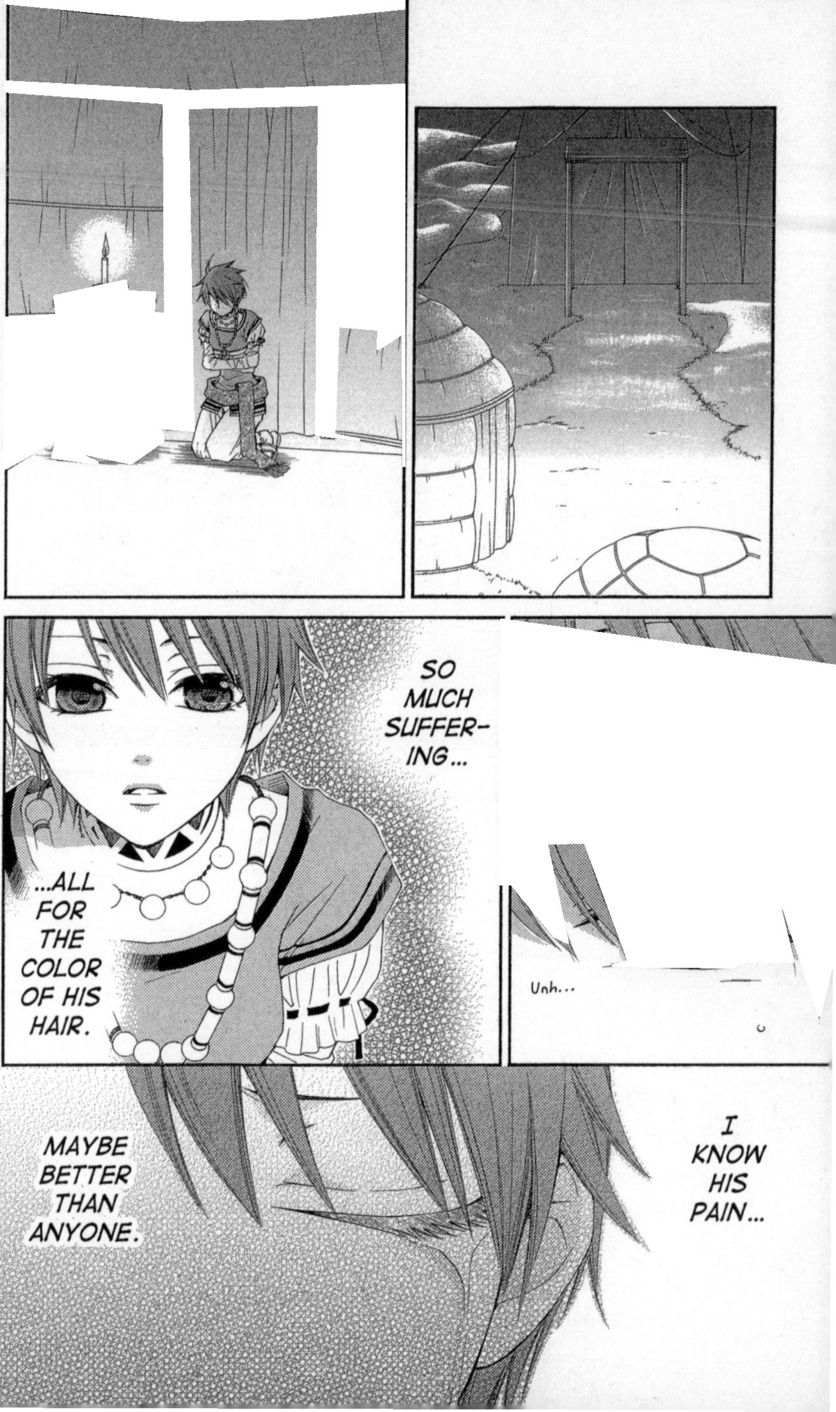
Unh...
SO MUCH SUFFER-ING...
...ALL FOR THE COLOR OF HIS HAIR.
I KNOW HIS PAIN...
MAYBE BETTER THAN ANYONE.

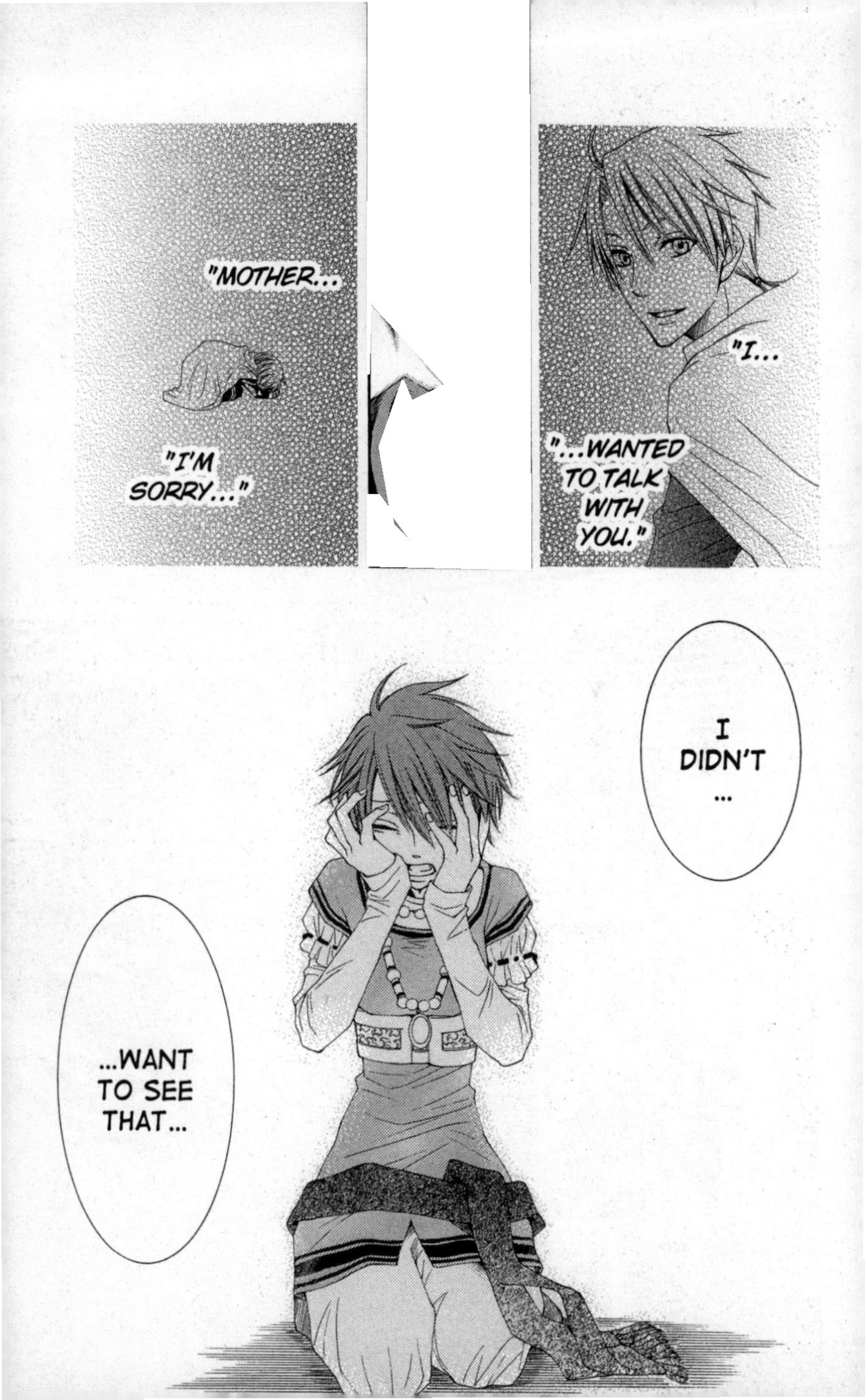
"I...
"...WANTED TO TALK WITH YOU."
"MOTHER...
"I'M SORRY..."
I DIDN'T ...
...WANT TO SEE THAT...

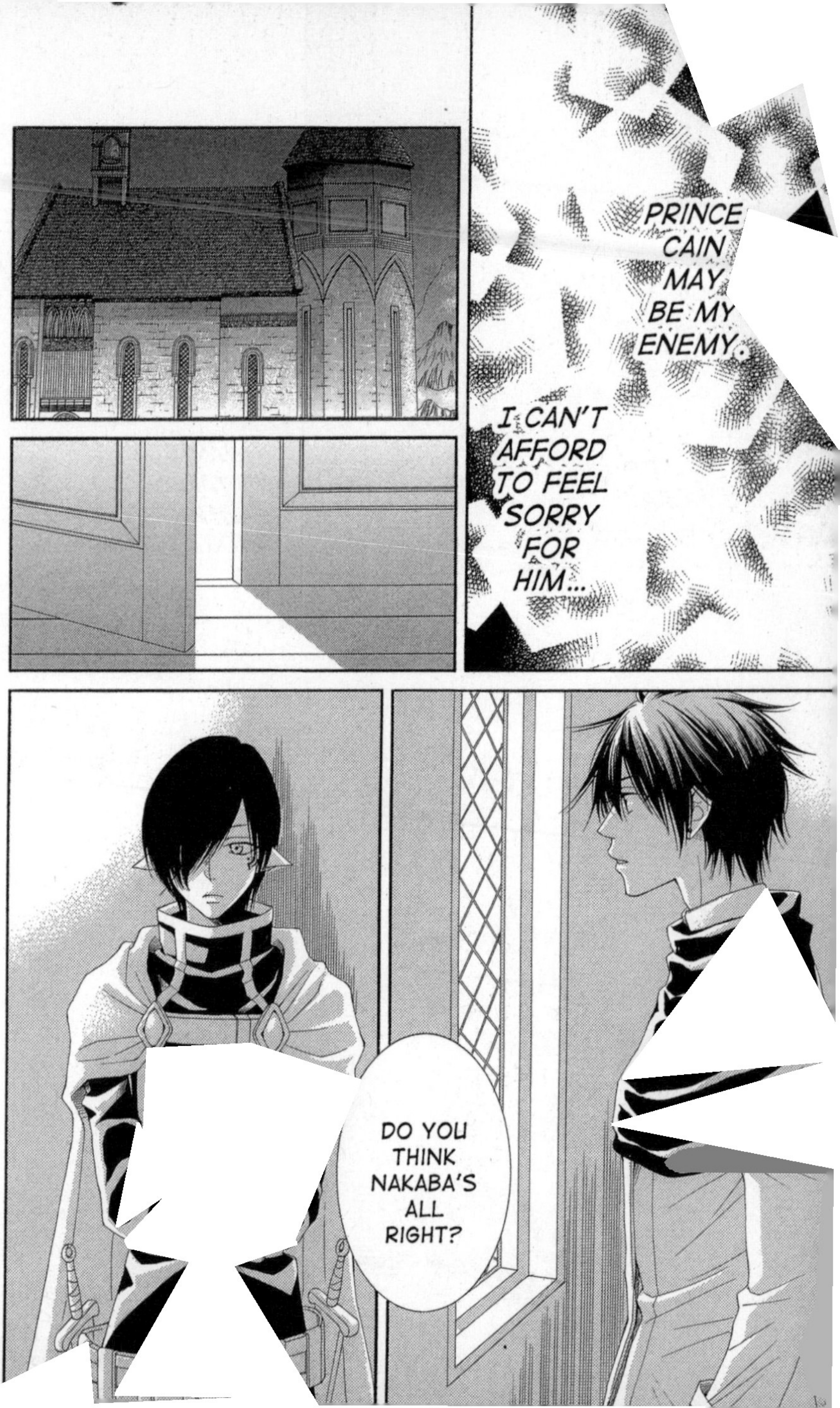
PRINCE CAIN MAY BE MY ENEMY.
I CAN'T AFFORD TO FEEL SORRY FOR HIM...
DO YOU THINK NAKABA'S ALL RIGHT?

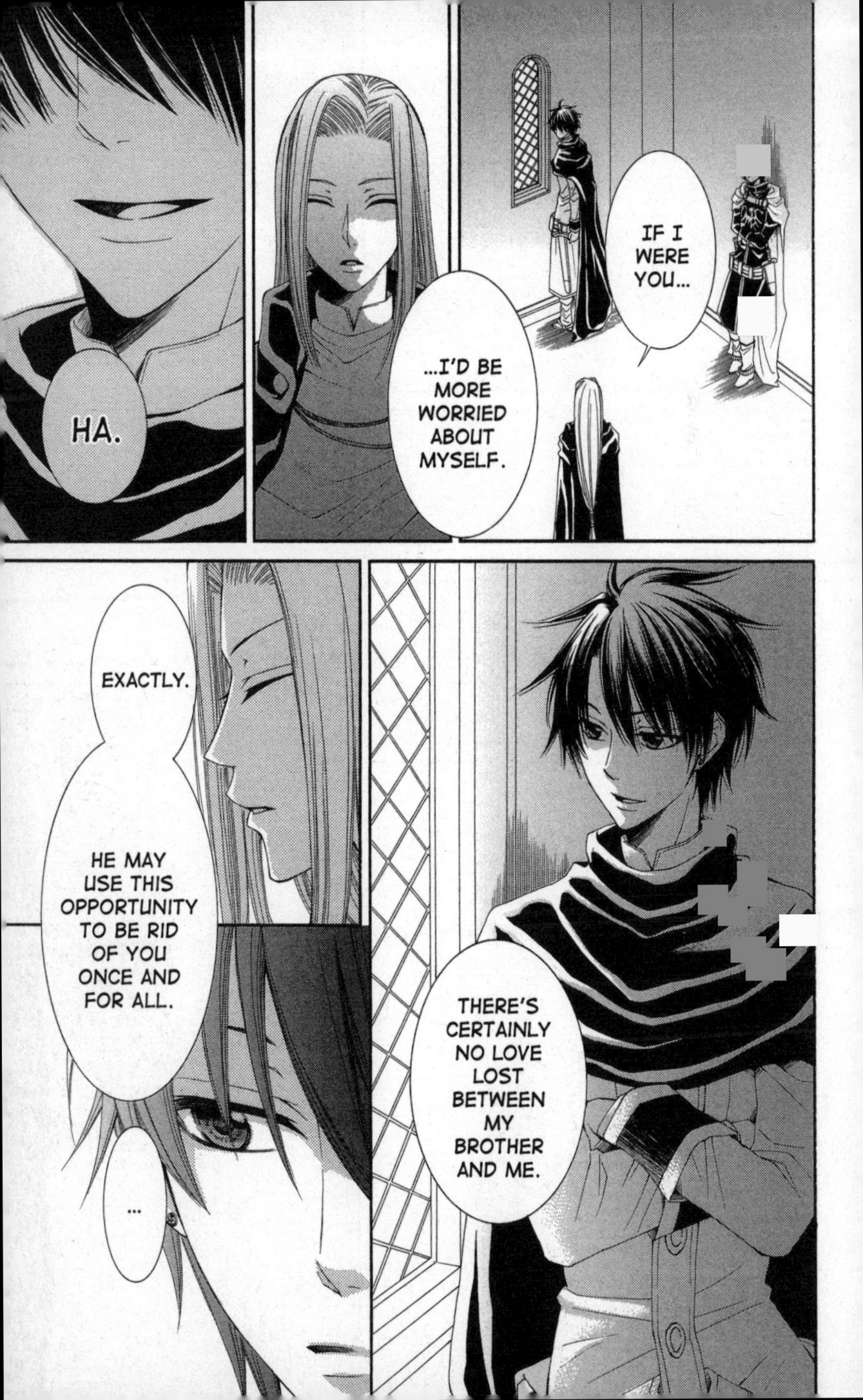
IF I WERE YOU...
...I'D BE MORE WORRIED ABOUT MYSELF.
HA.
THERE'S CERTAINLY NO LOVE LOST BETWEEN MY BROTHER AND ME.
EXACTLY.
HE MAY USE THIS OPPORTUNITY TO BE RID OF YOU ONCE AND FOR ALL.
...

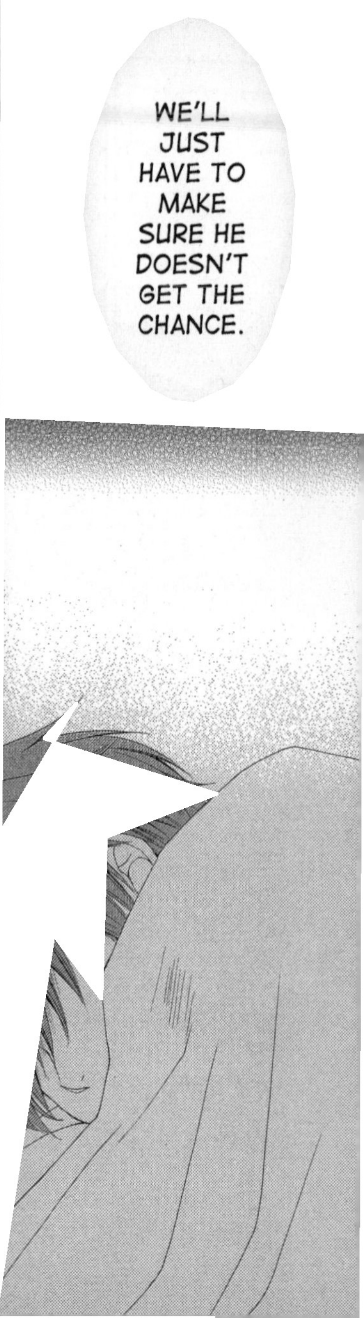
WE'LL JUST HAVE TO MAKE SURE HE DOESN'T GET THE CHANCE.
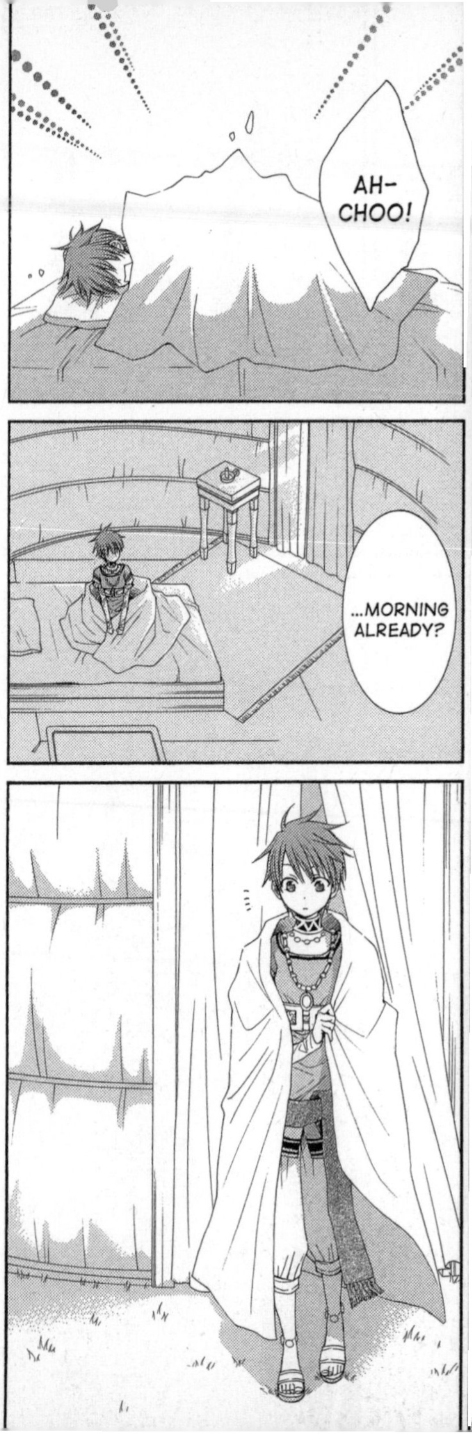
AH-CHOO!
...MORNING ALREADY?

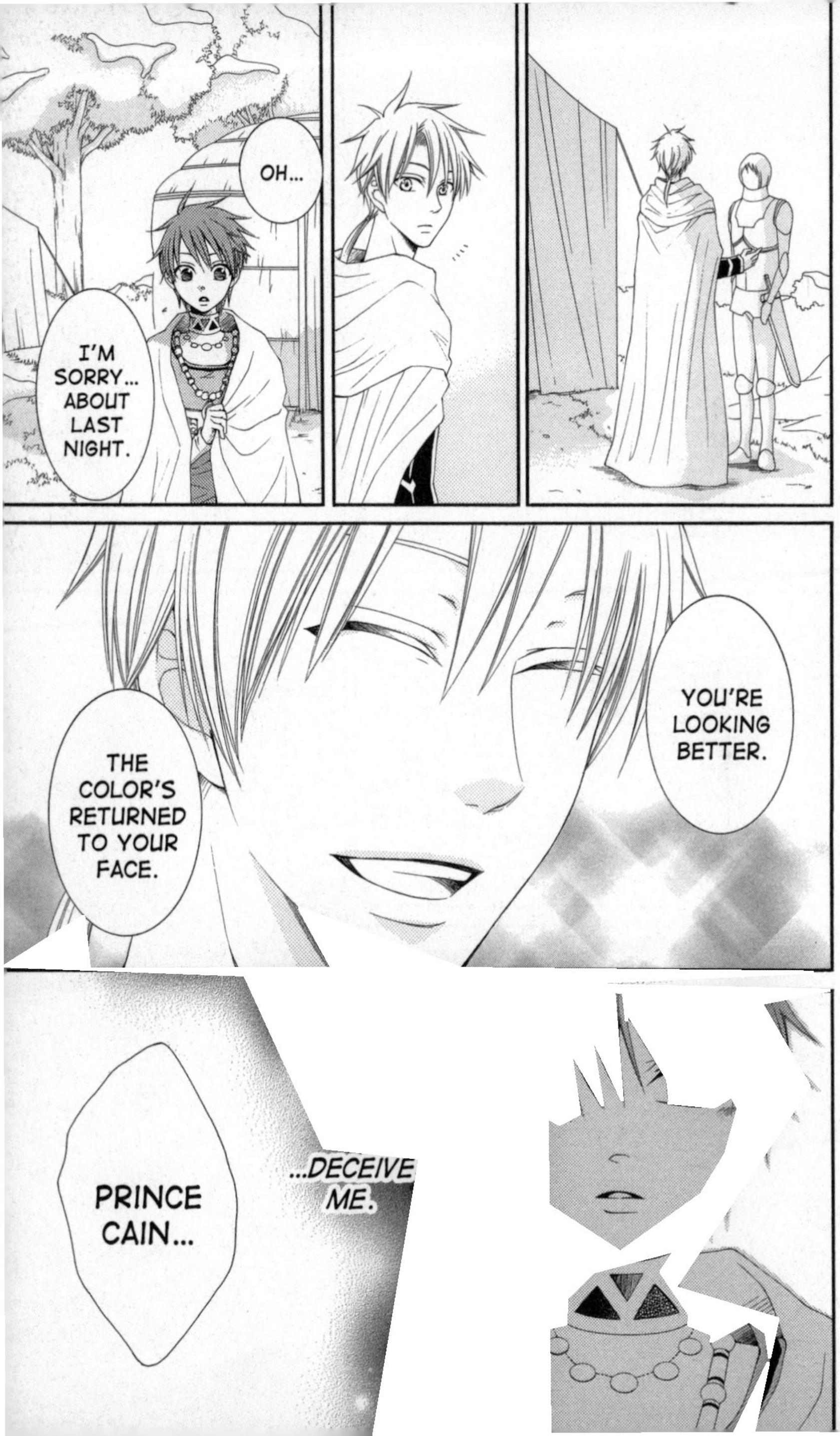
OH...
I'M SORRY... ABOUT LAST NIGHT.
YOU'RE LOOKING BETTER.
THE COLOR'S RETURNED TO YOUR FACE.
PRINCE CAIN...
...DECEIVE ME.

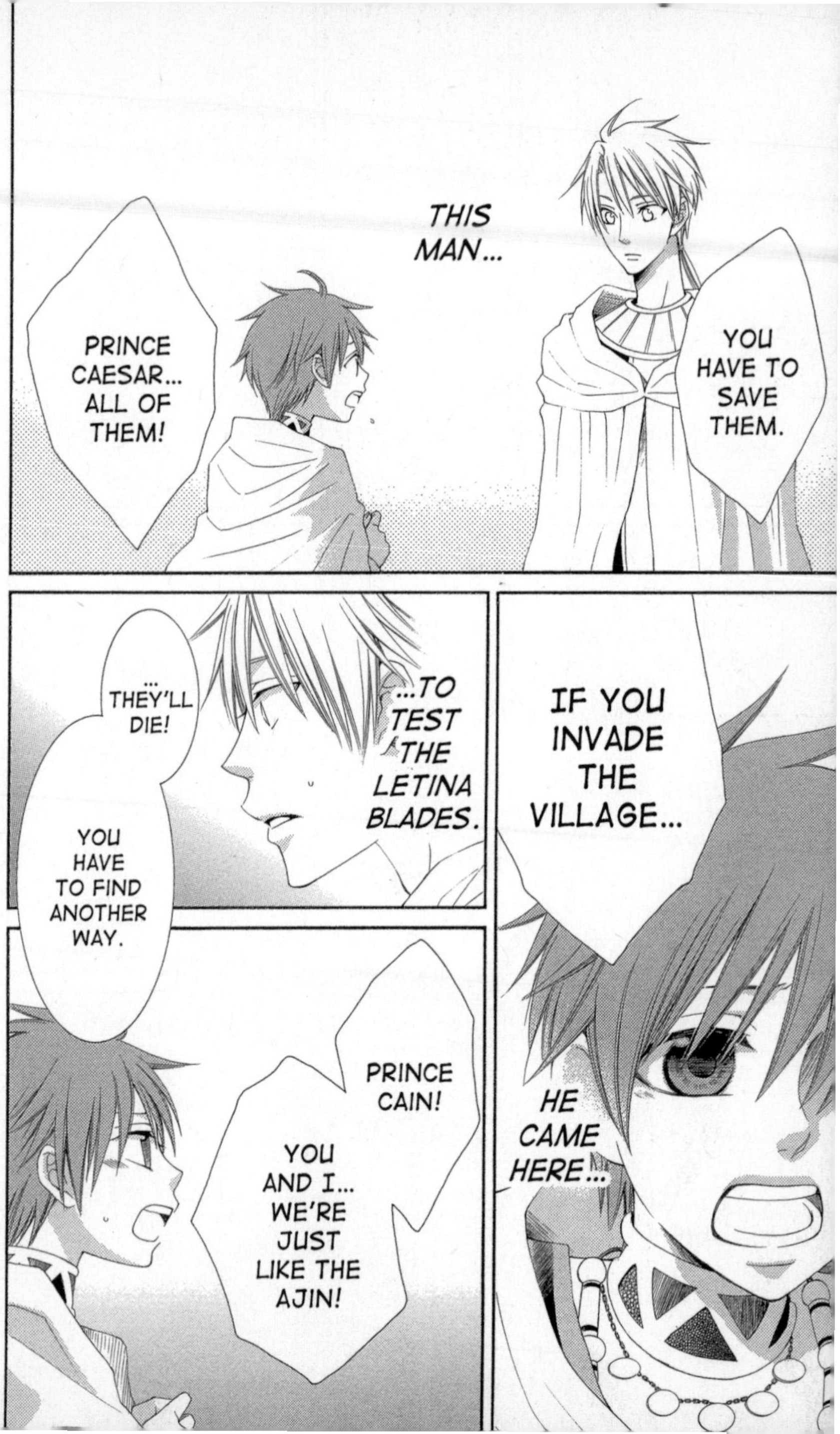
YOU HAVE TO SAVE THEM.
THIS MAN...
PRINCE CAESAR... ALL OF THEM!
IF YOU INVADE THE VILLAGE...
HE CAME HERE...
...TO TEST THE LETINA BLADES.
...THEY'LL DIE!
YOU HAVE TO FIND ANOTHER WAY.
PRINCE CAIN!
YOU AND I... WE'RE JUST LIKE THE AJIN!

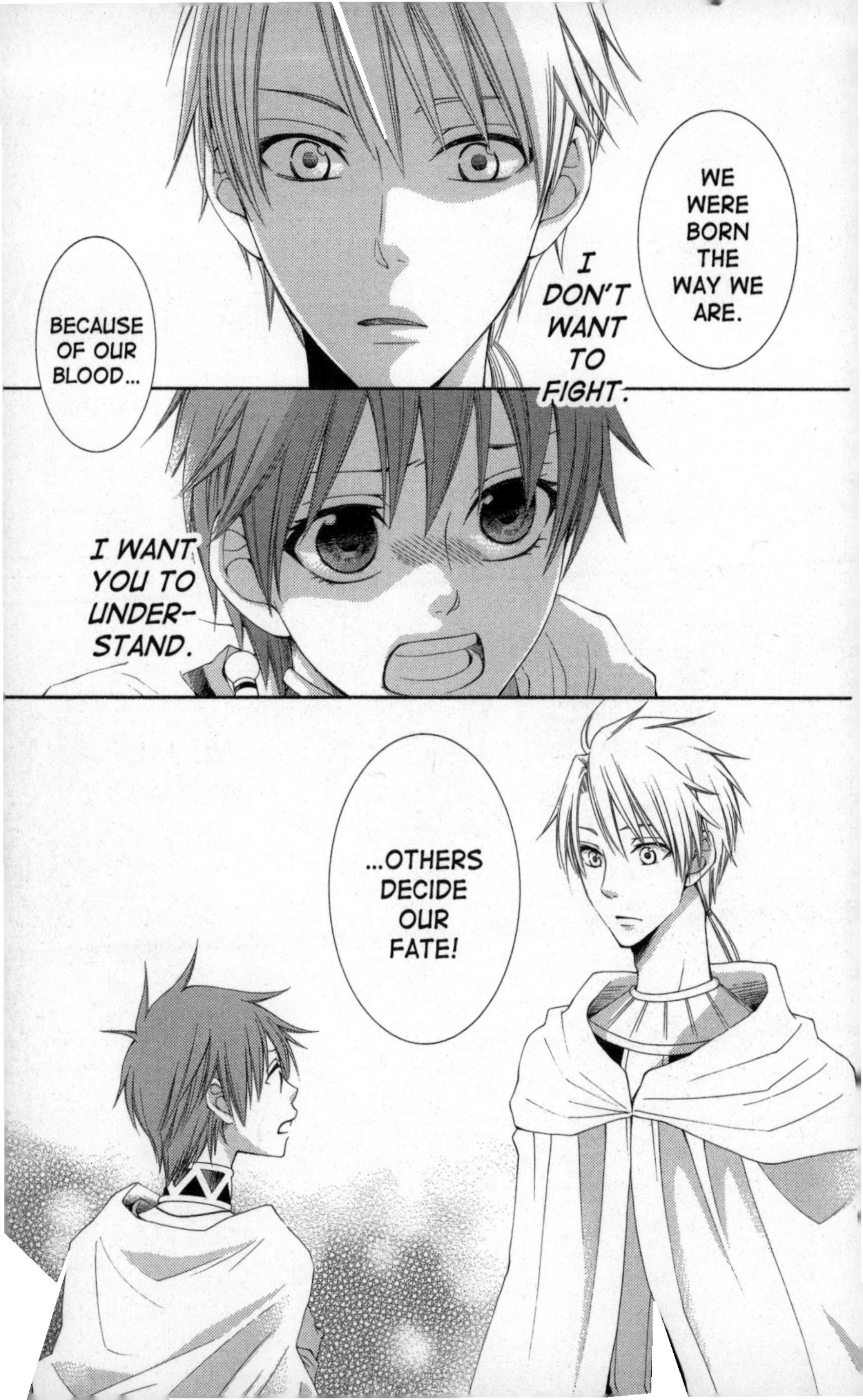
WE WERE BORN THE WAY WE ARE.
I DON'T WANT TO FIGHT.
BECAUSE OF OUR BLOOD...
I WANT YOU TO UNDER-STAND.
...OTHERS DECIDE OUR FATE!

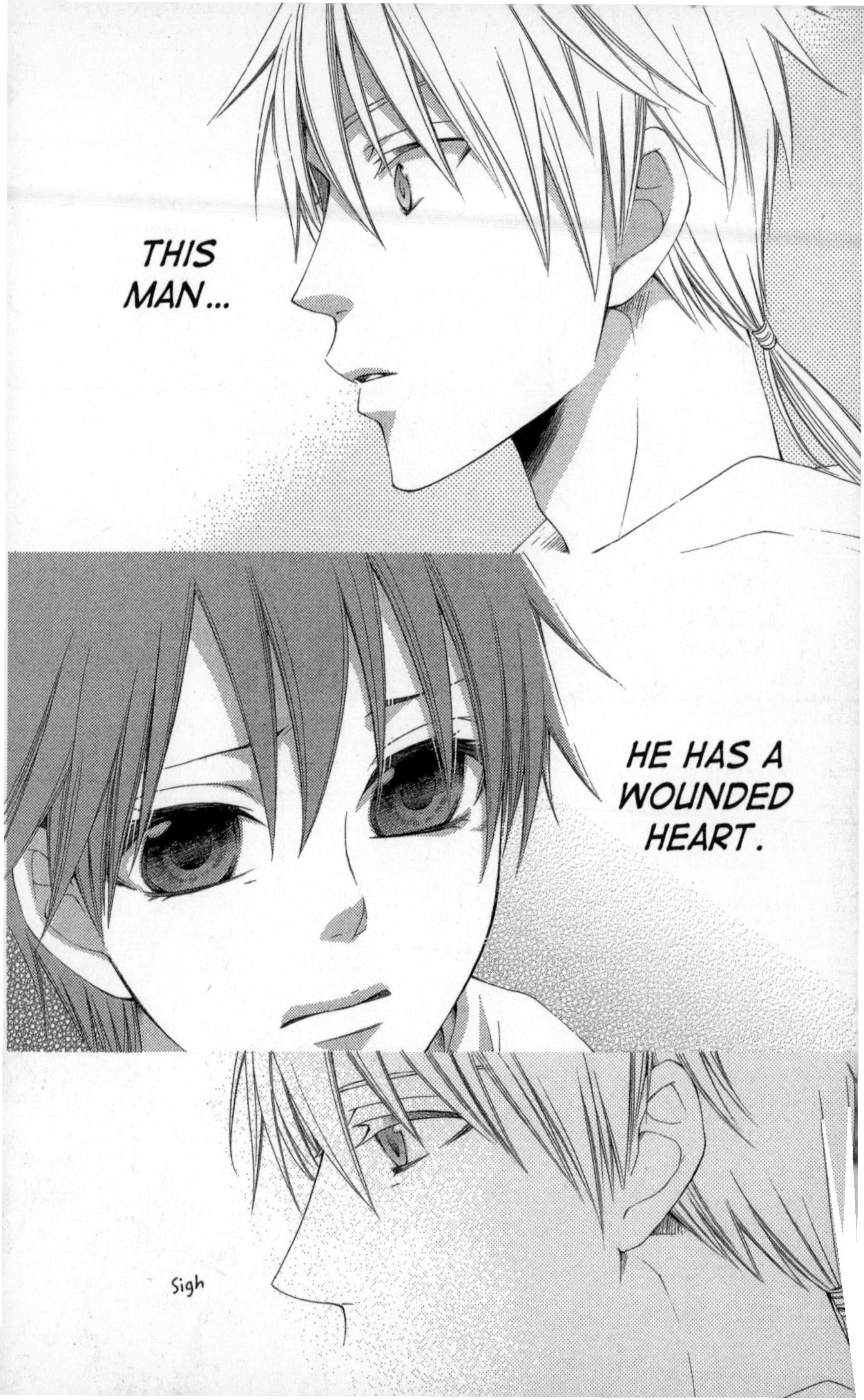
THIS MAN...
HE HAS A WOUNDED HEART.
Sigh

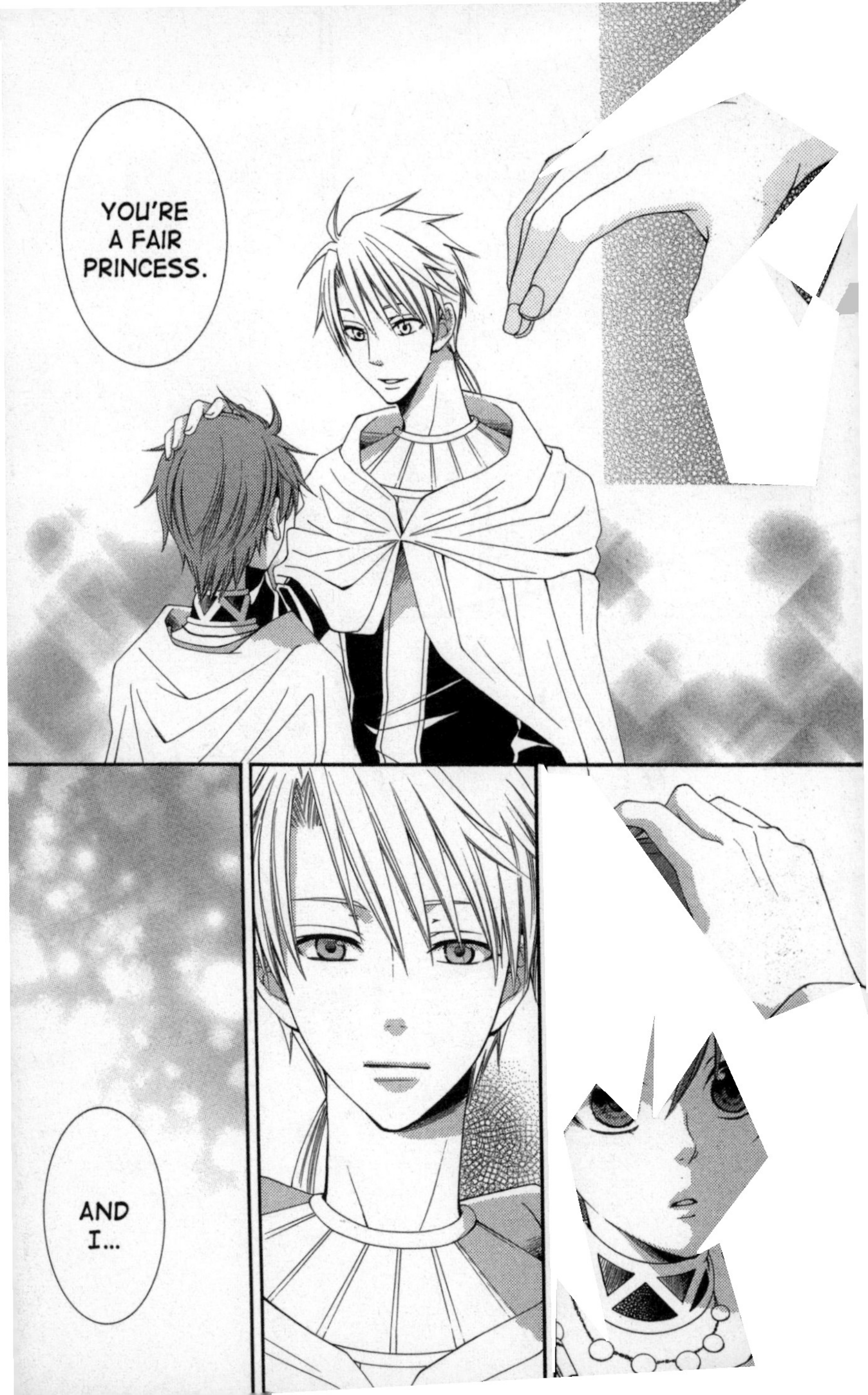
YOU'RE A FAIR PRINCESS.
AND I...

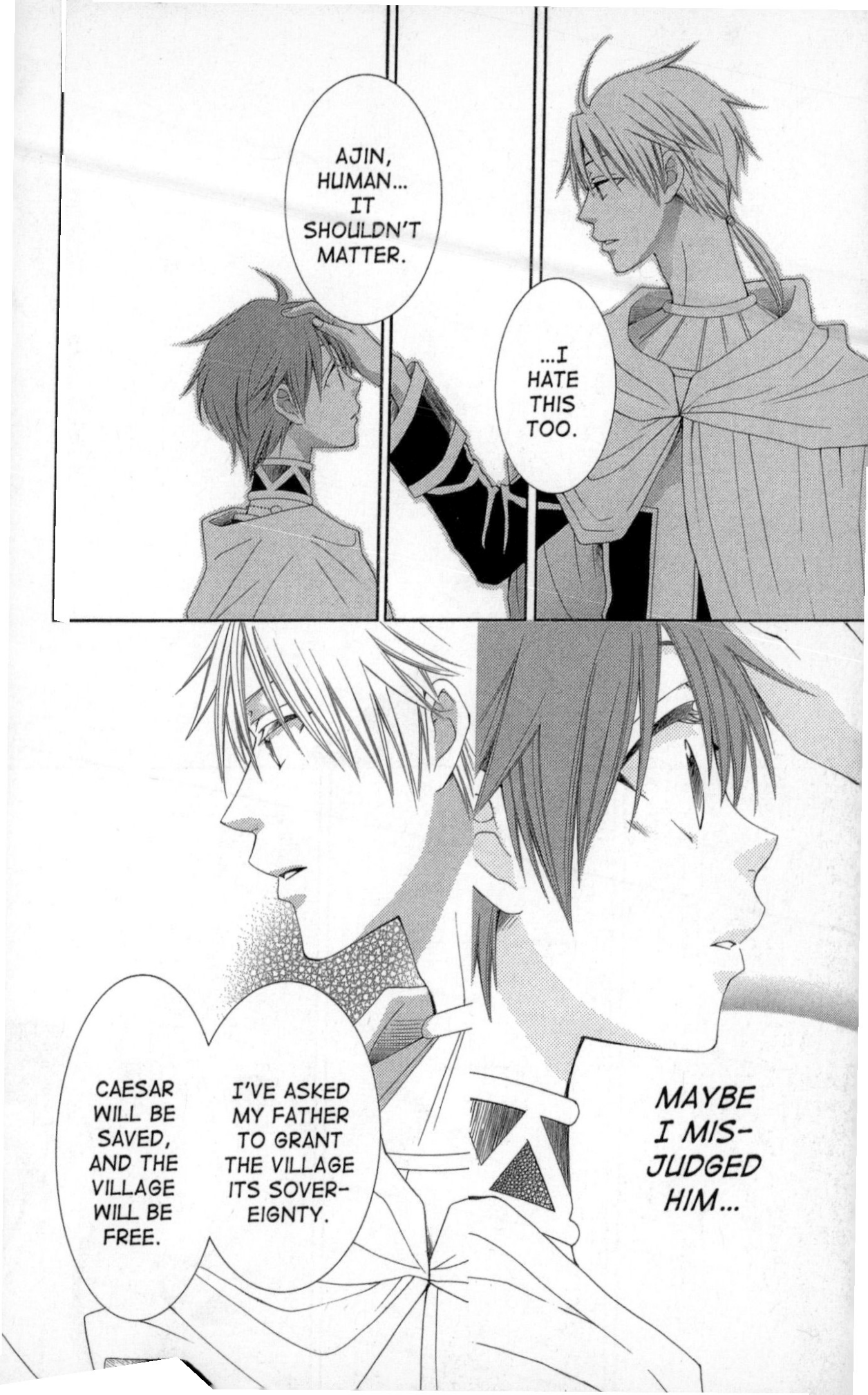
AJIN, HUMAN... IT SHOULDN'T MATTER.
...I HATE THIS TOO.
MAYBE I MIS-JUDGED HIM...
I'VE ASKED MY FATHER TO GRANT THE VILLAGE ITS SOVER-EIGNTY.
CAESAR WILL BE SAVED, AND THE VILLAGE WILL BE FREE.

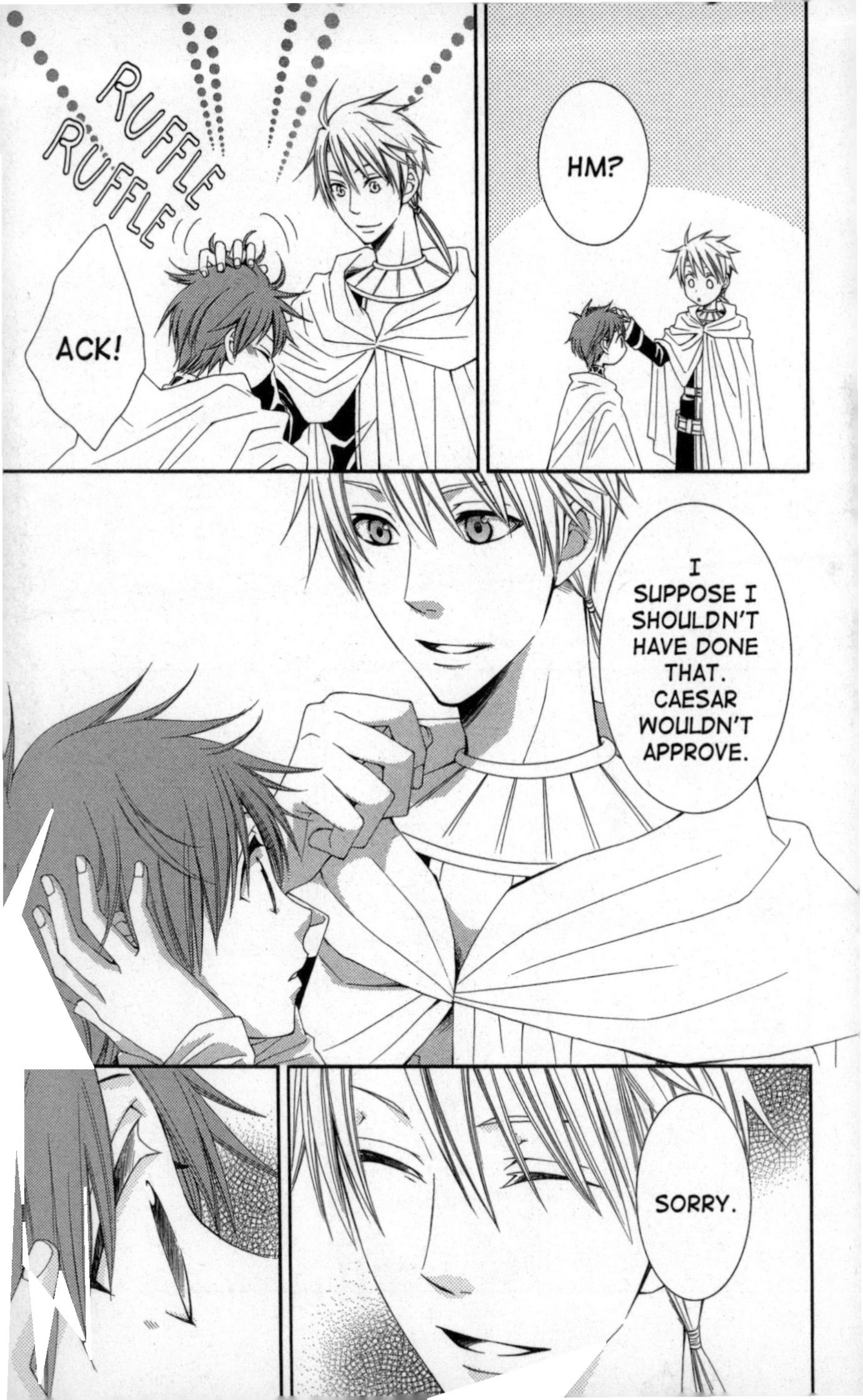
HM?
RUFFLE RUFFLE
ACK!
I SUPPOSE I SHOULDN'T HAVE DONE THAT. CAESAR WOULDN'T APPROVE.
SORRY.

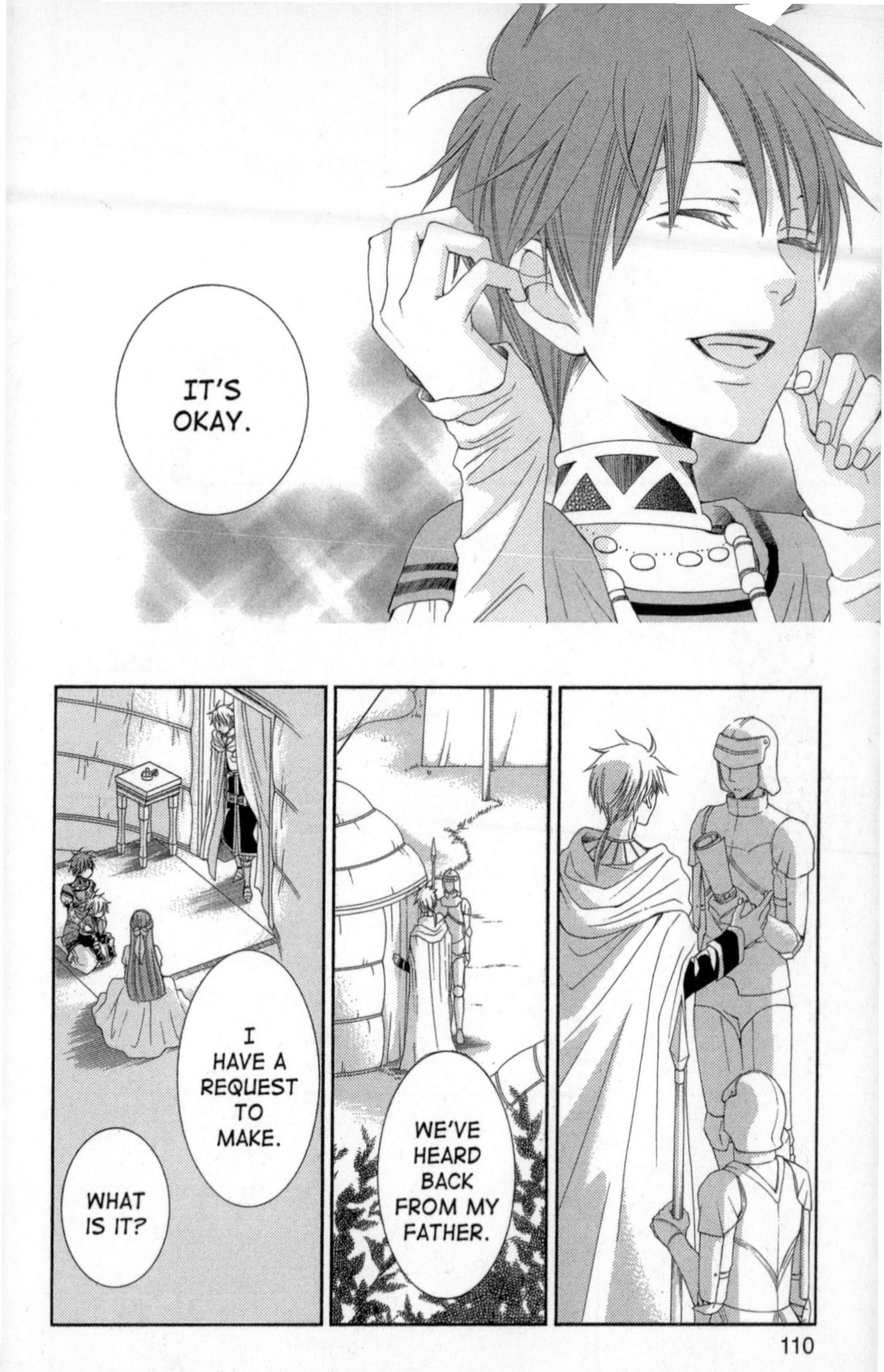
IT'S OKAY.
WE'VE HEARD BACK FROM MY FATHER.
I HAVE A REQUEST TO MAKE.
WHAT IS IT?

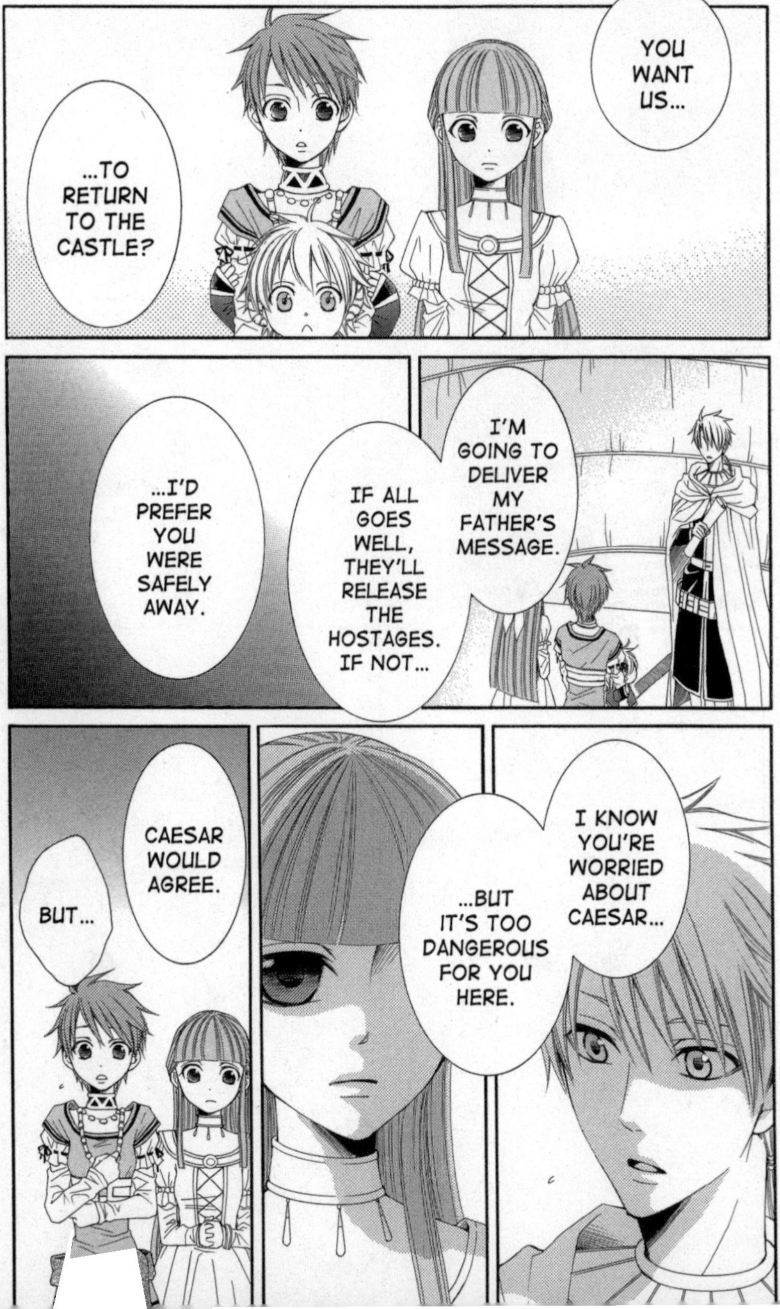
YOU WANT US...
...TO RETURN TO THE CASTLE?
I'M GOING TO DELIVER MY FATHER'S MESSAGE.
IF ALL GOES WELL, THEY'LL RELEASE THE HOSTAGES. IF NOT...
...I'D PREFER YOU WERE SAFELY AWAY.
I KNOW YOU'RE WORRIED ABOUT CAESAR...
...BUT IT'S TOO DANGEROUS FOR YOU HERE.
CAESAR WOULD AGREE.
BUT...

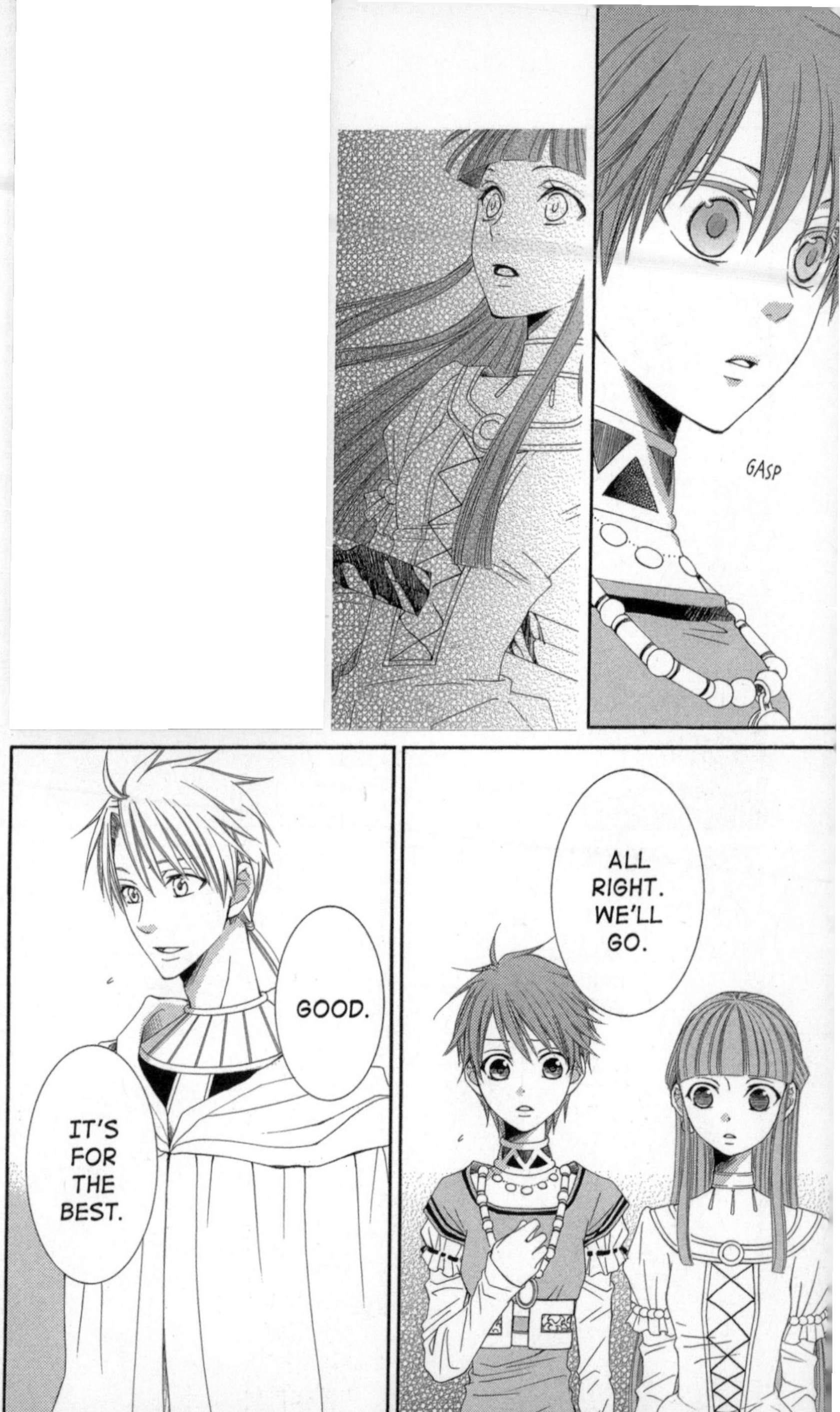
GASP
ALL RIGHT. WE'LL GO.
GOOD.
IT'S FOR THE BEST.

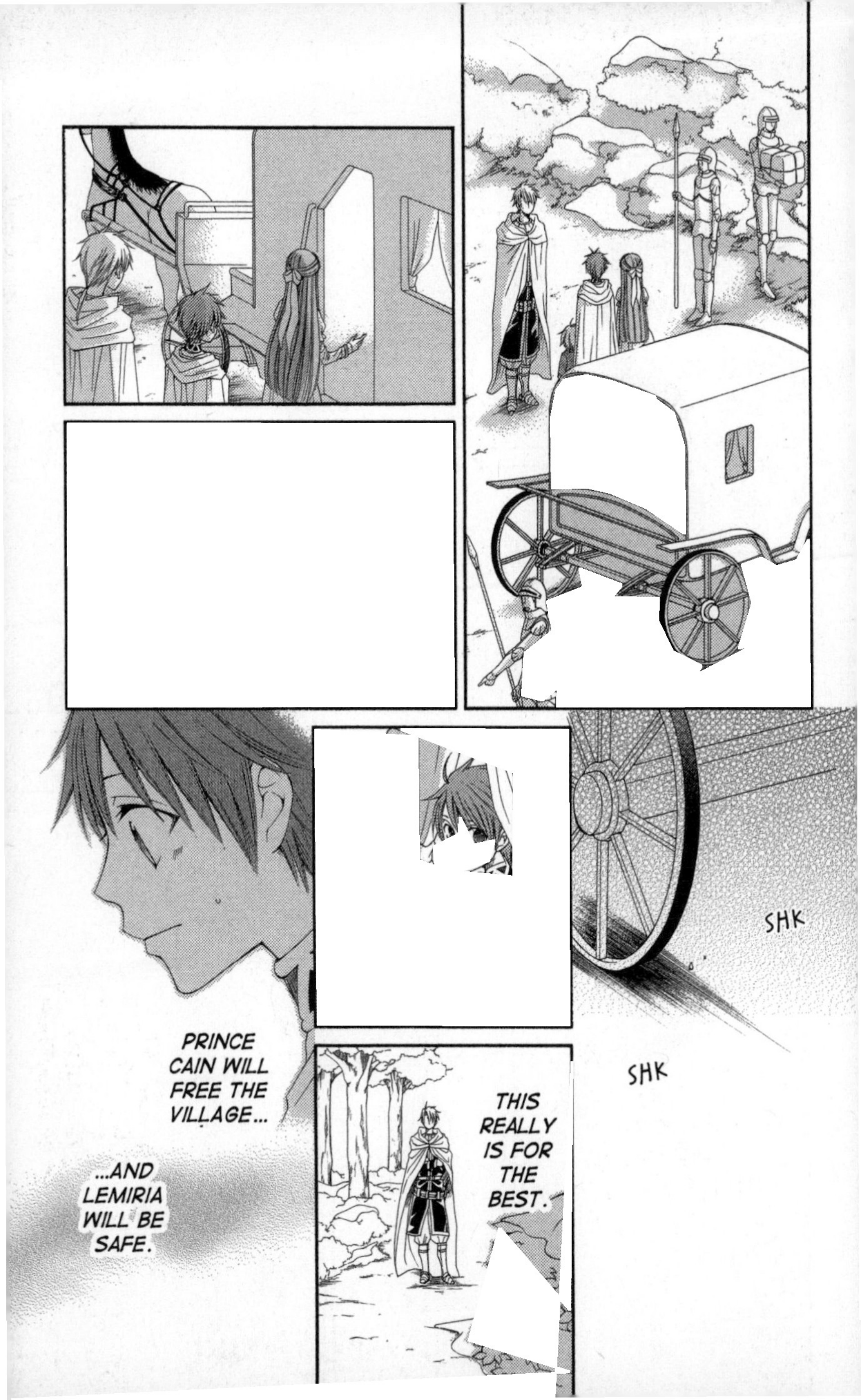
SHK
SHK
THIS REALLY IS FOR THE BEST.
PRINCE CAIN WILL FREE THE VILLAGE...
...AND LEMIRIA WILL BE SAFE.

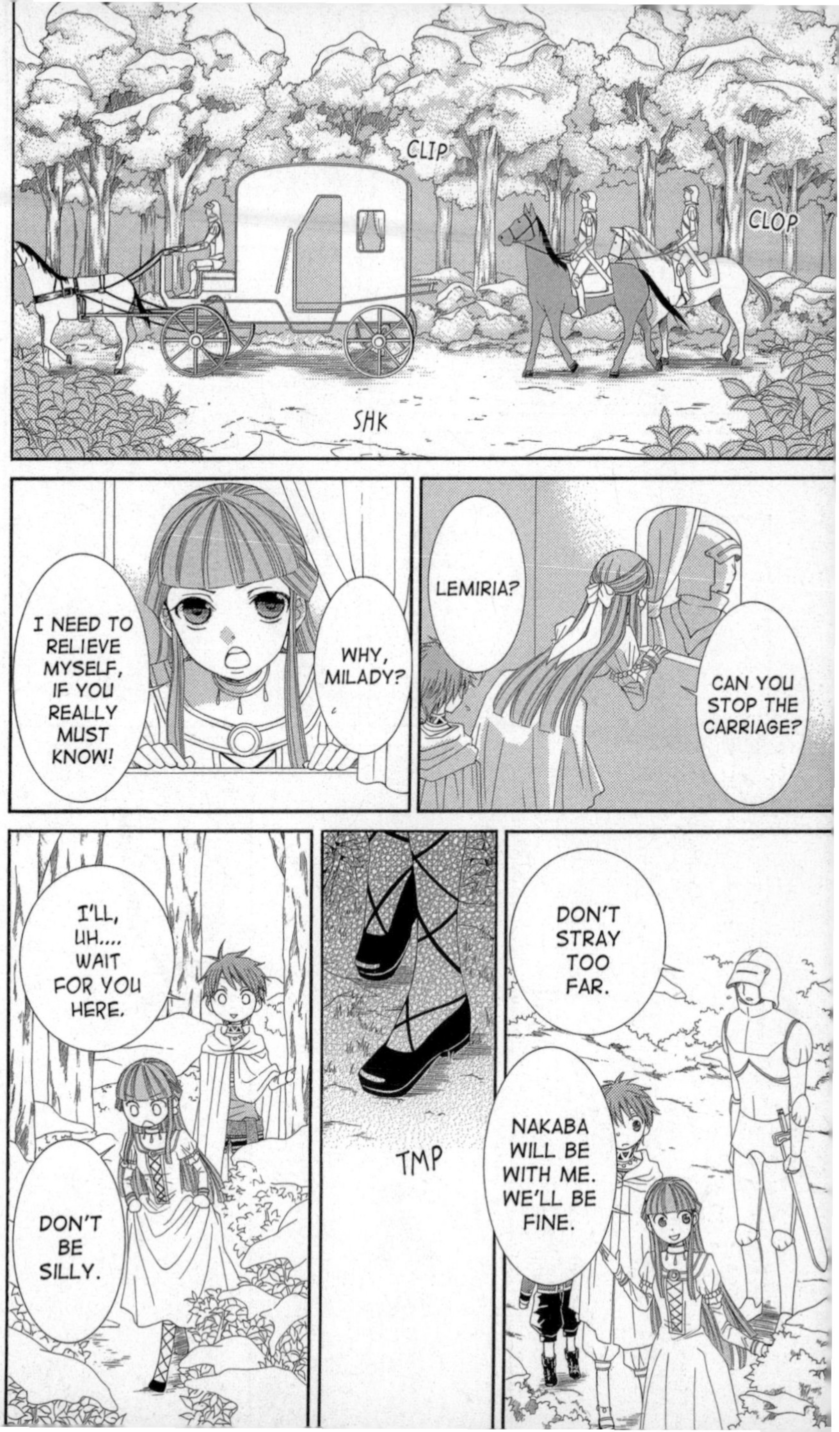
CLIP
CLOP
SHK
LEMIRIA?
CAN YOU STOP THE CARRIAGE?
WHY, MILADY?
I NEED TO RELIEVE MYSELF, IF YOU REALLY MUST KNOW!
DON'T STRAY TOO FAR.
NAKABA WILL BE WITH ME. WE'LL BE FINE.
TMP
I'LL, UH.... WAIT FOR YOU HERE.
DON'T BE SILLY.

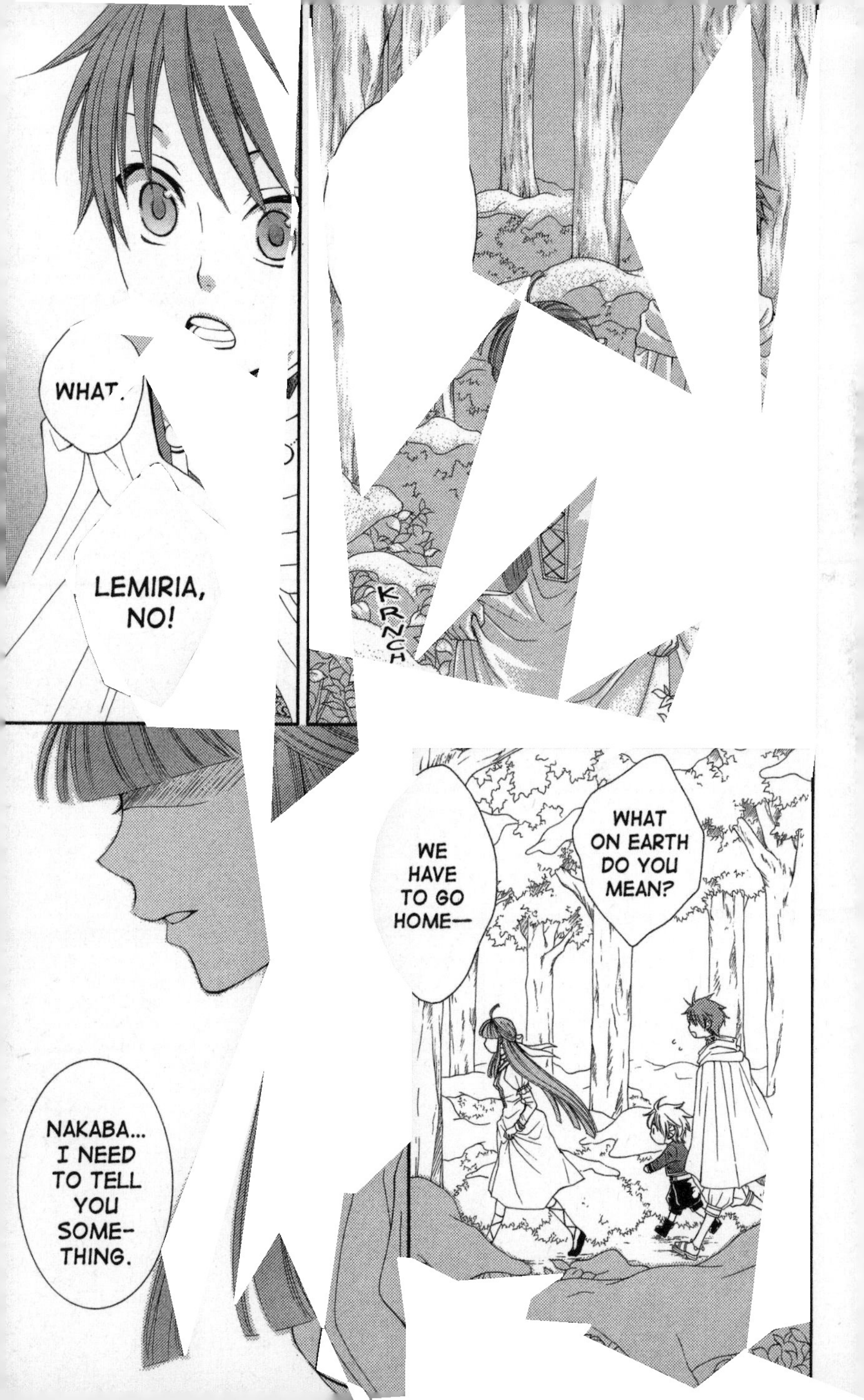
KRNCH
WHAT.
LEMIRIA, NO!
WHAT ON EARTH DO YOU MEAN?
WE HAVE TO GO HOME—
NAKABA... I NEED TO TELL YOU SOME-THING.

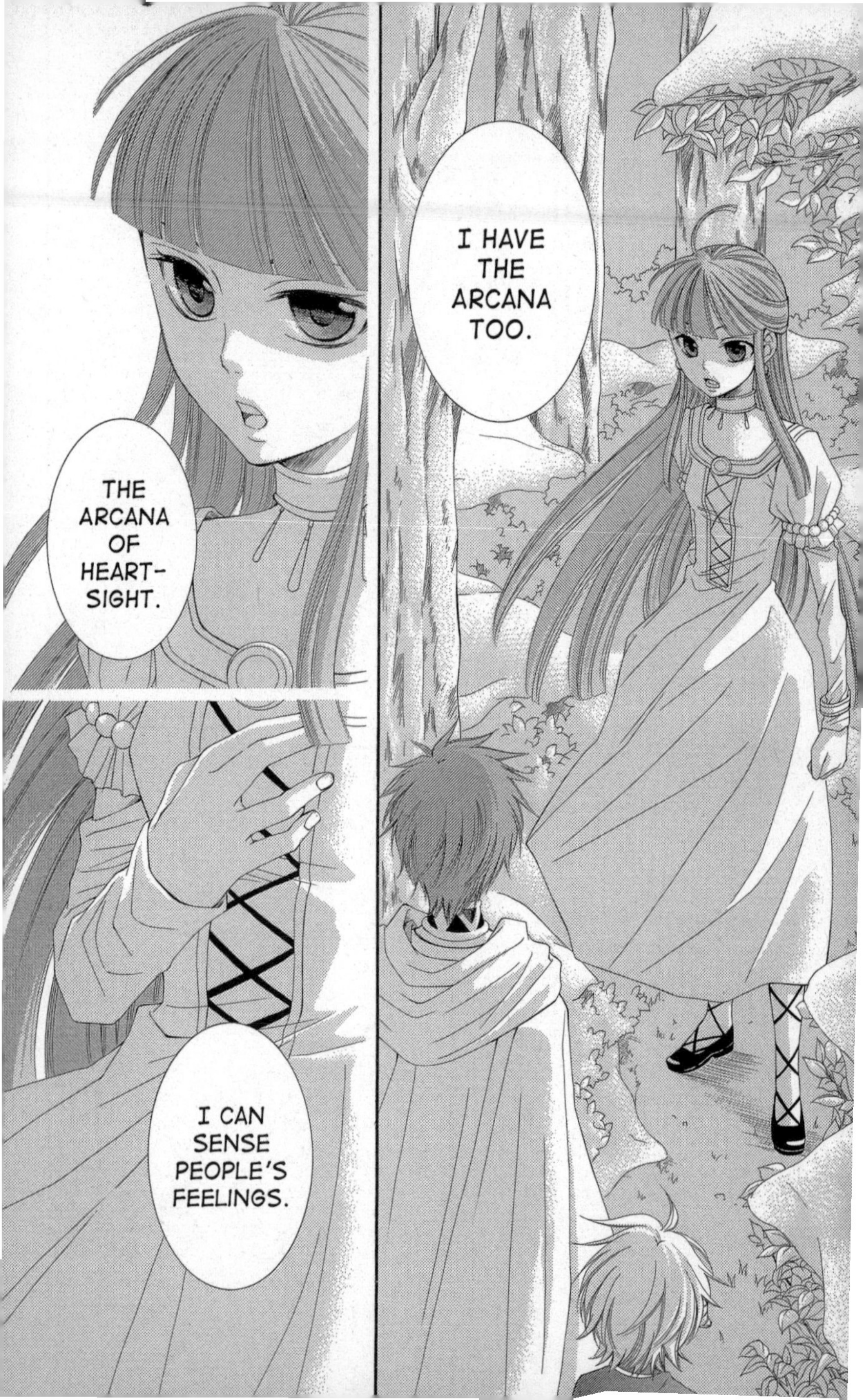
I HAVE THE ARCANA TOO.
THE ARCANA OF HEART-SIGHT.
I CAN SENSE PEOPLE'S FEELINGS.

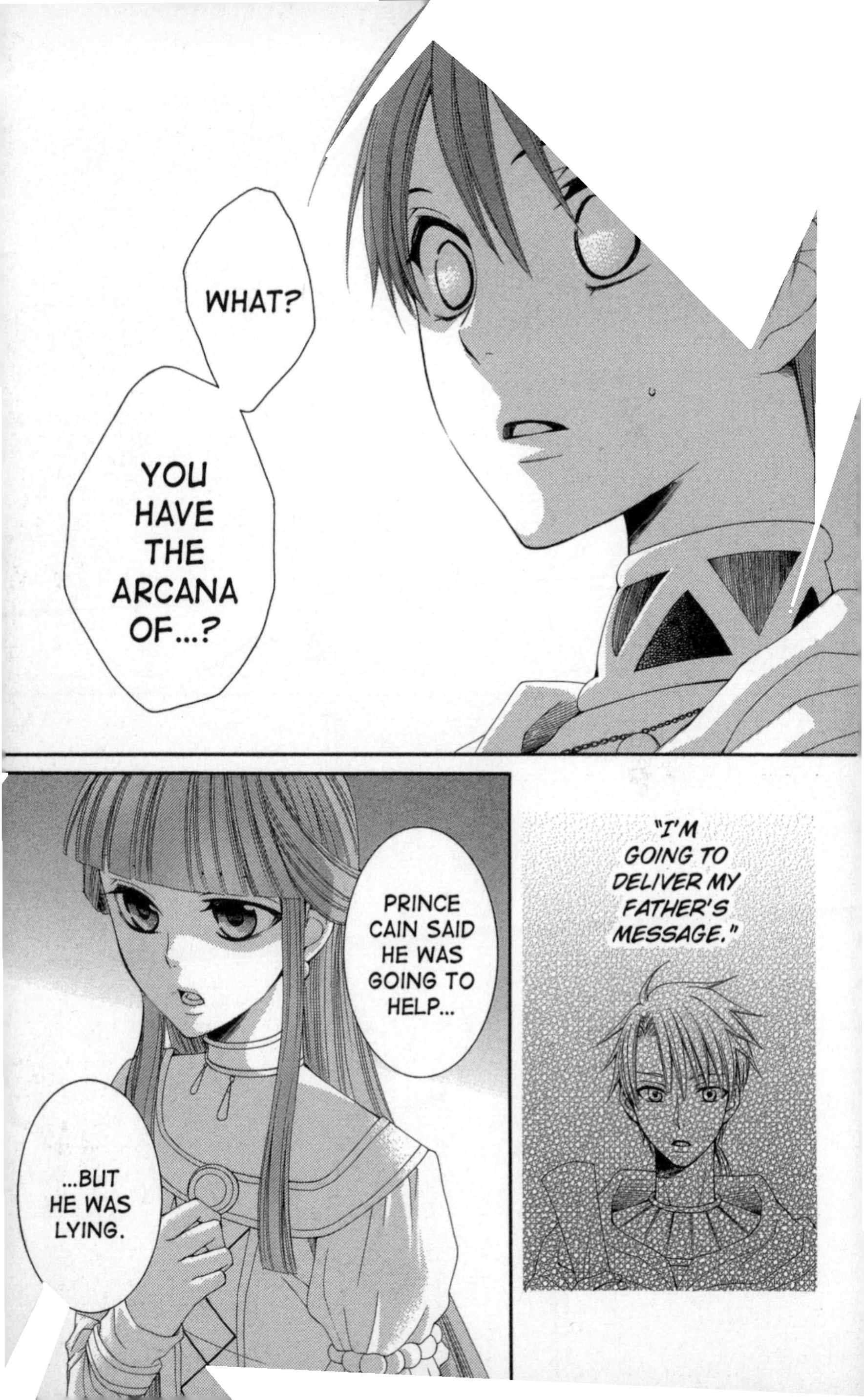
WHAT?
YOU HAVE THE ARCANA OF...?
"I'M GOING TO DELIVER MY FATHER'S MESSAGE."
PRINCE CAIN SAID HE WAS GOING TO HELP...
...BUT HE WAS LYING.

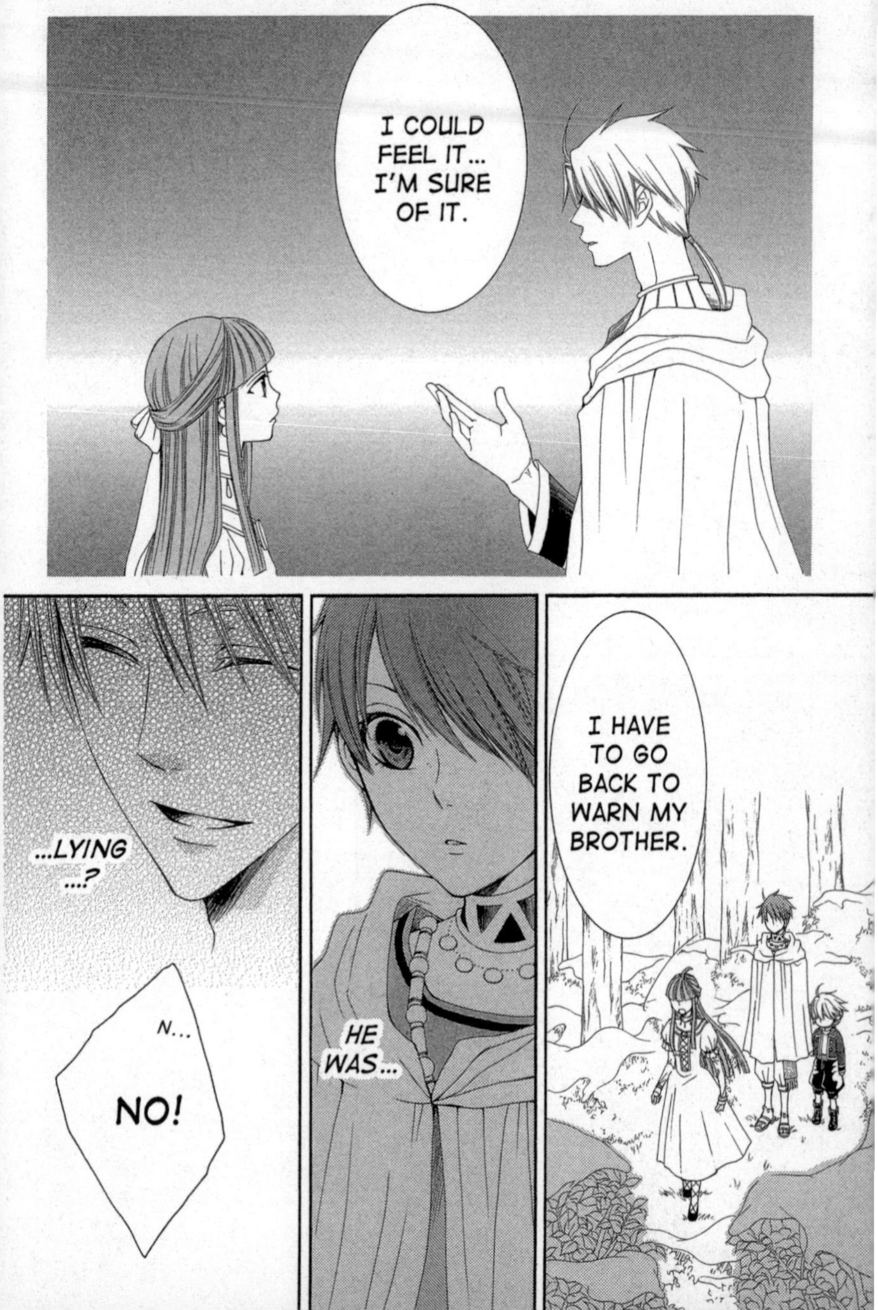
I COULD FEEL IT... I'M SURE OF IT.
I HAVE TO GO BACK TO WARN MY BROTHER.
HE WAS...
...LYING ...?
N...
NO!

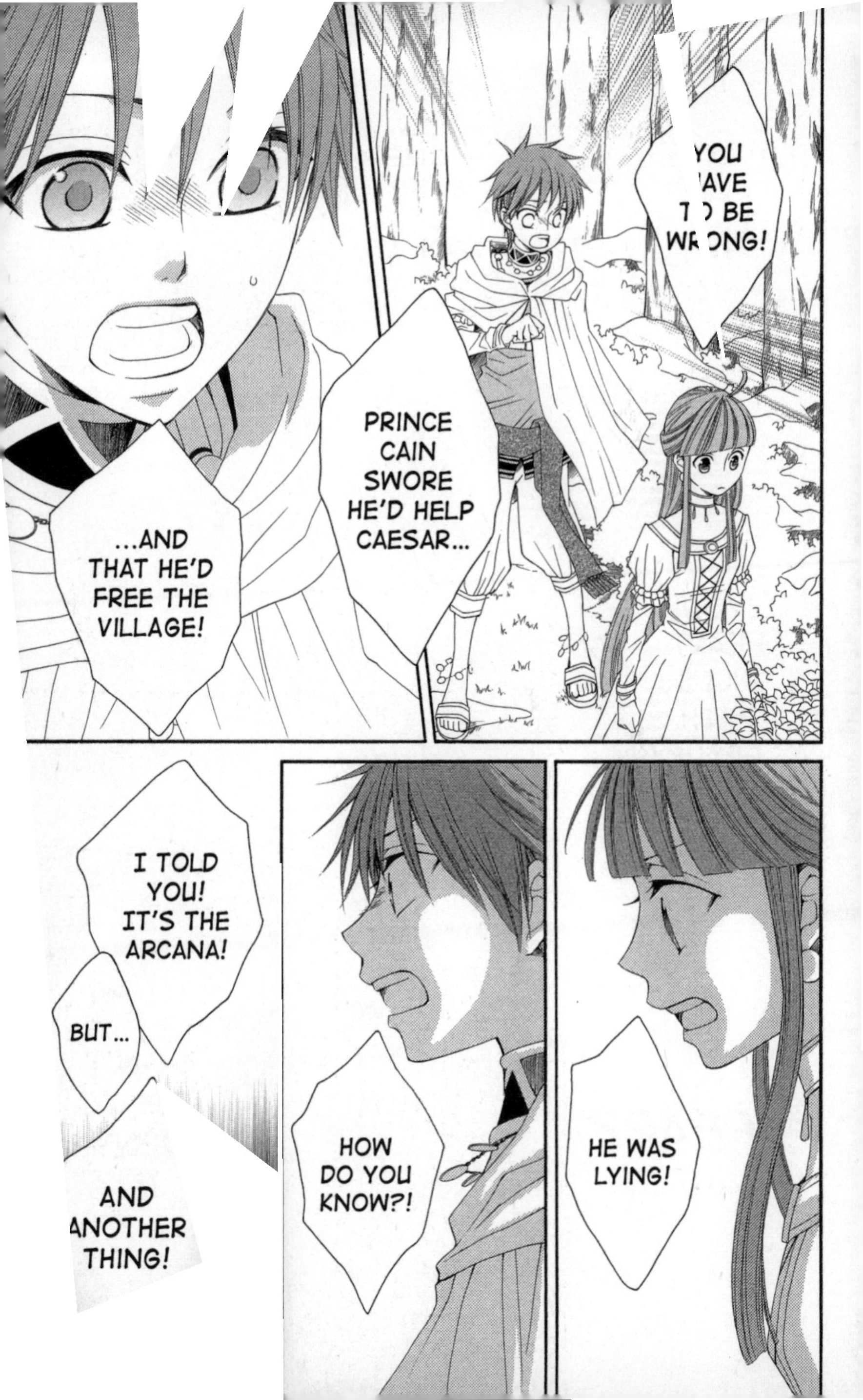
YOU HAVE TO BE WRONG!
PRINCE CAIN SWORE HE'D HELP CAESAR...
...AND THAT HE'D FREE THE VILLAGE!
HE WAS LYING!
HOW DO YOU KNOW?!
I TOLD YOU! IT'S THE ARCANA!
BUT...
AND ANOTHER THING!

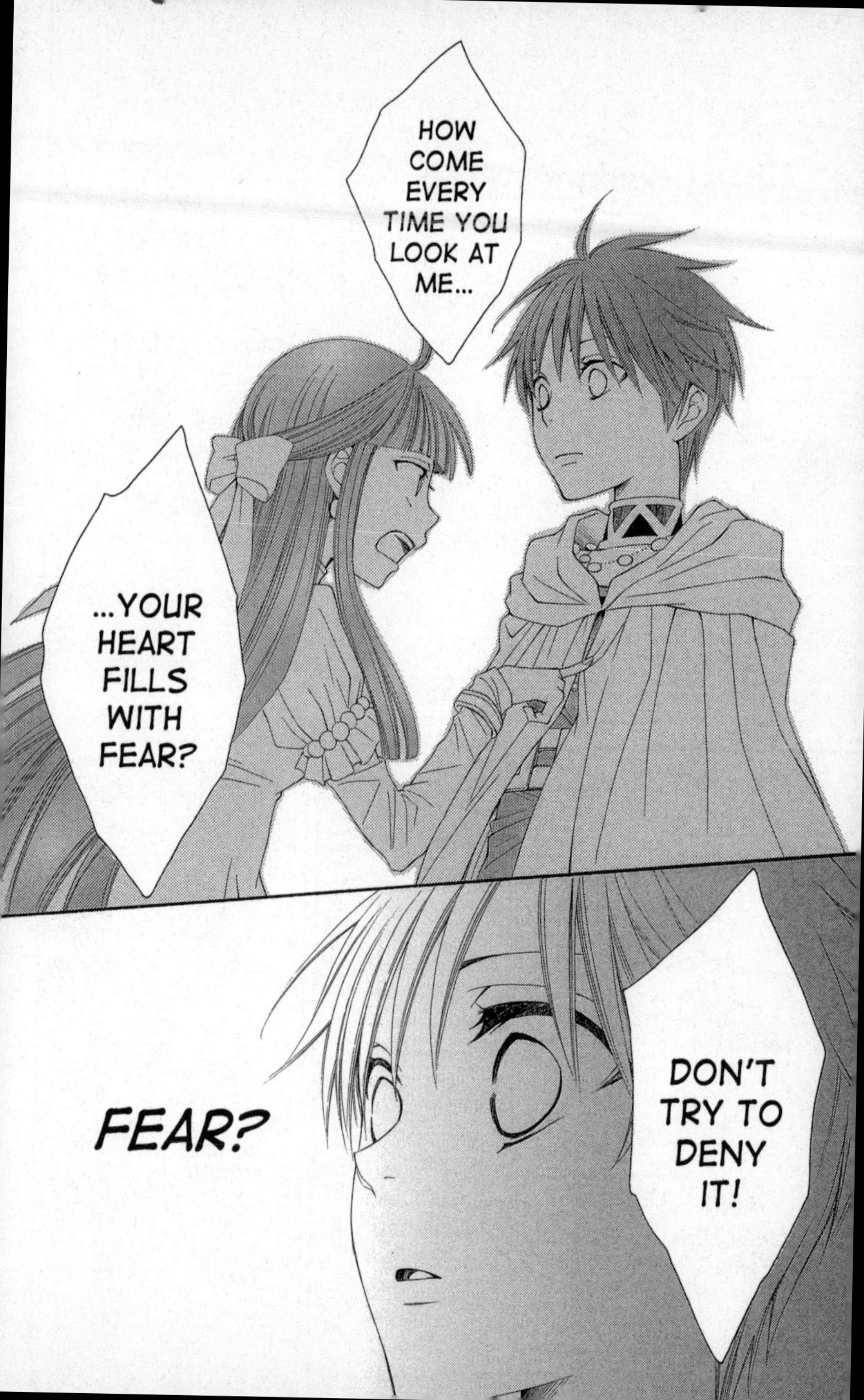
HOW COME EVERY TIME YOU LOOK AT ME...
...YOUR HEART FILLS WITH FEAR?
DON'T TRY TO DENY IT!
FEAR?

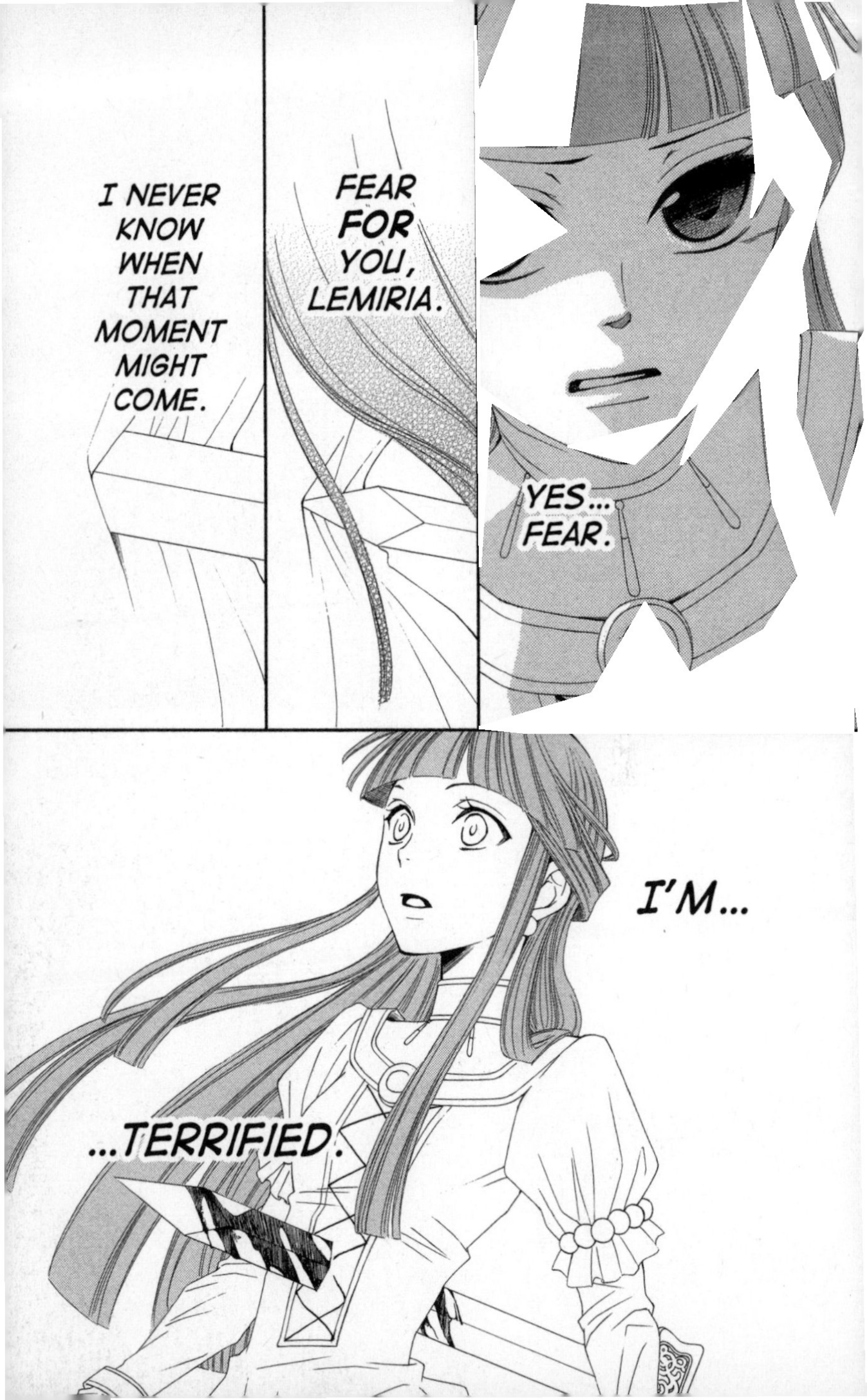
YES... FEAR.
FEAR FOR YOU, LEMIRIA.
I NEVER KNOW WHEN THAT MOMENT MIGHT COME.
I'M...
...TERRIFIED.

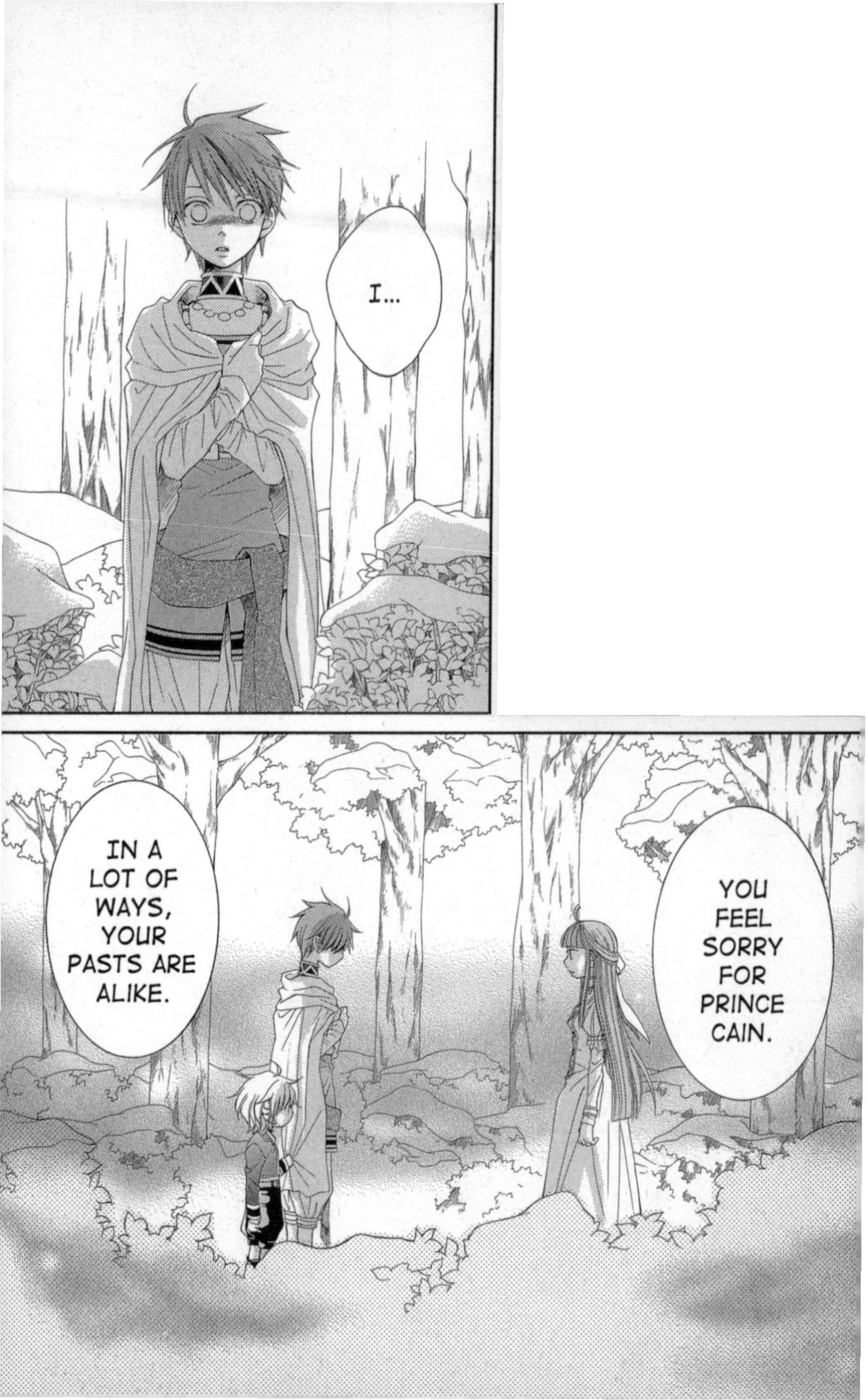
I...
YOU FEEL SORRY FOR PRINCE CAIN.
IN A LOT OF WAYS, YOUR PASTS ARE ALIKE.

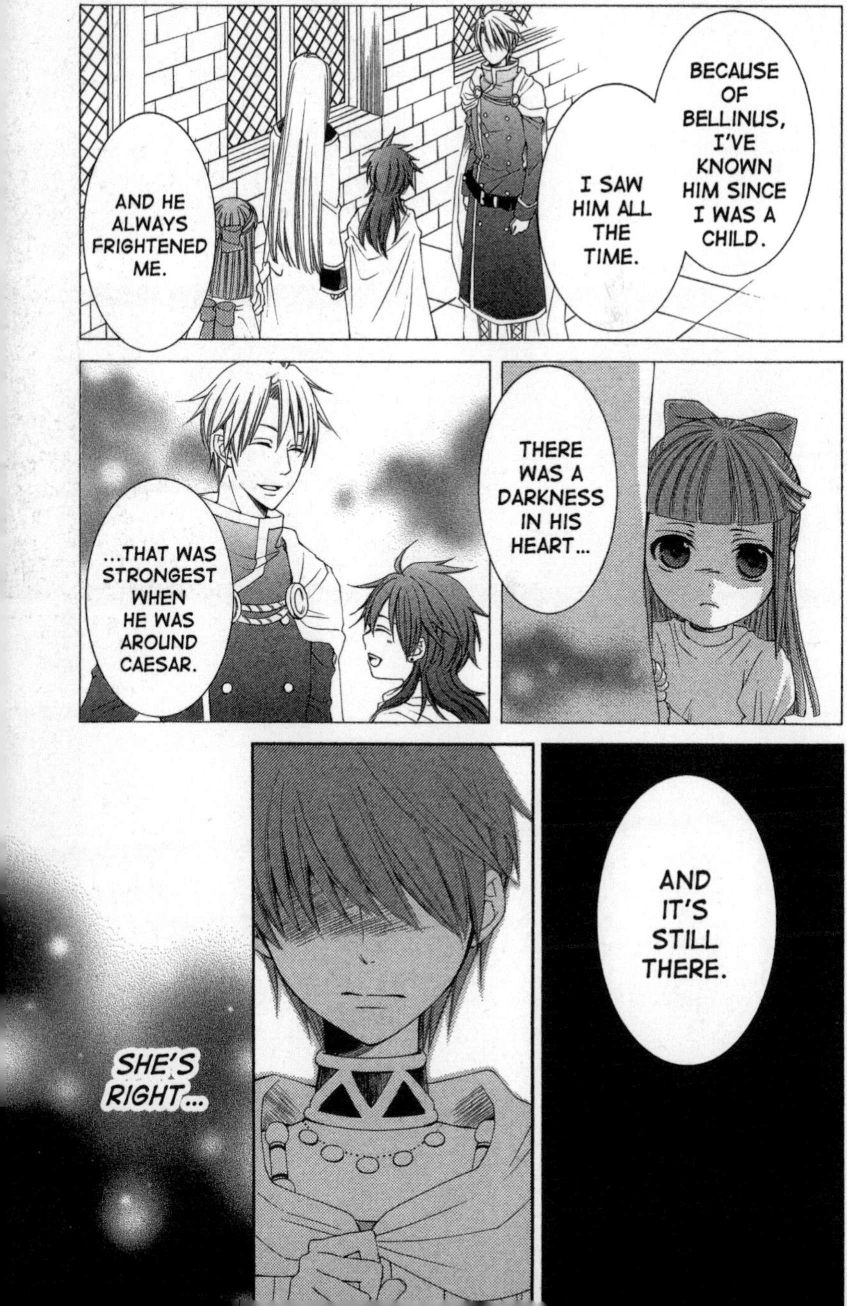
BECAUSE OF BELLINUS, I'VE KNOWN HIM SINCE I WAS A CHILD.
I SAW HIM ALL THE TIME.
AND HE ALWAYS FRIGHTENED ME.
THERE WAS A DARKNESS IN HIS HEART...
...THAT WAS STRONGEST WHEN HE WAS AROUND CAESAR.
AND IT'S STILL THERE.
SHE'S RIGHT...

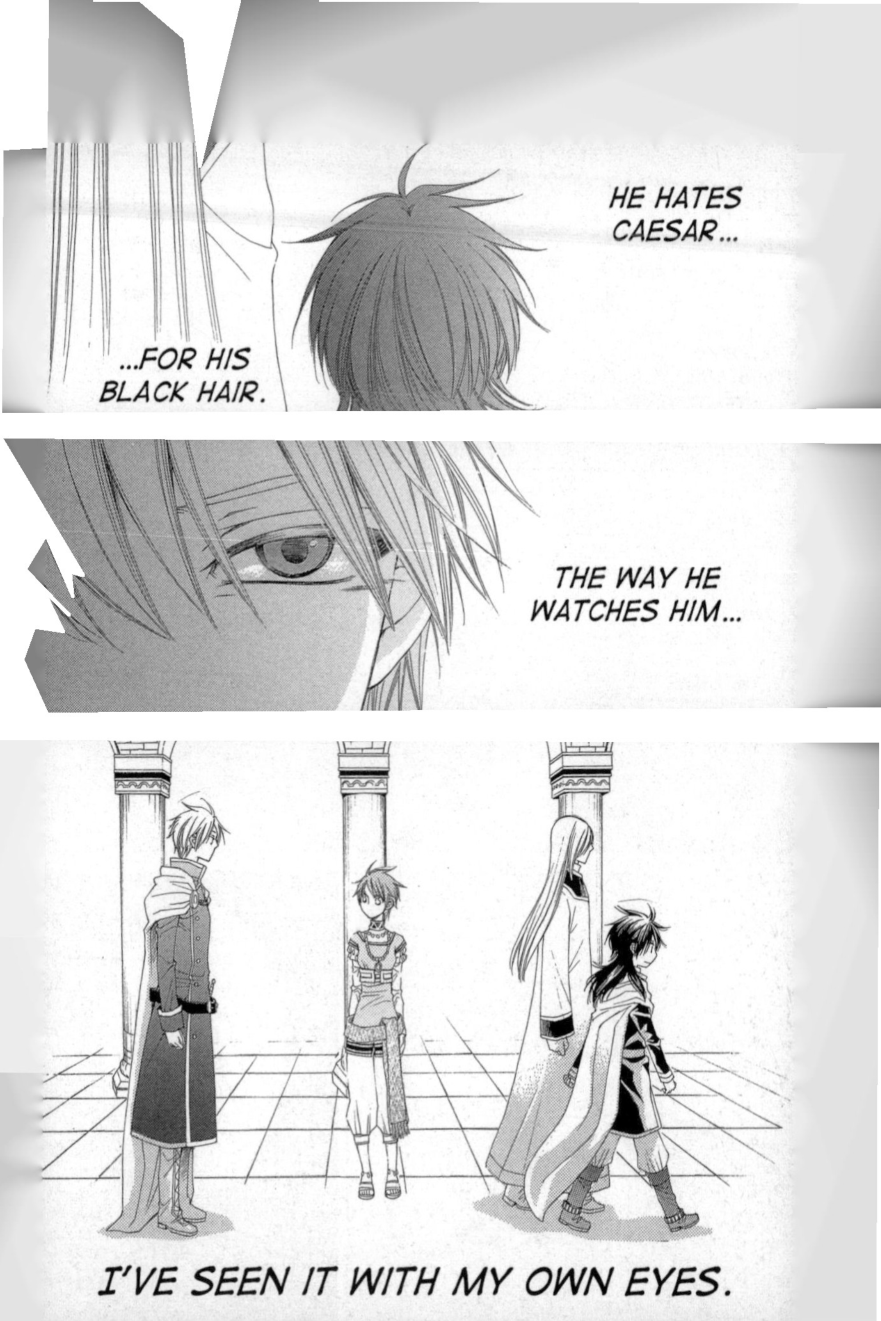
HE HATES CAESAR...
...FOR HIS BLACK HAIR.
THE WAY HE WATCHES HIM...
I'VE SEEN IT WITH MY OWN EYES.

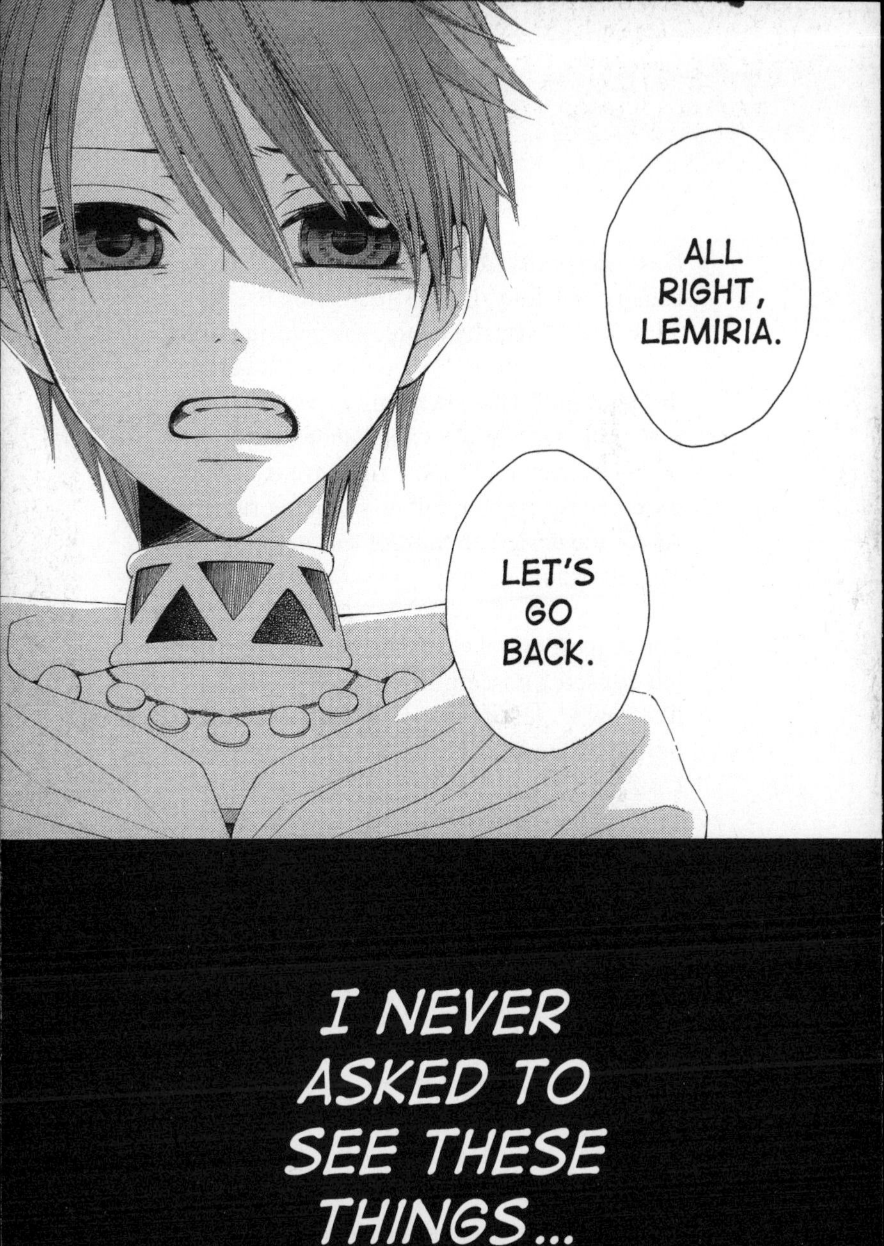
ALL RIGHT, LEMIRIA.
LET'S GO BACK.
I NEVER ASKED TO SEE THESE THINGS...

Next up is Loki, drawn by my assistant whom we usually call Tany. Before attempting the drawing, Tany said, "I usually handle the coloring of the clothes and such, so I'm confident I'll get the design right." That's why my expectations were high, but then she went and handed me a few whopper mistakes! Loki's right eye is usually obscured by his hair, but he's looking right at us! As for the design on the clothes, well... I guess she did okay!

The biggest mistake was the tattoo below Loki's left eye—it's missing! Heh heh heh… Oh. Kinda like how I…left it out…on the cover of volume 2… Sorry… That Tany is officially making a debut for *Cheese!* Let's all wish her success in her new career! (End commercial)

Princess Nakaba.

Chapter 19

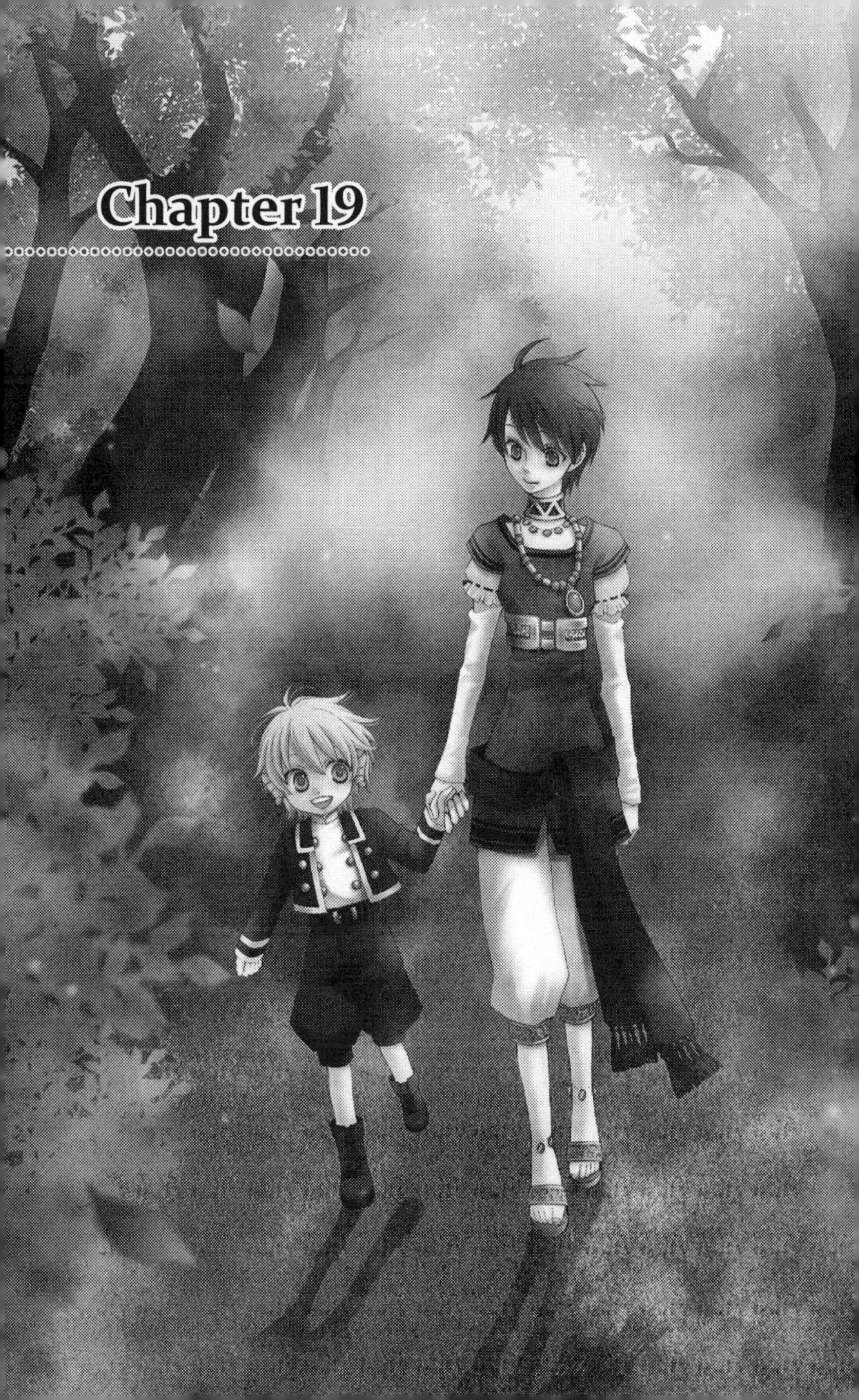

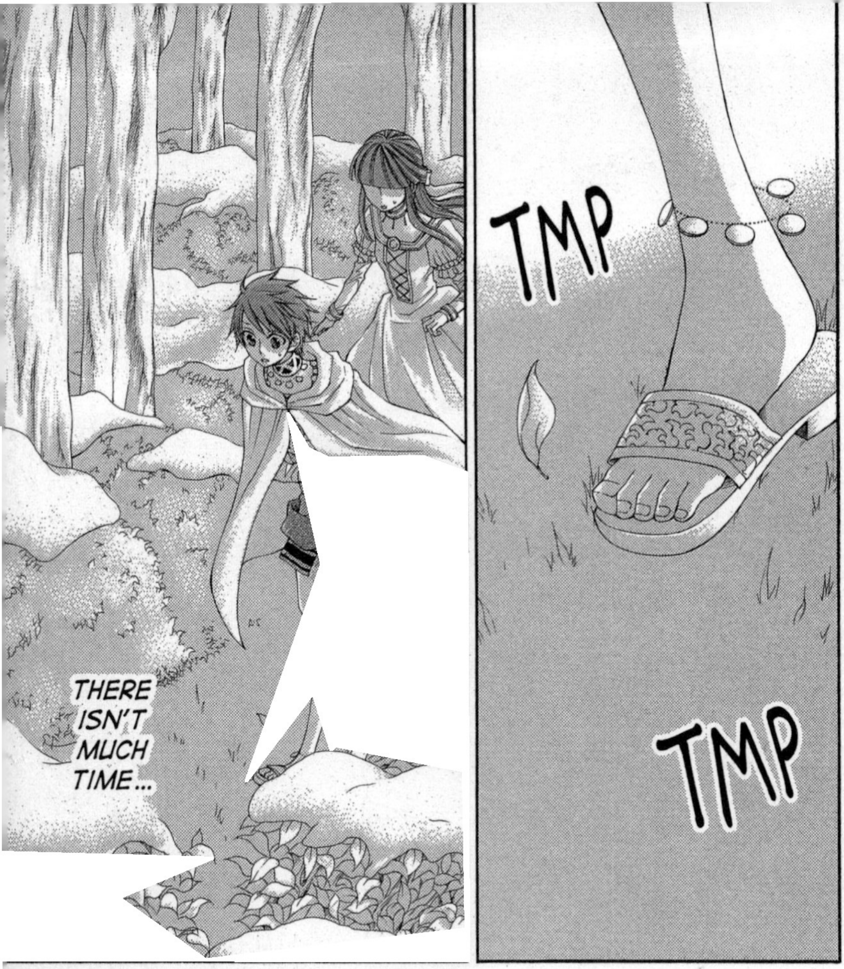
TMP
TMP
THERE ISN'T MUCH TIME...

Dawn of the Arcana

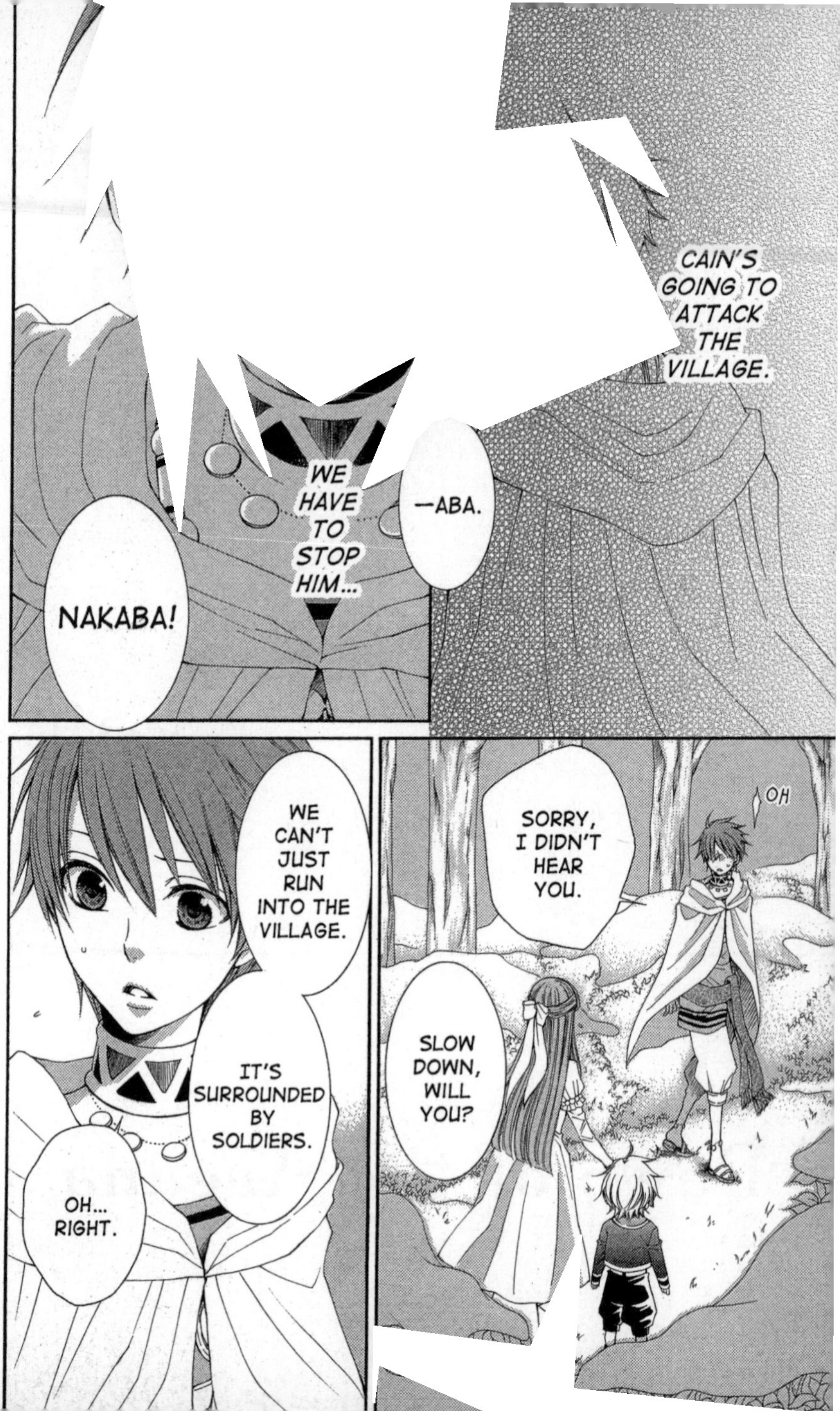
CAIN'S GOING TO ATTACK THE VILLAGE.
WE HAVE TO STOP HIM...
—ABA.
NAKABA!
OH
SORRY, I DIDN'T HEAR YOU.
SLOW DOWN, WILL YOU?
WE CAN'T JUST RUN INTO THE VILLAGE.
IT'S SURROUNDED BY SOLDIERS.
OH... RIGHT.

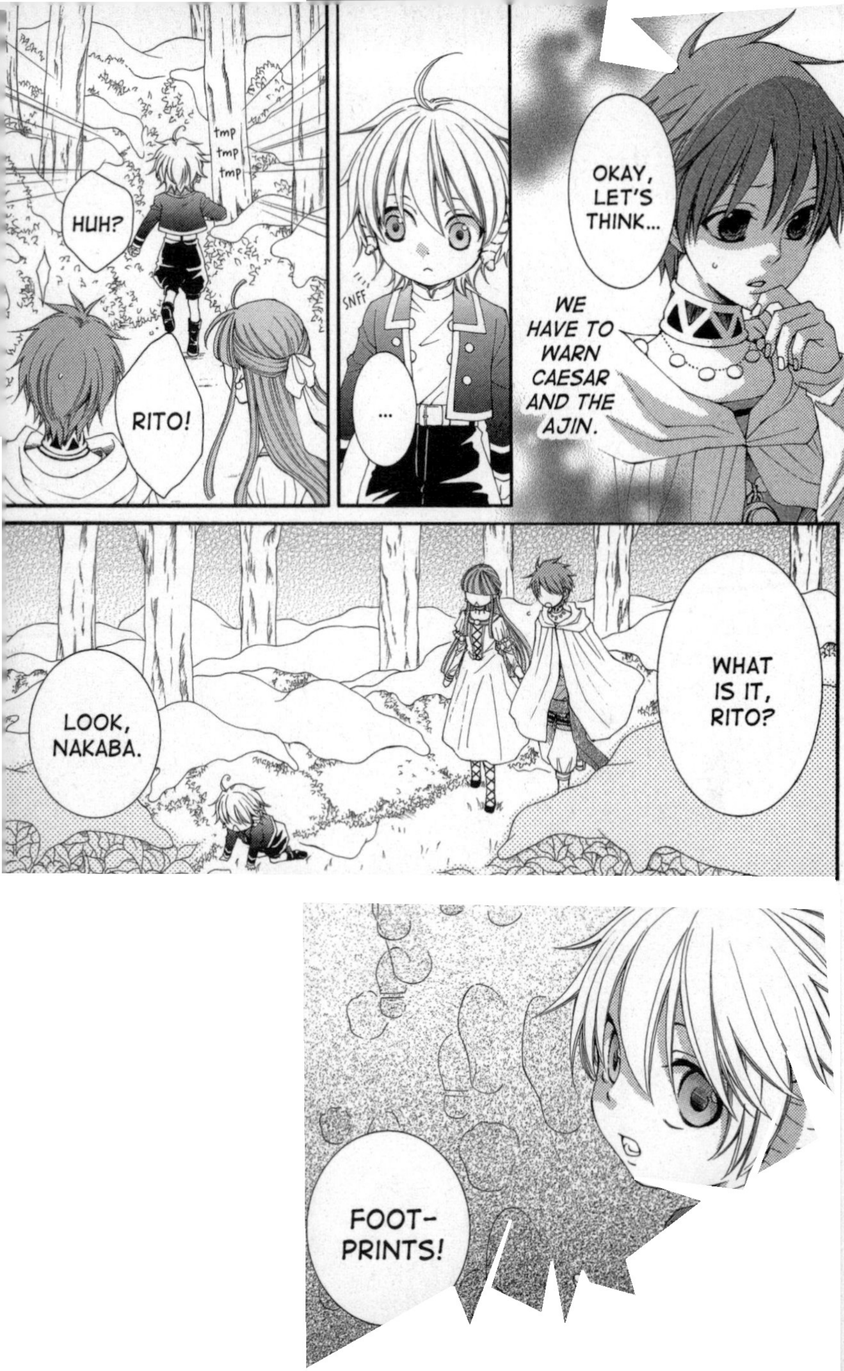
OKAY, LET'S THINK...
WE HAVE TO WARN CAESAR AND THE AJIN.
SNFF
...
tmp tmp tmp
HUH?
RITO!
WHAT IS IT, RITO?
LOOK, NAKABA.
FOOT-PRINTS!

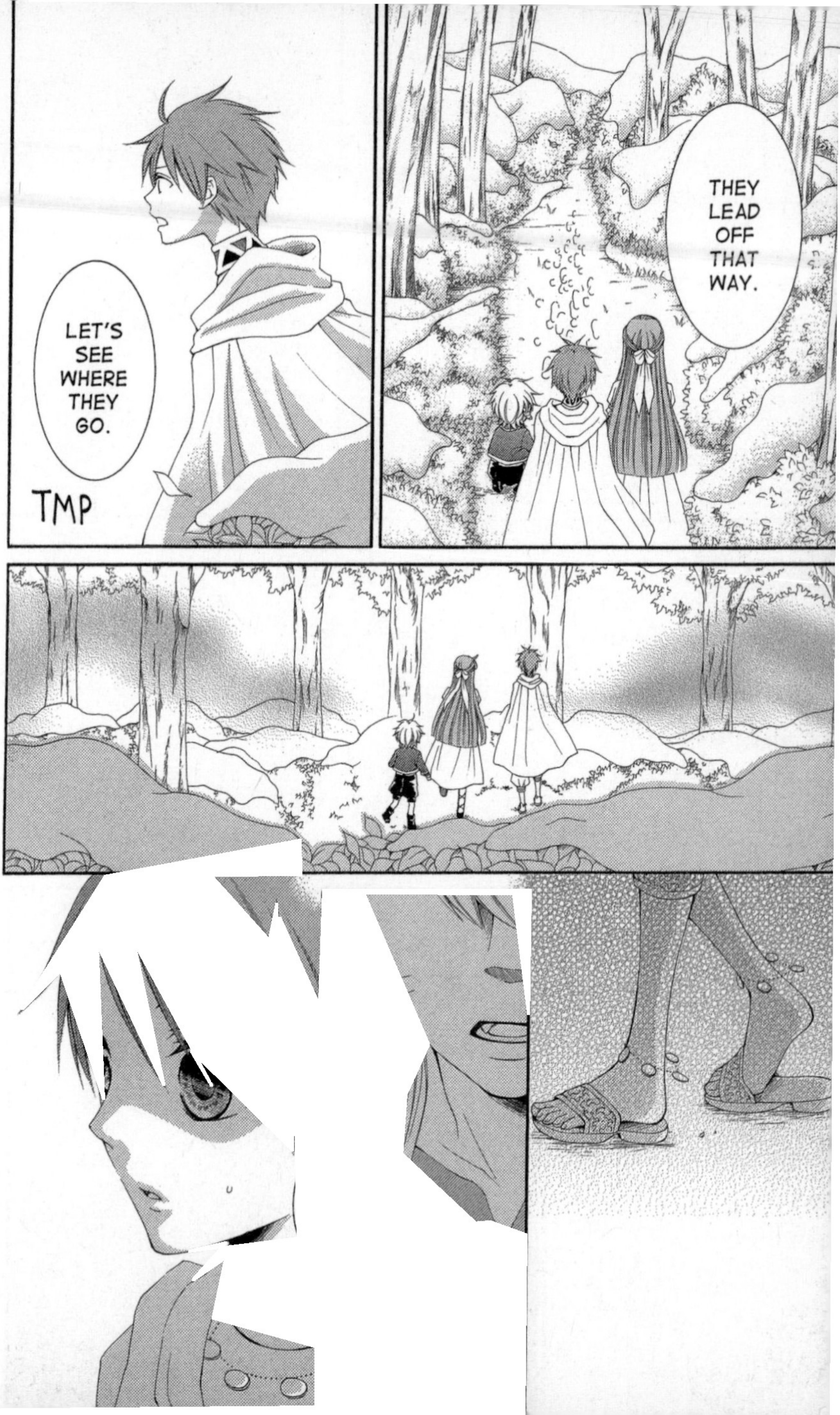
THEY LEAD OFF THAT WAY.
LET'S SEE WHERE THEY GO.
TMP

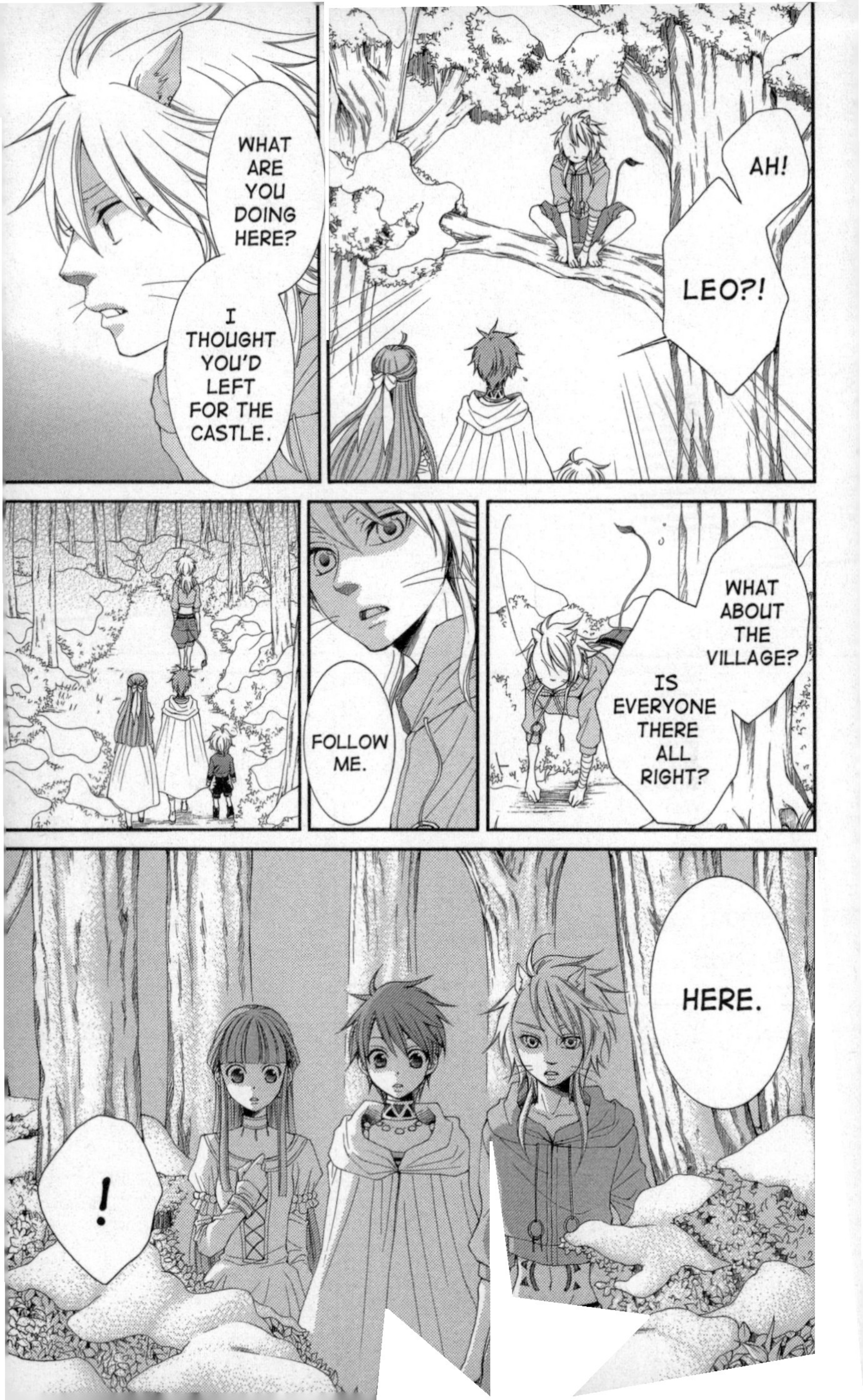
AH!
LEO?!
WHAT ARE YOU DOING HERE?
I THOUGHT YOU'D LEFT FOR THE CASTLE.
WHAT ABOUT THE VILLAGE?
IS EVERYONE THERE ALL RIGHT?
FOLLOW ME.
HERE.
!

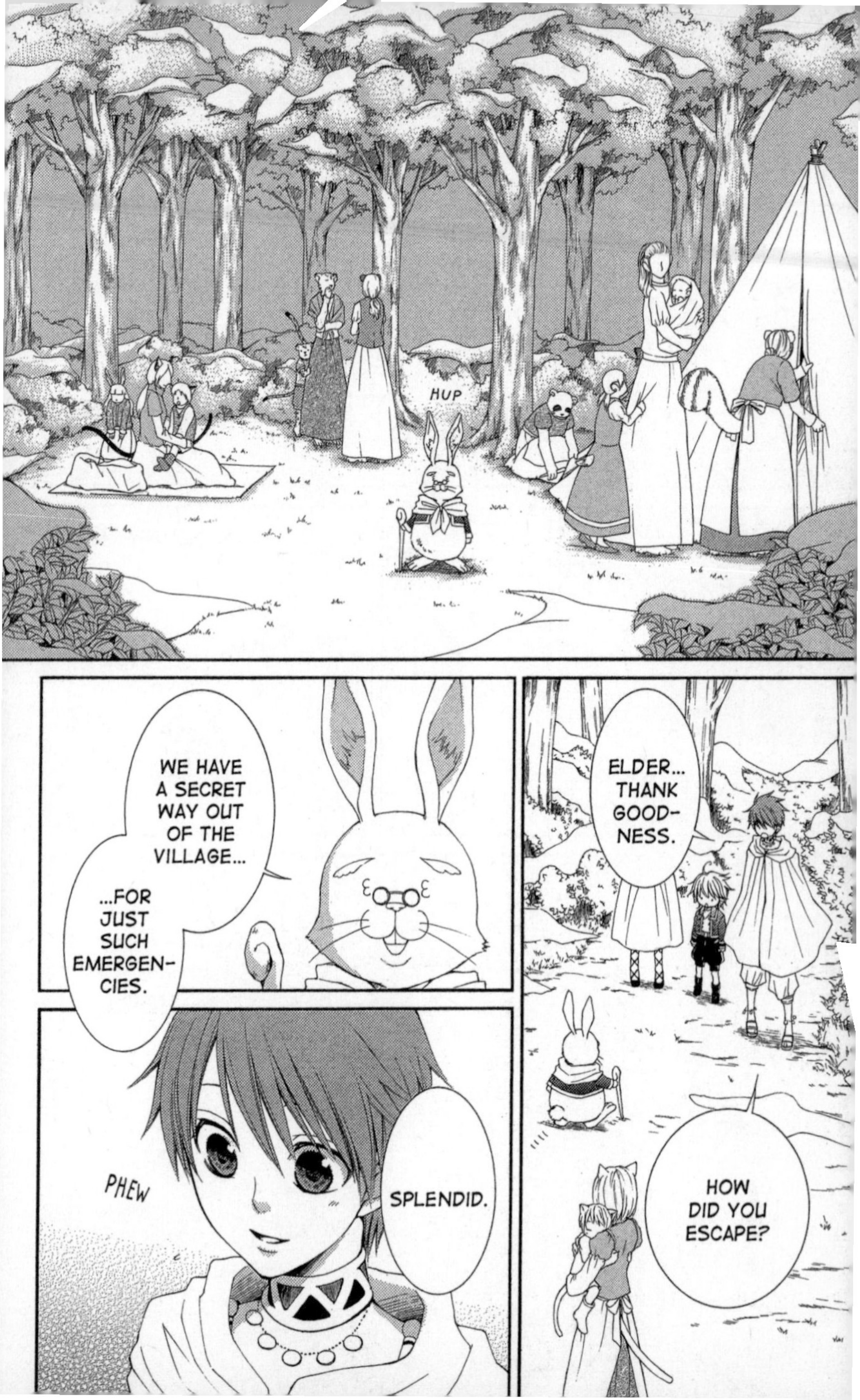
HUP
ELDER... THANK GOODNESS.
HOW DID YOU ESCAPE?
WE HAVE A SECRET WAY OUT OF THE VILLAGE...
...FOR JUST SUCH EMERGENCIES.
SPLENDID.
PHEW

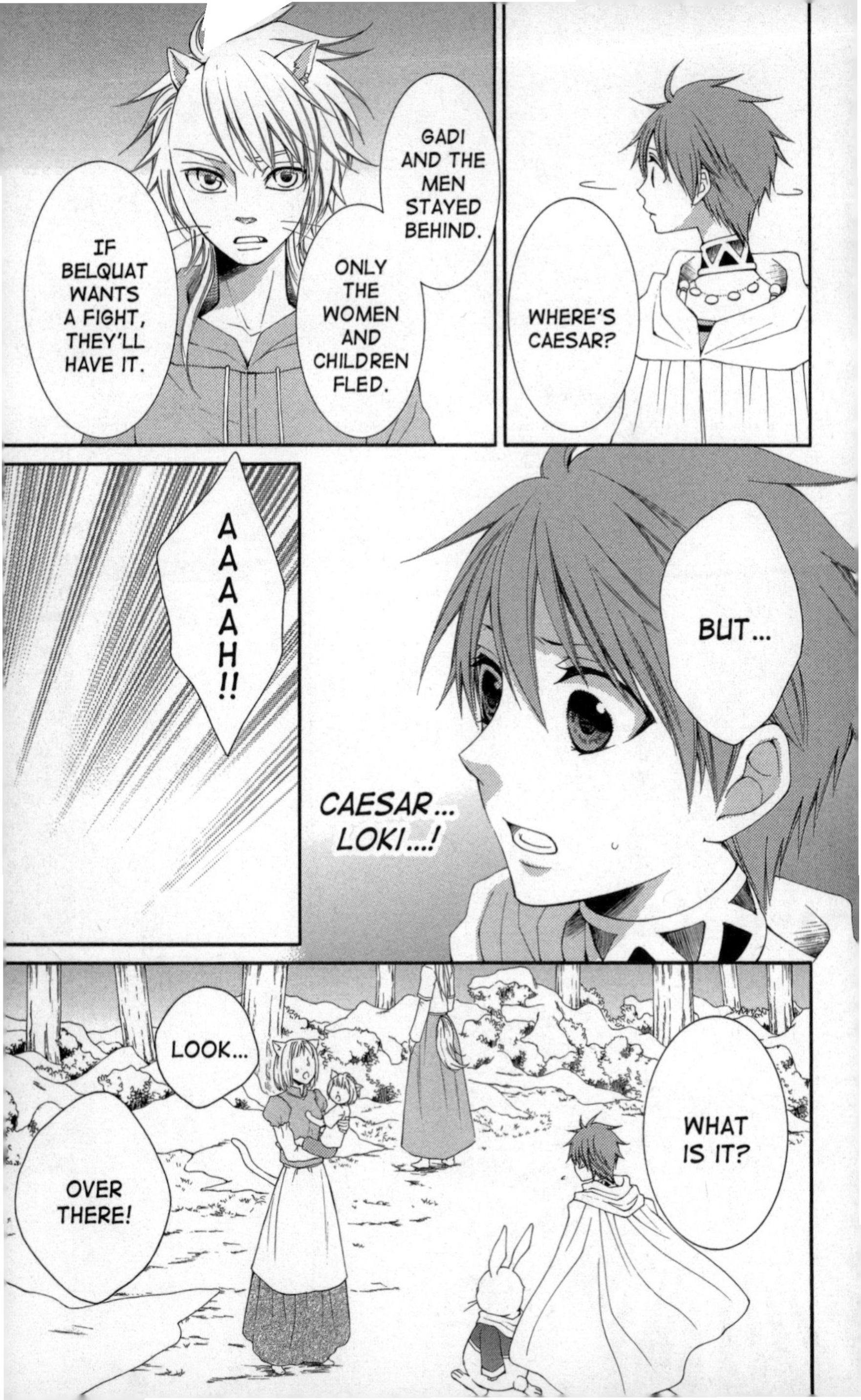
WHERE'S CAESAR?
GADI AND THE MEN STAYED BEHIND.
ONLY THE WOMEN AND CHILDREN FLED.
IF BELQUAT WANTS A FIGHT, THEY'LL HAVE IT.
BUT...
CAESAR... LOKI...!
AAAAAH!!
WHAT IS IT?
LOOK...
OVER THERE!

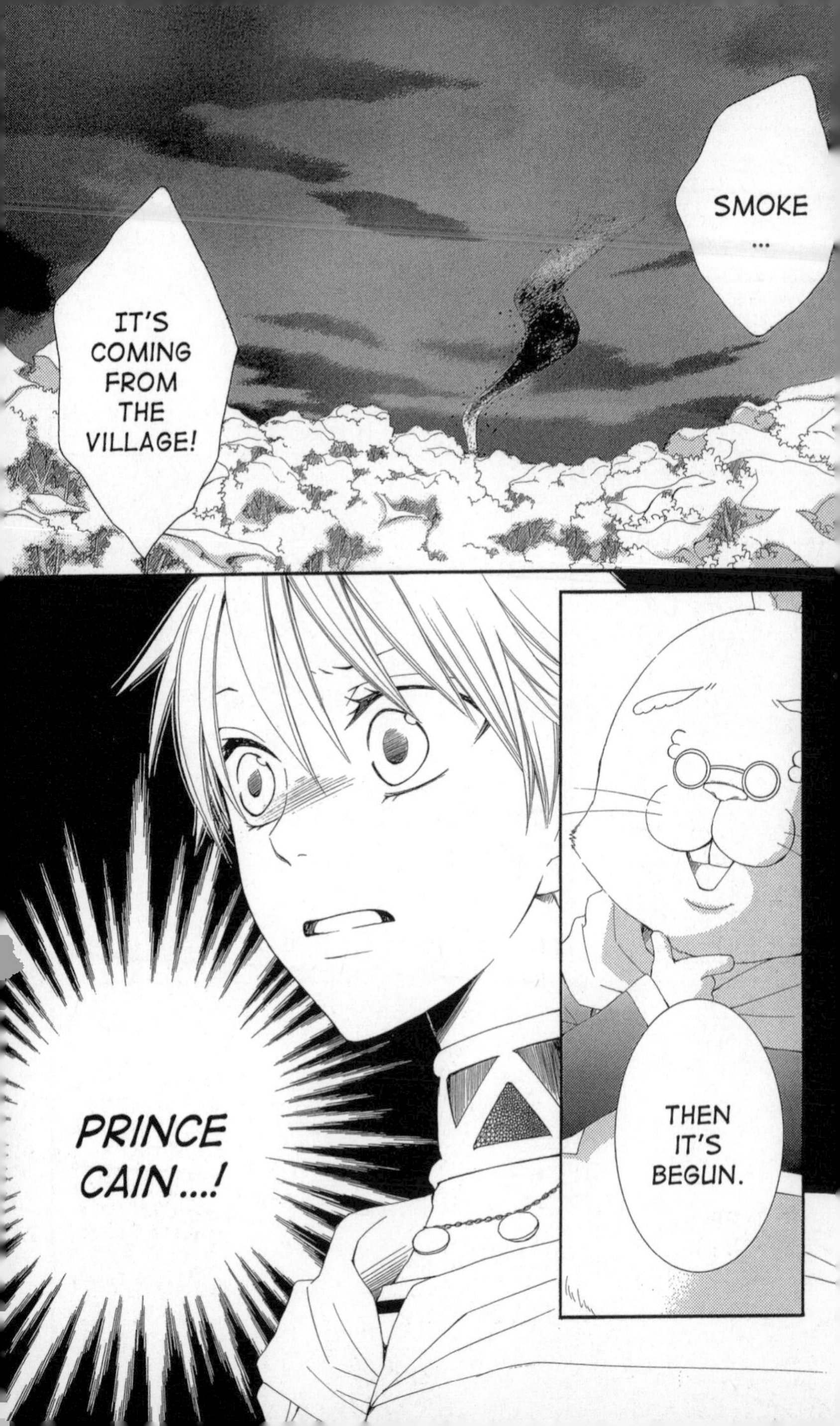
SMOKE ...
IT'S COMING FROM THE VILLAGE!
THEN IT'S BEGUN.
PRINCE CAIN...!

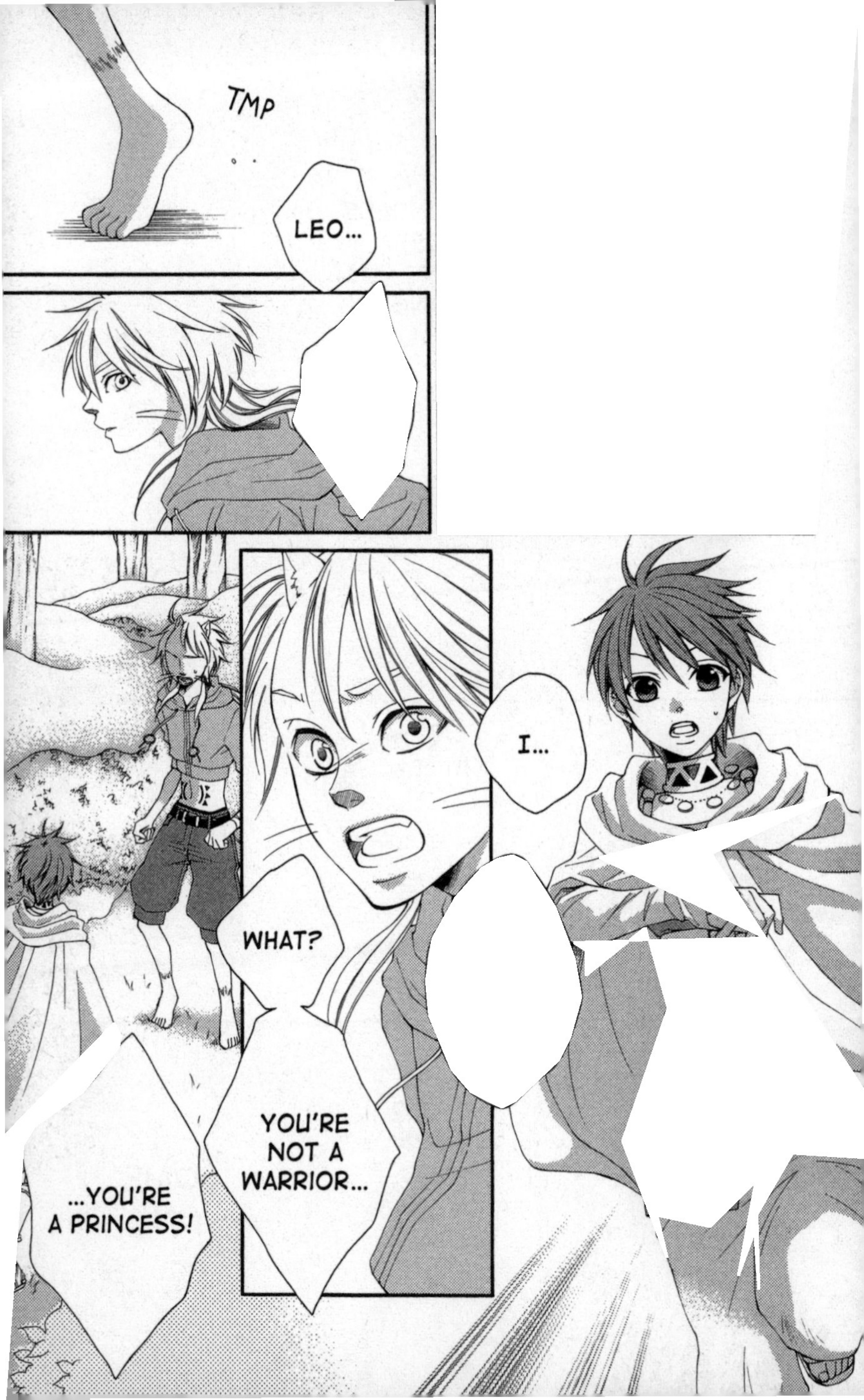
TMP
LEO...
I...
WHAT?
YOU'RE NOT A WARRIOR...
...YOU'RE A PRINCESS!

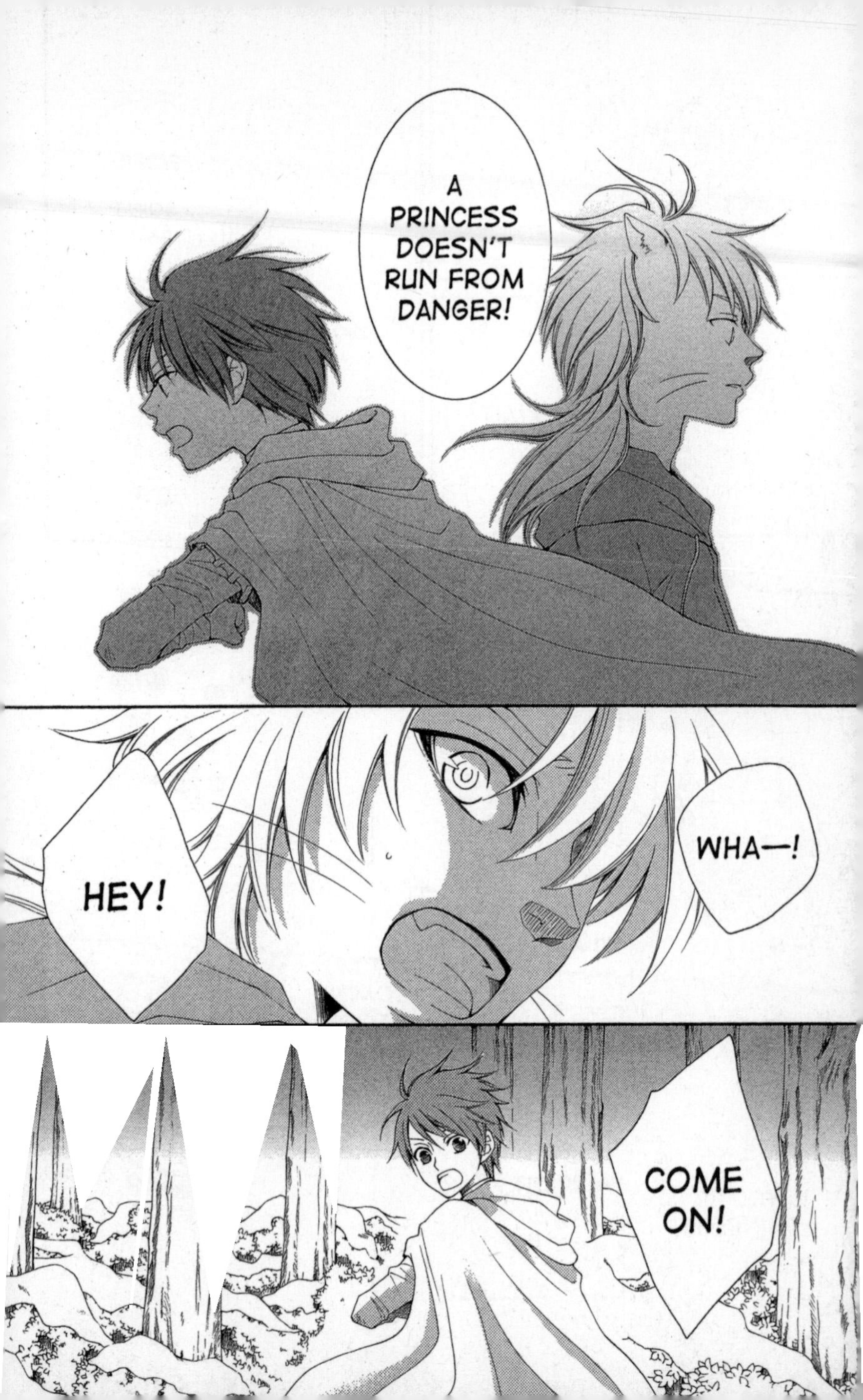
A PRINCESS DOESN'T RUN FROM DANGER!
WHA—!
HEY!
COME ON!

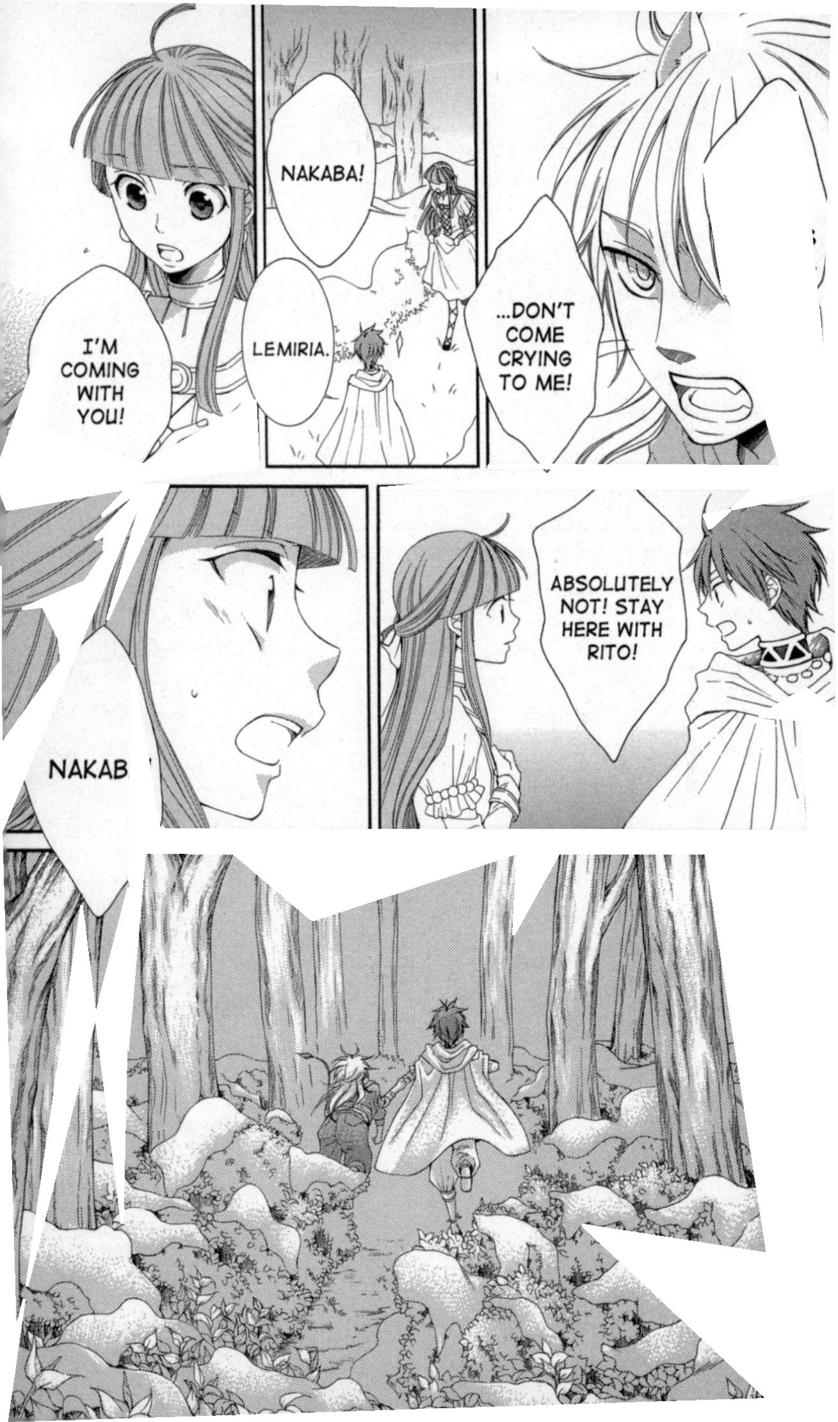
...DON'T COME CRYING TO ME!
NAKABA!
LEMIRIA.
I'M COMING WITH YOU!
ABSOLUTELY NOT! STAY HERE WITH RITO!
NAKAB

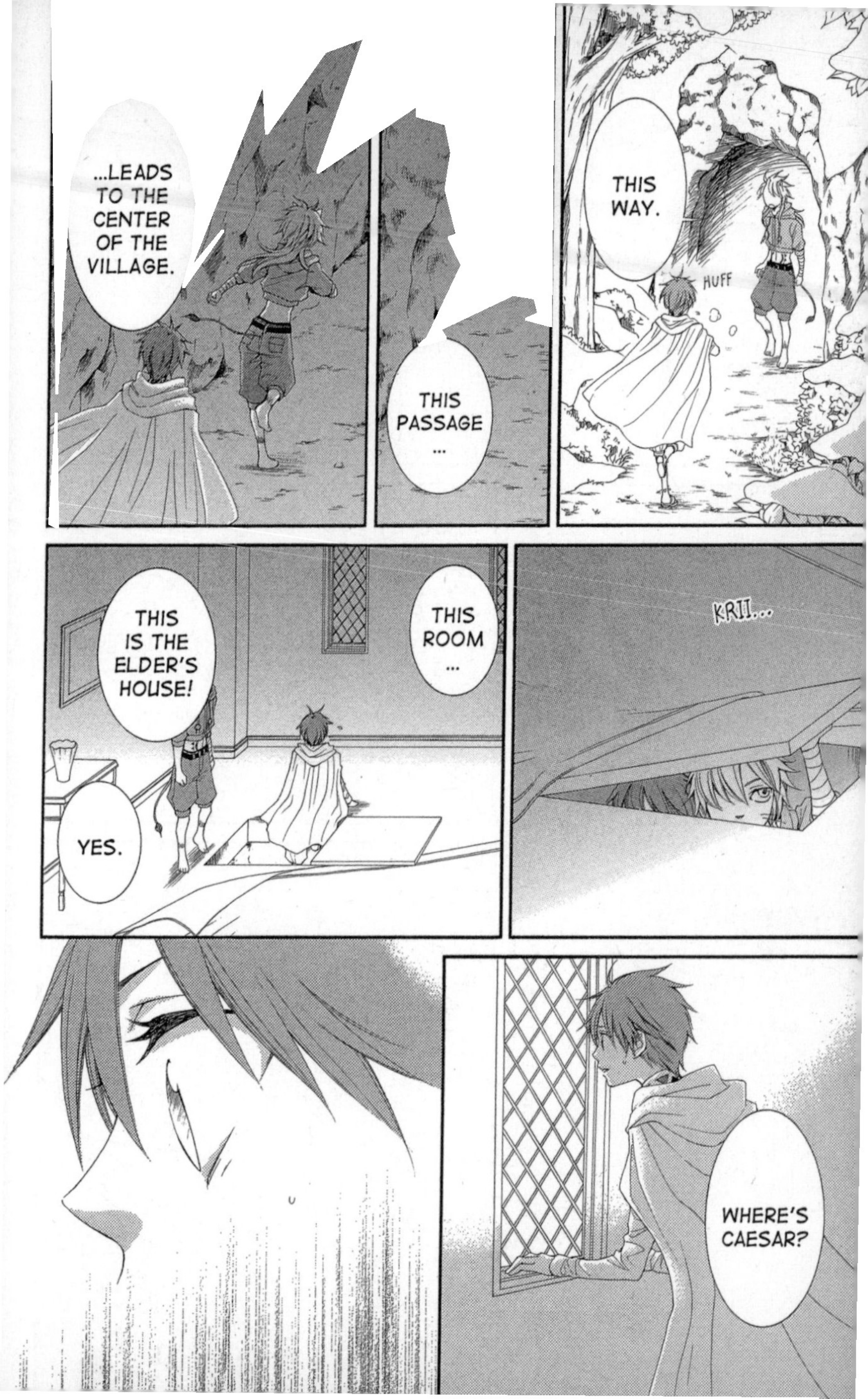
THIS WAY.
HUFF
THIS PASSAGE ...
...LEADS TO THE CENTER OF THE VILLAGE.
KRII...
THIS ROOM ...
THIS IS THE ELDER'S HOUSE!
YES.
WHERE'S CAESAR?

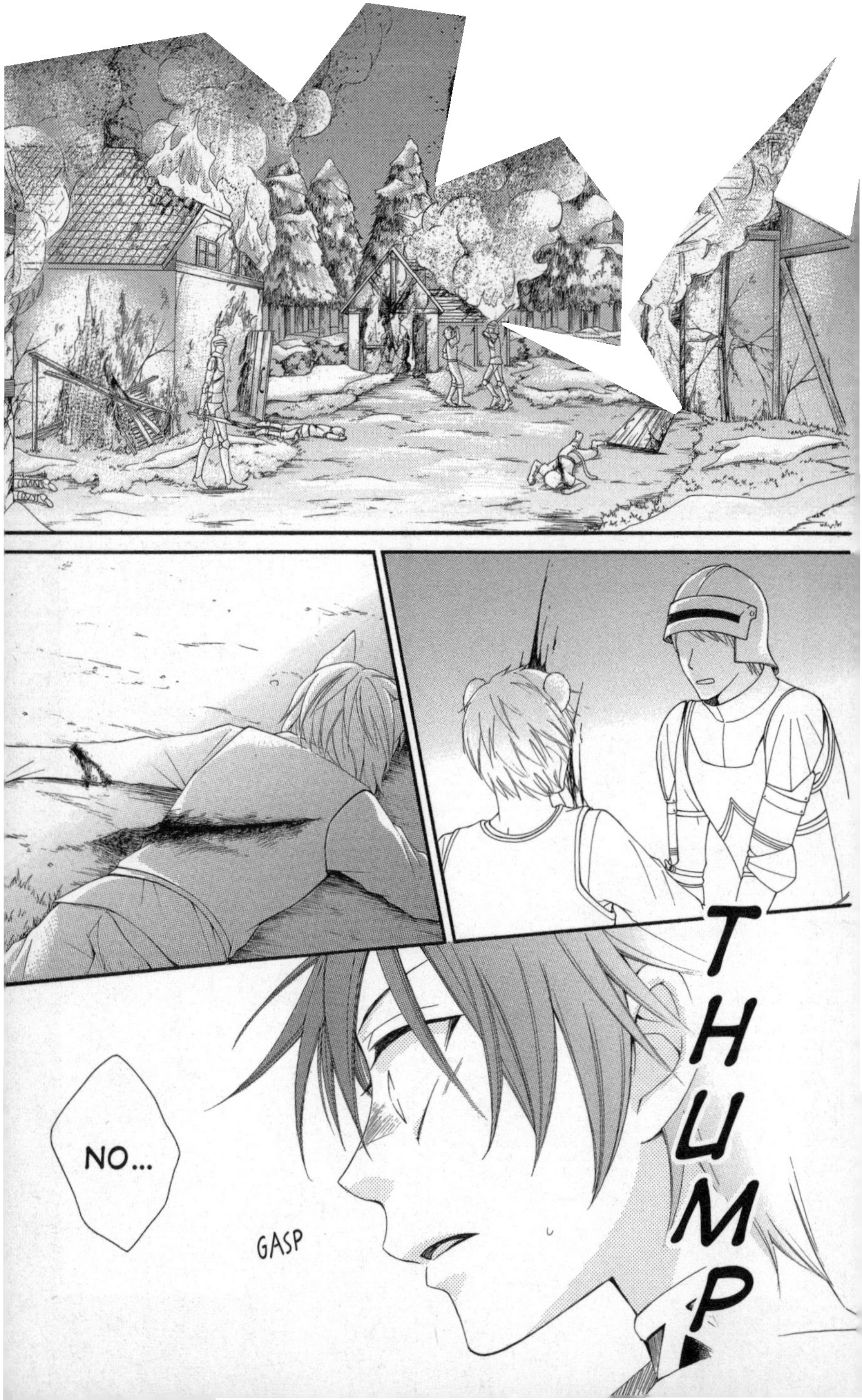
THUMP
GASP
NO...

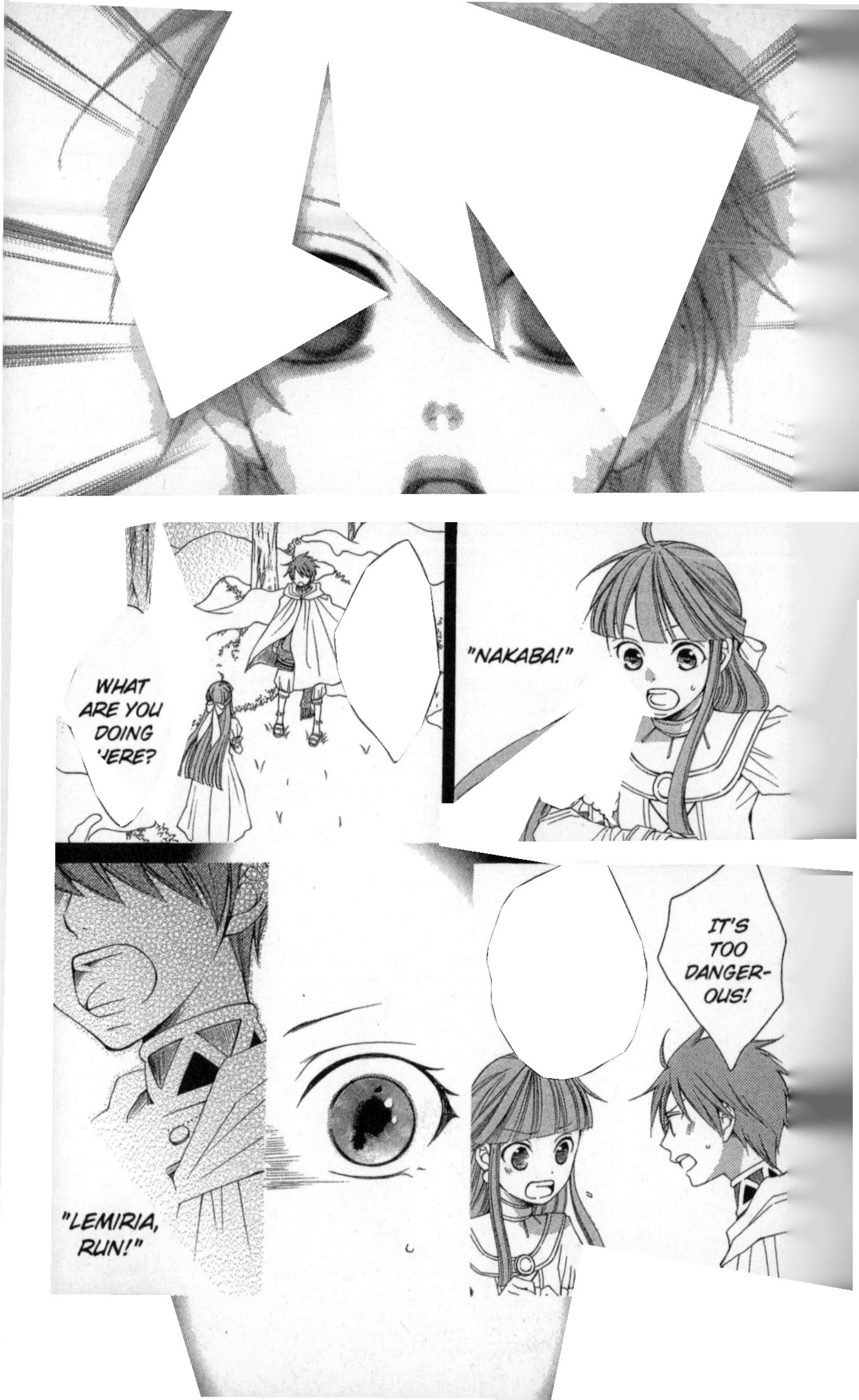
"NAKABA!"
WHAT ARE YOU DOING HERE?
IT'S TOO DANGER-OUS!
"LEMIRIA, RUN!"

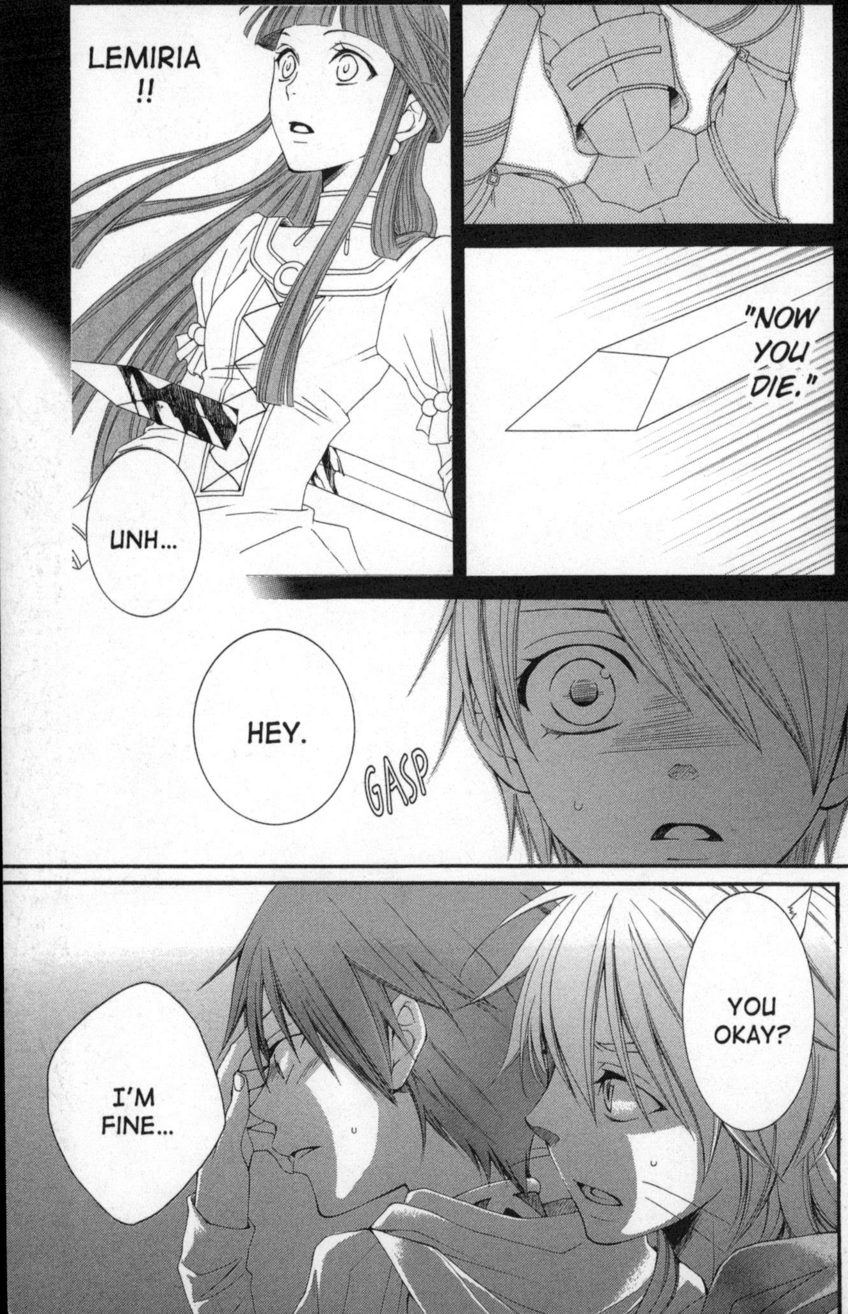
"NOW YOU DIE."
LEMIRIA !!
UNH...
HEY.
GASP
YOU OKAY?
I'M FINE...

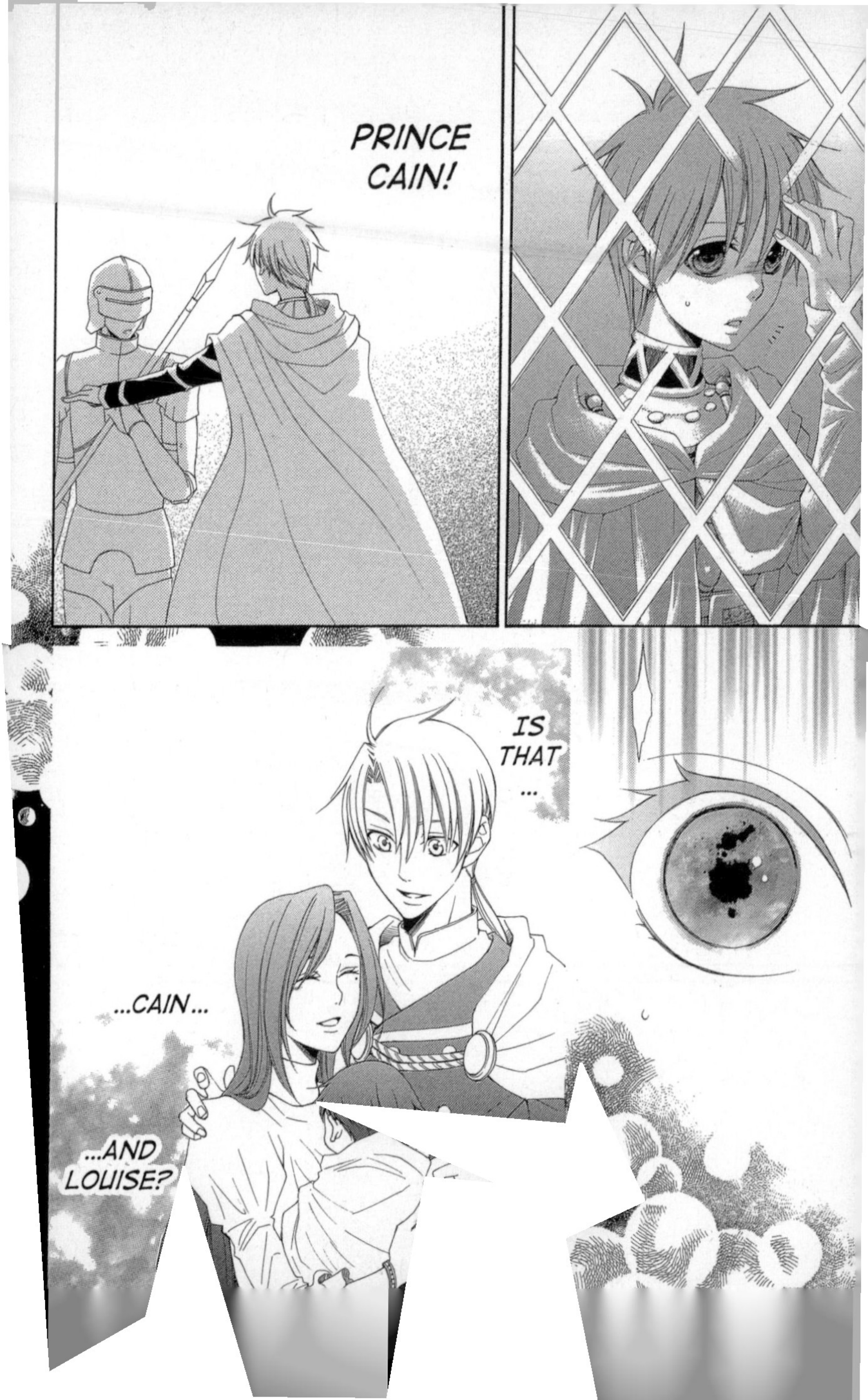
PRINCE CAIN!
IS THAT ...
...CAIN...
...AND LOUISE?

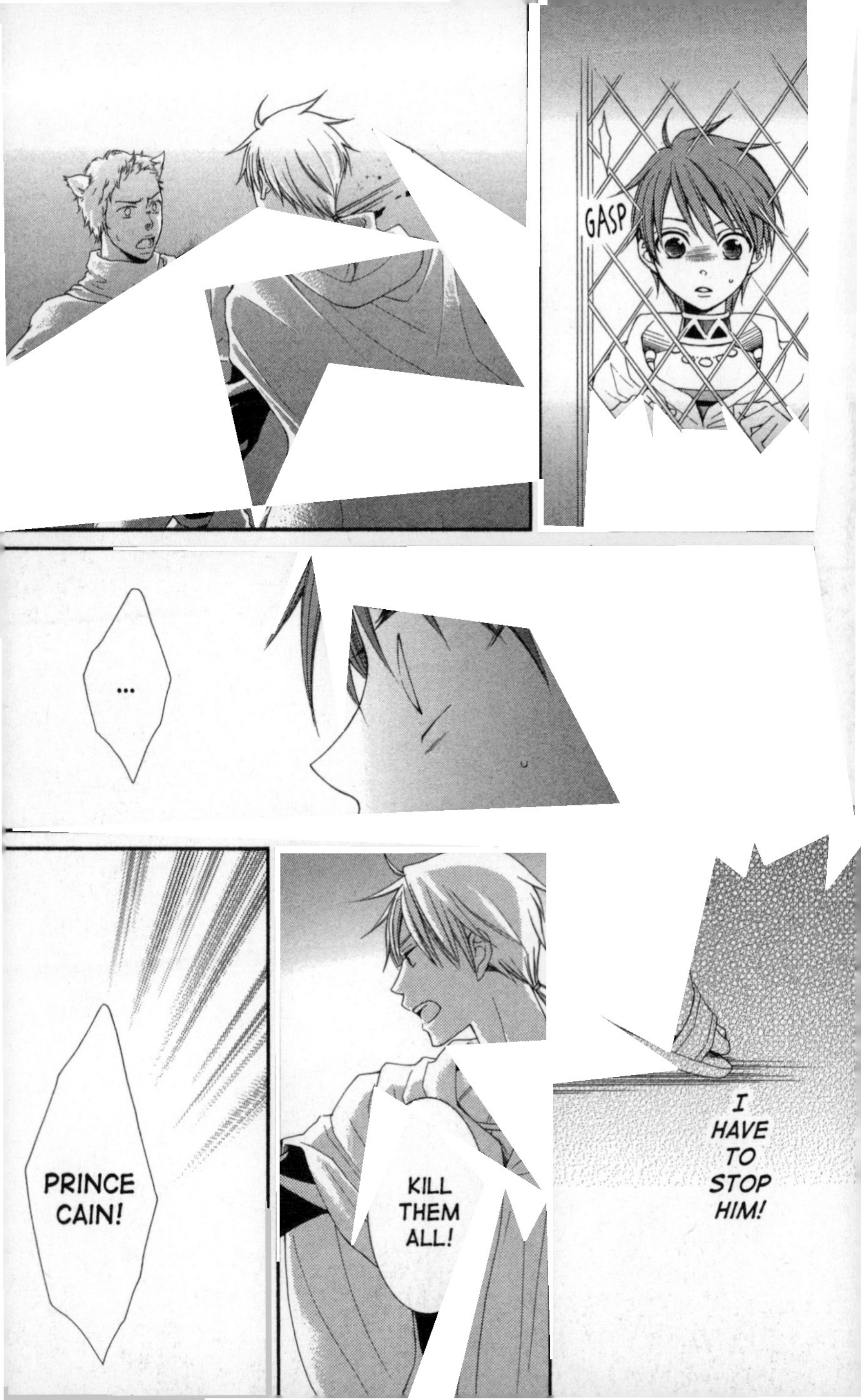
GASP
...
I HAVE TO STOP HIM!
KILL THEM ALL!
PRINCE CAIN!

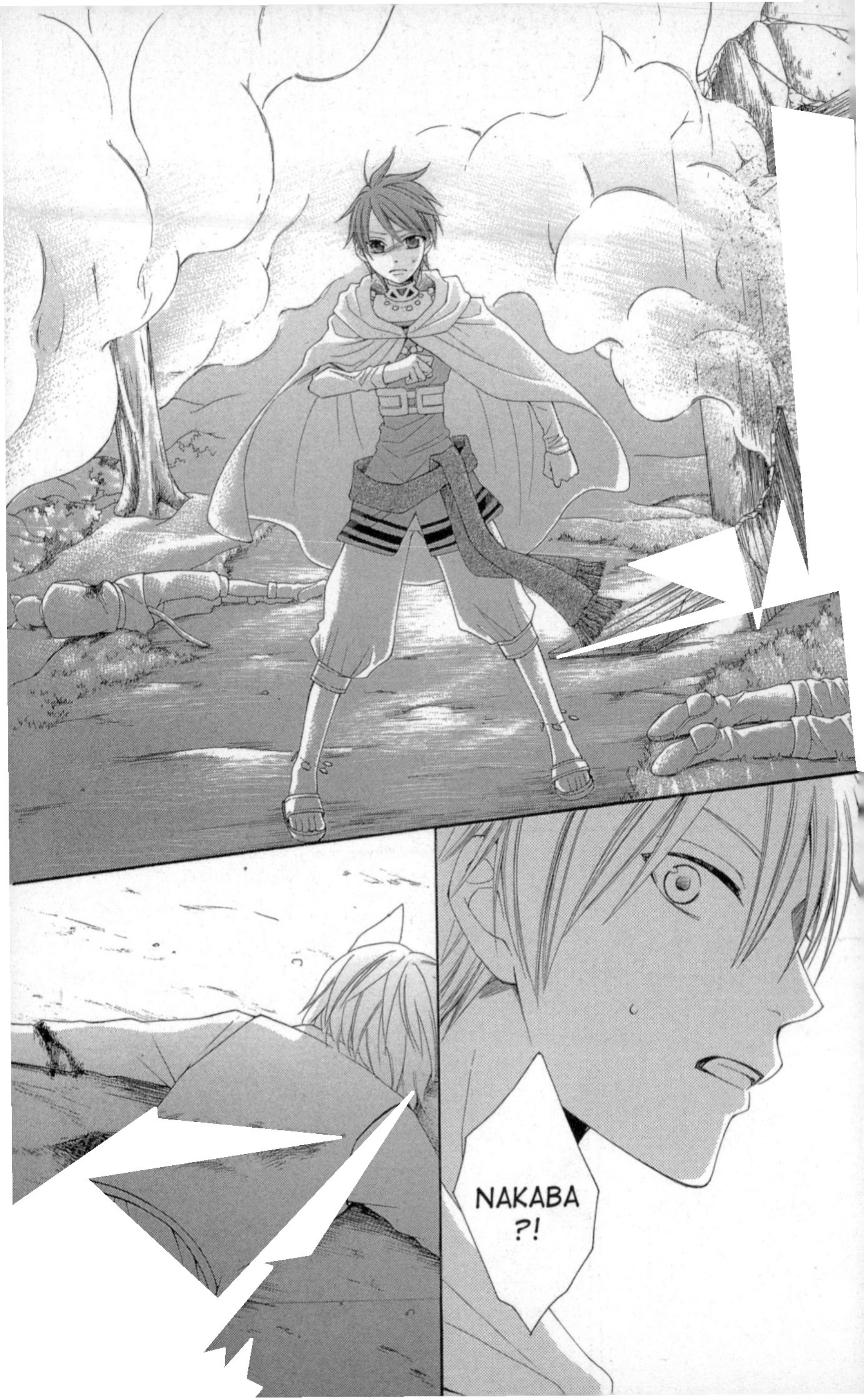
NAKABA
?!

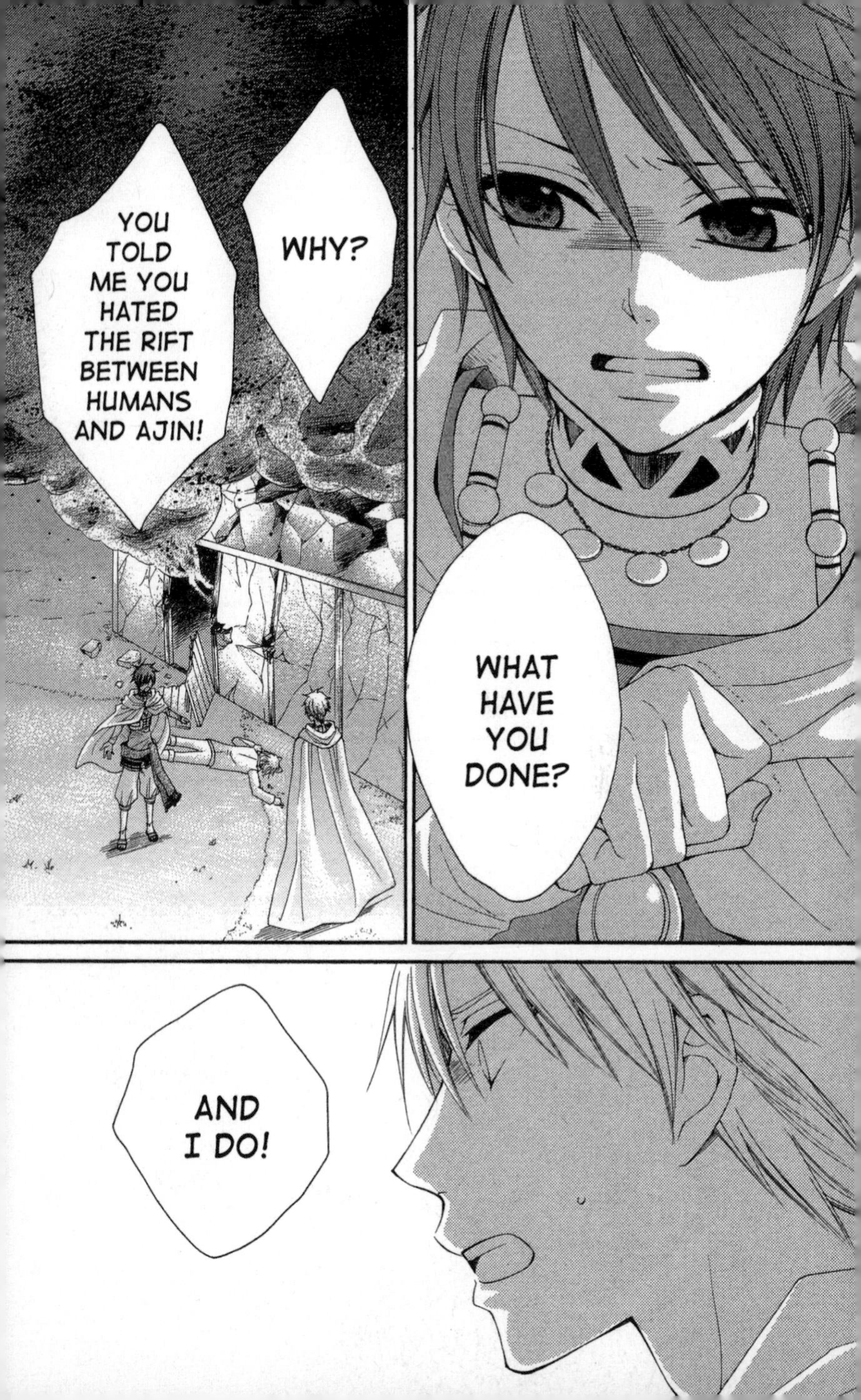
WHAT HAVE YOU DONE?
WHY?
YOU TOLD ME YOU HATED THE RIFT BETWEEN HUMANS AND AJIN!
AND I DO!

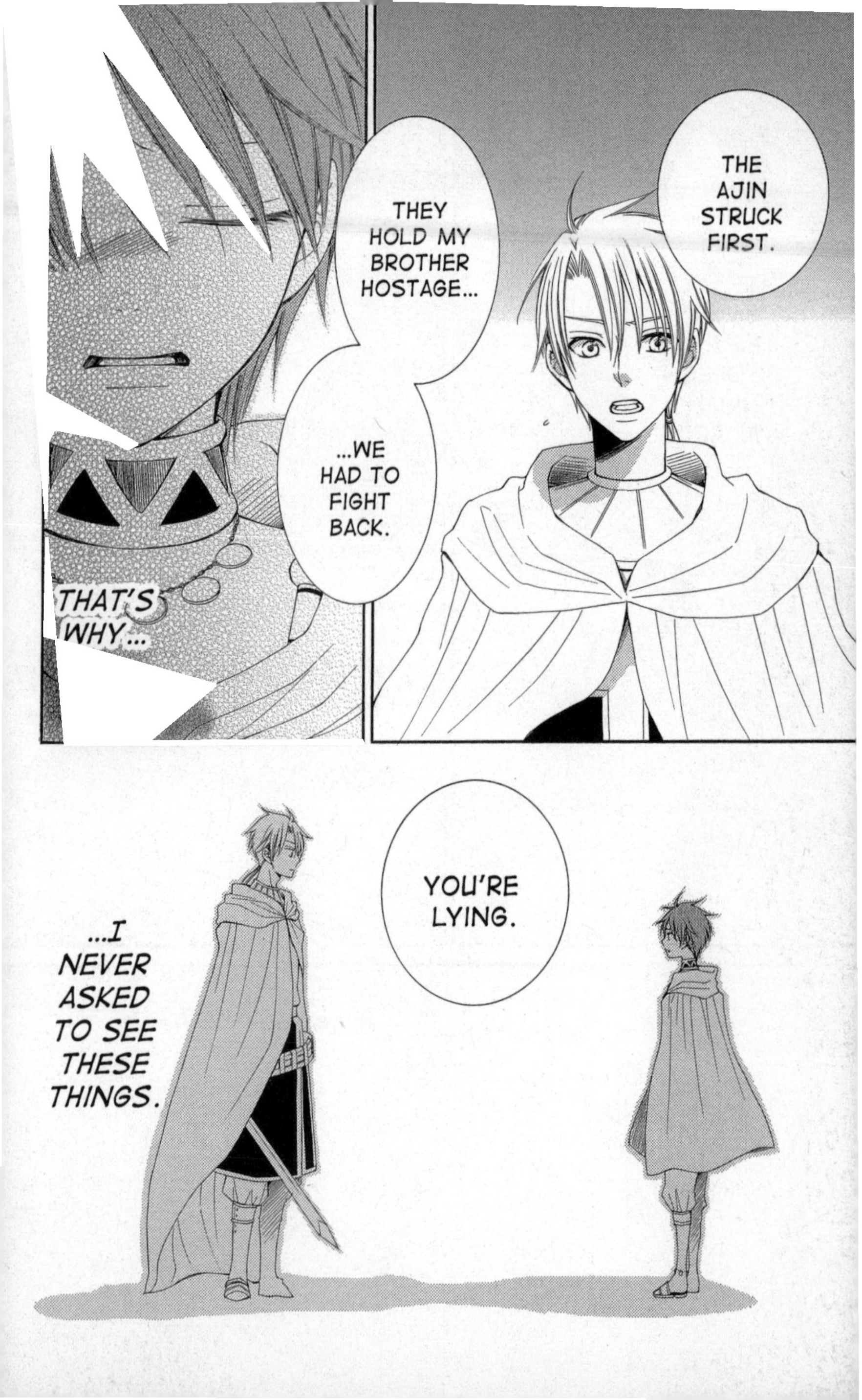
THE AJIN STRUCK FIRST.
THEY HOLD MY BROTHER HOSTAGE...
...WE HAD TO FIGHT BACK.
THAT'S WHY...
YOU'RE LYING.
...I NEVER ASKED TO SEE THESE THINGS.

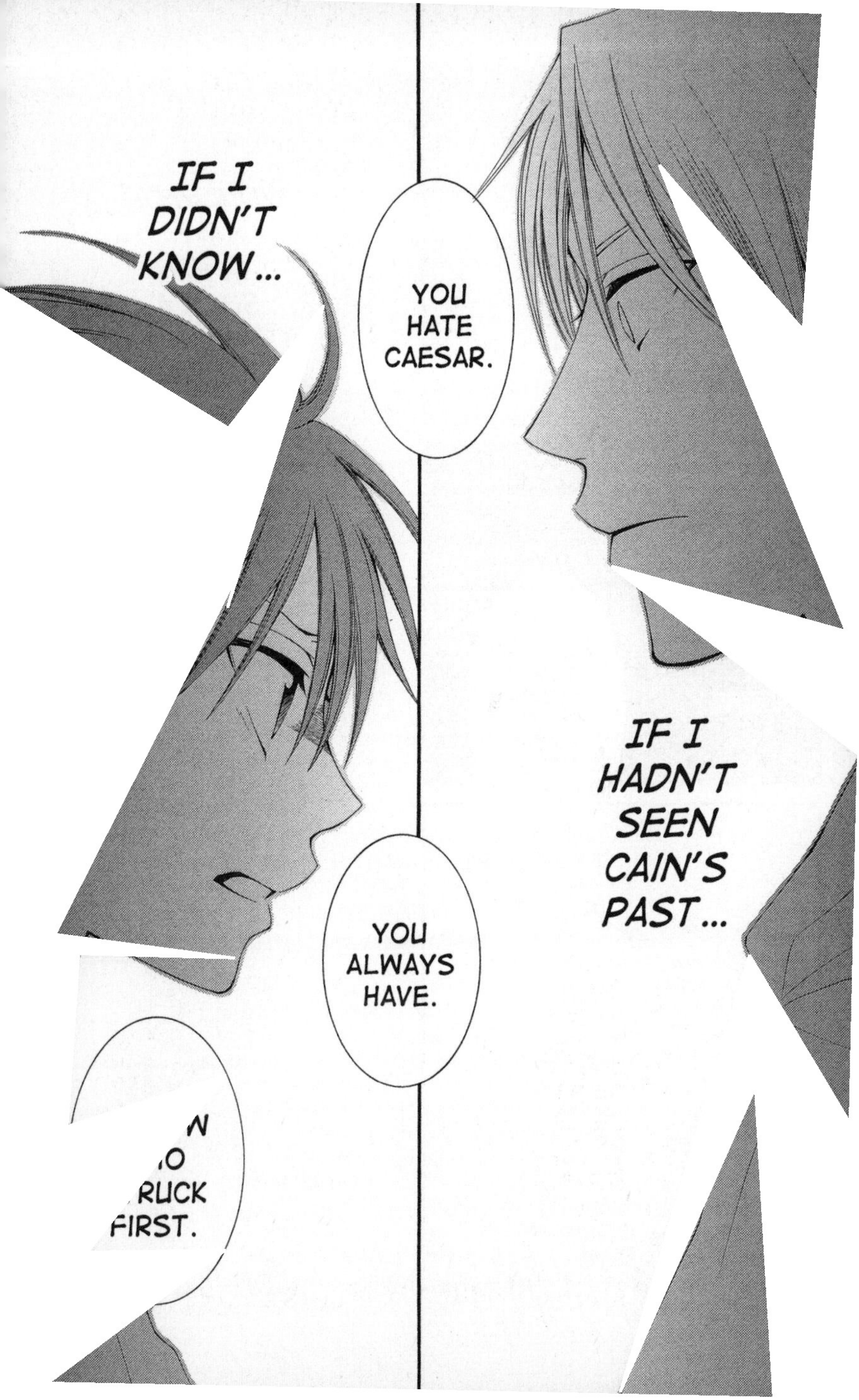
YOU HATE CAESAR.
IF I HADN'T SEEN CAIN'S PAST...
IF I DIDN'T KNOW...
YOU ALWAYS HAVE.
RUCK FIRST.

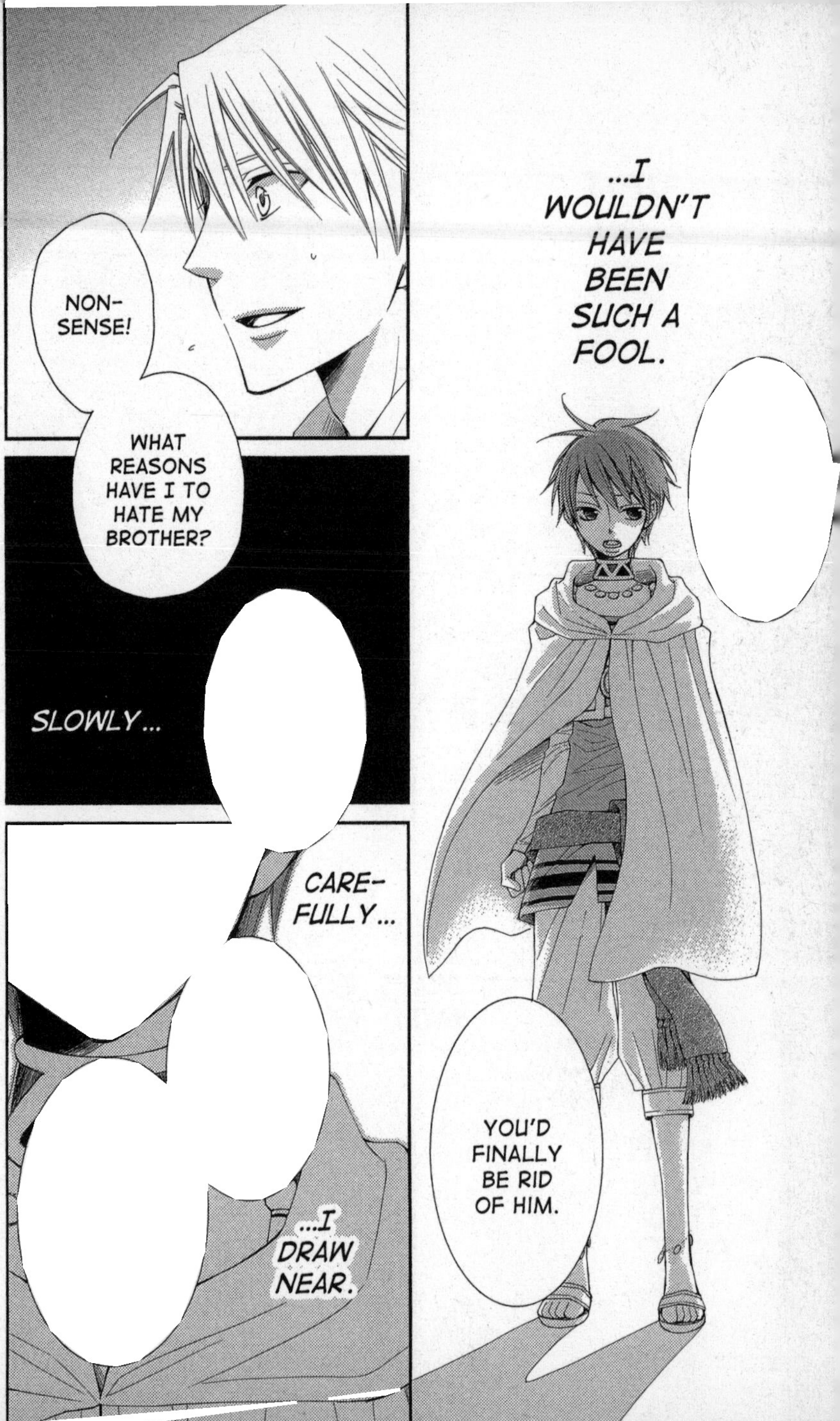
...I WOULDN'T HAVE BEEN SUCH A FOOL.
YOU'D FINALLY BE RID OF HIM.
NON-SENSE!
WHAT REASONS HAVE I TO HATE MY BROTHER?
SLOWLY...
CARE-FULLY...
...I DRAW NEAR.

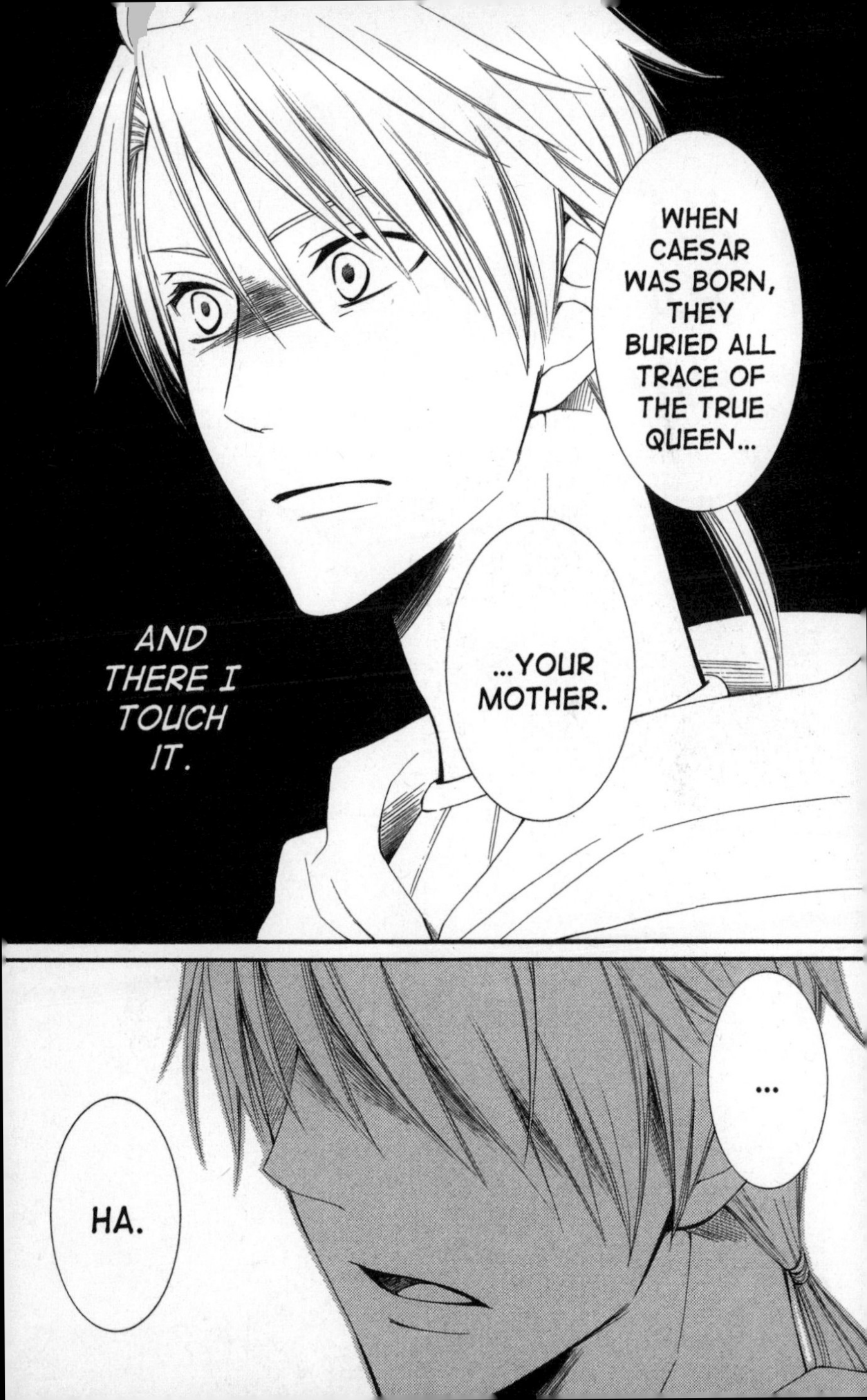
WHEN CAESAR WAS BORN, THEY BURIED ALL TRACE OF THE TRUE QUEEN...
...YOUR MOTHER.
AND THERE I TOUCH IT.
...
HA.

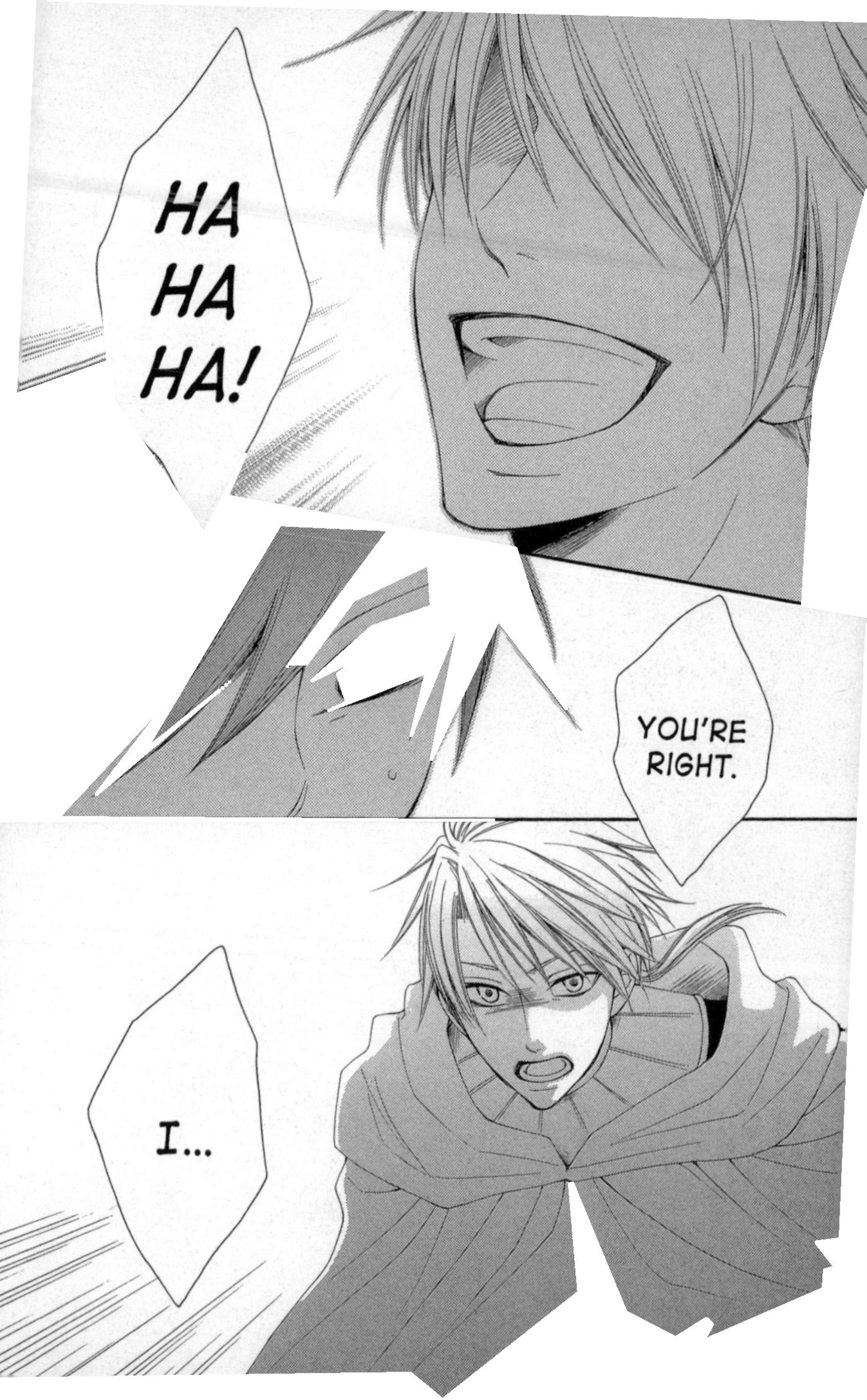
HA HA HA!
YOU'RE RIGHT.
I...

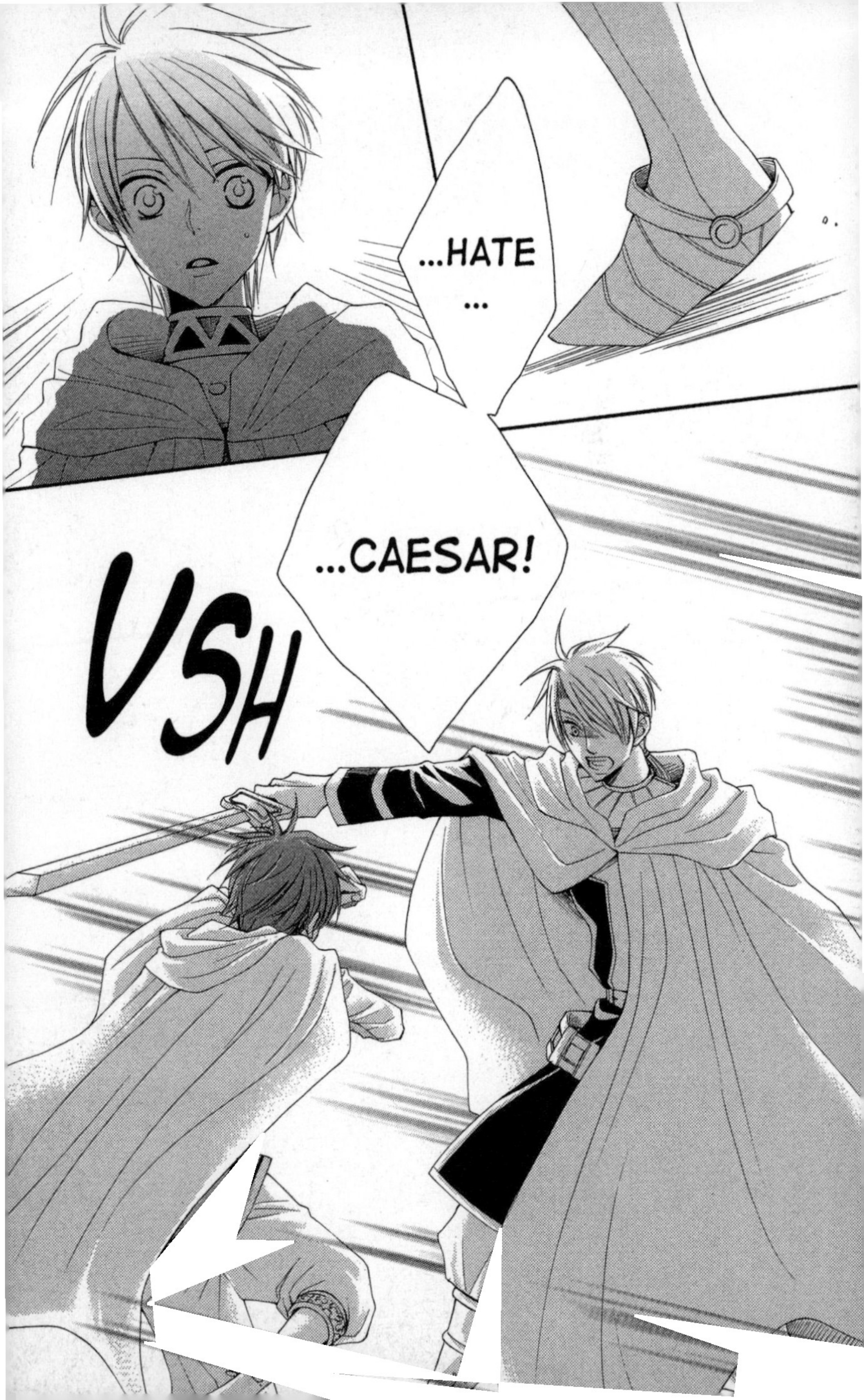
...HATE
...
...CAESAR!
VSH

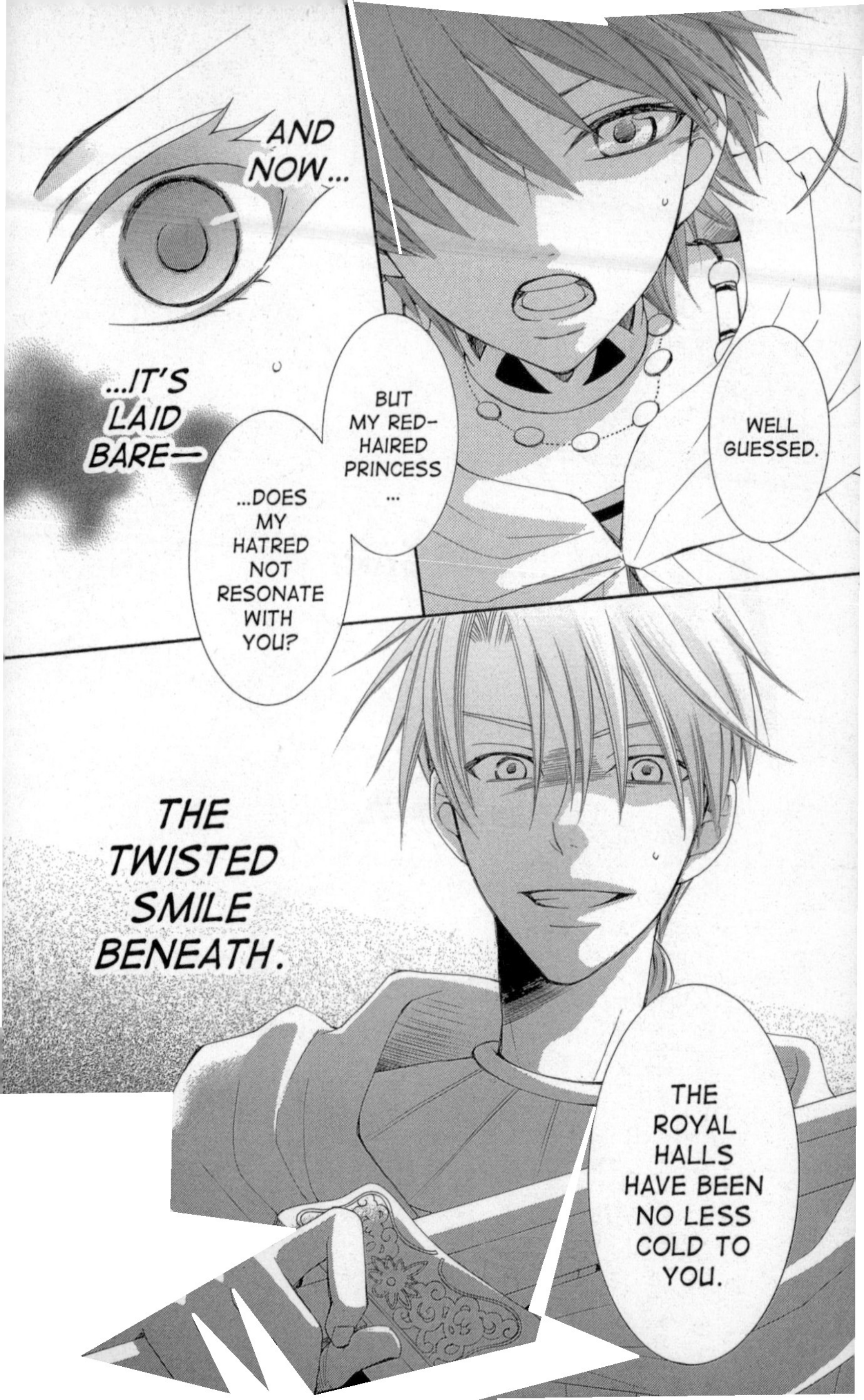
WELL GUESSED.
BUT MY RED-HAIRED PRINCESS...
...DOES MY HATRED NOT RESONATE WITH YOU?
AND NOW...
...IT'S LAID BARE—
THE ROYAL HALLS HAVE BEEN NO LESS COLD TO YOU.
THE TWISTED SMILE BENEATH.

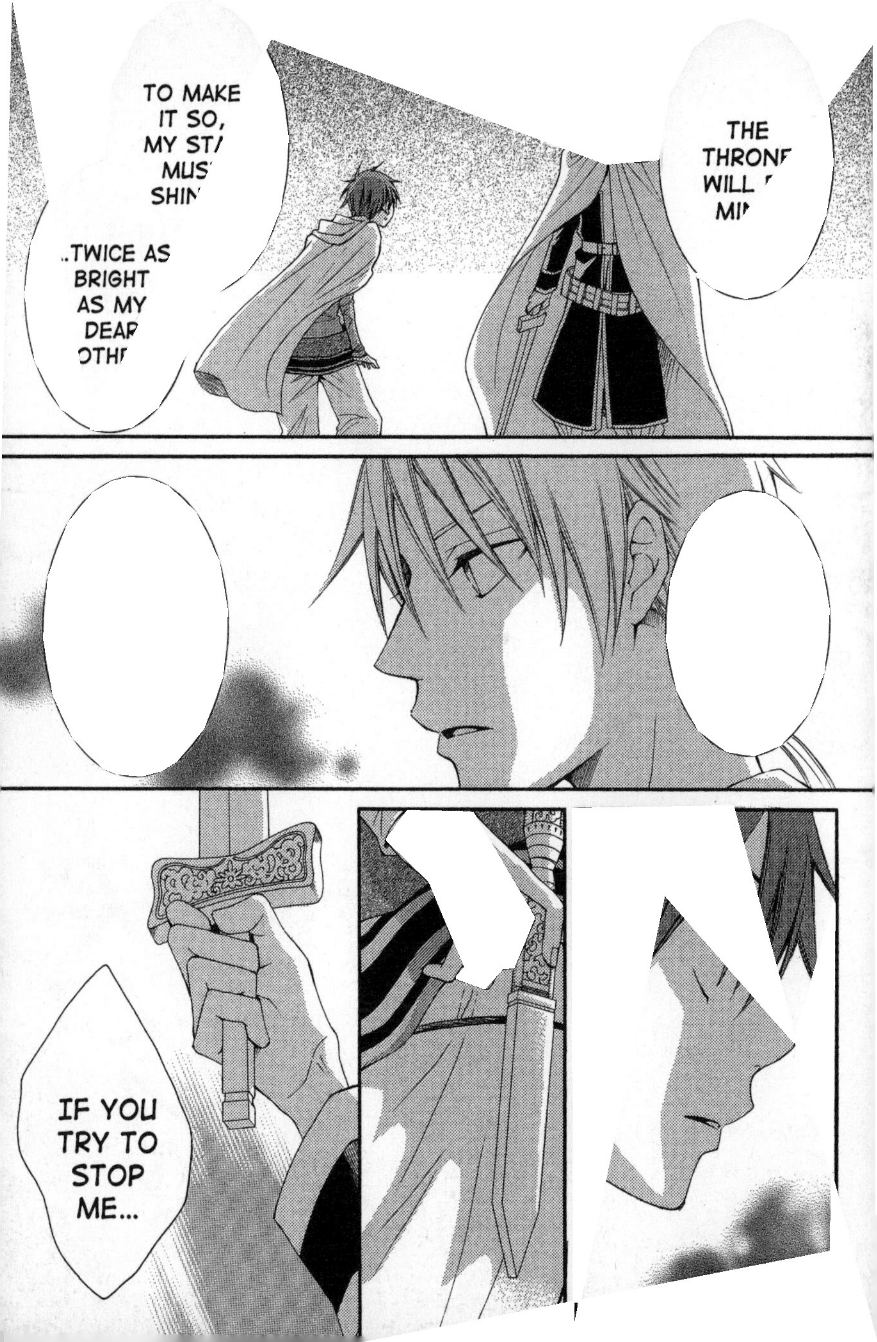
THE THRON WILL MI
TO MAKE IT SO, MY ST MUS SHI
..TWICE AS BRIGHT AS MY DEA OTH
IF YOU TRY TO STOP ME...

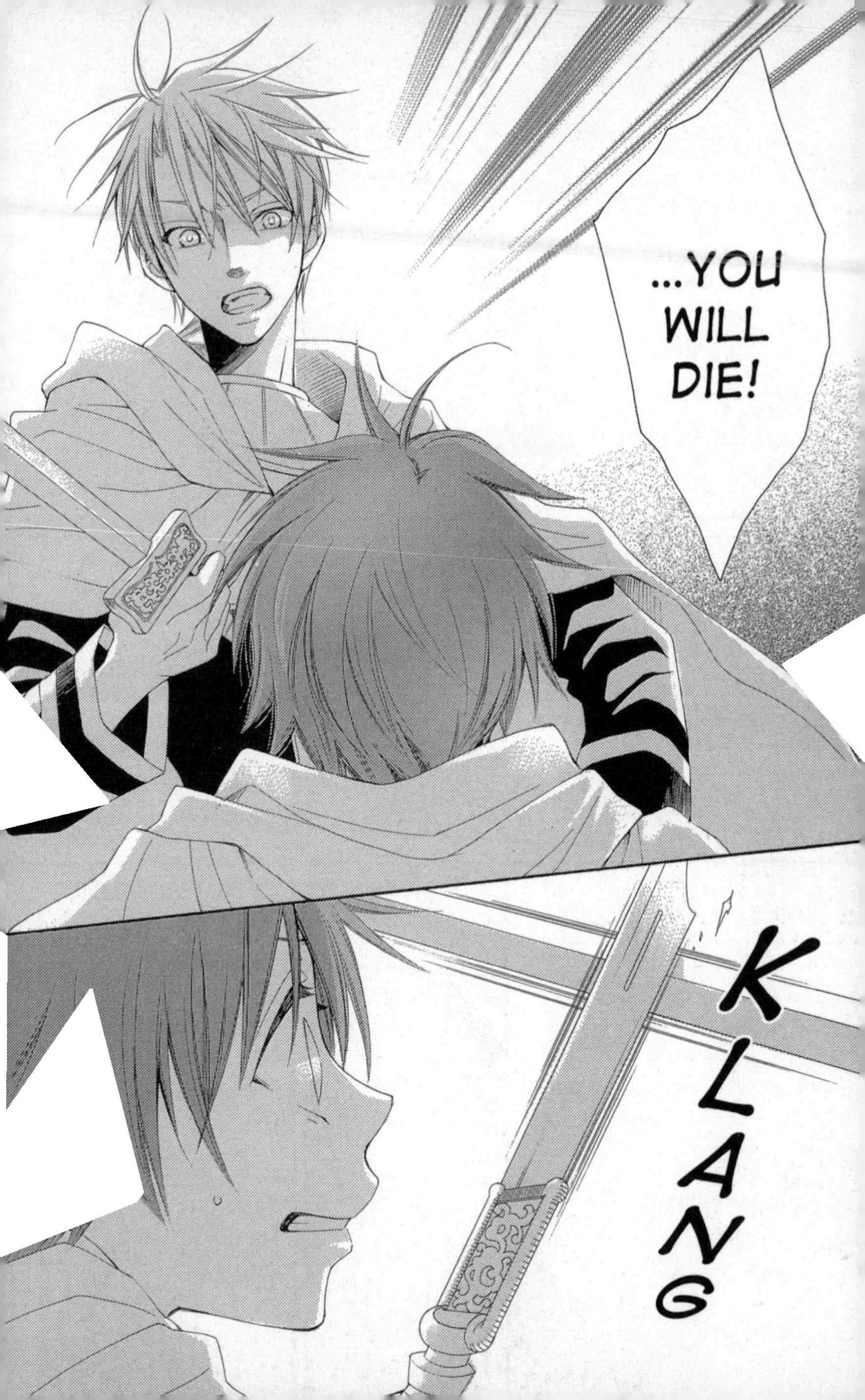
...YOU WILL DIE!
KLANG

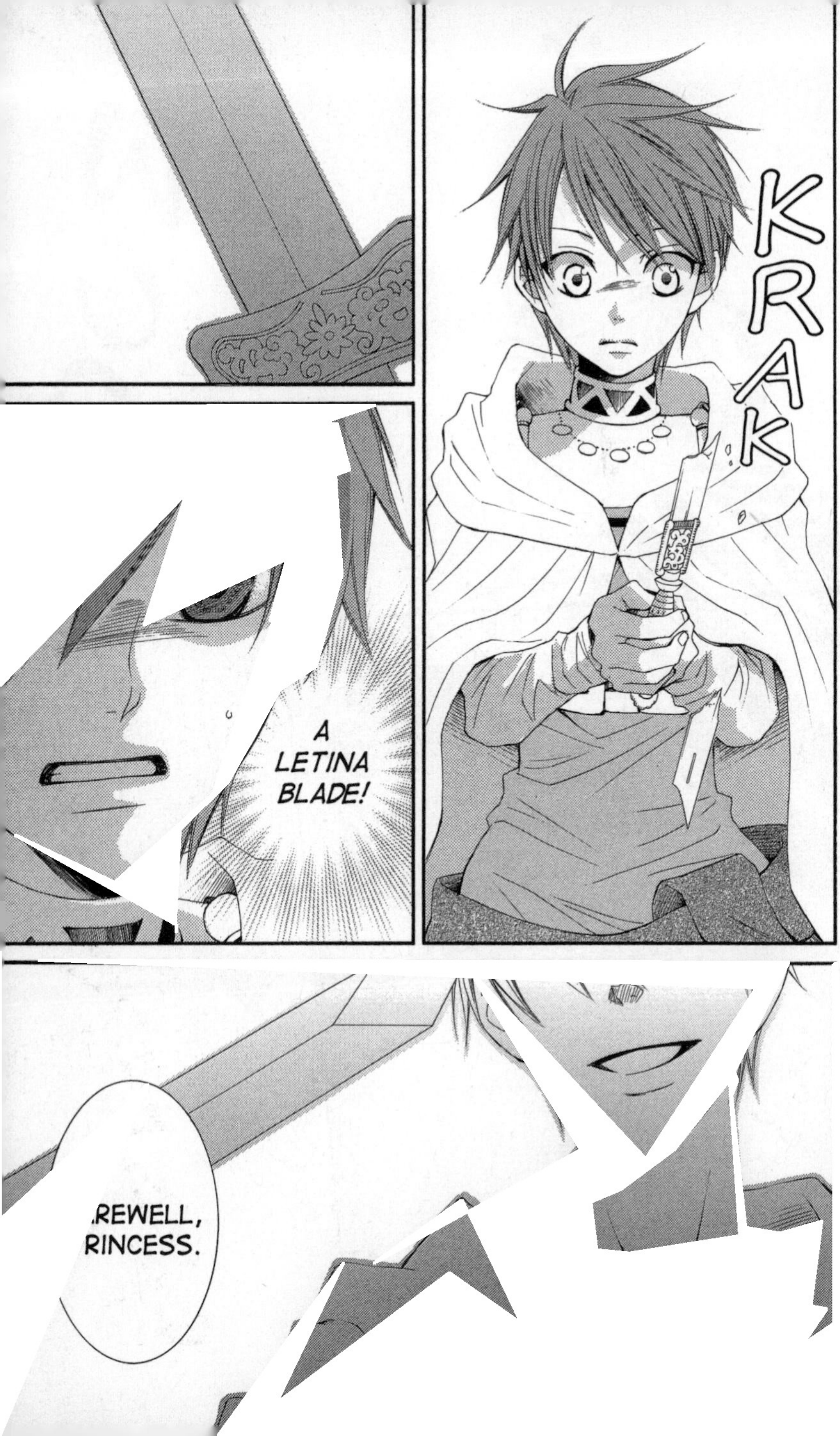
KRAK
A LETINA BLADE!
REWELL, RINCESS.

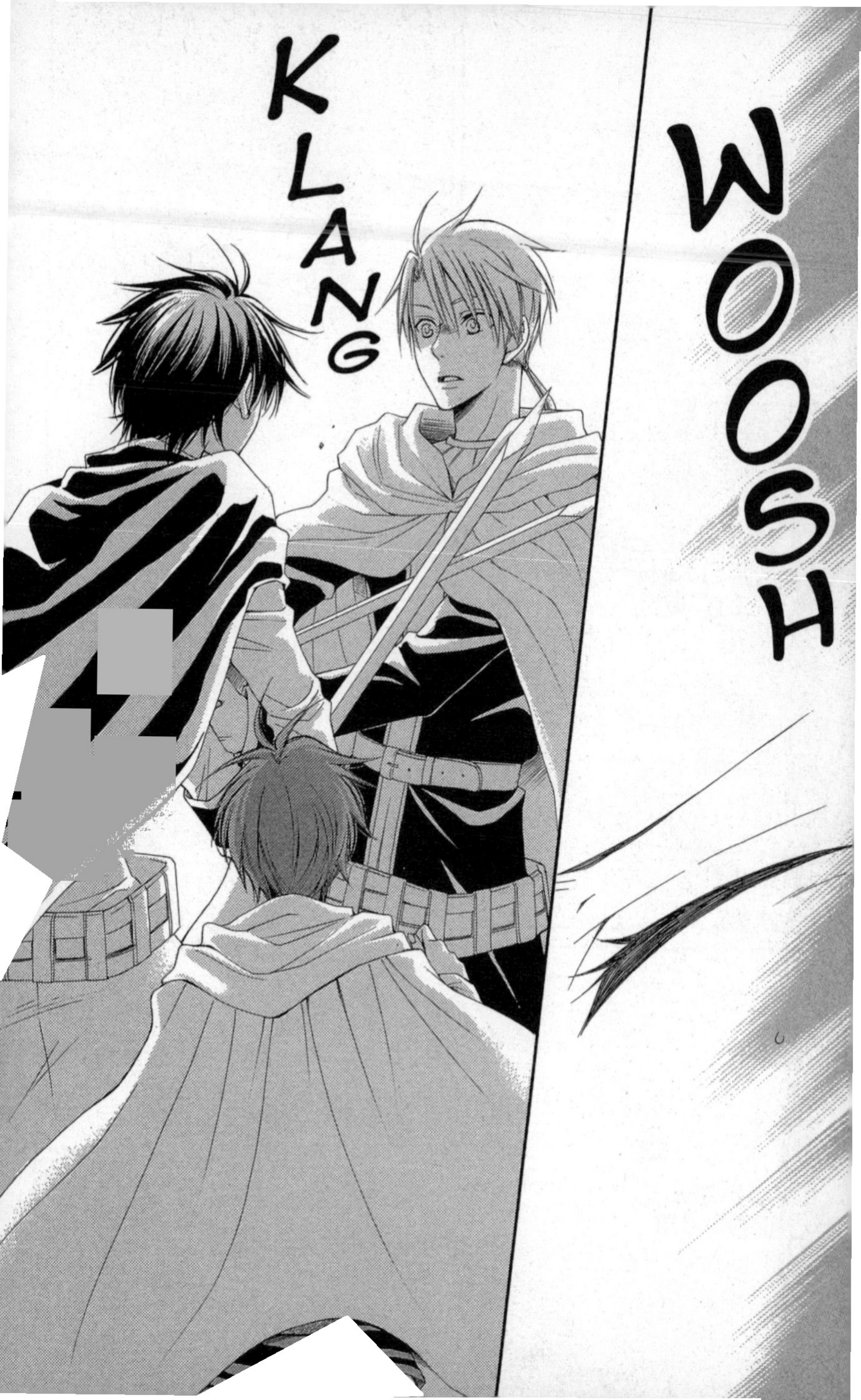
WOOSH
KLANG

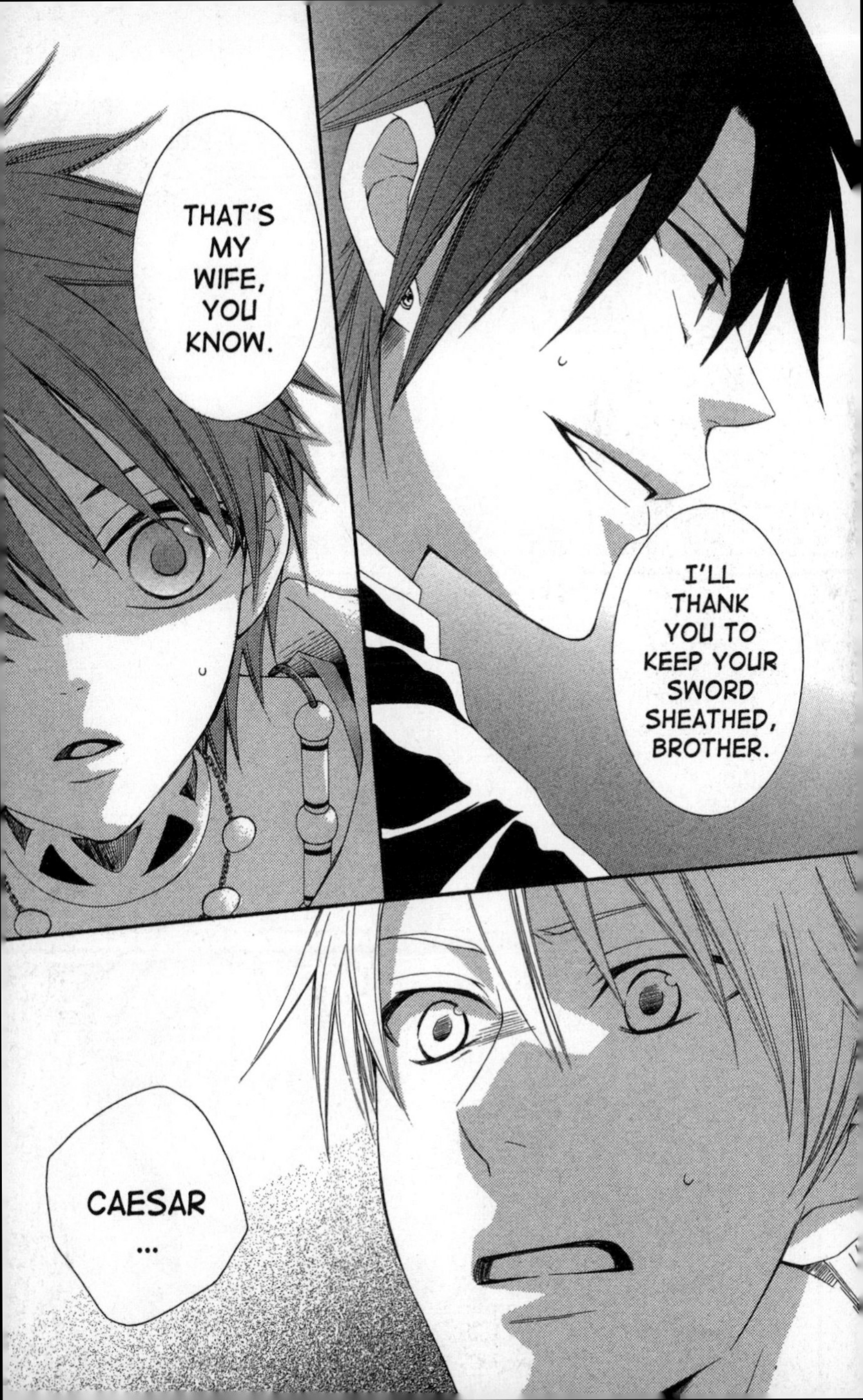
I'LL THANK YOU TO KEEP YOUR SWORD SHEATHED, BROTHER.
THAT'S MY WIFE, YOU KNOW.
CAESAR ...

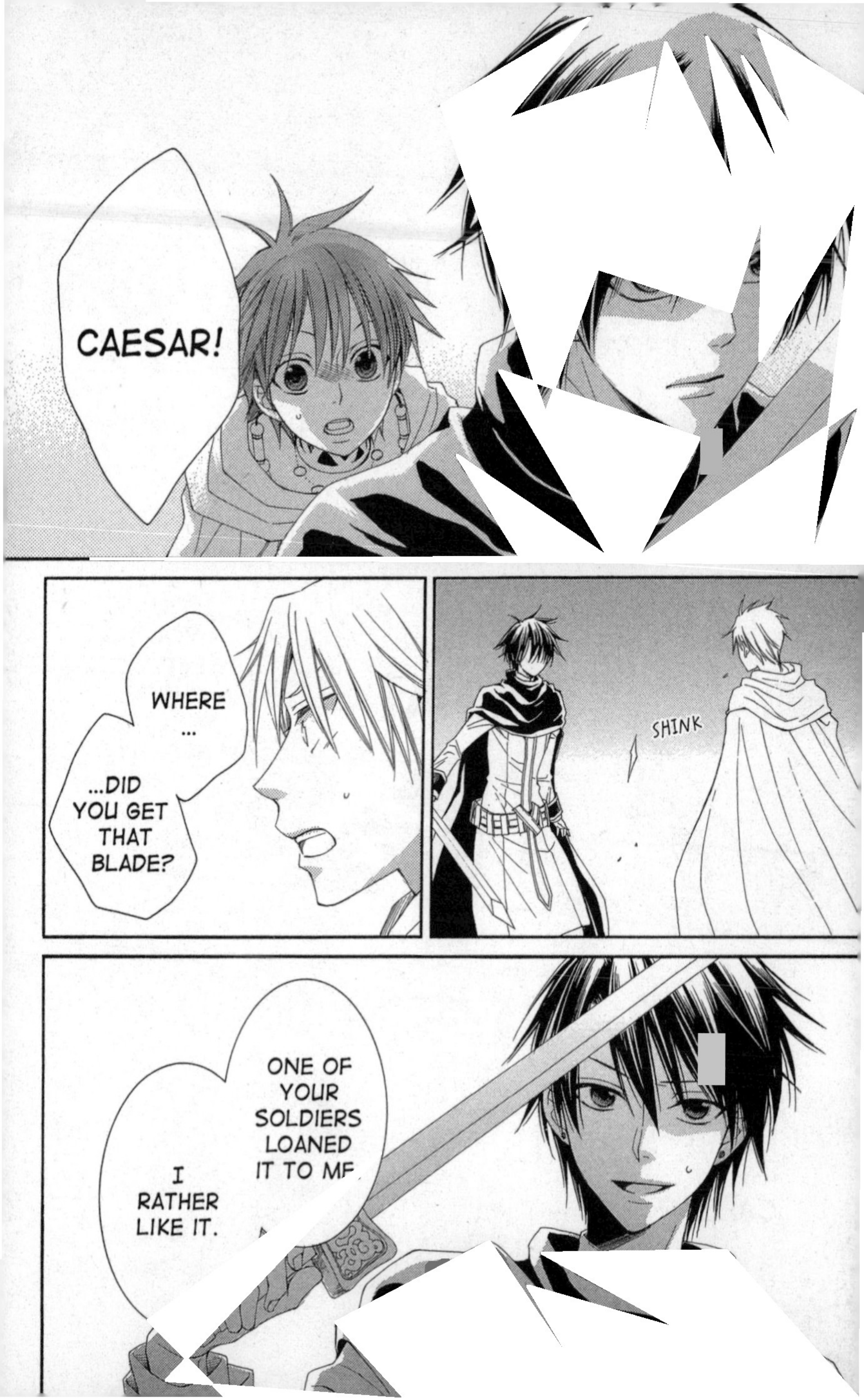
CAESAR!
SHINK
WHERE ... ...DID YOU GET THAT BLADE?
ONE OF YOUR SOLDIERS LOANED IT TO ME.
I RATHER LIKE IT.

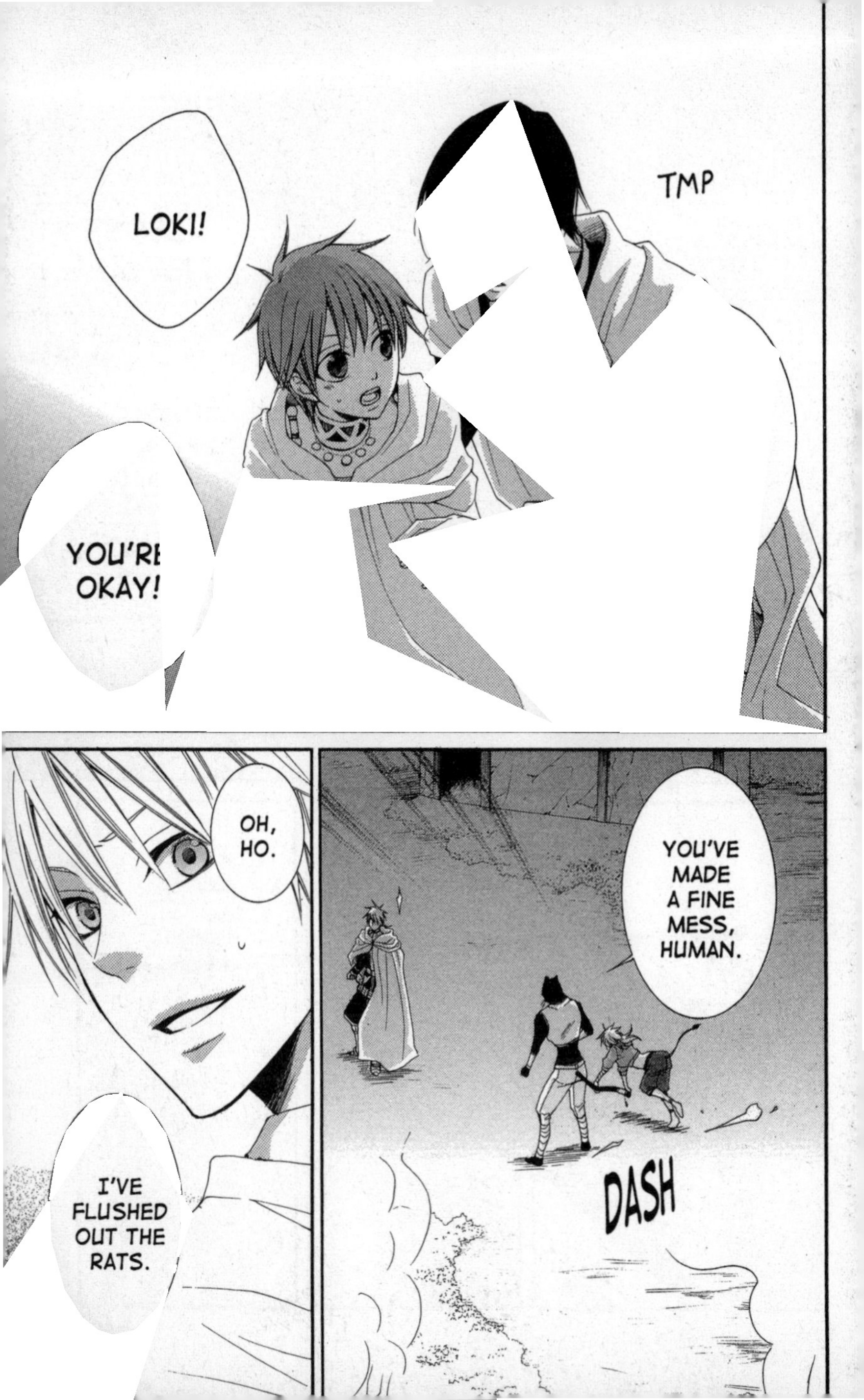
TMP
LOKI!
YOU'RE OKAY!
YOU'VE MADE A FINE MESS, HUMAN.
DASH
OH, HO.
I'VE FLUSHED OUT THE RATS.

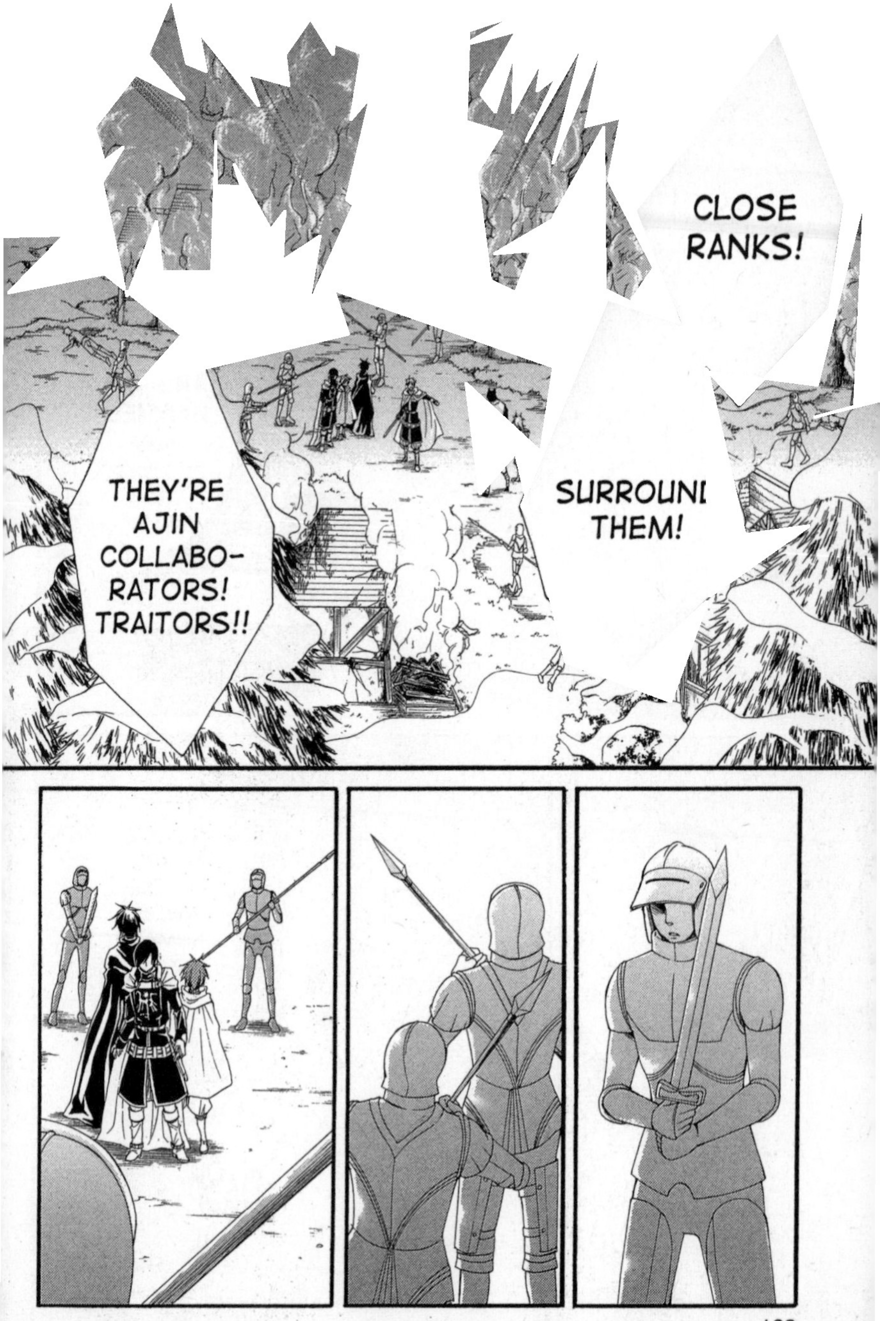
CLOSE RANKS!
SURROUND THEM!
THEY'RE AJIN COLLABO-RATORS! TRAITORS!!

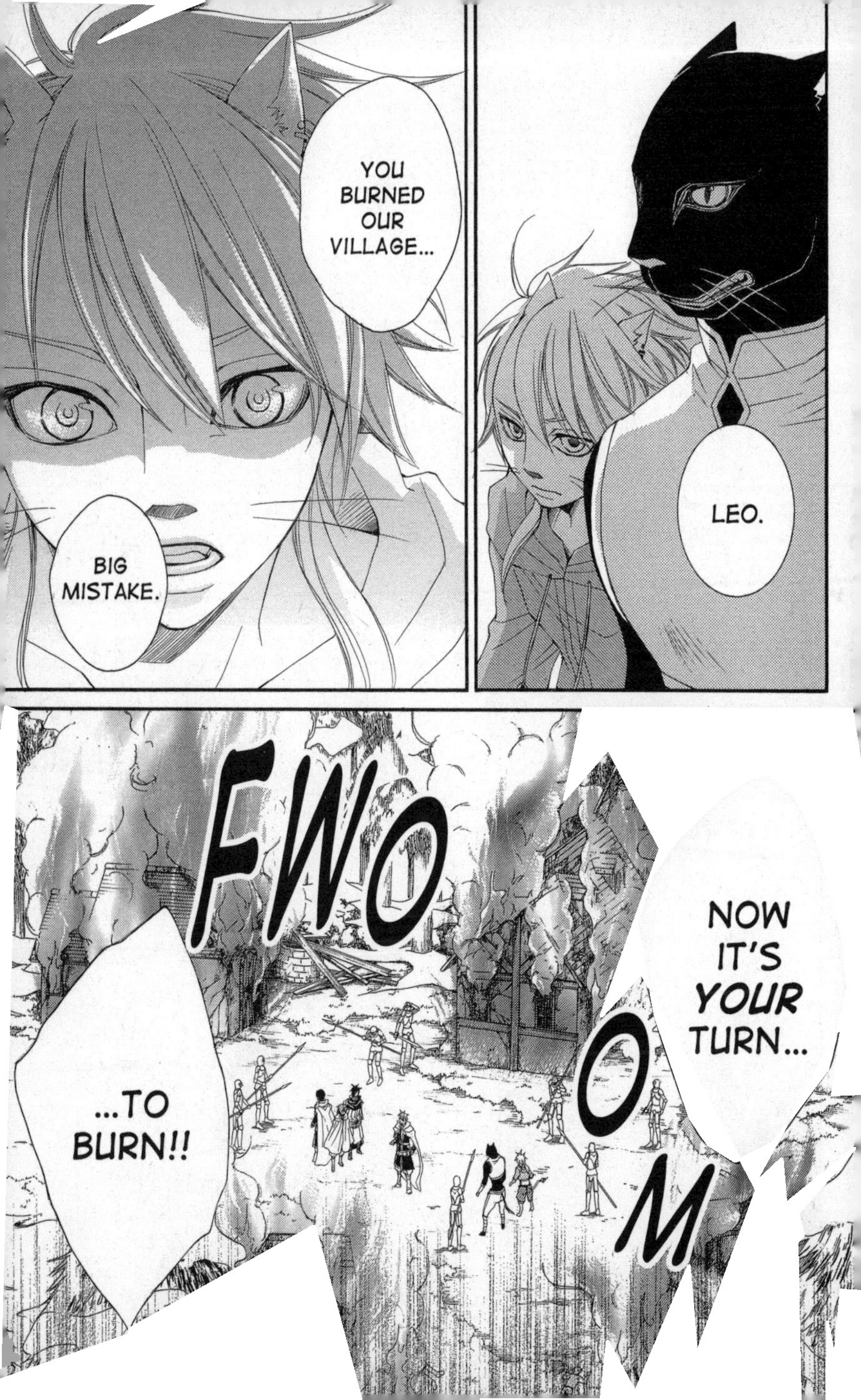
LEO.
YOU BURNED OUR VILLAGE...
BIG MISTAKE.
NOW IT'S *YOUR* TURN...
FWOOM
...TO BURN!!

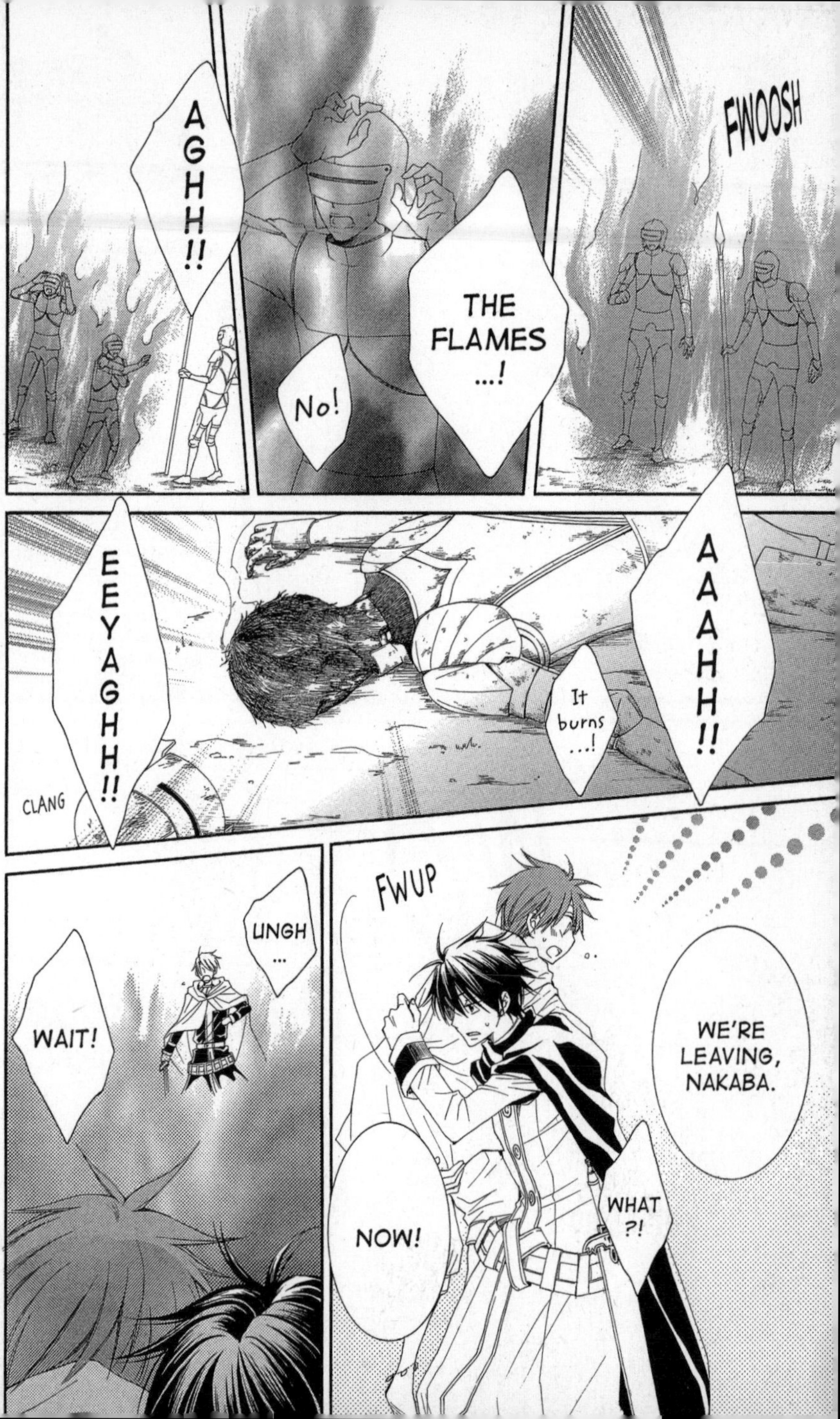
FWOOSH
THE FLAMES ...!
No!
AGHH!!
AAAHH!!
It burns ...!
EEYAGHH!!
CLANG
FWUP
WE'RE LEAVING, NAKABA.
WHAT ?!
NOW!
UNGH ...
WAIT!

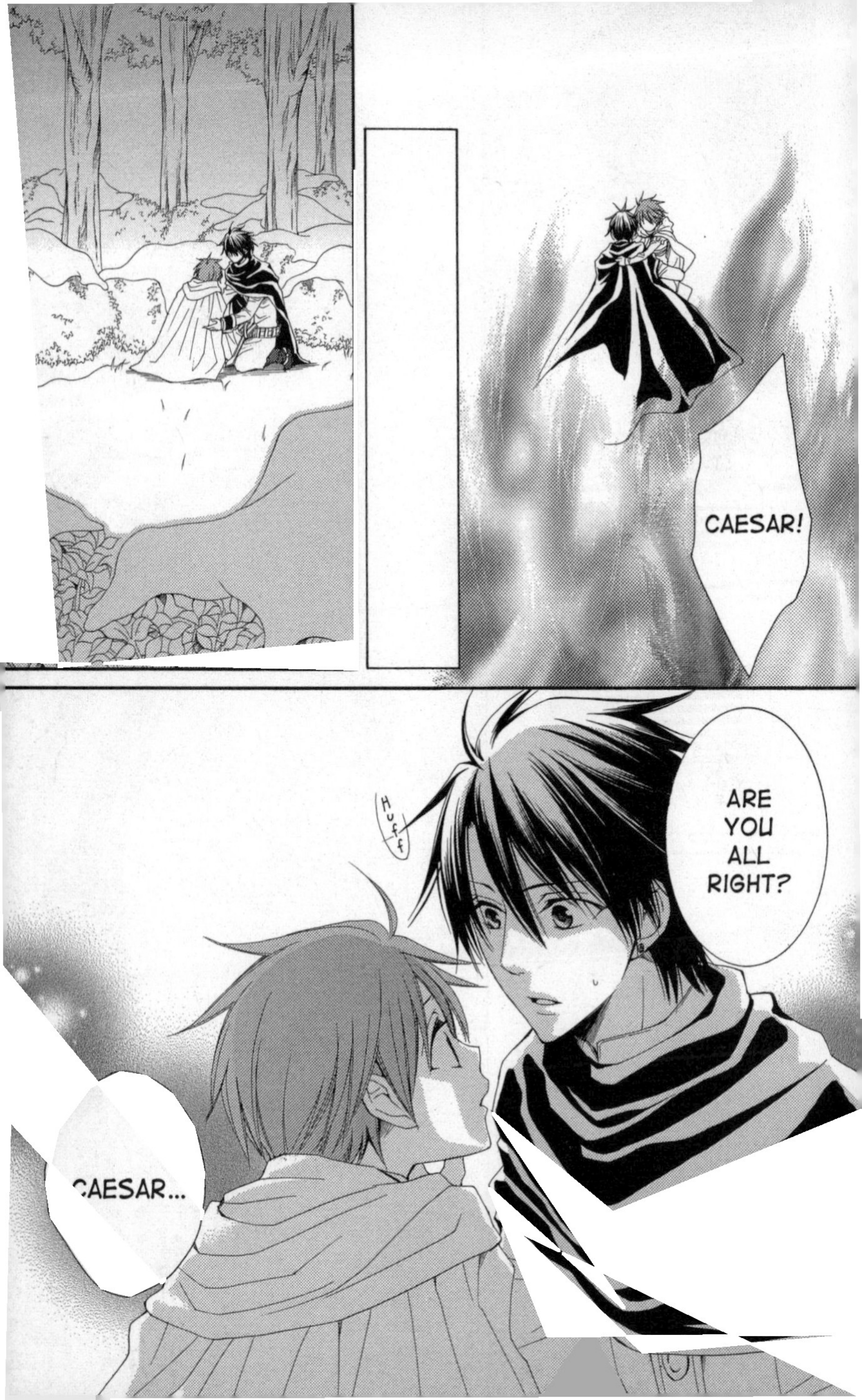
CAESAR!
ARE YOU ALL RIGHT?
Huff
CAESAR...

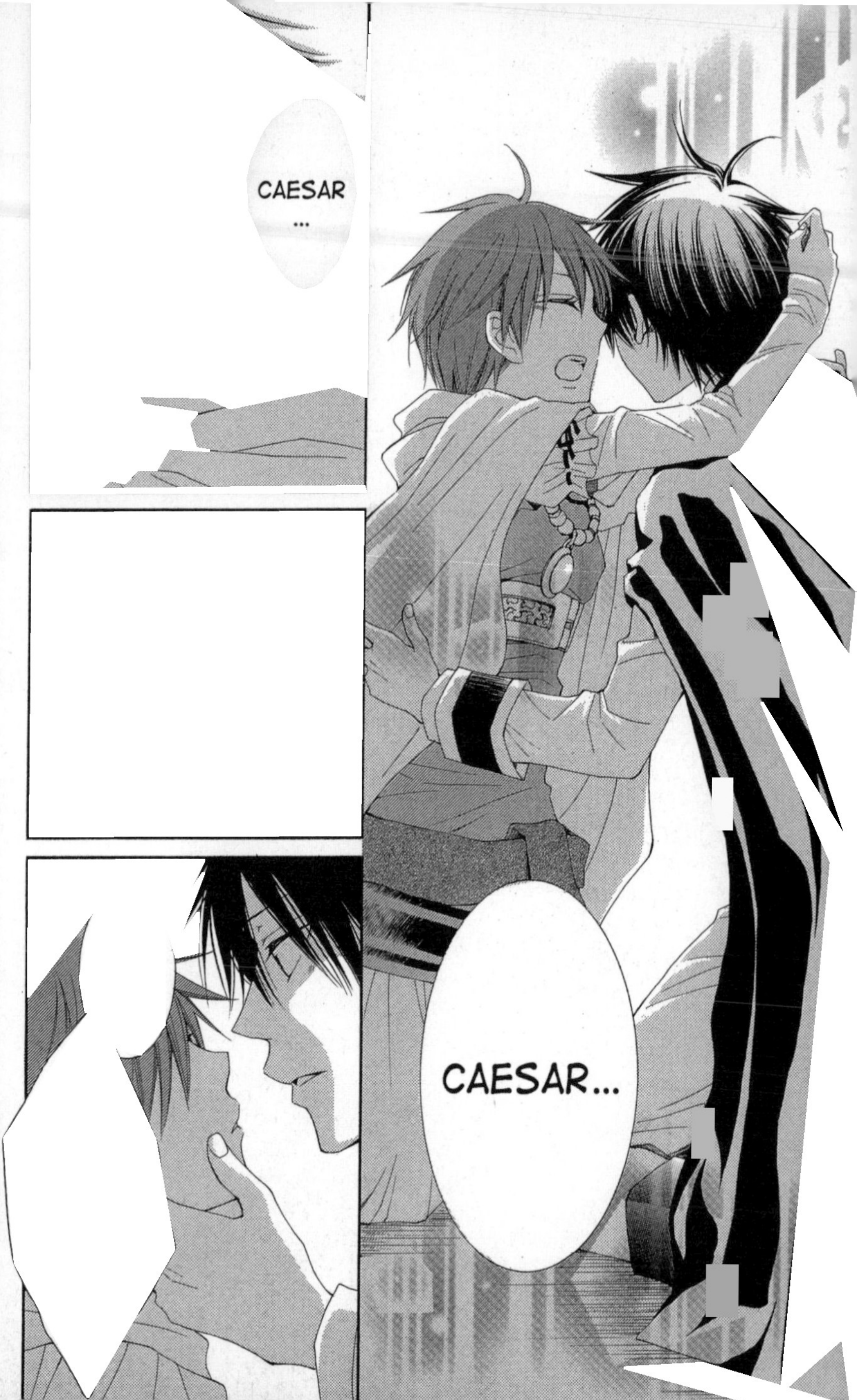

CAESAR...
CAESAR ...

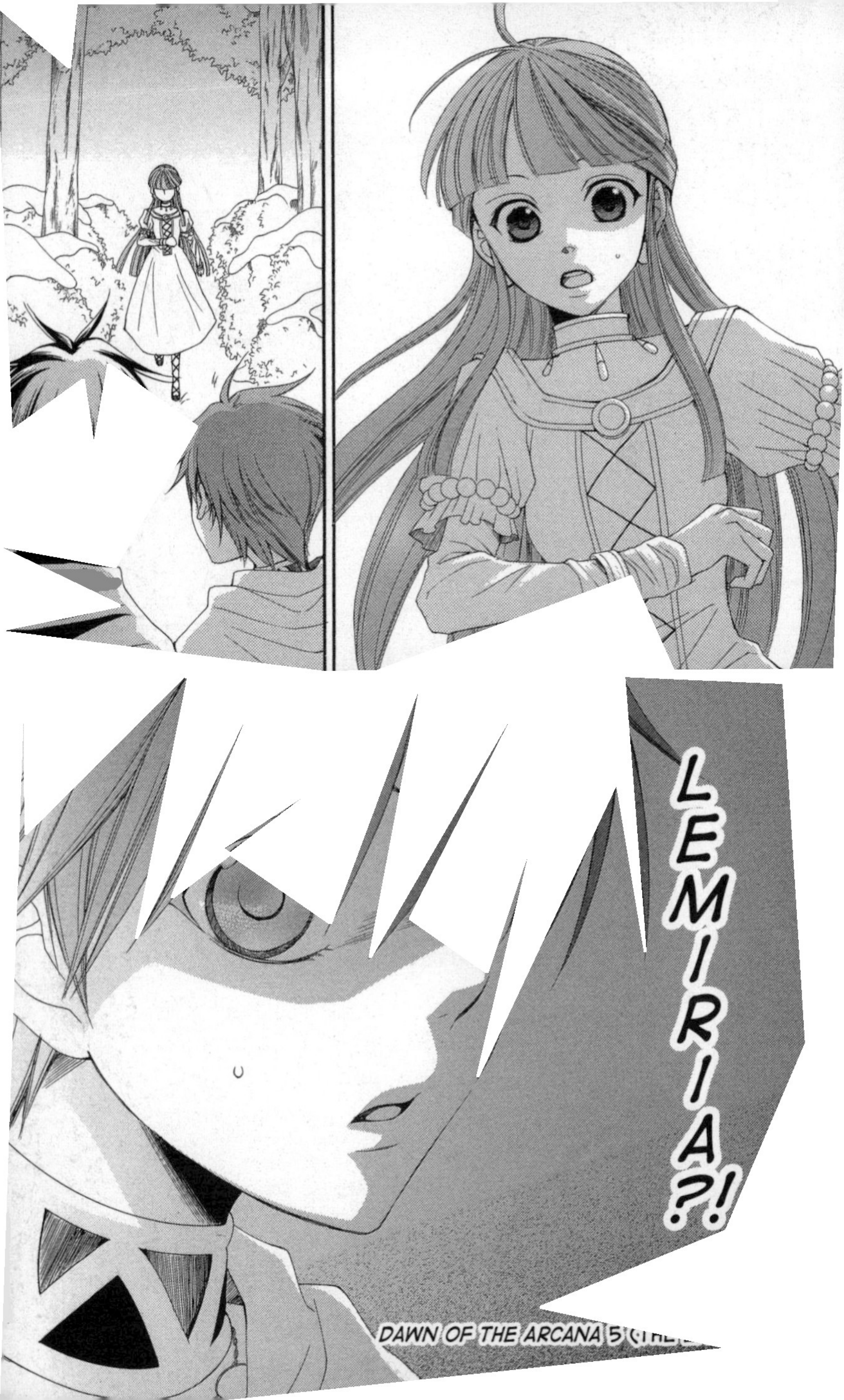
LEMIRIA?!
DAWN OF THE ARCANA 5 (THE

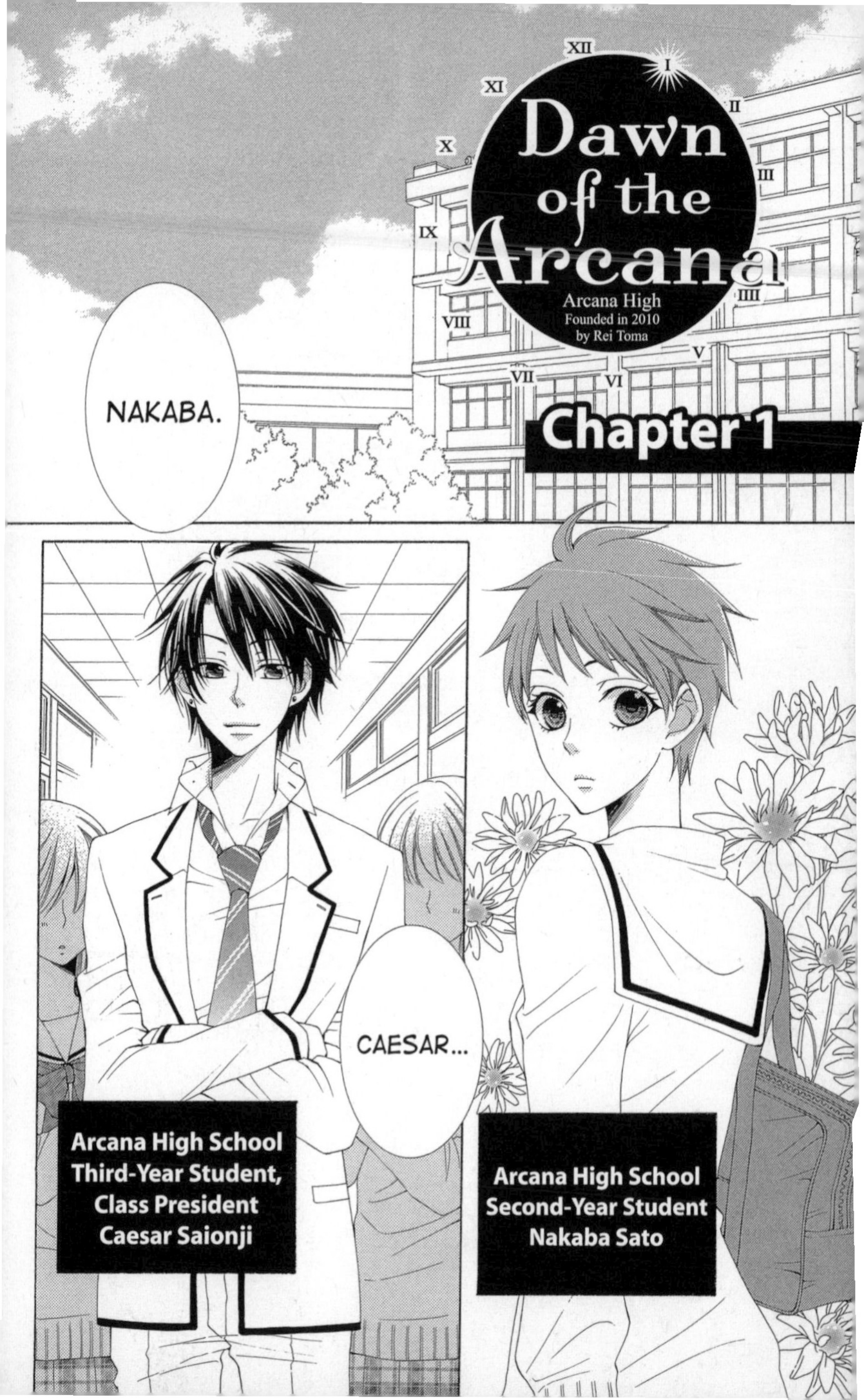
Dawn of the Arcana
XII I II III IIII V VI VII VIII IX X XI
Arcana High
Founded in 2010
by Rei Toma
Chapter 1
NAKABA.
Arcana High School
Second-Year Student
Nakaba Sato
CAESAR...
Arcana High School
Third-Year Student,
Class President
Caesar Saionji

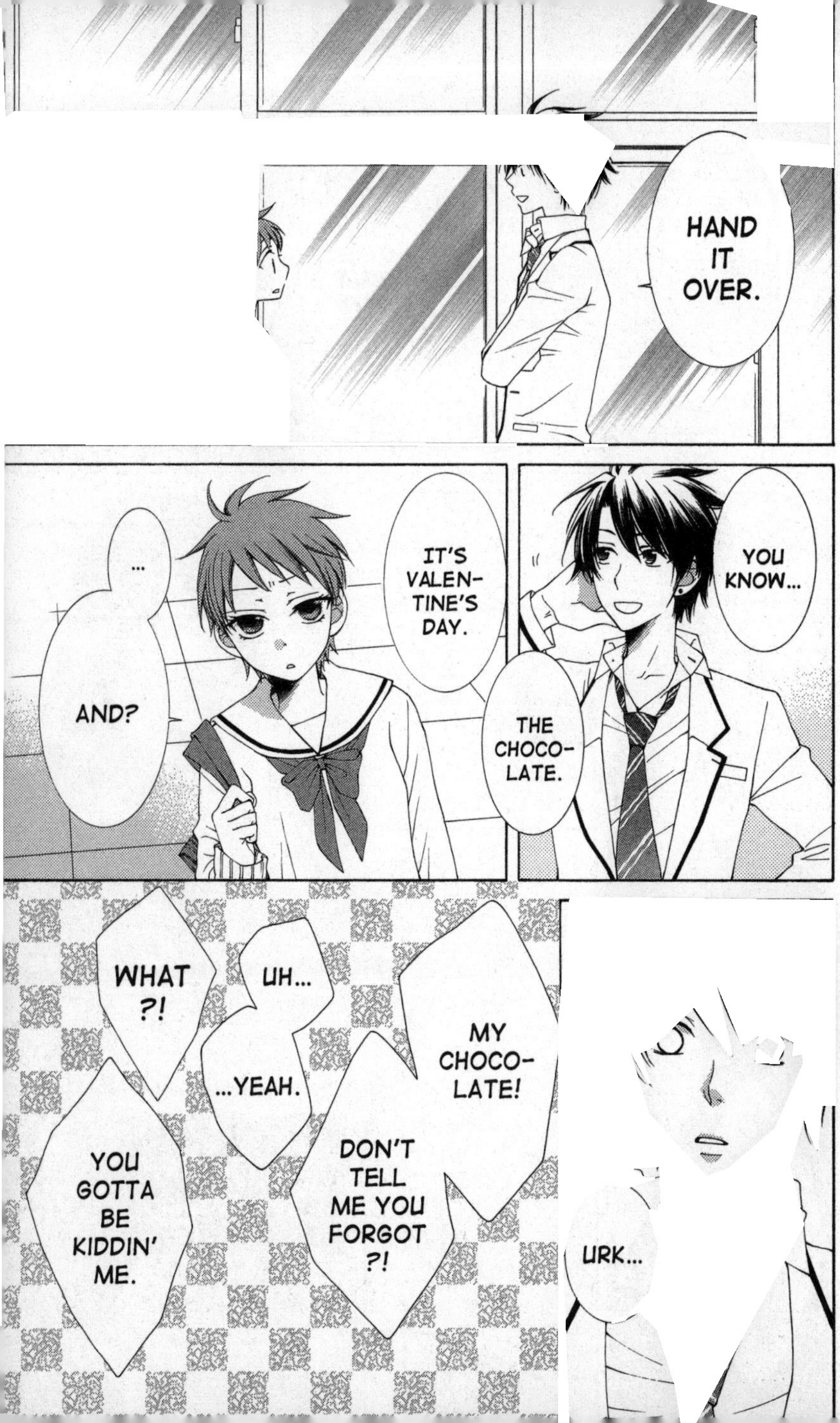
HAND IT OVER.
YOU KNOW...
THE CHOCO-LATE.
IT'S VALEN-TINE'S DAY.
...
AND?
URK...
MY CHOCO-LATE!
DON'T TELL ME YOU FORGOT?!
UH...
...YEAH.
WHAT?!
YOU GOTTA BE KIDDIN' ME.

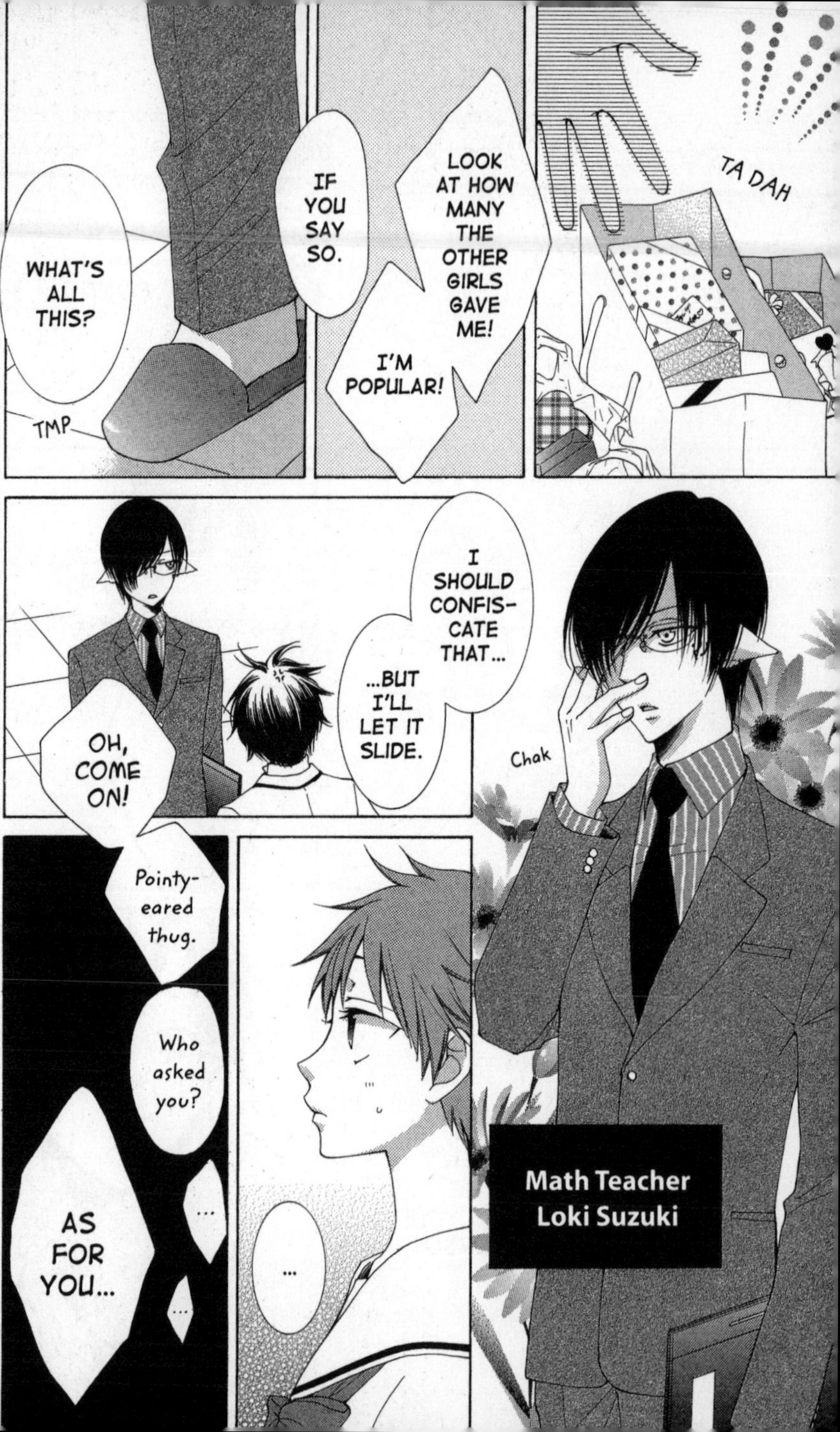
TA DAH
LOOK AT HOW MANY THE OTHER GIRLS GAVE ME!
I'M POPULAR!
IF YOU SAY SO.
WHAT'S ALL THIS?
TMP
Chak
Math Teacher Loki Suzuki
I SHOULD CONFIS-CATE THAT...
...BUT I'LL LET IT SLIDE.
OH, COME ON!
...
Pointy-eared thug.
Who asked you?
...
...
AS FOR YOU...

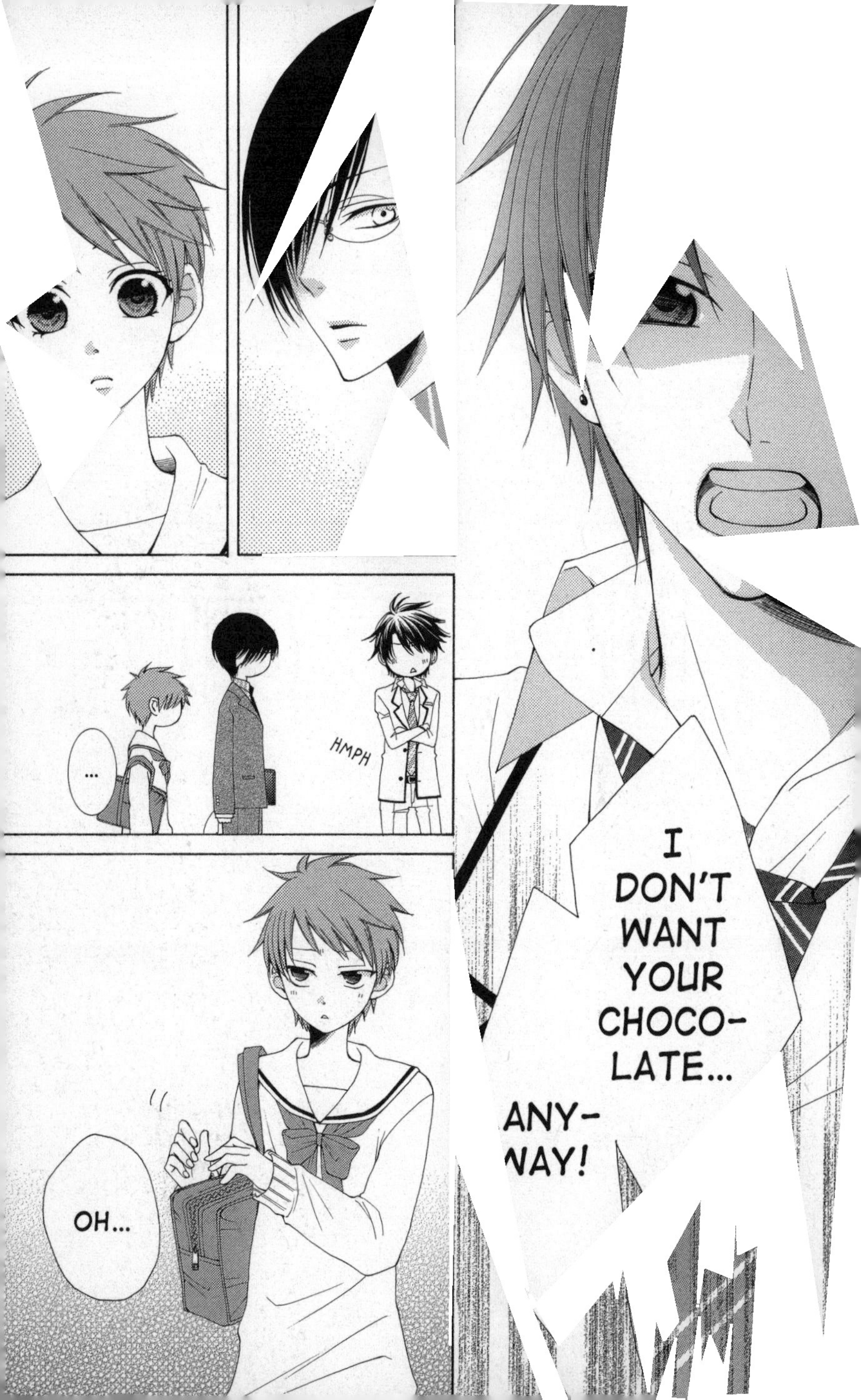
I DON'T WANT YOUR CHOCOLATE...
ANYWAY!
HMPH
...
OH...

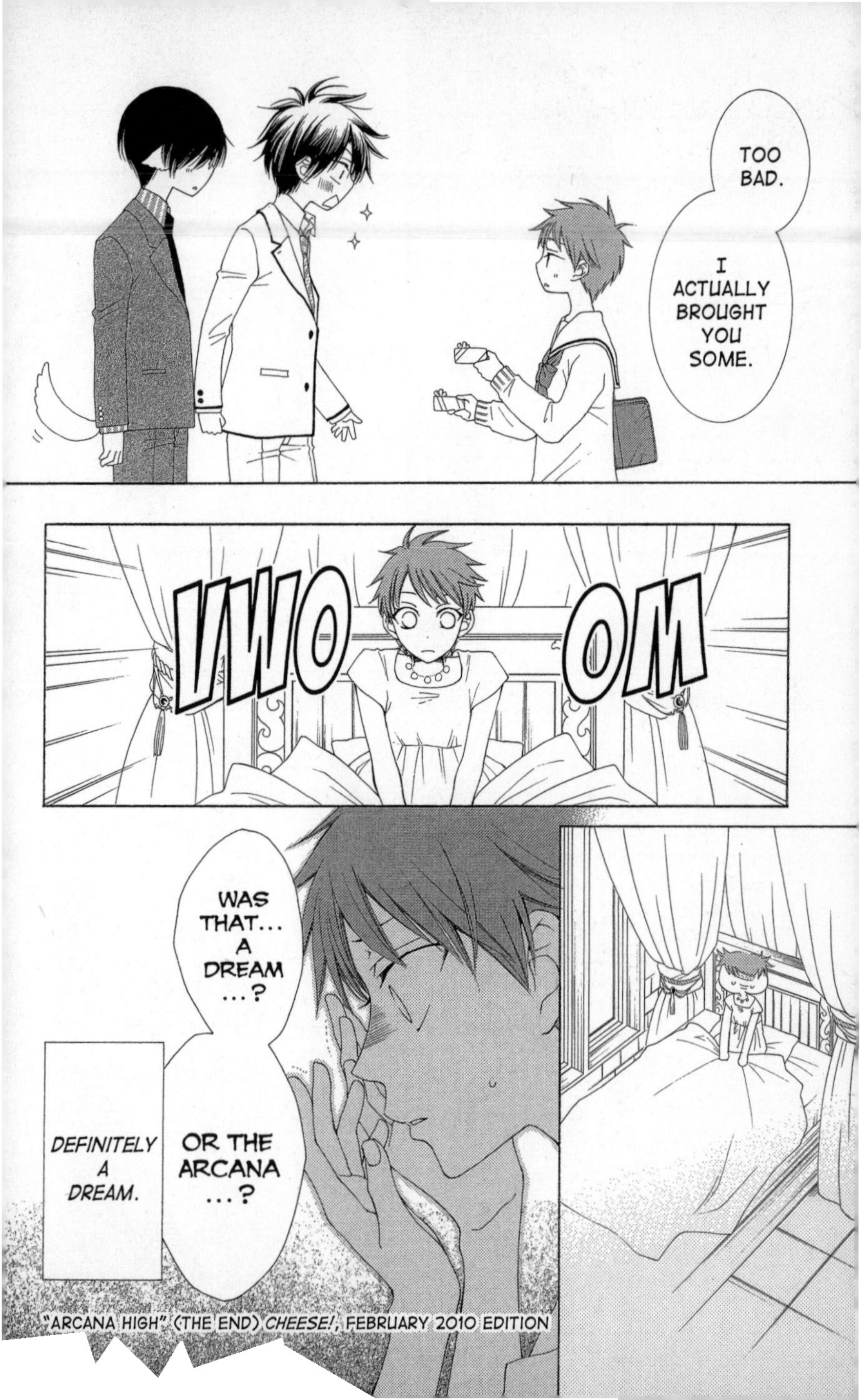
TOO BAD.
I ACTUALLY BROUGHT YOU SOME.
VWO OM
WAS THAT... A DREAM ...?
OR THE ARCANA ...?
DEFINITELY A DREAM.

"ARCANA HIGH" (THE END) *CHEESE!*, FEBRUARY 2010 EDITION

Chapter 2

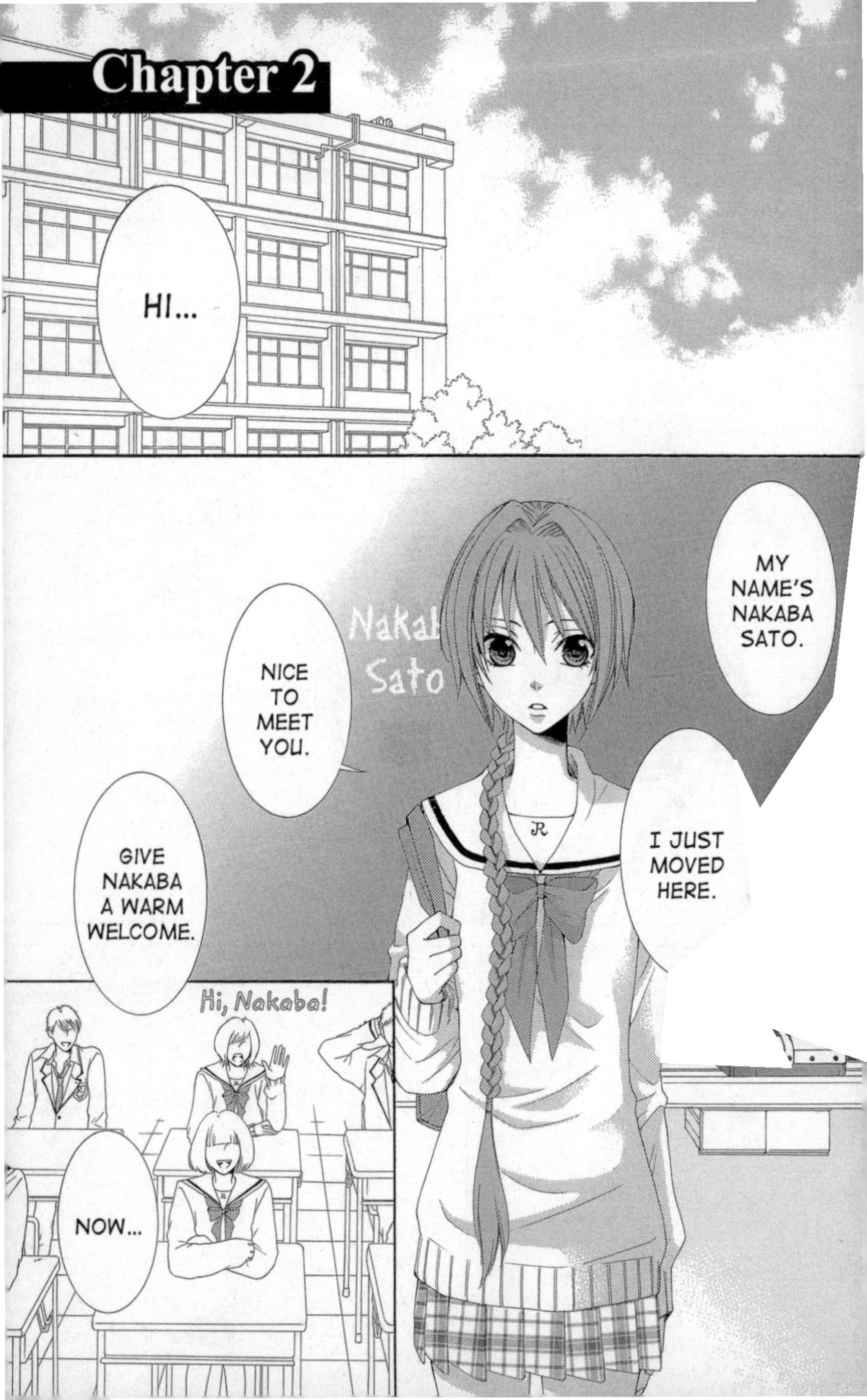
HI...
MY NAME'S NAKABA SATO.
Nakaba Sato
NICE TO MEET YOU.
I JUST MOVED HERE.
GIVE NAKABA A WARM WELCOME.
Hi, Nakaba!
NOW...

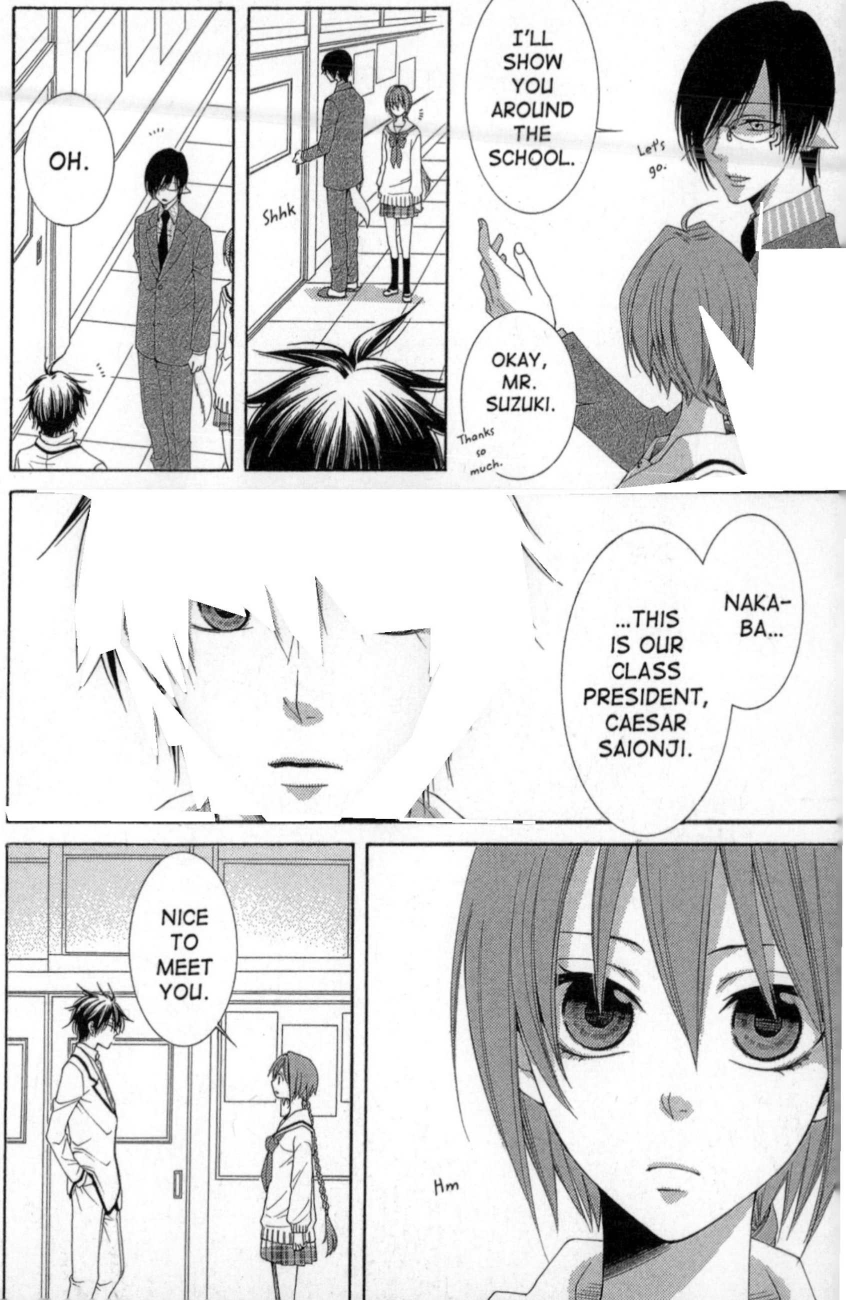
I'LL SHOW YOU AROUND THE SCHOOL.
Let's go.
OKAY, MR. SUZUKI.
Thanks so much.
Shhk
OH.
NAKA-BA...
...THIS IS OUR CLASS PRESIDENT, CAESAR SAIONJI.
Hm
NICE TO MEET YOU.

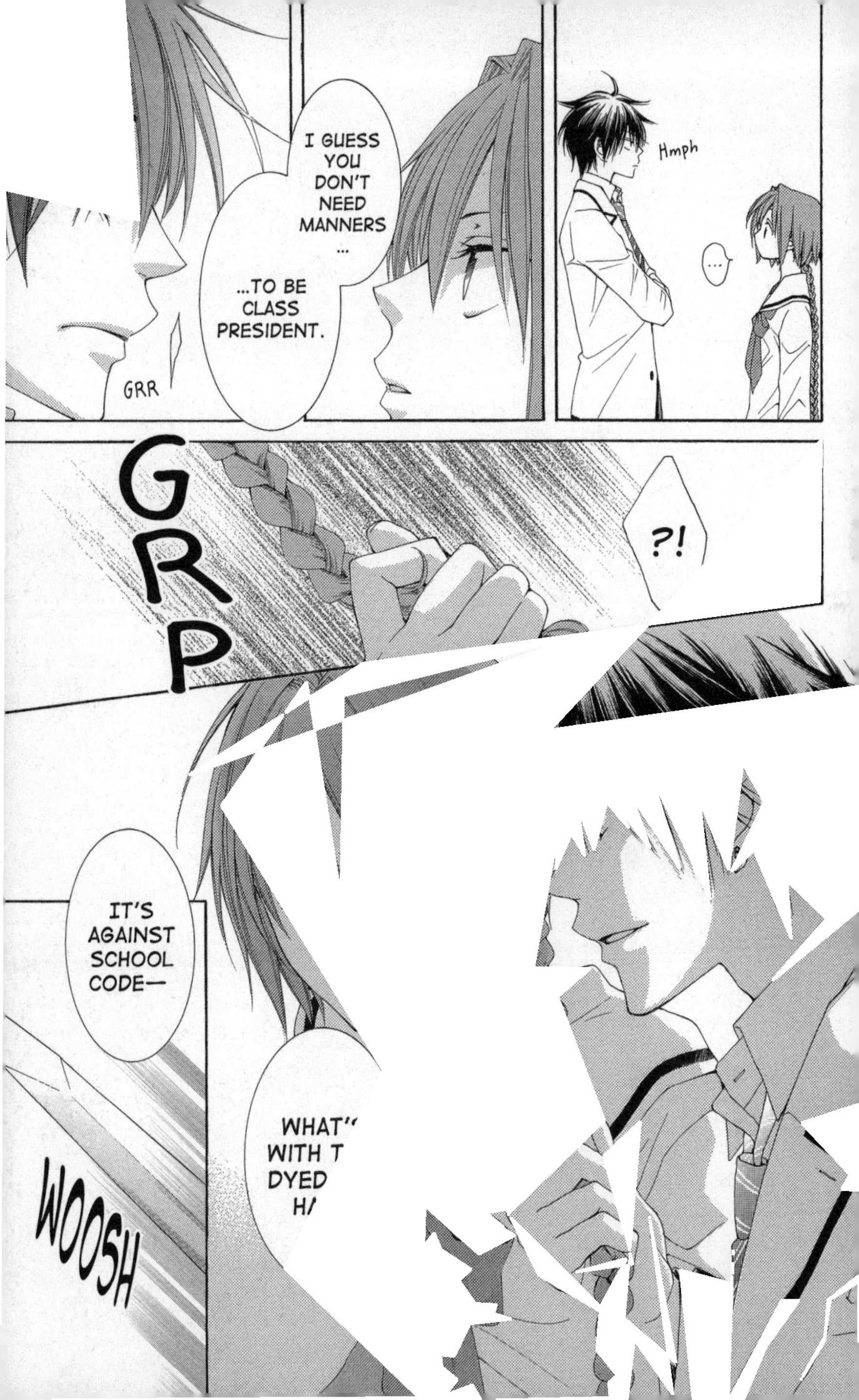
Hmph
...
I GUESS YOU DON'T NEED MANNERS...
...TO BE CLASS PRESIDENT.
GRR
?!
GRP
WHAT'
WITH T
DYED
HA
IT'S AGAINST SCHOOL CODE—
WOOSH

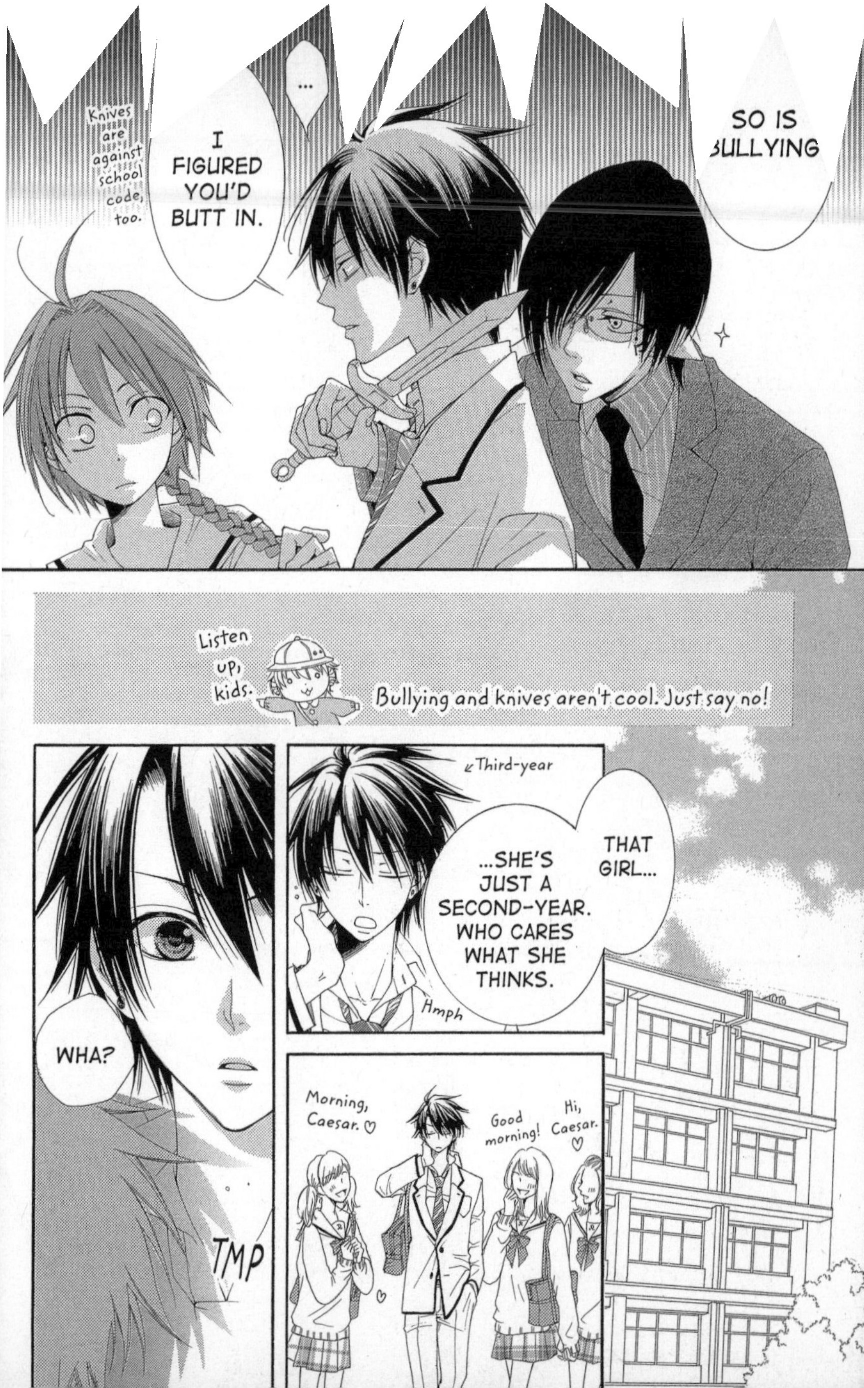
SO IS BULLYING
...
I FIGURED YOU'D BUTT IN.
Knives are against school code, too.
Listen up, kids.
Bullying and knives aren't cool. Just say no!
Third-year
THAT GIRL...
...SHE'S JUST A SECOND-YEAR. WHO CARES WHAT SHE THINKS.
Hmph
Hi, Caesar.
Good morning!
Morning, Caesar.
WHA?
TMP

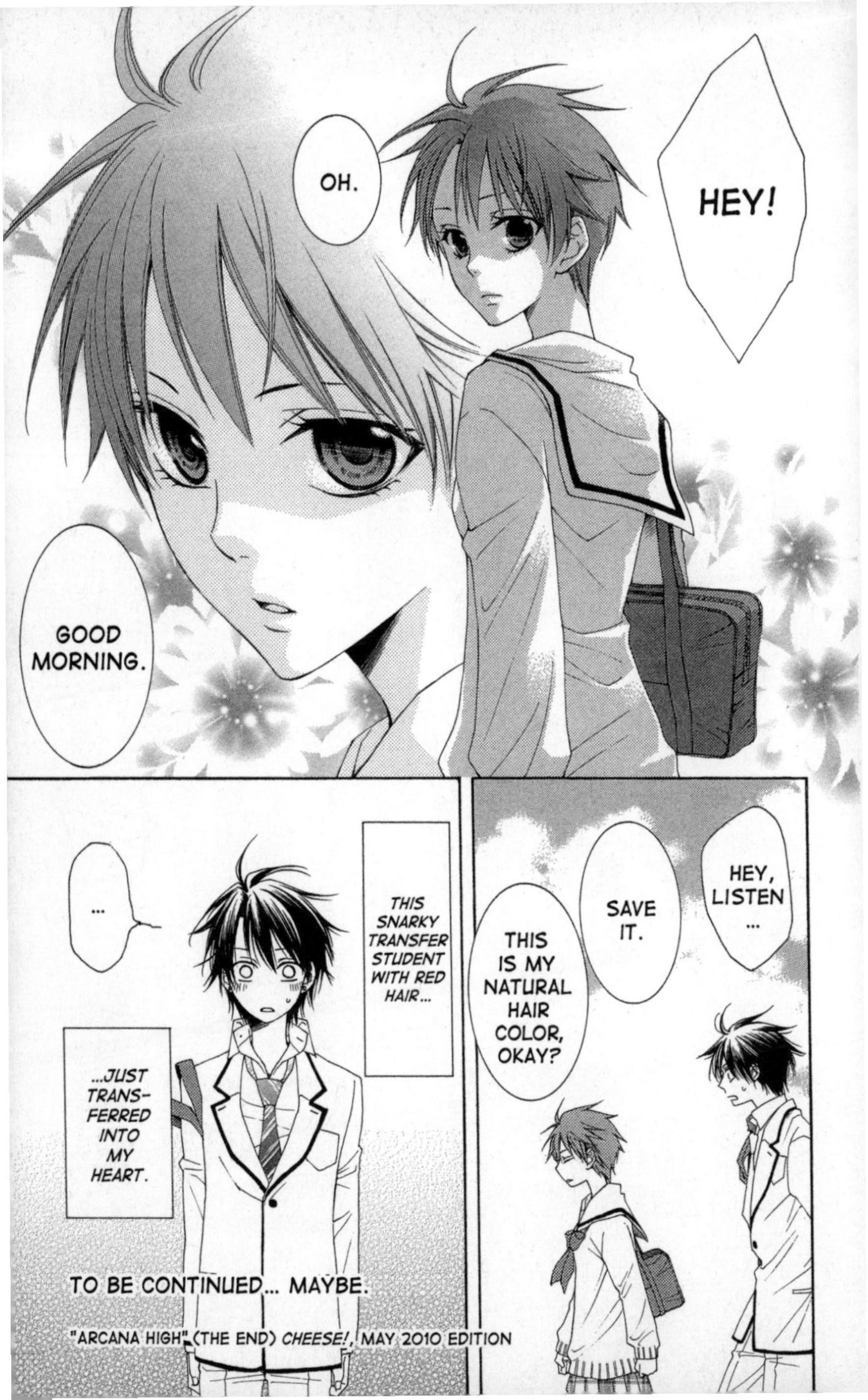
HEY!
OH.
GOOD MORNING.
HEY, LISTEN ...
SAVE IT.
THIS IS MY NATURAL HAIR COLOR, OKAY?
THIS SNARKY TRANSFER STUDENT WITH RED HAIR...
...
...JUST TRANSFERRED INTO MY HEART.
TO BE CONTINUED... MAYBE.
"ARCANA HIGH" (THE END) CHEESE!, MAY 2010 EDITION

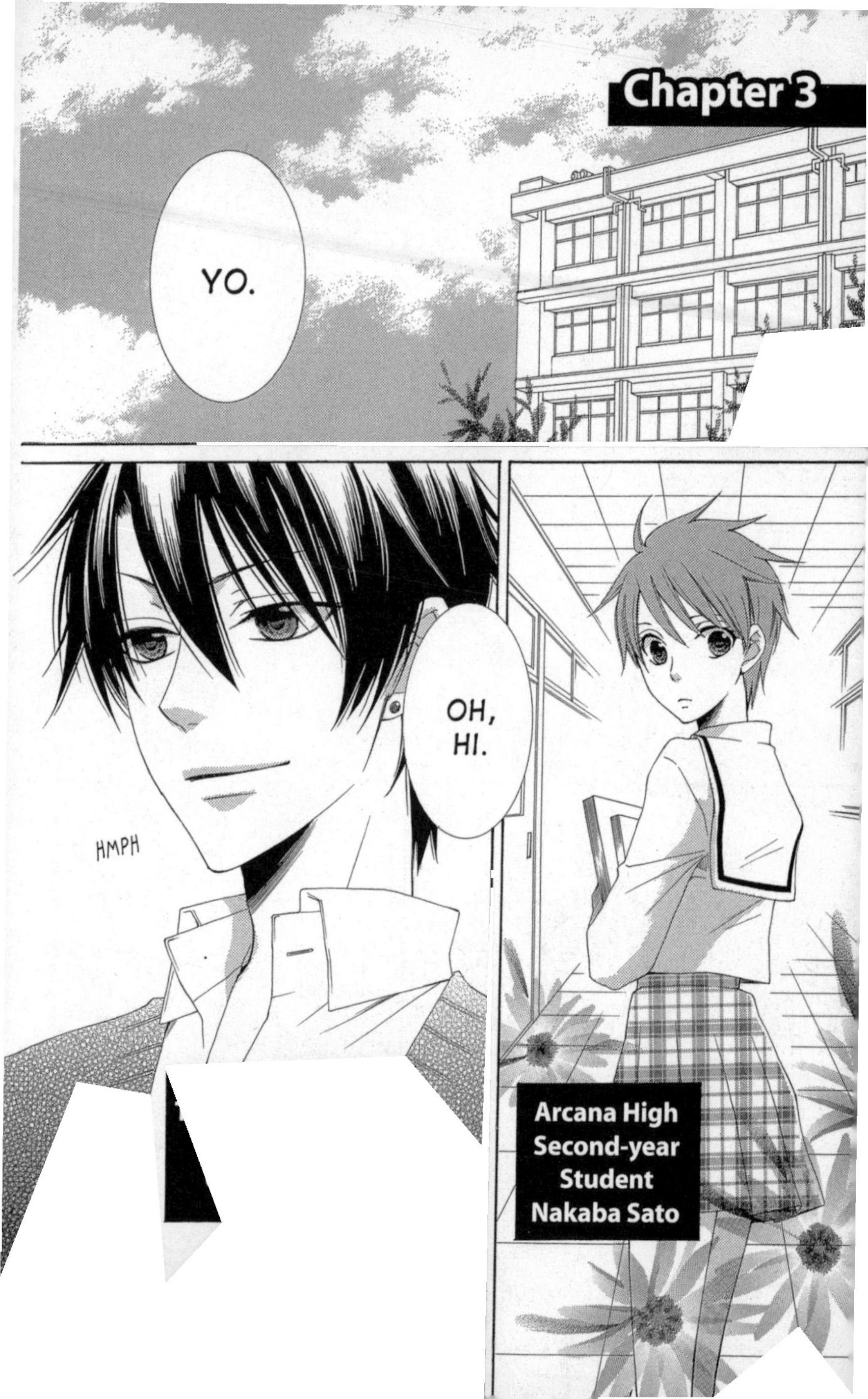
Chapter 3
YO.
Arcana High
Second-year
Student
Nakaba Sato
OH, HI.
HMPH

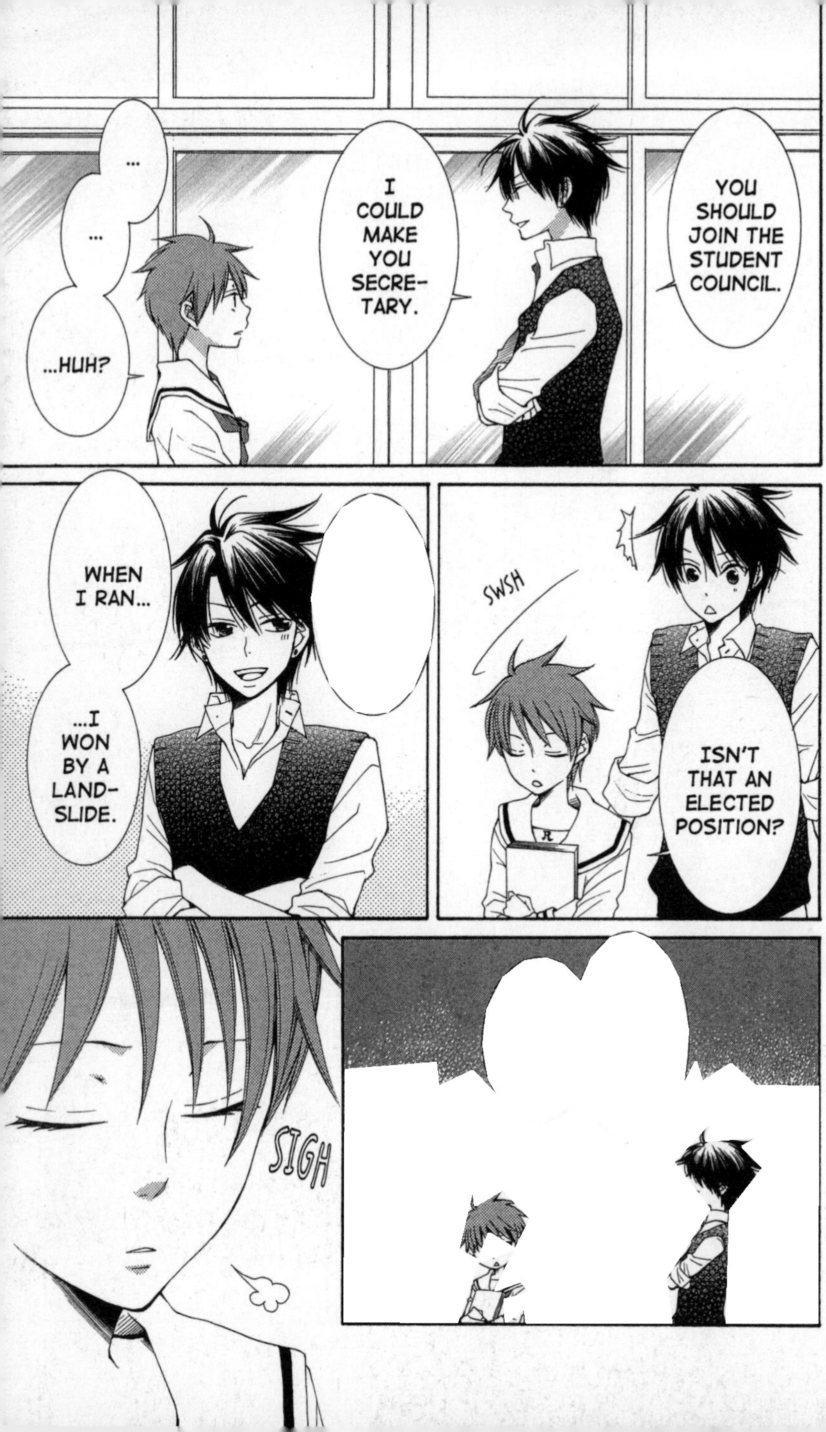
YOU SHOULD JOIN THE STUDENT COUNCIL.
I COULD MAKE YOU SECRE-TARY.
...
...
...HUH?
SWSH
ISN'T THAT AN ELECTED POSITION?
WHEN I RAN...
...I WON BY A LAND-SLIDE.
SIGH

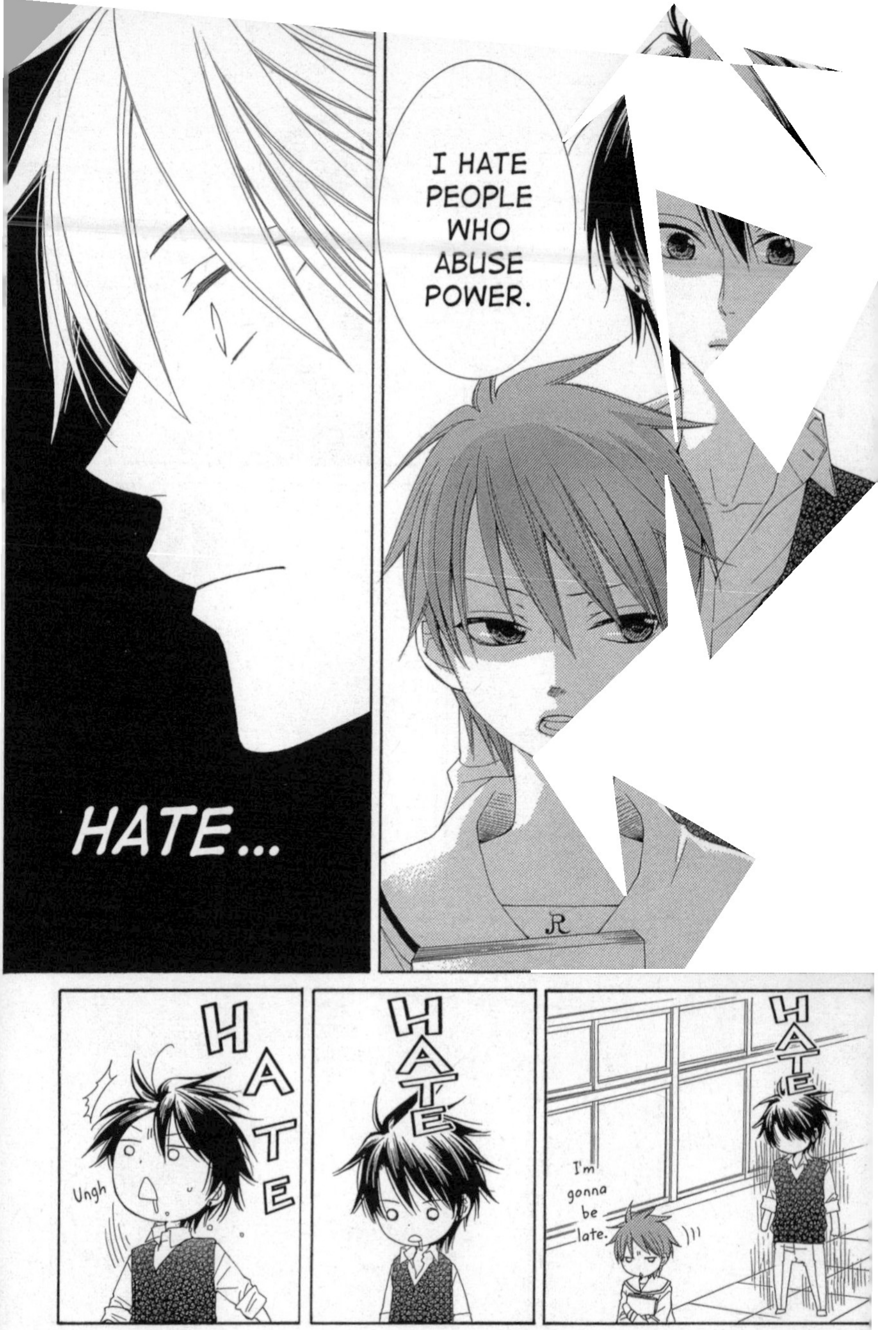
I HATE PEOPLE WHO ABUSE POWER.
HATE...
HATE
I'm gonna be late.
HATE
HATE
Ungh

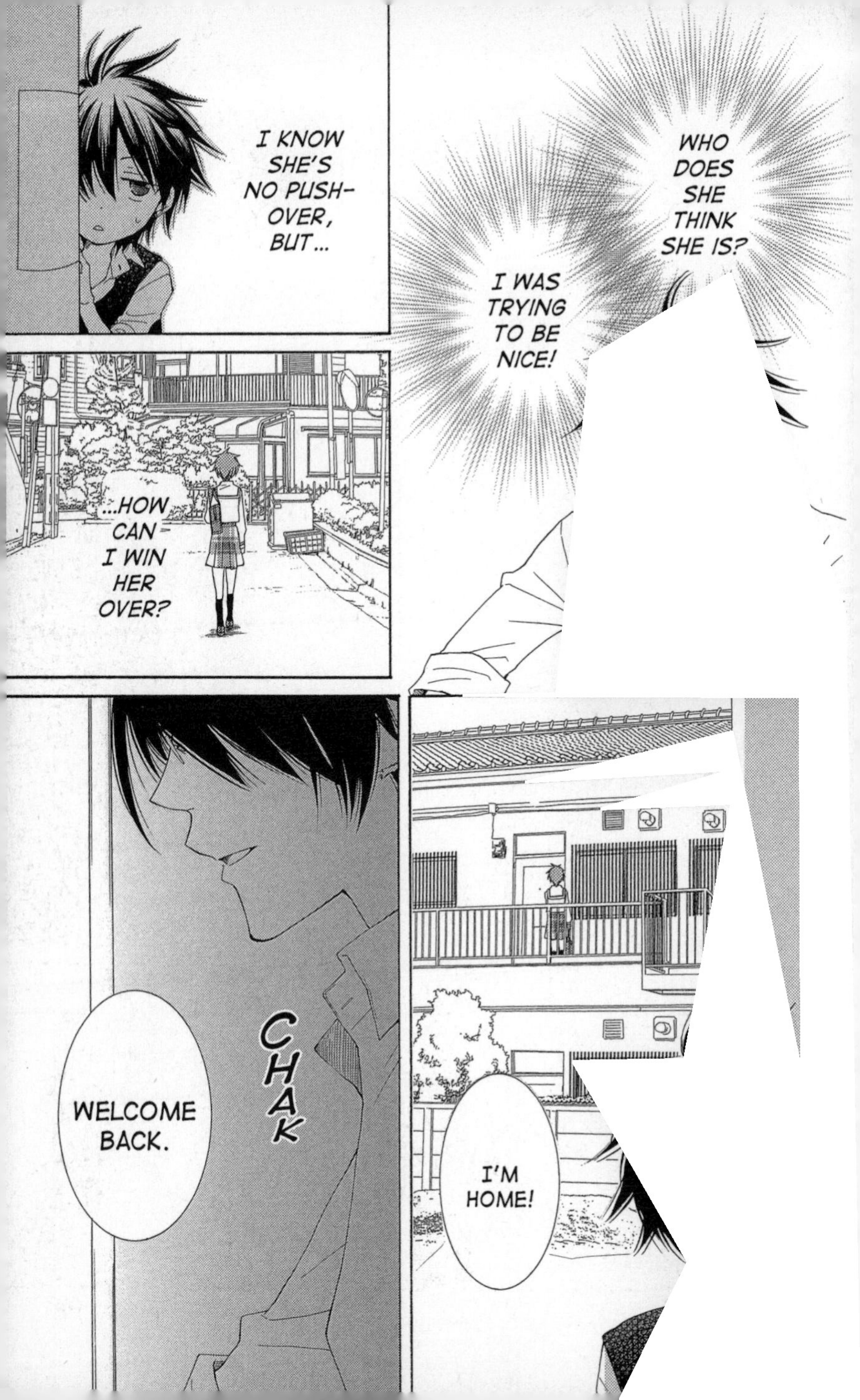
WHO DOES SHE THINK SHE IS?
I WAS TRYING TO BE NICE!
I KNOW SHE'S NO PUSH-OVER, BUT...
...HOW CAN I WIN HER OVER?
I'M HOME!
CHAK
WELCOME BACK.

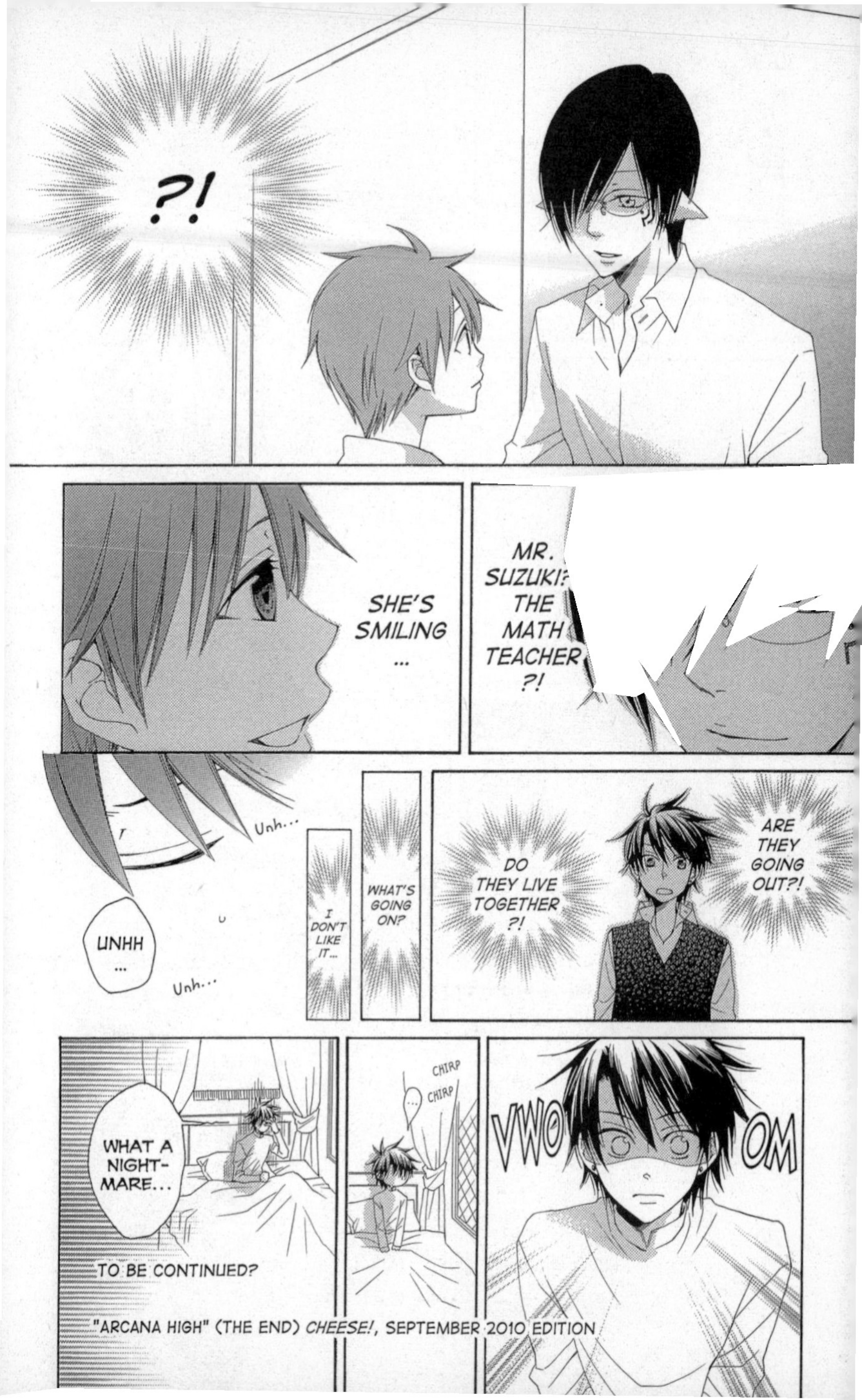
?!
MR. SUZUKI? THE MATH TEACHER?!
SHE'S SMILING ...
ARE THEY GOING OUT?!
DO THEY LIVE TOGETHER?!
WHAT'S GOING ON?
I DON'T LIKE IT...
Unh...
UNHH ...
Unh...
VWOOOM
CHIRP
CHIRP
...
WHAT A NIGHT-MARE...
TO BE CONTINUED?
"ARCANA HIGH" (THE END) CHEESE!, SEPTEMBER 2010 EDITION

I'll be the king of follicles!

Loves flair

Next is a drawing from *Cheese!* mangaka Sei Aoki, who's been helping me out lately. And it's the king! The king!…The king?

Long flowing hair, puffy pants, a mysterious wand... The king's nuts. Well done. Tany wound up with a character no one wanted to draw, hence this mess. I suppose it's even more amusing when you make fun of the serious characters. (*Laugh*)

This brings volume 5 to a close. The "Arcana High" collection is included in this volume. (*Laugh*) That started out as a short Valentine's Day special, and it just kept going... It's in the special edition sometimes. Don't expect much, and neither of us will be disappointed!

I always enjoy reading your letters. They're my nourishment.

Rei Toma
c/o Dawn of the Arcana Editor
Viz Media
P.O. Box 77010
San Francisco, CA 94107

Prince Cain... I have to admit, he's one of my favorite characters.

–Rei Toma

Rei Toma has been drawing since childhood, but she only began drawing manga because of her graduation project in design school. When she drew a short-story manga, *Help Me, Dentist,* for the first time, it attracted a publisher's attention and she made her debut right away. Her magnificent art style became popular, and after she debuted as a manga artist, she became known as an illustrator for novels and video game character designs. Her current manga series, *Dawn of the Arcana,* is her first long-running manga series, and it has been a hit in Japan, selling over a million copies.

DAWN OF THE ARCANA
VOLUME 5
Shojo Beat Edition

STORY AND ART BY
REI TOMA

© 2009 Rei TOMA/Shogakukan
All rights reserved.
Original Japanese edition "REIMEI NO ARCANA"
published by SHOGAKUKAN Inc.

Translation & Adaptation/Kajiya Productions
Touch-up Art & Lettering/Freeman Wong
Design/Yukiko Whitley
Editor/Amy Yu

Printed in the U.S.A.

Published by VIZ Media, LLC
P.O. Box 77010
San Francisco, CA 94107

10 9 8 7 6 5 4 3 2
First printing, August 2012
Second printing, August 2014

www.viz.com   www.shojobeat.com

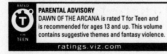

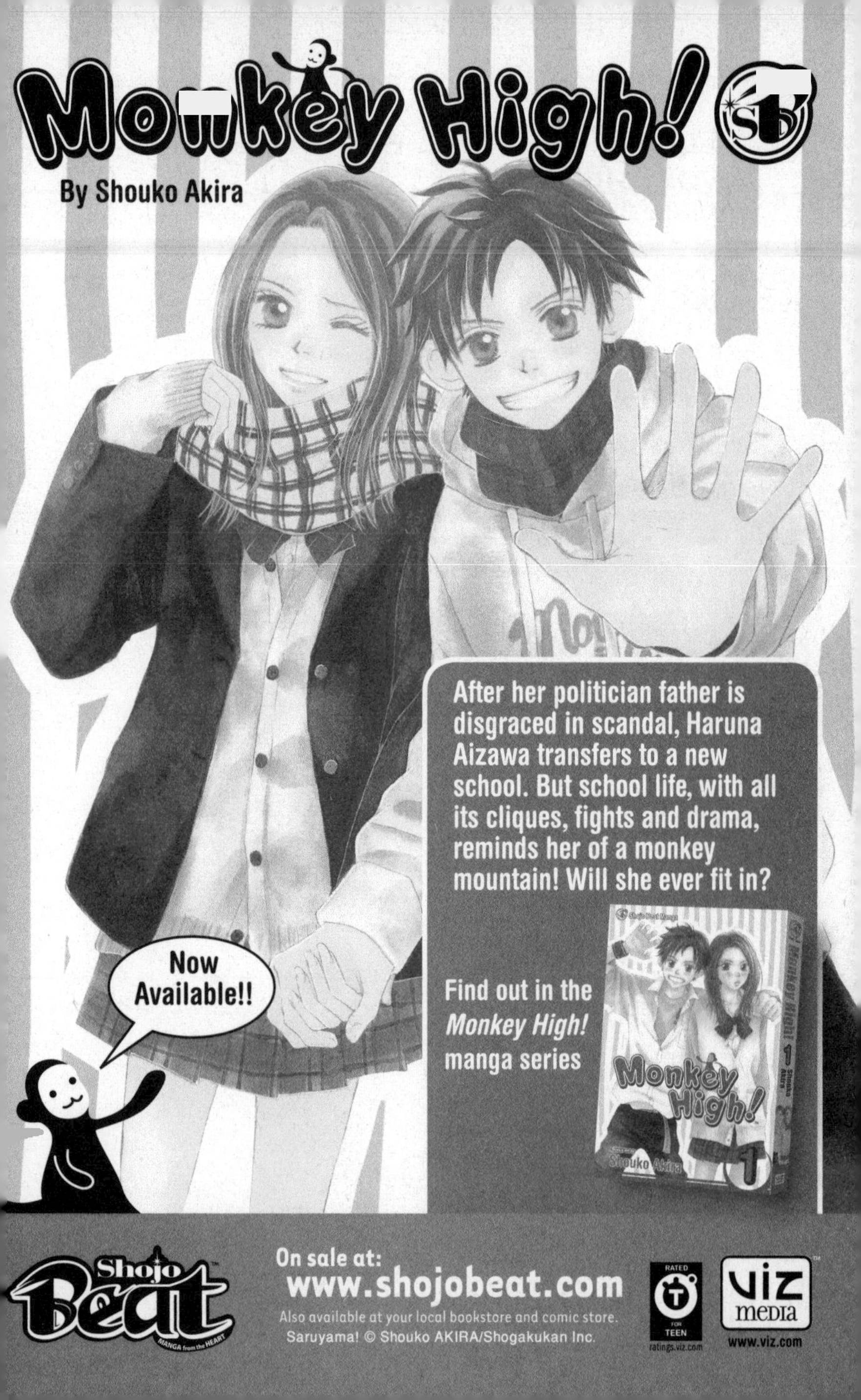
Monkey High!
By Shouko Akira
After her politician father is disgraced in scandal, Haruna Aizawa transfers to a new school. But school life, with all its cliques, fights and drama, reminds her of a monkey mountain! Will she ever fit in?
Now Available!!
Find out in the *Monkey High!* manga series
Monkey High!
Shouko Akira
1
Shojo Beat
MANGA from the HEART
On sale at:
www.shojobeat.com
Also available at your local bookstore and comic store.
Saruyama! © Shouko AKIRA/Shogakukan Inc.
RATED T FOR TEEN
ratings.viz.com
VIZ MEDIA
www.viz.com

We Were There

By Yuki Obata
Also known as the award-winning series *Bokura ga Ita*

Get to the Bottom of a Broken Heart

It's love at first sight when Nanami Takahashi
falls for Motoharu Yano, the most popular boy in
her new class. But he's still grieving his girlfriend
who died the year before. Can Nanami break
through the wall that surrounds Motoharu's heart?

Find out in *We Were There*—
manga series on sale now!

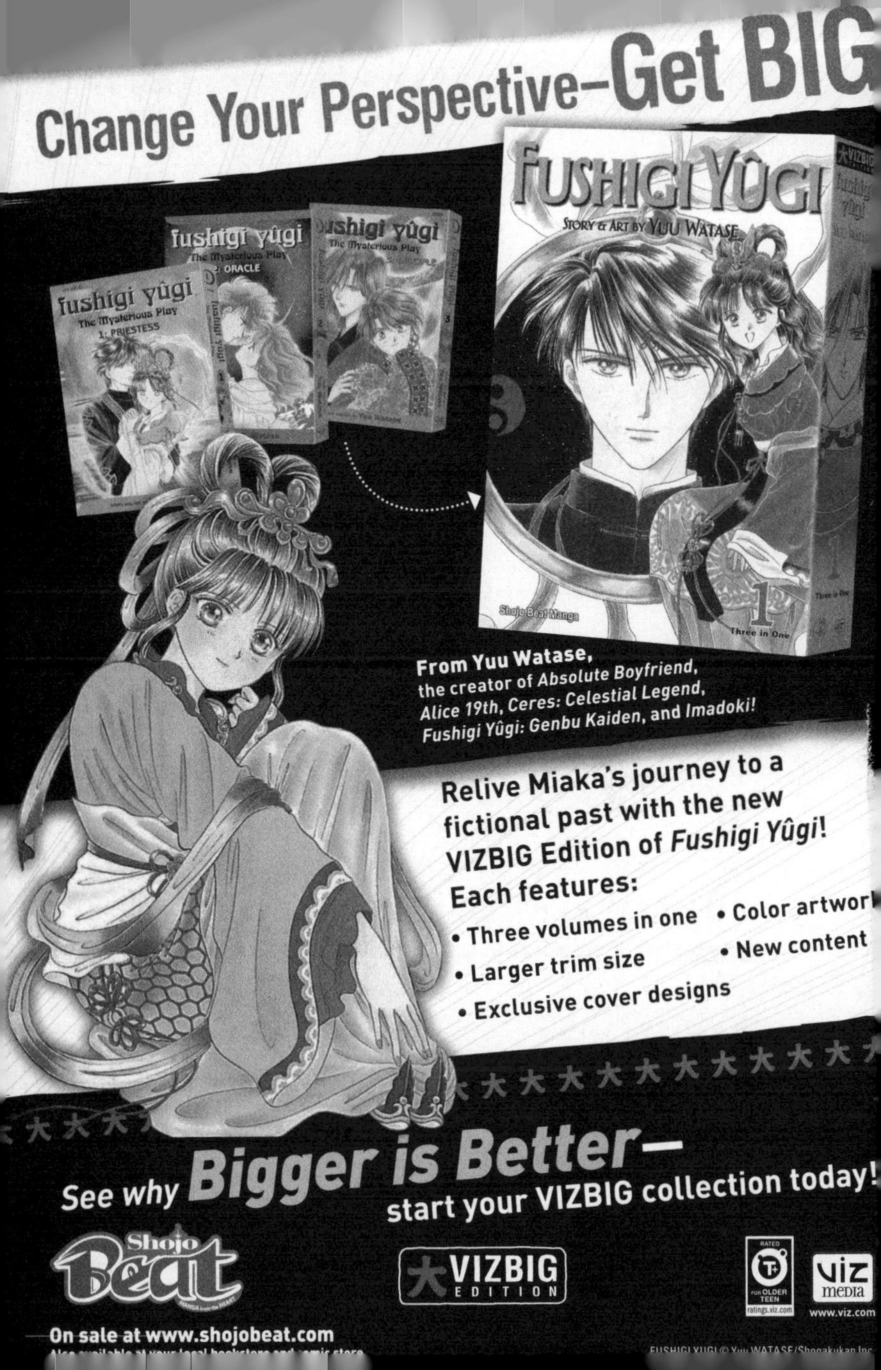
Change Your Perspective–Get BIG
FUSHIGI YÛGI
STORY & ART BY YUU WATASE
Shojo Beat Manga
Three in One
fushigi yûgi
The Mysterious Play
1: PRIESTESS
2: ORACLE
From Yuu Watase,
the creator of Absolute Boyfriend,
Alice 19th, Ceres: Celestial Legend,
Fushigi Yûgi: Genbu Kaiden, and Imadoki!
Relive Miaka's journey to a fictional past with the new VIZBIG Edition of Fushigi Yûgi!
Each features:
• Three volumes in one
• Larger trim size
• Exclusive cover designs
• Color artwork
• New content
See why Bigger is Better–
start your VIZBIG collection today!
Shojo Beat
MANGA from the HEART
VIZBIG EDITION
RATED T+ FOR OLDER TEEN
ratings.viz.com
VIZ media
www.viz.com
On sale at www.shojobeat.com

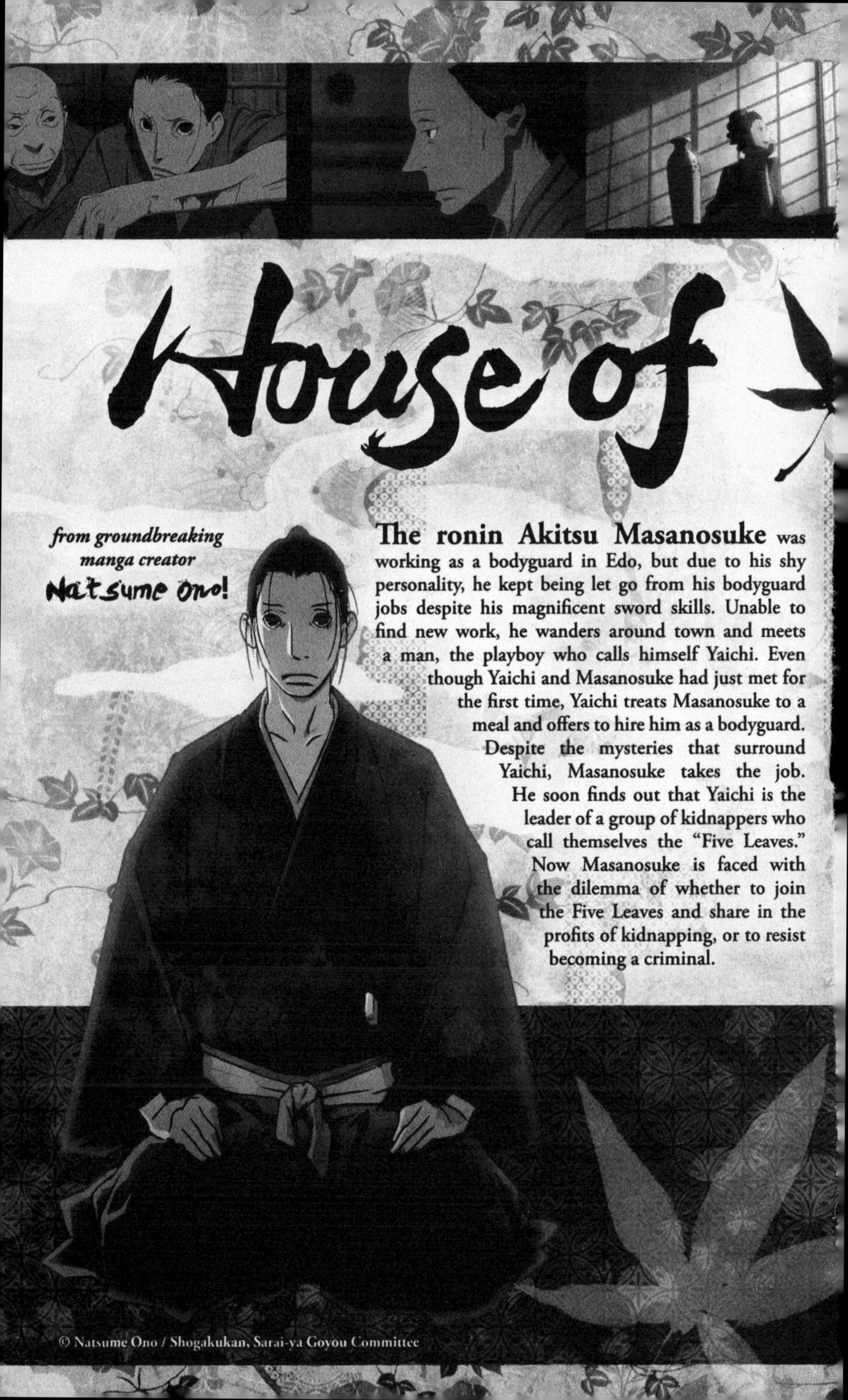
House of
from groundbreaking manga creator
Natsume Ono!
The ronin Akitsu Masanosuke was working as a bodyguard in Edo, but due to his shy personality, he kept being let go from his bodyguard jobs despite his magnificent sword skills. Unable to find new work, he wanders around town and meets a man, the playboy who calls himself Yaichi. Even though Yaichi and Masanosuke had just met for the first time, Yaichi treats Masanosuke to a meal and offers to hire him as a bodyguard. Despite the mysteries that surround Yaichi, Masanosuke takes the job. He soon finds out that Yaichi is the leader of a group of kidnappers who call themselves the "Five Leaves." Now Masanosuke is faced with the dilemma of whether to join the Five Leaves and share in the profits of kidnapping, or to resist becoming a criminal.
© Natsume Ono / Shogakukan, Sarai-ya Goyou Committee

This is the last page.

In keeping with the original Japanese comic format, this book reads from right to left—so action, sound effects, and word balloons are completely reversed. This preserves the orientation of the original artwork—plus, it's fun! Check out the diagram shown here to get the hang of things, and then turn to the other side of the book to get started!

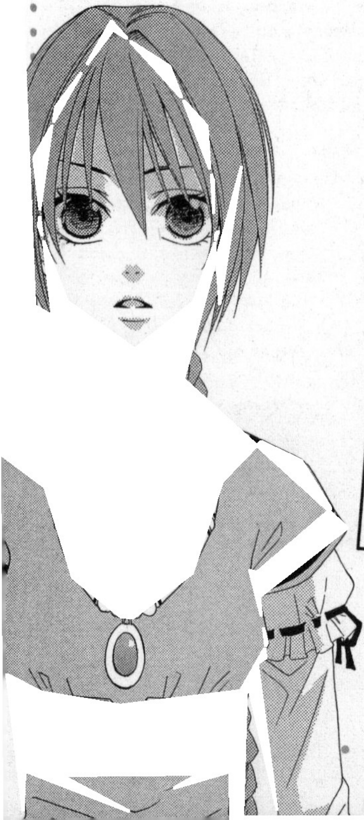

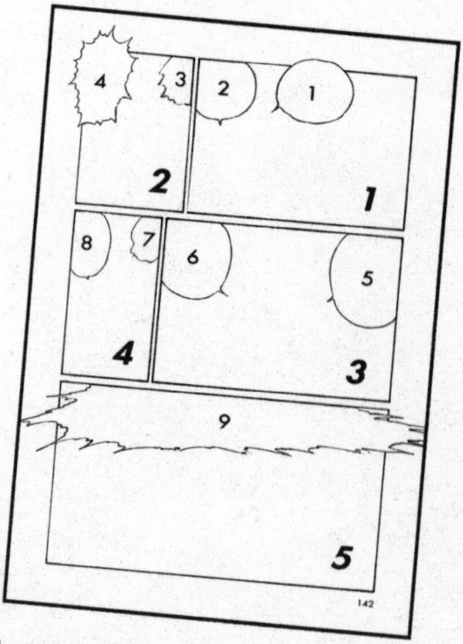
1
2
3
4
1
2
5
6
7
8
3
4
9
5
142